Btrieve Complete

A Guide for Developers and System Administrators

Jim Kyle

Addison-Wesley Publishing Company

Reading, Massachusetts • Menlo Park, California • New York
Don Mills, Ontario • Wokingham, England • Amsterdam
Bonn • Sydney • Singapore • Tokyo • Madrid • San Juan
Paris • Seoul • Milan • Mexico City • Taipei

Library of Congress Cataloging-in-Publication Data

Kyle, James, writer on electronics
    Btrieve complete : a guide for developers and systems
administrators / Jim Kyle.
      p. cm.
    Includes index.
    ISBN 0–201–48326–2 (alk. paper)
    1. Computer software—Development. 2. Database management.
3. Btrieve. I. Title.
QA76.76.D47K95 1995
005.74—dc20   95–18692
                                                       CIP

ISBN 0–201–48326–2

Sponsoring Editor: Kim Fryer
Project Manager: Eleanor McCarthy
Production Coordinator: Deborah McKenna
Cover design: Suzanne Heiser
Set in 11 point Palatino by A&B Typesetters, Inc.

2 3 4 5 6 7 8 9 10 MA 00999897
Second printing, March 1997

Addison-Wesley books are available for bulk purchases by corporations, institutions, and other organizations. For more information please contact the Corporate, Government, and Special Sales Department at (800) 238-9682.

Table of Contents

Introduction

For a product that's in its second decade of life, is the *de facto* standard for its corner of the PC network market, supports nearly 50,000 registered software developers worldwide, and is the foundation upon which tens of thousands of applications are built, Btrieve remains almost unknown outside the close-knit community of those who use it. I hope that this book does its part to correct that situation!

I must admit at the outset, though, that I find it impossible to play the role of unbiased observer and simply report what the product can do and how you can get maximum benefit from it. Although I came into the ranks of Btrieve developers quite recently (less than four years ago), I've discovered in that time many of the qualities that have propelled this package to its current enviable position and consequently must list myself as an ardent champion of the product. (I do, on occasion, use competing products; no single tool can be best of breed for all tasks, although in many respects the Btrieve package comes close.)

I *will* make every attempt to present only facts in these pages and to place as much emphasis on problem areas as on features. As a buyer of this book you have every right to expect that and I've attempted to deliver it to you. However, you also have the right to know that I think this product enjoys its position atop the heap for the simple reason that it's earned that position!

This achievement has come about the hard way, too. When I found it necessary to become fully competent at working with Btrieve in mid-1990 so that my programs could interface with other products that already used it, my first thought was to get the best reference books about its use that I could obtain and use them to help me understand the official manuals provided by Novell (which had purchased the product several years earlier). It was then that I discovered, to my great dismay, that no such reference books existed, either good or bad! The only sources of information available were the product manuals, and those folks already using the package. And the product manuals, unfortunately, were written as reference books rather than as tutorials, leaving me no way to get started other than the classic technique known as "trial and error" aided by frequent questioning of other developers both in my company and elsewhere who were already familiar with Btrieve.

In a very real sense this book dates from that time. However, many other things had to happen before I could interest any publisher in the subject. All market studies indicated that titles such as *An Idiot's Guide to Computing* were in much greater demand than were books devoted to such an out-of-the-way subject as record management. I must express my appreciation to Phil Sutherland at Addison-Wesley for having the courage to consider my proposal and to eventually bring it to pass!

In the meantime, other things were happening, all of which contributed to making this book possible. Novell's strategic plans apparently did not include active competition with any of their database-oriented customers. As a result, the networking giant dropped all advertising and promotion of the Btrieve product line sometime around 1992. This, in turn, led many folks in the industry to believe that the product was either already dead or in its death throes.

Actually, Novell continued to support improvements, but was unwilling to release them to customers. This led the original Btrieve team, who had come into the Novell organization with the product, to initiate efforts to regain control of the product. In April 1994, Btrieve Technologies Inc. took over both Btrieve itself and its related product, Netware SQL (which was renamed Scalable SQL, both to eliminate the Novell trademark and to indicate its broader scope).

I go into much more detail about these events below, but I must mention at the outset what I consider the most remarkable thing about Btrieve, which I believe to be the reason it has become the standard and remained there for so many years. As one of my first steps of research for this book, I attended the Btrieve Technologies "Summit Conference" in their home city of Austin, Texas, in October 1994 and met many of the people who have built the product. I found that almost without exception, they had a close-knit feeling of "family" and looked on the product as their personal responsibility. Unfortunately, that's a rare situation in today's software industry!

Many of those now building Btrieve and its related products have been connected with the package from its earliest days. Two of the three people in the top positions of the new company were the co-founders of the original company; one of these designed the program initially. The vice-president of customer service is also a Soft-Craft veteran. Of the more than sixty persons involved with the package at the time of my visit, almost all had long experience with Btrieve under the Novell banner; I met no one who was a newcomer to the family.

The almost universal concern I encountered was a fear that the potential marketplace considered Btrieve to be an "old," or even dead, technology because of the lack of promotion efforts. Many of those attending the conference recounted tales of their managers' questions about whether it was wise to continue using Btrieve. As I hope to show in the following pages, I consider these fears unjustified. The current versions of the product reflect an entirely new microkernel architecture that's specifically designed to retain compatibility while providing full freedom to evolve in any direction future computing needs may take. Customers now have the benefit of those developments that had been bottled up for the final two years of the Novell-owned era, and even newer developments are in the offing.

The server package for Windows NT, which is scheduled for public release at about the same time as this book, features full multi-threaded operation, making an already responsive system even snappier. Other servers following the same principles are in the pipeline. Even the plain MS-DOS versions, which cannot use true multithreading techniques because the operating system fails to support such, have a pseudo-threaded foundation that greatly increases speed in comparison with older versions.

Despite all these advances, current versions of Btrieve provide full support for files written with any earlier version, dating all the way back to version 1.0 released in early February of 1982. One promise I heard over and over at the Summit Conference was that such compatibility would be retained in all future versions, thus giving developers full protection against any possibility of future upgrades breaking existing applications. I find this commitment most commendable!

Btrieve's Development

As a first step in the education process, this section describes the history and current industry position of Btrieve. I will trace the product's development through its three distinct stages: SoftCraft (founded by Doug and Nancy Woodward in 1982), the years as part of Novell (1987 to 1994), and Btrieve Technologies (an independent firm established in 1994).

The Product

The history of Btrieve closely matches that of the MS-DOS-based desktop computing industry.

As Figure I.1, a chart of significant milestones, reveals, Btrieve began just six months after IBM's entry into "personal computing"

Figure I.1   *Btrieve's history closely matches that of the PC itself.*

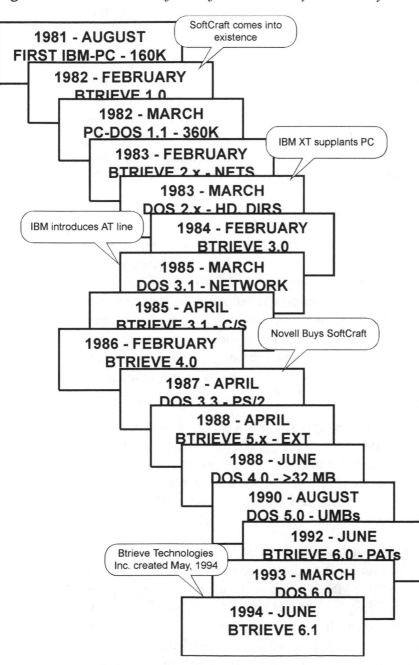

gave authenticity to the fledgling industry, and a month *before* introduction of the double-sided floppy diskette with its amazing 360K storage capacity.

Originally, Btrieve was the sole product of a small company named SoftCraft, located in Austin, Texas. Actually, both Btrieve and SoftCraft itself came from the creative minds of a pair of young programmers working as a husband-wife team. Doug and Nancy Woodward saw the need for a professional-quality record management system to run with the new IBM PC and jointly created the software. Then they established SoftCraft to develop and market the product, with Nancy becoming president and Doug taking the office of VP, Software Development.

From the beginning, several policies guided development of the Btrieve products: first and foremost was that of providing reliable operation. Early magazine ads emphasized Btrieve's capability to protect users' data against even power failures (frequent happenings in those days before uninterruptible power supplies became commonplace). Almost as important was the policy of keeping an open ear tuned to the developers who used the product and responding to their needs and desires as rapidly as possible consistent with keeping the package reliable.

Finally, with the first major upgrades came a policy of total backward compatibility. This policy makes it possible to run applications that were written for version 1.0 under the latest version 6.0 and later engines. Try doing the same with any other software that's available, including MS-DOS itself. And keep in mind that Btrieve's version 2.0 was released before MS-DOS introduced directories or file handles.

During the first half of the 1980s, Btrieve's technical advances appeared more frequently than did those in the operating system itself. Just a month after MS-DOS made uniform network support possible by standardizing the internal hooks (at version 3.1), Btrieve released an upgrade providing full client-server operation on any network. And a full year before DOS 3.3 appeared, Btrieve's version numbers had advanced to 4.0. The first minor upgrade of this, to version 4.1, introduced extended key types and supplemental indexes, setting the pattern for widespread adoption of the package by the financial industry.

By 1987, the Btrieve developer base had grown to some 5,000 and the package had become known as the leading player in the financial area, due largely to its emphasis on reliable and secure operation. As competition grew hot in the closely associated network-software market, Novell found that many of their customers used Btrieve, and the Utah company moved to acquire SoftCraft in order to bundle Btrieve as part of the Netware package.

Initially the only effects of the Novell acquisition were the addition of the phrase "A Novell Company" to the copyright notices in the user manuals and the change of manual covers from blue-gray to Chinese red. The offices remained in Austin, most of the development and support staff remained in place, and the Woodwards stayed on as key players: Nancy became VP and General Manager of Novell's Austin operations while Doug became VP of Advanced Database Technologies. Several months later, the SoftCraft name quietly vanished into history and Btrieve became simply a Novell product.

However, all members of the Btrieve product family (with one exception) were born under the SoftCraft banner. Only NetWare SQL (now renamed Scalable SQL) dates from a time after the Novell acquisition, and even that product is based on XQL from the SoftCraft days.

The first version of Btrieve released under the Novell name was 5.0, in early 1988. This version introduced a number of features: auto-increment key types, the BROUTER network process server, data-only and key-only files, and optional data compression all first appeared in version 5.0. By this time, both the network and the standalone version of Btrieve had come into widespread use. Addition of the new capabilities and the tie-in with NetWare caused the developer base to skyrocket from the 5,000 in 1987 to more than 40,000 just seven years later.

Nearly two years passed before another upgrade came about. In 1990, version 5.1 brought a 50 percent increase in the number of files allowed in one transaction and added capability for logging and roll-forward actions. Significant enhancements to the API resulted in extended operations that could return multiple records with a single server request. This version of Btrieve became, and remains to this day, the industry standard for record managers.

With the added organizational overhead that's inescapable in any large corporation, Btrieve's development pace slowed somewhat during the Novell years. More than twenty-four months went by between the release of version 5.1 and the appearance of version 6.0. During that time, Novell's promotional and marketing efforts for the Btrieve product line were minimal. Consequently, when version 6.0 appeared in mid-1992, industry reaction was also minimal.

The list of features added at version 6.0 is long. It includes:

1. Introduction of microkernel architecture
2. Additional information in STAT response
3. AutoIncrement duplicate-key error eliminated
4. Concurrent transactions allowed
5. Duplicate-key pointer reservation and reuse enabled
6. Key Allocation Table created in header
7. Locking of extended operations permitted
8. More than 24 key segments permitted
9. New file format for microkernel architecture
10. NoCase key option added
11. Optional renumbering of keys enabled
12. Permanent keys can be dropped
13. Relational Integrity enforcement put into kernel
14. Shadow paging replaces pre-imaging
15. Specific key-number assignment allowed
16. Update and Delete enabled for key-only files

17. Three new API functions added: Get by Percentage, Find Percentage, Update Chunk

18. Several existing API functions enhanced: Get Direct, Stat

Many developers, your author included, chose to ignore 6.0 despite the added capabilities and continued developing applications with version 5.1. By doing so, they denied themselves improved shadow imaging, better interfacing with Windows applications, and the ability to handle individual records longer than 64K.

Not all the coolness toward the new version resulted from lack of promotion, however. To provide still better reliability, the Btrieve engineers had violated a critical part of the compatibility policy. File format changed so drastically that files written to use the advanced features in version 6.0 were unreadable to older versions. While a configuration option retained backward compatibility for the engine, using that option was effectively equivalent to staying with version 5.1. Although an effective file-conversion utility came as part of version 6.0, the very popularity of version 5.1 turned out to be the biggest enemy of the new version. Until all applications had moved to the new file format, nobody wanted to be first!

The lack of enthusiasm for version 6.0 apparently caused Novell to reduce its promotional efforts to nearly nothing, although product development continued unabated. For the next two years, the near-total lack of mention in the industry press caused many observers to conclude that Novell had quietly killed the package. Although nothing could be less true, the myth spread rapidly. Those who had brought the product line to life grew alarmed. Quietly, they began working on a plan to regain control of the entire technology involved and to revive it.

The plan took almost two years to reach fruition, but on January 26, 1994, Novell announced its decision to transfer ownership of the database product line to Btrieve Technologies Inc. The new company's management lineup included Nancy Woodward as Chairman and Doug Woodward as Chief Technical Officer. On April 29, 1994, the transfer closed and BTI became a reality. By June 1, version

6.15 of Btrieve for Windows began shipping, followed closely by the matching version of Btrieve for DOS.

This version of Btrieve represents a total rewrite of the software, which not only corrected a number of minor problems noted in version 6.0 but also made it much easier to add features in future versions. Several such features are already scheduled to appear in the next version, due by mid-1995. However, the major strengths of the package (reliability, speed, and low resource requirements) remain unchanged.

Several years ago, a major cosmetics manufacturer based an entire ad campaign on the slogan "You're not getting older, you're getting better!" That slogan would be appropriate for Btrieve. While some of its enthusiasts worry that potential buyers view the package as being "old and obsolete," the facts are that the latest versions are as far ahead of the standard 5.1 product as that version was when compared to version 1.0. Later in this book I go into more detail about many of the new features.

The People

A primary reason for the excellent performance and extreme compatibility of the Btrieve product line is the simple fact that all the key people involved in it have lived with this package for many years and have a personal dedication to its success. Few other firms in the software industry can match BTI in this respect.

The company is well aware of this fact and considers their team the most important corporate asset because of its sharp focus and complete commitment.

To illustrate the situation, consider the Woodwards. Without Doug and Nancy Woodward, Btrieve would never have existed. Together with Ron Harris, whom we'll meet a bit later in this section, they worked as junior programmers at Texas Instruments in the late 1970s.

Doug was the original architect, and through the sequence of different companies has always provided the guiding vision for the

Btrieve package. While Nancy and he worked jointly on the first versions, Nancy moved out of software development early in the SoftCraft days to take responsibility for other aspects of the business. Asked in a magazine interview whether she missed coding, she replied, "I really don't. I enjoyed it while I was doing it, but I enjoy the challenges of the business side just as much." She became CEO of SoftCraft when it came into existence.

It's obvious that her move from programming to administration was a good one. By the time SoftCraft became a Novell company, annual revenues exceeded $2 million. At Novell, she became VP and General Manager for the entire Austin operation, and as such was a key spokesperson for the firm in addition to managing some two hundred employees in marketing, support, software engineering, and administration.

At BTI she continues as a key executive with the title of Chairman (company press releases use that term rather than the recent gender-free "Chairperson"), while relinquishing the CEO role to Ron Harris. Ron had stayed at Texas Instruments for twelve years, then moved on in 1989 to help launch Citrix Systems, Inc., in Coral Gables, Florida. At Citrix, he rose from Director of Strategic Planning to VP of Marketing and finally to Product Group VP where he was responsible for all product development, marketing, and customer support. Though not directly involved with either SoftCraft or the Novell database technology group, he maintained close connections with the Woodwards over the years. As President and CEO for BTI as one of its three principals, he brings solid technical background and an additional perspective to the new firm.

His goals for the company are simple and direct: "Our focus is on developing lean and mean engines," he says. "We're going to continue doing what we do best: developing serious back-end engines." When talking to developers, he's adamant about maintaining the compatibility that has become such a major feature in Btrieve. "The version 1.0 API is still supported in version 6.15," he reminded a group during a recent meeting, "and we're going to keep it forever!"

Another team member whose tenure dates from SoftCraft is Mad Poarch, now VP of Customer Service. Mad (whose name is familiar to all readers of the Novell "Bullets" newsletter) was the very first technical support person hired at SoftCraft. She moved to Novell with the rest of the staff in 1987. Three years later she became director of the Developer Support Operation, with a staff of approximately forty. This group had responsibility for worldwide support of all developer SDKs.

Though a more recent member, coming to Novell in 1989, Lori Baldwin drove implementation of the company's database strategy as director of the Database Market Development organization and saw revenues increase by more than 35 percent yearly as a result. At BTI, she's VP of Sales and Channel Marketing with responsibility for worldwide sales and marketing activities.

Another longtime key person is Kristin Burkland, now director of Business Development with the task of developing relationships, joint development agreements with partners and key industry players, and marketing opportunities. At Novell, she spent five and a half years in similar efforts and was senior manager of Development Technologies before moving to BTI.

In all, some sixty top people from the Novell operation moved over to BTI, and in nearly every case continued doing the same things they had been doing before. Only a few of BTI's personnel came from elsewhere, and most of those (such as Bo Holland, director of Product Marketing) came with Ron Harris from Citrix.

Whenever one talks with any member of the BTI team, whether face-to-face at a conference, by telephone, or via E-mail, it's obvious that the group considers itself to be an extended family, all working toward a single goal and that's the one expressed by Harris: "Keep doing what we do best!" It's not at all uncommon in the BTI support forum on the CompuServe network (GO BTRIEVE, naturally, to access it) to find technical questions being answered directly by Doug Woodward, or policy questions being settled by Ron Harris. Few other firms of comparable or larger size allow customers direct contact with top management, but at BTI, that's a way of life.

Related Products

As the fledgling Btrieve product gained popularity among developers, the absence of any user interface layer turned out to be a bit of a problem in some cases. Exacerbating the situation was the fact that the other major data-management products available in those years all included menu-driven interface capabilities, leaving SoftCraft as the only firm not providing a user-friendly package. Consequently, once Btrieve's initial growing pains were past, Woodward and company turned their attention to creating a front-end that would simplify Btrieve for end-users.

The result, introduced to the world in September of 1984, was Xtrieve. Xtrieve provides a totally menu-driven interface, based on a data dictionary that attempts to comply with the twelve rules of relational databases. This dictionary, comprising a number of different Btrieve files with the common file type ".DDF", remains in wide use to the present day even where Xtrieve is not used; it's the hook used by Microsoft's Open DataBase Connectivity (ODBC) standard to deal with Btrieve files.

With Xtrieve, users can build data requests, views, and so on by navigating through its menus. Although these constructs result (behind the scenes) in creation of a relational expression similar to those used in SQL, the user remains unaware of that. This allows casual operators to deal with data in terms of records and fields as with non-relational systems rather than being forced to think in terms of tables, rows, and columns.

The core of Xtrieve is a set of primitive operations that mimic SQL actions, but not in a totally compliant manner. By the time Novell acquired SoftCraft in 1987, Xtrieve had undergone two major revisions and was at version 3.0. Along the way, the rising popularity of SQL for accessing relational databases had not gone unnoticed. An additional product called XQL made its appearance at almost the same time as the acquisition.

XQL provided a developer's tool, similar to Btrieve itself, consisting of three different sets of primitive operations. The lowest level, known as XQLP functions, consists simply of the primitives already existing in Xtrieve. Atop this layer lies another set, XQLL, which provides the SQL language layer. Developers wishing to embed SQL within an application can use XQLL to do so.

The third set of operations, XQLI, implements an interactive SQL statement executor. Using XQLI, the user can type in any SQL statement and then request its execution. None of the user-friendly Xtrieve interface appears; the intent of XQLI was that it be used by experienced data retrieval operators rather than by the casual user.

By the time that Btrieve had made it to version 2.1, network support appeared. Initially the network version's name was Btrieve/N (for networks); when Novell acquired everything, the name changed to Btrieve for NetWare. The original Btrieve became Btrieve for DOS to differentiate the two.

Although development had begun on a network version of XQL, nothing had reached release before Novell took over. The embryo product became NetWare SQL instead. Version 1.0 reached the market in early 1989, with a beta copy reviewed in the March 1989 issue of PC Tech Journal magazine (competing against SQL Server, Gupta's SQLBase, Oracle's ORACLE Server, and XDB Server from XDB Systems).

This original version supported IBM's version of SQL with no extensions; all the competing products added at least a few extras such as date, time, character, and math operations. Consequently, the review gave only faint praise to the newcomer, although it did note that NetWare SQL was "attractive to Novell's large and active Btrieve user base."

Any shortcomings of version 1.0 were remedied over the ensuing years; version 3.0 now supports both ANSI SQL and the IBM SAA version, plus Microsoft's ODBC interface. The name, too, has changed to remove Novell's trademark. It's now Scalable SQL (abbreviated to SSQL). By the time this book sees print, it should be available in a single-user non-networked version.

A company brochure describes SSQL as a relational database technology that seamlessly scales your applications from mobile notebook computers, up to the largest client/server environments, without requiring that you rewrite so much as a single line of code. Still based on the reliable Btrieve engine, SSQL provides relational integrity enforced at the engine level. This means that although the Btrieve API itself has no RI features, no Btrieve program can violate the integrity of a relational database created by SSQL.

Conclusion

In the pages that follow, I concentrate primarily on the features of the current versions, but also cover the differences in file formats for versions before 6.0. My purpose is to provide you the volume I could not find in 1990: an independent overview and tutorial for the product together with details of its internal workings adequate to let you fine-tune your application. In this effort I have had full cooperation from the crew at Btrieve Technologies Inc., but they have made no attempt to censor my opinions in any way. Words are inadequate to express my appreciation of their assistance.

Although the Btrieve staff did review the manuscript for possible technical errors, responsibility for any errors that may have slipped through are mine alone. If you should locate any, I want to know about them so that they can be fixed in any future printings. I can be reached on CompuServe at 76703,762 and via Internet at 76703.762@compuserve.com, in addition to the usual route via the publishers.

Jim Kyle
Oklahoma City, Oklahoma
February 1995

1

A Brief Overview of Btrieve

One might expect that the system most widely used for storage and rapid retrieval of data would be familiar to anyone in the desktop computing industry. One would be wrong. That system, Btrieve, is the foundation for seven of the top ten professional accounting systems. What's more, it forms the backbone of countless other software packages in widespread use. Yet at a recent meeting of leading Btrieve developers, the most common complaint voiced was that their customers, and their managers also, have absolutely no idea what Btrieve really does.

Because of this lack of comprehension, the developers were under severe pressure to abandon their most reliable tool. Managers were insisting that they convert all applications to run under a more popular DBMS such as Oracle, Paradox, or dBase IV. Although such action would greatly increase resource requirements and at the same time reduce accuracy and reliability, executives and customers alike remain blissfully unaware of such facts.

The purpose of this book is twofold: One goal is to provide the developer and the system administrator with ample information to let them take full advantage of the power inherent in the Btrieve system. The second goal is to breach the veil of ignorance concerning just what Btrieve is and what it does, thus helping developers educate their customers and their managers. With adequate education, the pressure to abandon a useful tool should significantly subside.

What's in It Today

Let's examine the product as it exists at this writing. (Another major upgrade is in the pipeline and could appear by the time this book reaches you, but BTI operates on very short upgrade cycles; as I write this, I've not yet had a chance to examine the new version.)

The introduction lists new product features added in version 6.15, but a more accurate view of Btrieve's current capability is given by the full list, including both new and old capabilities. Version 6.15 is available both for DOS and for Windows, each as either a client-based package or a server-based system. The client-based packages come both as developer kits or client engine kits. The server-based package comes only as the engine kit; development for the server environment is identical to that for the client environment, so the same developer kit applies in both.

The developer kits include a copy of the client engine that is limited to five concurrent users to allow developers to test their applications. Engine kits (both client and server) are licensed for various numbers of users and are priced accordingly. Server engine kits include copies of the applicable Btrieve requester packages for use at individual workstations.

What's in Version 6.15

Some of the key features present in all variations of version 6.15 include the ability to support up to 119 key segments per file (in contrast to the 24-segment limit of older versions) and to add or drop any index at any time. Btrieve supports a full range of data types and a long list of key attributes, including the ability to use different alternate collating sequences for different keys in the same file. Index numbers no longer change automatically when an index is dropped and can be assigned out of the normal sequence when a new index is added.

Files are still limited to a maximum of 4 GB (the limit imposed by NetWare), although this restriction is expected to vanish in the near future. The number of records within a file is limited only by the file's size and the amount of storage space available. File definition and management functions are independent of the operating system in use, allowing simple conversion from one platform to another.

Btrieve provides its own memory cache algorithm, independent of any caching performed by the operating system. System administrators can specify the size for this internal cache.

Single-record and multiple-record locking occur automatically or under program control, as desired. Both concurrent and exclusive transactions are now possible. Shadow paging within the same file holding data provides increased reliability by eliminating an entire set of copy operations formerly required. Logging of all operations that modify any file is possible, and this in turn provides a Roll-Forward capability to recover data corrupted by a system or server failure. Dynamic encryption and decryption of data remain available, as do owner-names, which can be used to force data access to be read-only.

New for version 6.1 and later are the choice of single engine file sharing (SEFS) and multiengine file sharing (MEFS) modes. By default, SEFS applies when files are on a local drive; MEFS applies when files are on a remote (network) drive. For the first time, individual records can exceed 64K in length, making possible storage of document images and other huge items. Collating sequences can be made locale-specific, and the ACS is no longer necessary in order to eliminate case sensitivity in key fields. The Btrieve requester for NetWare servers now supports MAP ROOT drives and NetWare's file level security features.

Only one operation supported by older versions is missing from version 6.0 and later. That dropped operation is Extend, which could split a single file across two separate drives. This operation was quite useful in the early days of the product, when Btrieve ran on systems with nothing but floppy disks. By allowing a data file to span drives A: and B: at the same time, applications could have files as large as 700K. In current use, where a 250MB fixed disk is now considered small, the extend operation has become obsolete.

Obsolescence alone, though, was not why it was dropped. The function was simply not compatible with platform independence since it required that the filename of the file containing the second half of the data be written into the file holding the first half. In addition, the shadow-imaging technique made it impossible to predict which half of a file might hold a given logical page at any instant.

Comparing the Features

A major problem facing developers who want to use Btrieve in new applications is that misinformed managers persist in thinking of it as a database management system (DBMS) and evaluating the product in those terms. In point of fact, as Nancy Woodward has described it, "Btrieve is a database engine that provides the underlying data management functions required by application programs." The difference is significant.

In their 1976 classic, *Software Tools* (Addison-Wesley, ISBN 0-201-03669-X), Brian Kernighan and P. J. Plauger enunciated what they called the first principle of programming: "Keep it simple." They expanded this to: "At all levels, be as clean as possible, and write the simplest, clearest thing that will do the job." The entire book promoted this theme, presenting in a clear and concise fashion one of the most elegant sets of tools ever published.

In the years since that milestone, the principle of working with tools that do just one thing but do that task superlatively well has become known as the UNIX philosophy because so much of that operating system was based on it. It applies everywhere, though, and Btrieve furnishes an example of just such a tool.

By contrast, a DBMS must by its very nature do many more things and cannot be as simple. Figure 1.1 shows the major difference between a record manager, such as Btrieve, and a full DBMS: in principle it's the presence of a user interface layer in the DBMS that distinguishes the two, but in practice the differences are more marked.

The designers of most DBMSs have allowed some of their user-interface concern to affect the implementation of the record management layer, consequently preventing some types of actions. One popular entry-level DBMS, for instance, makes no provision whatsoever for storing numeric values in binary form. This forces record sizes to be much larger than necessary. That DBMS also allows variable-length records in only a few special cases, again contributing to oversize records and consequent slow retrieval of data.

Figure 1.1   *The difference between a DBMS and a record manager is that a record manager does not have the user interface layer and its associated limitations.*

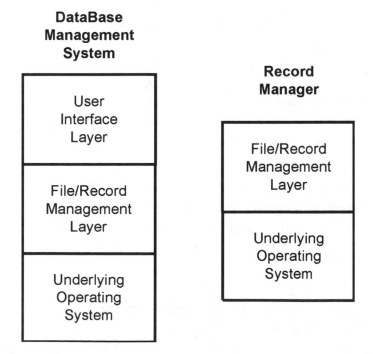

Because the difference between a record manager and a DBMS is so crucial, Chapter 2 explores the characteristics that differentiate DBMS methodologies. Chapter 3 then examines indexing techniques, and Chapter 4 introduces Btrieve itself.

Who Uses This Package?

More than 50,000 software developers around the world use Btrieve in their applications. This number merely accounts for those developers known to BTI. It's quite likely that at least that many more may be using the package illicitly. If Software Publishing Association estimates are to be believed, on average every legitimate user of a software product is matched by five or more who use it illegally. Applying that factor to the list of registered users would bring the total to almost a quarter of a million!

Note that this count is of *application developers*, not of *end users* (most of whom are blissfully unaware that they are using Btrieve at all, unless they happen to see an error message that the application fails to trap and handle properly).

Why does Btrieve have so many users? The universal comment among those who earn their livings with the product is that they prefer it for three reasons: It's reliable, it's fast, and it's small. The reliability is especially important in the area of financial applications, where downtime of only a few minutes can result in cash losses measured in the tens of thousands of dollars. Those who work in the financial community are among the most enthusiastic backers of Btrieve.

To close out this chapter, we present brief descriptions of how a few Btrieve developers use the product (and, in some cases, its close relatives based on the same underlying engine). Most of these descriptions come from presentations given at a worldwide conference of Btrieve developers.

Solomon Software

Seven of the top ten professional-level accounting packages for the desktop environment are built on Btrieve or its engine as the foundation. Among these is Solomon Software, of Findlay, Ohio, one of the leaders in the NetWare-based field. The Windows version of their product, released in early 1994, uses Scalable SQL. Senior marketing manager Skip Reardon explained why: "It gives you all the benefits of the 'big boy' SQL products," he said, "but it's a lot less expensive and a lot easier to maintain."

To prove to a Fortune 200 customer that SSQL could deliver the needed performance, Reardon created a test network capable of handling some 4,000 accounts-payable vouchers each month, involving some 12,500 customers and vendors. Since SSQL uses the Btrieve engines as its foundation, full compatibility with any other Btrieve-based applications is retained by choosing SSQL. Such flexibility was a major consideration in choosing the product, according to Reardon, since previous versions of the Solomon packages had also been built on Btrieve.

Arctco, Inc.

Arctco, Inc. (located 60 miles east of Grand Forks, North Dakota, and 60 miles south of the Canadian border) has in the past few years moved its payroll, personnel, accounting, shipping, and manufacturing bills-of-material systems from a Unisys mainframe to a distributed network based on Btrieve. The manufacturer of Arctic Cat snowmobiles and Tigershark watercraft had used some 150 remote terminals throughout its plant and had found it necessary to upgrade the mainframe hardware every twenty-four to thirty-six months just to meet the need for increased processing capacity.

Rather than continue the upgrade spiral, Arctco installed a distributed network involving five servers and using Novell's NetWare versions 3.11 and 3.12. Raymond Koukari, Jr., the MIS director, explains that the company already owned its mainframe source code, all written in COBOL-74 using the Unisys DMS-II database. To simplify conversion, they chose to do the network development using Visual COBOL from MBP with Borland's ObjectVision providing a simple user-interface tool. "Our database choices were many, all claiming superior performance," said Koukari. However, in his seventeen years as programmer, analyst, consultant, and teacher before coming to Arctco, he had become quite familiar with Btrieve, and he recommended it strongly. "The programmers took to Btrieve like ducks to water," he reports. Part of their easy transition was due to the presence of transaction processing, record locking, and logging, all of which were features of DMS-II that they had used heavily.

As a first step in the total conversion, the company converted the payroll and personnel systems. A full year was scheduled for the changeover, and (like most conversion projects) it was barely adequate. However, the project finished on time and users were highly pleased. This gave the rest of the conversion a green light.

The first phase taught Koukari's developers one lesson: their choice of tools had been too limited. For the major task, they had geared up by learning C and C++, but decided these languages would be too cumbersome to deal with the rapid changes necessary to match company growth. The final choice was Visual Basic, which could meet performance requirements when augmented with appropriate controls. This included Btrieve controls from both Classic Software and Smithware, making the underlying Btrieve files available to all applications developed for the system.

While developers were stocking their toolboxes, the hardware for all three plants was going into place. Fiber-optic backbones connected separate LANs in each plant, and training for all terminal operators began. With the network up and running, the conversion began in earnest.

More than 400 user functions required rewrite, as did some 1,000 reports. After more than two years of effort (including the year-long first phase), July 5, 1994, marked I-day. Despite the usual initial problems encountered with any conversion of such magnitude, it was a success. After eight weeks of having the mainframe standing by in case fallback was needed, Koukari's department powered it down. "Wow, was our computer room quiet!" Koukari recalls.

Benefits from the conversion were many: shipping capacity (limited by the system's ability to generate manifests) tripled, and an additional bonus was the ability to automatically select the best shipping method for every case. Engineers who had formerly spent ten minutes listing each bill of materials on the mainframe as the first step toward making a design change are now able to do complete processing of the same bill in less than 45 seconds because of Btrieve's rapid retrieval capability. Several days were trimmed from the annual budgeting exercise because of the new system's ability to interface spreadsheet calculations and the database files. "By far the most important accomplishment," says Koukari, "is that we are now in a better position to change *with* the business, rather than following behind."

Greater Illinois Title Company

Greater Illinois Title Company, in just nine years, has grown to twenty times its original size. Starting in 1985 with nine employees and one office, the firm now employs 180 and maintains nine offices. In 1993, it was the largest independent policy issuing agent of Chicago Title Insurance Company, both in the number of policies issued and the total value of premiums remitted.

During all this growth, Btrieve has been at the base of the company's data files. Barry Loveland, VP for MIS, spearheaded the efforts, developing programs to streamline operation systems and procedures. He credits the application independence of Btrieve files, together with the speed and efficiency of the system, with making this possible.

Starting with databases relating customers and orders, Loveland was able to add additional tables providing names, legal descriptions, and activity details associated with each order. He then linked both the customer and order datasets to an invoicing application, which in turn feeds into a database of fees, payments, and expenses.

The next step was to add closings, linked to customers and invoices, followed by policies (linked only to closings). Also linked to closings, finally, was a file of checks deposited.

For each of these datasets, front-end applications meet specific business needs. Loveland and his staff use Realia Cobol, C, and Visual Basic to create the front ends. Ten LAN servers (interconnected through 56K lines) provide autonomy at each office together with a central master site. Currently this system contains more than 5 million records spread over 2 gigabytes of storage, with two database servers. Client platforms include DOS, Windows, and OS/2.

ThinkNet, Inc.

ThinkNet is a team of innovative technology consultants specializing in databases and communications. For remote data collection situations involving disconnected databases spread across the entire nation, with high volume and multiple platforms, they routinely choose Btrieve and SSQL.

Directors Paul Pavlik, Jr. and Edward S. Kress say they chose Btrieve for its ability to deal effectively with large data volumes and its support of multiple platforms. The data integrity features, support for referential integrity, and ability to handle full transactions as a unit, all provided additional reasons for its use. Because of the large number of remote sites involved, ability to use the client engine free of royalty payments was an added bonus. Finally, Btrieve's rapid access times aided in maintaining the required performance levels.

By choosing SSQL to work with the Btrieve foundation, Pavlik and Kress made the data dictionary independent of the databases themselves and allowed the developers to concentrate on the application rather than on database administrator functions. In addition, SSQL was simple to install, configure, and use, and like Btrieve itself, was small, fast, and efficient in use of resources.

Using these tools, ThinkNet is able to provide one-way replication over such huge networks to collect all data changes from remote sites and channel them into a single master database, while retaining a detailed audit trail. This replication occurs automatically and is independent of the individual applications at the remote sites. Future plans include addition of bi-directional replication and customizable rules to help resolve timing issues, but customers are quite happy with current systems.

Gates Rubber Company

Another example of a massive system built on Btrieve is the Gates Advanced Information Network (GAIN) created by Gates Rubber Company of Denver, Colorado, a leading maker of belts and hoses for transportation and other industries since 1911. An outgrowth of cooperative processing begun in the 1980s after IBM decided to discontinue the 8100 system that Gates had been using, GAIN now serves not only the huge Denver facility through a MAN but also connects to distribution centers across the continent via a WAN.

Along with the IBM decision, another impetus for development of GAIN was a growing dissatisfaction with the centralized application development imposed by classic mainframe practices. The system still includes a mainframe that holds corporate data (using IDMS) and can act as either a client or a server in the Denver MAN, but the vast majority of workstations are PCs. Each remote site has its own local server and local database built on Btrieve.

Gates serves some 20,000 customers with 150,000 products involving more than 130,000 different raw materials and does over $1 billion in annual sales; thus, GAIN is not a small system by any stretch of the imagination. It serves twenty-four plants and twenty-eight distribution and service centers across the continent, by means of the North American WAN. Each of these centers includes a LAN that connects to the WAN, providing full access to GAIN.

Fred Meier, manager of systems architecture for Gates, lists forty-five distinct Btrieve tables used in the Denver MAN. Eighteen of these are shared with the WAN and the remaining twenty-seven are available only in Denver. Ten of the twenty-seven support customer operations, eleven are for distribution operations, and six belong to manufacturing operations.

Meier describes GAIN in terms of three software layers called Red, Blue, and Green. The Red layer consists of corporate data and business rules. Blue contains applications that interface only with both apps and data in the Red layer. These layers both exist only in the headquarters MAN. The Green layer contains everything on the continent-spanning WAN, including local databases and applications developed locally at each site to meet specific needs. Applications in the Green layer have access to both Red and Green data as required to meet business requirements.

The List Goes On

These sketches provide only a small sample of the total user base. For instance, in the financial community alone, such firms as Great Plains Software, Macola, Inc., Platinum Accounting, Princeton Financial Systems, Inc., and even the Bank of England were among those sending representatives (at their own expense) to a recent planning conference in Austin hosted by BTI.

David Fry, CIO of Fry's Electronics (a West Coast electronics retail distribution giant) uses Btrieve-based systems to maintain not only accounting data but also to provide inventory control and to track hot-selling items.

Joe Dyer, project manager for Windows at Micro-MRP, Inc. in Foster City, California, uses Btrieve to handle the involved multilevel data access necessary to support manufacturing requirements prediction (MRP) calculations. MRP makes possible just-in-time ordering of inventory by accurately forecasting need for assemblies and their component parts and taking into account all lead times involved. Here again reliability and speed are essential characteristics since failures in an MRP system can literally force a plant to shut down and send all workers home.

Other users are legion. Many health-care support firms (such as IPS Summit of Dallas, Texas) use Btrieve to track all types of information. Vinzant, Inc. creates decision support systems based on Btrieve. Even IBM builds document imaging applications on a Btrieve base. Magic Software, a general-purpose application development system created in Israel, originally used only Btrieve as its foundation. The latest versions of the Magic package now support other record management systems along with Btrieve, but the Btrieve engine remains the backbone of most Magic applications because of its ability to provide other programs access to the same files with no problems.

Although most of the firms and organizations mentioned in this chapter are at least moderately large (and some are giants), the vast majority of the 50,000 registered Btrieve developers work in small companies or as individual consultants. They create custom applications to meet specific needs of a single client. Providing these solo operators with full information about the program, its use, and the internal structure of its files was the primary reason for creating this book.

Conclusion

In this chapter you've met Btrieve itself and a cross-section of the companies and developers who use the package. In Chapter 2 we turn our attention to the differences between a record manager, such as Btrieve, and the more familiar database management systems, such as dBase, Paradox, or Oracle.

2

Database Versus
Record Management

Mention "Btrieve" to anyone not yet familiar with the package, and the response (if it's not a puzzled "What did you say?") is likely to be, "Oh, yes, it's a database manager, isn't it?" From Btrieve's first days, that's how the software industry has perceived the product.

Competing database technologies have taken full advantage of this general perception by emphasizing how much more they provide in the way of end-user interfaces and ad-hoc queries, in comparison to "plain old Btrieve." Unfortunately, these efforts have been all too successful in some cases, causing Btrieve to be dismissed prematurely from consideration. The comparison is not just a case of "apples to oranges"; it's more like comparing apples to potatoes, because the fact of the matter is that Btrieve is not a database management system (DBMS) at all!

Instead, Btrieve is a record management system and functions at a lower level of system architecture than does a DBMS. Because of this, it's possible to build any of several different varieties of DBMS atop the common foundation provided by Btrieve, yet all of them can simultaneously access the underlying data. As far as I am aware, no other record management techniques even begin to approach this flexibility.

Because the distinction between a record management system and a DBMS is so crucial to proper understanding of Btrieve and what it does, this chapter explores in detail the differences between the two. First, let's use a number of widely known products to examine conventional DBMS capabilities. We'll then see how Btrieve's functions differ, yet can be (and are) used to provide equivalent capabilities in a seamless fashion.

Database Management Systems

Before we can even begin to establish any kind of definition for database management systems, we must first determine just what a database might be. Although nearly everyone who deals with data in any way seems to feel this concept is so obvious that it doesn't need a specific definition, the result of this widespread attitude makes itself evident in the wealth of contradictory advertising claims concerning database management in general. For instance, one group of experts insists that only a fully relational DBMS can validly be described using the phrase "data model," while other equally vocal authorities dismiss such claims as nonsense.

What Constitutes Data?

Let's attempt to avoid the religious-war overtones that seem to spring from nowhere when anyone tries to discuss database theory and see if we can come up with useful definitions of the terms we're using in this chapter. A logical place to begin is with data itself.

One way to look at data is as "a sequence of bits residing on storage media," to take a phrase from a 1983 reference book (see Figure 2.1). However, by this definition, a stream of random noise would be

Figure 2.1   *A bit stream as data?*

considered as data having equal validity with any other sequence of bits. Therefore, this definition is far too general to be useful in describing the kind of data intended to be managed by any DBMS or similar system.

That same reference book defines a record as "an organized and identifiable aggregate of data," which comes much closer to describing the data we deal with in our information systems. But a better definition, since it also applies outside the computer-specific domain, is based on Webster's Unabridged Dictionary's definition of datum. To paraphrase, data consists of the permanent (or relatively so) transcription of facts that result from observation of physical events.

Although this definition may appear unduly limited (how can my name be an observation?), it really isn't as restrictive as it looks. Any item of data can be traced back to some physical event. In the case of a person's name, the physical event occurred shortly after birth, when the parents chose a name for their offspring (see Figure 2.2). Other seemingly abstract data items similarly result from physical events that took place at some past time.

Figure 2.2   *One item of data*

With a usable definition of data itself, we can turn our attention to deciding just what a database might be. A starting point might be the once-popular but now obsolescent equivalent data bank, which immediately draws the mental analogy of a place where things can be deposited and withdrawn, and which has some system of accounting for the items deposited.

Banks or Bases?

In fact one definition of data bank is that it's a file of data from a variety of sources, stored for ready access by a range of possible users. The only thing I find wrong with this definition is its use of the term *file,* since most data banks consist of many files rather than just one.

Thus, we can consider a database to be something like a data bank, or a collection of data items originating from many sources and retained for use by multiple clients. Such a database may consist of either a single file or of thousands of different files spread out across tens or hundreds of computer sites. The defining characteristic is that the database contains many data items and is accessible by a variety of potential users of its content.

Notice especially that this definition for a database makes no mention at all of the technique by which the content is managed, nor does it even necessarily imply that any management at all exists. A recycling dumpster full of old newspapers, tossed in at random, could be considered a database under this definition—and it *is* one in fact (see Figure 2.3). Such a random collection, with no means for locating any desired item, isn't very useful, of course. But it's still a database, and if nothing better is available, is even a usable one.

When you want to locate any specific item, such as the bid and asked values of a single stock issue on the New York Stock Exchange on the 23rd of last month, you must first search all the newspapers in the bin, one by one, until you find the one for the desired day. Then you must search that paper, page by page, until finding the market quotations, and finally you must search that list for the issue in which you are interested.

Figure 2.3   *The dumpster as database*

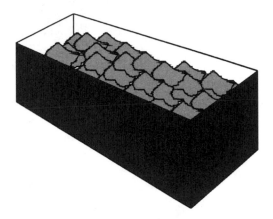

If you are especially lucky, you'll find the right item on your first try. If you're very unlucky, you may not find it until the last paper in the bin (I'm assuming that the bin actually does contain the paper you need, but even this isn't guaranteed in reality). Thus your retrieval time for the data can range from a matter of minutes to an upper limit measured in days or months, if ever. And the average time to locate any specific item turns out to be half of the maximum time. We'll get back to these figures later when we look at indexing techniques. For now, let's try to refine our definition a bit.

A somewhat more restrictive definition of a database (which would *not* include our dumpster full of discarded newsprint) is that presented by Al Stevens in his tutorial book, *C Database Development*. He defines a database as an integrated collection of data files related to each other in support of a common purpose (see Figure 2.4).

This definition brings us back to the universe of computers and data files and adds the extremely important qualification that all the data in the database be related (somehow) in support of a common purpose. This common purpose may, however, be rather broadly defined itself. For instance, one of the dreams of many corporate information officers is to create a single massive database that contains every shred of data necessary for the business to operate and achieve its goals.

Figure 2.4 *Even this can be a database.*

One significant distinction between a simple file of data and a true database is that the database usually comprises a number of files, each related to the others in various ways. This does *not* mean that all databases are **relational** (a technical term we'll explore later in this chapter) but it *does* mean that they all involve relations between different data items.

For now, let's accept Stevens's definition as adequate if not exhaustive and move on to examine the factors and functions involved in database management. Obviously, any real database requires management of its content in order to be useful. The wide range of retrieval times we encountered in that bin full of newsprint underscores the necessity of both properly organizing storage techniques and making it easy to get data back out of the database once it's there.

Managing the Material

More specifically, a serviceable system for managing databases (or a DBMS) needs to provide as a minimum four major functions. These are methods for

1. Creating data items within the database

2. Retrieving those items once they are created

3. Updating the content as required to keep the information current

4. Deleting unwanted items once they are no longer required

Even though some DBMS policies may forbid change or removal of data, requiring instead that new correction entries be added in order to maintain historical records (a frequent requirement in accounting and legal data systems), the DBMS must still provide those capabilities if for no other reason than to permit testing of the system with dummy data and subsequent removal of that dummy data before putting the system into production use.

In the information industry's jargon, the creation-retrieval-update-delete capability is known by the homely acronym CRUD, and this quartet of functions is at the heart of every DBMS (see Figure 2.5). Although the methods by which each function is accomplished may vary widely from one DBMS to the next, the functions themselves are present. In fact, the earliest examples of DBMS provided just those facilities and little if anything more.

Figure 2.5   *CRUD: The heart of every DBMS*

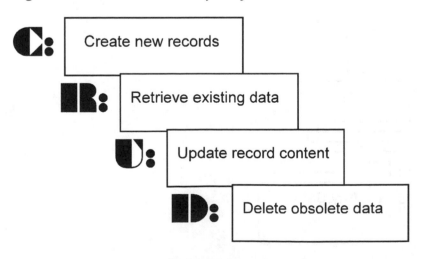

Early Efforts

Many early attempts at database organization were modeled upon either the card file, such as that used by a public library for its catalog, or the conventional office filing cabinet (see Figure 2.6). In both cases, a single card or file folder contained all necessary information about a single subject and was stored in accordance with a specified sequence (usually alphabetical). This made retrieval of the data simple as long as no misfiling occurred.

In the computer, the card becomes a **record.** The entire collection of records becomes a **file,** and the individual items of interest within each specific record are called **fields.** Most data management models use these terms. However, the relational model we'll encounter soon employs alternate terms that shift the emphasis away from physical structure to its logical domain.

When it became necessary to provide multiple sequences (as in the library card catalog where books were filed by title, by subject, and by author) a problem loomed. To solve it, either multiple copies of the record were created and inserted into the file, or "see also" reference cards were located strategically in the other sequences.

Figure 2.6   *One of the earliest database prototypes*

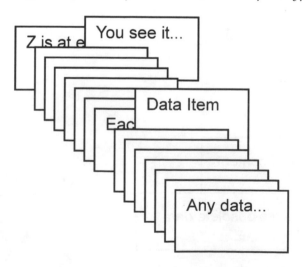

In the computer versions of such data organization techniques, multiple copies quickly proved impractical. If three copies of a record existed in the file, it rapidly became apparent that at least one and possibly two of the three would fail to be updated with critical information. The result was a loss of data integrity; it became impossible to trust any data retrieved from such a file unless all copies were retrieved and compared to each other.

On the other hand the "see also" technique became extremely easy to implement, since multiple entries could be placed in an index, all referring to a single data record; the computer could access that record almost instantly once its address was known, making it possible to provide many more "see also" references for each data item. This approach evolved into the multiple-index databases in near-universal use today. It also provided impetus for development of rapid, reliable indexing systems, leading in turn to the B-tree approach, which is the basis of Btrieve.

However, even with indexing, a DBMS can be organized along many different lines. Let's look at some of the most significant such organization models, in historical sequence, to see how they compare in terms of advantages and disadvantages.

Keep in mind as we do so that only purists care much about the finer points of database theory. The people who use, and pay for, the database put their emphasis on accuracy, reliability, and efficiency, usually in that order. The world's most theoretically perfect database is useless if it cannot deliver accuracy, is unavailable more than available, or takes years to provide a response.

The Hierarchy Approach

One of the earliest organizational models was to store data as a hierarchy of related records in a format closely resembling the traditional organization chart. This level-based approach imposed serious constraints on freedom to establish relations between specific items of information: each record type can have only one relation to a parent; even more restrictive is the fact that any two record types can have only one relation linking them.

For instance, a company with many offices might establish the
office location as the topmost level of the hierarchy, with the various functional divisions in each office (accounting, sales, and so on)
as the next lower level (see Figure 2.7). This organization makes it
simple to retrieve all data concerning a specific office, but falls
short of the ideal when it's necessary to gather accounting data
from all offices at once to create, as an example, a month-end profit-
and-loss statement.

Figure 2.7   *Hierarchical organization of data*

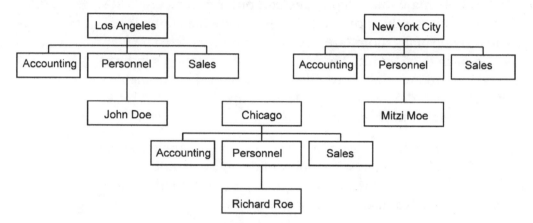

A real headache present in the hierarchy-based model, though, is
the problem of handling transfers from one lower-level area to
another. Consider the movement of personnel records if John Doe,
Richard Roe, and Mitzi Moe all transfer to different locations. The
single-relation rule makes it necessary to copy their records from
the old area to a new one. In the process of moving all records for
each employee from one personnel group to another, errors are virtually certain to occur.

The problem of gathering company-wide data for reports is easy to
solve. Just arrange the hierarchy in a different sequence, placing the
functional divisions at a higher level than the office locations, as in
Figure 2.8.

However, this merely brings a new obstacle into existence. Although it's easy to gather accounting or sales data company-wide,

Figure 2.8   *Revised hierarchy still finds transfers a problem.*

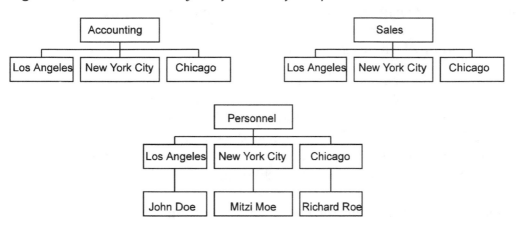

it becomes more difficult to create a complete report of operations for any specific location. The transfer situation, meanwhile, remains a headache for all concerned.

That's the major problem with the hierarchical model for database organization. No matter how the levels are initially arranged, some critical needs are almost certain to be made difficult to achieve simply because of the organization layers themselves. The restriction to a single relation between different record types, necessary in order to define the hierarchy, makes the problem inescapable.

A secondary problem is nearly as serious (and may in some cases even be worse): Such a database becomes all but impossible to expand or modify, except after total redesign from the top down. This total redesign requirement often proves too costly to even be considered. The database then remains static while the business changes. Eventually the database becomes completely outdated. This is a major reason why *legacy system* is often considered synonymous with *problem*.

The Network Model

Another early organization method known as the network model places essentially no restrictions upon the number of relations in which a record type may participate. A single record in such a database may be, all at the same time, related to two different **parent** records while having a number of **siblings** and even **children.** The family-based terms that describe the levels involved reflect the metaphor from which this model came.

To a large degree, the network model embodies concepts first popularized by M.V. Wilkes's invention of linked lists, in the earliest days of computer research. The total generality of the list idea appealed to researchers in all areas of the industry. Language developers came up with IPL-V and LISP based on the list structure. Systems theorists developed processor architectures using the idea of list linkage, and most of our modern CPU designs descend from these. And those most concerned with data processing applied the idea to help organize their collections of data items.

One of the most influential of these network-model systems was the Integrated Data Store (IDS). Charles Bachman developed IDS at the General Electric Company's computer division in Phoenix, Arizona, during the late 1950s and early 1960s, making it public in 1961. In this design (which eventually became a major part of the COBOL standards), records of the database are linked into **chains.** Links can be **masters, slaves,** or **details,** and the only limit to the number of links allowed for any single record is the record size itself (see Figure 2.9).

Any diagram of a production-level IDS organization tended to resemble a spiderweb because of the large number of links between record types. The sketch shown here only approaches the complexity of actual structures that have been a mainstay of many industries for more than a quarter-century. Even in this simplified form, the detail tends to become overwhelming. To retrieve information from an IDS database, one first traverses the master chain to find the record type involved in the search. With the type's master record located, tracing out its slave and detail chains leads to the desired specific record.

Although the process may sound cumbersome when described in words, it took full advantage of the capabilities of then-new disk storage devices. Consequently, a well-designed IDS system's performance usually surpassed that of competing data organizations.

Figure 2.9 *This spiderweb represents an IDS database organization.*

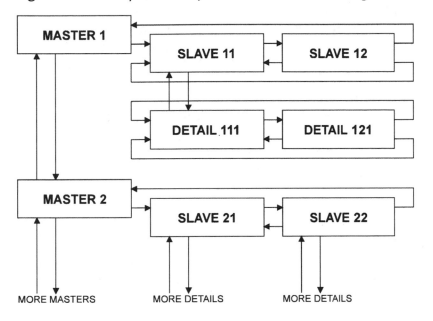

Another example of the network model is Raima's Data Manager.

A Navigational Approach

According to some authorities, the navigational model includes both the hierarchical and network models within its bounds. In this book, though, I use the phrase to refer specifically to the flat-file, card-index-oriented type of database most widely known in the desktop computer industry. Examples of commercial products based on the navigational model include xBase (including dBase, FoxPro, Clipper, Phase3, and a number of others using the DBF file format) and Vulcan/EB. Some other popular products, such as Access, Paradox, and Clarion, can be used as navigational structures, although their architecture is not necessarily that of the flat file. The navigational-model product on which I focus, though, is Btrieve itself. For the original version and all subsequent releases, the built-in application programming interface (API) is completely navigational in nature.

To describe the characteristics of the navigational model, let's go back to the first popular desktop program built on this model, dBASE. In the March 1991 issue of *Data Based Advisor* magazine, this program's originator, C. Wayne Ratliff, told how the package came into existence.

It began in 1975, when he was working on the Viking Mars-lander project at the Jet Propulsion Laboratory, in charge of database management for the spacecraft's ground support system. Although JPL had developed a database tool called JPLDIS, he did not use it in his work. Ratliff first became interested in creating an English-like interpretive language for extracting statistics from data sets. This was not a part of his job, but originated from his participation in office football pools. Within only days, however, his emphasis shifted from football to the possibilities inherent in the language itself.

By November 1976, Ratliff had become the owner (and builder) of an IMSAI computer, and the next fifteen months went by as he brought it up to full operational capability. During this time he came across the JPLDIS manuals in the lab's library and thought it might be a good starting point for his effort. And in January 1978, he began writing a program that would interpret a simplified subset of the JPLDIS commands.

The DBF file format, according to Ratliff's account, came into existence on January 29, 1978, "probably around midnight." With a file format established, Ratliff went on to implement the commands CREATE, DISPLAY STRUCTURE, DISPLAY, APPEND, and EDIT. In the months that followed, he added additional commands, mostly modeled on the keywords present in BASIC.

Ratliff called his original program Vulcan; the name became dBASE in 1980 when Ratliff joined forces with George Tate in late 1980 and Ashton-Tate was formed to distribute it as a commercial product. By 1983 relations between Ratliff and A-T had begun to sour and he eventually left to create his own Emerald Bay / Vulcan product line. The dBASE legacy, however, had been established by that time. Its features have constituted a benchmark for compatibility in the desktop database industry ever since.

These features, present in virtually all navigational-model approaches, include the standard CRUD capabilities. Multiple indexes not only are permitted but are encouraged. All data items within a specific file share the same record format, and the only relations established are those implied by the appearance of different fields within the record. This single-format restriction gives the model its common name, **flat file.**

Navigation from one record to another within the file uses the current index to establish which records are first, last, previous, next, and current. Changing the index in use thus changes the effective sort order of the file although no physical data movement occurs (see Figure 2.10).

The industry's vocabulary includes a number of terms other than **navigational model** to describe this structure and technique. General Electric and Honeywell Bull labeled it the Index Sequential Processor (ISP). IBM applied the label indexed sequential access method (ISAM), as did some Microsoft products.

The navigational model is unsurpassed for such sequential tasks as repetitive data entry, and its machine-level primitives are virtually required for implementation of all other data models. That is, any other data model can be constructed on top of the foundation that the navigational primitives provide. This simple fact is the heart of Btrieve's microkernel approach: the microkernel provides the

Figure 2.10 *Navigational: One file, two sequences, via indexes*

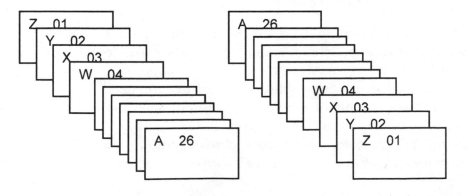

primitives while a higher-level layer provides an appropriate model implementation.

Relational Theory and Practice

Although most discussions of database management systems (including this one) view the relational model as an entity totally distinct from all other data models, at least one expert sees it as a special case of the network model. Ben Shneiderman has written that a relational database is a network database in which the relations between data types are handled in a quite specific manner.

The apparent distinction, in Shneiderman's view, stems from the terminology used to describe relational databases, which is quite different from that in everyday use for all other models. For example, the everyday relation between data types becomes, in the RDBMS vocabulary, an interrelational dependency. The word relation itself then refers to the record type. Although this may remind some readers of Humpty Dumpty's attitude toward words, as described by Lewis Carroll, it's not as arbitrary as it might seem.

The relational theory of database organization made its first public appearance in a 1969 IBM Research Report by E. F. Codd, titled "Derivability, Redundancy, and Consistency of Relations Stored in Large Data Banks." The actual model was described by Codd the following year in the *Communications of the ACM* and quickly attracted interest from many parts of the industry. A major reason for the model's rapid acceptance was its solid base in mathematical theory; nearly all previous database models had simply evolved pragmatically based on empirical experience.

Because of the theoretical underpinnings, Codd felt it essential to use the mathematical vocabulary rather than the existing database jargon. Thus, instead of files of records with each record composed of fields, a relational database contains tables, organized into rows and columns. The metaphor is that of a matrix or a multidimensional array. Each data item may be (and usually is) spread across several tables, as one row of each table. The collection of rows composing a single data item then becomes a relation, since it's expressed in terms of interrelational dependencies between the tables that identify which row (or rows) of table A is related to a specific row of table B.

Relationships, in other words, are represented by including certain data items in more than one table. These specific matching data items, or keys (not to be confused with the keys used in Btrieve), take values from a shared domain of possible values. All rows with matching values in such key fields participate in the same relationship.

In practice, one column in the rows of each table (known as the **primary key** for the table) uniquely identifies each row within that table. This primary key establishes the domain of possible values for dependencies in which it participates. Other columns within each table establish any dependencies. These columns contain values that are in domains established by other tables within the database, and are called **foreign** keys.

Figure 2.11, though greatly simplified, shows the basics of the relational model. Much more is required before a database can be considered fully relational, however. In 1985, Codd published a set of twelve rules he said must be met before a system could be considered fully relational. Paraphrased from a May 1986 report written by Codd (and revised a year later), these rules are as follows.

1. All information in the database must be represented explicitly, by values in relational tables, and in no other way.

Figure 2.11   *Simple three-table RDBMS organization*

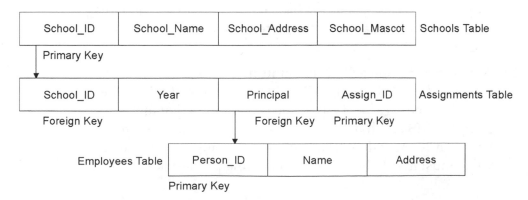

2. Every atomic value of information in the database must be logically accessible through a combination of table name, primary key value, and column name.

3. Indicators for "missing" information, distinct from blank or empty space, must be supported and must be independent of data type; the DBMS must also be capable of dealing with these indicators as if they were actual data.

4. The database must be fully described in a data dictionary, which must be represented in the same manner as all other data so that users can deal with it in the same way.

5. At least one language must be provided for dealing with the database, and this language must support data definition, definition of views, manipulation of data both interactively and by program, integrity of information, security of the data, and establishment of transaction boundaries.

6. An algorithm to determine (when a view is defined) whether that view is capable of modifying data both at the row level and for each column within the view must be provided; results of this determination must be recorded in the data dictionary (rule 4) entries for the view.

7. The DBMS must be able to deal with both base relations and derived relations as a single operand during retrieval, insertion, update, and deletion operations.

8. Changes made to either storage formats or access methods must have no logical impact on application programs.

9. Any kinds of changes to the base tables that are capable of preserving information unimpaired must do so without affecting application programs.

10. Any applicable integrity constraints must be capable of definition in the data language (Rule 5) and must be stored in the data dictionary (Rule 4). Two such constraints that apply to every DBMS are that no component of a primary key may have a missing value, and each non-missing foreign key's value must match the value of an existing primary key in the

same domain. These are known as **entity integrity** and **referential integrity** respectively.

11. The database must preserve all applications without impairment if data distribution is introduced or if data is redistributed.

12. If the database can be accessed by a low level language, that low level must not be able to bypass or subvert the integrity constraints of Rule 10.

Few, if any, commercially available systems completely meet more than eleven of these requirements. The stumbling block, in most cases, is Rule 12, since any data can be modified by machine-language intervention. This failure, however, has not prevented anyone from claiming full RDBMS functionality for a product.

Among products based primarily on the relational model we find IBM's DB2, Oracle, Paradox, Access, and many others. The most widely used data query language, Structured Query Language (SQL), presumes the relational organization and meets the requirements of Rule 5. Little doubt exists that the RDBMS is, today, the standard for information technology.

So what does this portend for the Btrieve approach? I see no serious impact here. As noted earlier, every RDBMS must be based on a functional record management engine of some sort, even though that engine may be carefully concealed from users of the system. No other record manager begins to approach Btrieve in the three areas of most importance to paying customers: accuracy, reliability, and efficiency.

Btrieve's creators seem to share this feeling. Their Scalable SQL product provides an effective RDBMS interface to underlying data that need not necessarily follow all of Codd's twelve rules and provide fully relational organization. The microkernel that forms the foundation of both Btrieve and SSQL in their most recent versions provides full relational integrity of data (one of the most difficult of the twelve rules to deal with) at the engine level. The outlook is bright.

Future Possibilities

Most of today's pundits seem to consider object orientation the next "silver bullet" for solution of all software problems. Although I've worked with it to some degree, I felt my knowledge was incomplete. To put Btrieve into context with regard to such future possibilities, I asked Rud Merriam, a Houston consultant who specializes in object-oriented programming and is working on theoretical justification for object data base management systems, to explain for me just how an ODBMS differs from the more conventional variety.

"Data management research didn't stop with the advent of the relational model," he explained. "A specific area of continuing interest involves complex objects. To deal with these, several workers have extended the relational model, by relaxing its implied normalization requirements while maintaining a rigorous mathematical foundation. This led to the development of object database management systems (ODBMS).

"Currently, ODBMS are used primarily as application specific data management tools. In the applications where ODBMS are being used they are of great value. One area of common use is for storage of graphic information such as that in CAD, CAM, and CASE tools. Such an application contains well-defined object classes and well-defined relationships between those objects. In these applications, too, retrieving one object normally draws upon relationships to bring in many other objects.

"In a CAD drawing, bringing in a Widget also brings in a multitude of lines, arcs, figures, and notations. Using other database forms to access all these other objects by indexes is horribly time consuming."

The jury is still out as to the advantages of the ODBMS for general use, however. Only a few commercial products yet exist, and user reaction to them has been mixed at best. However, should this turn out to be a significant part of the future for database developers, Btrieve will be ready to support them. The latest versions of Btrieve's microkernel engines were designed specifically to permit these kinds of application interface layers (plus others not even dreamed of as yet) to be grafted seamlessly into an effective system.

An Often Overlooked Item

If each of us had only a penny for every hour wasted in religious-war debate between proponents of the different distinct database models, we would all be independently wealthy and would have no need to be concerned about the differences. I hope that the brief descriptions of each model given in this chapter show clearly enough that each of the techniques has both strengths and weaknesses. Granted, some approaches have more in the way of weakness than strength, and others tilt the balance in the opposite direction. However, in specific cases, each model outperforms all others. This means that a system having the ability to mix models and use each with the application for which it's best suited always maximizes application effectiveness. Btrieve's possession of this ability has played a significant role in the product's rise to its current level of acceptance.

Structured Query Language and the DBMS

Shortly after Dr. Codd published his relational database theories, IBM's research center put together something called Structured Query Language (SQL, now pronounced "sequel") to comply with Rule 5 of the twelve rules. Thus, the RDBMS model significantly influenced the structure and syntax of SQL. As a result, SQL and RDBMS became almost synonymous to most computer users. However, even though SQL is built on the relational model, a database need not be relational in itself to use SQL.

As the relational model grew in popularity, SQL advanced right alongside. Originally confined to IBM's mainframe databases, it became more generic when Oracle introduced its version in 1979. By 1986 the language became an ANSI standard (revised in 1989 and again in 1992). At least 140 different database products with SQL capability had been counted by 1993, according to Martin Gruber's book, *SQL Instant Reference.*

SQL differs significantly from conventional programming languages. Possibly the most striking difference is its nonprocedural approach. Where programming languages specify step by step every action required to solve a problem, SQL merely states what result is required and leaves the rest up to the DBMS.

Because of this generality, SQL is probably the most widely known information-retrieval method in use today. The 1992 version of the standard is five times as long as the original 1986 document. The creators of Btrieve are fully aware of the importance of SQL and have met the implied challenge, as we shall see near the end of this chapter.

Record Managers

The record manager differs significantly from the DBMS. The DBMS, regardless of model, puts its primary emphasis on the organization of data. The record manager, on the other hand, concentrates on rapid and effective storage and retrieval of data; it need have no concern with details of data layout within each record. All other considerations remain the responsibility of the application that uses the manager's services.

This difference permits direct access to data for those applications not requiring true database features. It also allows developers to build both navigational and relational DBMS models atop the same set of data files and thus obtain the best of all worlds.

Runtime Functions

Earlier in this chapter we met the four primary functions required by any database: creation, retrieval, update, and delete capabilities, or CRUD. Many DBMS packages (such as the original dBASE, Fox-Pro, and Access) depend upon a **runtime module** to provide these primary functions. Others (such as FairCom's C-Tree) employ a static library approach and link the functions into each application from that static library. Today's advanced systems include much more than the elementary primitives, of course, and the differences in feature lists are among the major competitive points when choosing a system.

However, all systems share the basic elements. One way of categorizing the primitives is to divide them into groups: File Management functions, Data Management, Index Management, and so forth.

Using this approach, the File Management group might include functions to create a new database, to open an existing database thus permitting access to its content, to close the database once created or opened, and finally to destroy the entire database. Data Management could include writing new records, reading existing ones, rewriting or updating a record to change its content, and deleting a record. This group might also include the functions to permit searching for a record according to any desired criteria. Index Management could provide procedures for adding entire new indexes to the database, deleting an existing index, or setting one of several indexes to be used for subsequent data retrieval searches.

By no means is this the only possible organization of a set of DBMS primitive operations. Additionally, today's need for shared access to data within a database adds a need for functions to manage concurrent access, particularly when two or more users need to modify the same record at the same instant. Such concurrency management should be built into the file and index management routines at the lowest levels, so it too needs to be part of the package of primitives.

Once such a functional package is available, any of the described database models can be implemented on top of the package, in exactly the same way that the primitives themselves are built on top of an operating system. We'll look at this layered approach in more detail throughout this book.

The Btrieve Microkernel

From its earliest version, Btrieve has provided just such a functional package upon which any type of interface can be built. Effective with version 6.0, however, the technology has been modularized in a way calculated to make the construction process simpler than ever before. A **microkernel engine** now encapsulates the necessary primitive functions. This engine can support any of several interface modules. At the same time, the engine acquired capabilities beyond the minimum requirements (such as enforcement of referential integrity even when not running a SQL application) to strengthen the support it provides.

The microkernel architecture introduced at version 6.0 is intended to provide not only data model independence, but platform independence also (see Figure 2.12). For each supported platform, a microkernel engine tailored to that platform's capabilities achieves maximum performance. Meanwhile, the data model layers remain unchanged from one platform to the next.

At the time of writing, engines for three platforms are shipping to developers and end users. By the time you read this, the Btrieve creators expect to support two additional platforms, with even more potentially coming in the future. The first three platforms are MS-DOS, 16-bit Windows, and Novell NetWare. The two scheduled to ship in early 1995 are OS/2 and Windows NT.

All platforms share several features of the microkernel engine. These include set operations, support for huge records, percentage operations, a plethora of data types, integrity enforcement at the engine level, true multithreading of the engine (even in a single-thread operating system), and complete management of transactions.

The set operations can deliver partial records and filter results. Huge record (BLOB or Binary large object) support permits storage of document images and similar large records within a database. Percentage operations assist developers in the use of **slider** controls to browse through multiple records. The many data types help in

Figure 2.12   *The microkernel architecture*

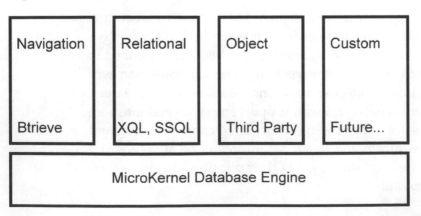

standardizing internal representations of such quantities as dates or financial data.

Enforcement of integrity at the engine level overcomes objections that availability of nonrelational interfaces violates Codd's Rule 12. Multithreading greatly improves system performance. Finally, transaction management eliminates the need to verify that no other user has changed a record that is being updated.

New features planned for addition to all microkernel engines in the near future include transparent two-phase commit actions, nested transactions, support for files larger than the present 4-GB limit, and improved support for continuous operation while allowing system backups to proceed unimpaired. No announced date for these plans exists, however. Also in the mill are additional specialized data types including arrays and messages, object storage capabilities, a scripting language providing stored procedures and event triggers, ability to replicate databases to remote sights, and versioning (which retains old information when new data is added).

The microkernel architecture provides five significant benefits, in comparison to the capabilities of older versions of Btrieve. Concurrent access to data while using different data models is now possible. New types of applications to allow information collaboration are supported. Existing applications achieve improved performance. Applications are easily transported to other platforms so long as a microkernel engine for the new platform is available. And best of all, these capabilities remain fully compatible with all older products. Even the original file formats are supported, although using them prohibits an application from taking advantage of the newest features.

Introducing Xtrieve

The need for a DBMS-style interface was recognized by the Btrieve development team as early as 1984, resulting in the introduction of the companion product Xtrieve, which provided an interactive SQL-like capability for retrieving data from Btrieve-based files. Xtrieve also introduced the data dictionary concept to Btrieve, in the form of DDF files that define the structure of the entire database (which can and usually does consist of many different files and indexes).

These DDF files serve the same purpose as the built-in file structure headers of xBase files, and are needed by many modern applications.

Xtrieve's menu allows users to build requests, views, and other relation-based constructs. The core of Xtrieve consists of a number of primitive functions that translate the SQL-like queries created by the user's menu into appropriate calls to the Btrieve engine operating invisibly behind the scenes. Although the primitive functions actually provide a relational expression statement, the user is unaware of the translation process and, as a result, can think purely in terms of table construction and table updates.

Xtrieve itself is positioned as a direct competitor to dBASE, FoxPro, and other xBase-like products that simplify ad-hoc inquiries from casual users and is inherently interactive. The only programming support available is the command file, which allows a sequence of interactive commands to be stored then played back for action sometime later.

As Figure 2.13 shows, Xtrieve-Plus is a DOS command-line application, although it conforms more closely to standard SAA user interface rules than do most products from its era. At this writing, the future of Xtrieve itself is somewhat uncertain although it's still included in the product line.

XQL and Scalable SQL

As demand for a true SQL capability grew, the primitives at the heart of Xtrieve were extracted into a separate package, and a SQL Language layer was added atop the primitives. This combination became the XQL product, released in 1987.

XQL comprises three different layers of software, known as XQLP, XQLM, and XQLI. The XQLP layer consists of the Xtrieve primitives and provides the actual interface with the underlying Btrieve

Figure 2.13   *Xtrieve dictionary listing, captured from screen*

```
    FILE: Appointments                                    RECORDS:    15
  LOCATION: patapp.dta                                   PAGE SIZE: 2560
 Field                  Type       Size   Dec Delimiter Case
  ID                     String       6                  No
  Appointment Date       Date         4
  Appointment Time       Time         4
  AM/PC                  String       4                  No
  Doctor                 String      12                  No
  Procedure Code         String       3                  No
  Amount Paid            Money        8
  Date Paid              Date         4




















  SWITCH
  Use ↑,↓ to view fields, ENTER for indexes, ESC when finished      Browse
```

engine. XQLM (XQL Manager) consists of the SQL Language layer, implementing the translation of SQL statements into a series of XQLP primitive calls. This translation is done by means of function calls to the XQL Manager code and therefore requires that the SQL statements be embedded in compiled programs. Finally, XQLI (the interactive layer) allows direct execution of individual SQL statements one by one.

The difference between Xtrieve and the XQLI functionality may be difficult to envision without having both packages available to experiment with. Briefly, it's this: Xtrieve presents a menu interface from which the user selects the desired actions, but XQLI simply accepts a SQL statement from the user and executes it. Thus, the Xtrieve user has no need to know SQL syntax or even that such a language exists, but a user of XQLI must be familiar with SQL to get anything done.

As business systems migrated from the original single-computer designs inherited from mainframe days into the current network-based client/server architecture, the XQL package evolved into something originally called Netware SQL but now known as Scalable SQL.

Conclusion

In this chapter you've explored the many different methods for organizing and storing information that comprise database technology. Chapter 3 focuses on the "rest of the story" (to steal Paul Harvey's phrase) and examines indexing techniques usable for gaining rapid access to any data we've stored away.

3

Indexing Methods, An Overview

In Chapter 2 you saw that a primary requirement for any DBMS is the ability to accurately retrieve any desired item of data upon demand. This chapter explores the techniques commonly used to meet this requirement. Beginning at the most basic level of physical data structure and storage—the nonautomated card catalog and its linear search—the discussion culminates with the highly effective B-tree technique employed by Btrieve.

Although techniques even more advanced than those of the B-tree exist, none has proved general enough to supersede this algorithm. You can find descriptions of some in the references listed at the end of this chapter.

Physical Storage Essentials

Before examining indexing techniques with any precision, we must establish exact definitions for the terms we'll be using to describe units of data storage and data structures themselves. These units and structures are related to, but separate from, the DBMS models we looked at in Chapter 2.

The significant difference is that, in this chapter, the units and structures are at a much lower level of abstraction, usually (but not always) referring to physical entities rather than to logical constructs.

Units of Data Storage

In the dim dark ages before the arrival of automation, collections of data took the form of boxes full of index cards. When Herman Hollerith invented the punched-card automaton to help process the 1890 census data, the card remained supreme. Not until well past the middle of the twentieth century did magnetic storage media force these pieces of pasteboard from their position of dominance in data processing.

The names we apply to units of data storage quite naturally descend from those used to describe the layout of a handwritten or typed index card. Each unit of information, such as the card itself, is known as a record. Each record consists of one or more (usually many more) fields. Each field deals with a single subject. A collection of records all having the same field layout is known as a file (derived presumably from the filing cabinet in which card indexes were usually housed).

Cards finally gave way to magnetic storage in the late 1960s and early 1970s. Today's dominant storage media include magnetic tape, floppy disks, and fixed disks. Optical storage devices are coming into use but are not yet widespread.

For all these devices, the same terms are used to describe units of data storage. It may be helpful to relate these units to the physical units of a disk storage unit: each disk surface contains several concentric tracks of data, each of which is divided into regular sectors, and a disk unit usually has at least two surfaces. Thus, the sector is similar to a field, the track to a record, and the surface to a file (see Figure 3.1).

Figure 3.1 *Elements of physical storage media*

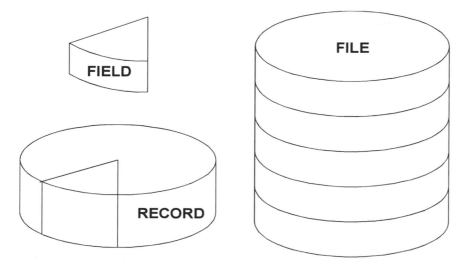

Some early database designs put this physical equivalence directly into practice by assigning a separate track to each record of their files. Although efficient, the extravagance of this technique with regard to storage resources kept it from ever achieving wide popularity. When operating systems became the norm, all use of direct physical mapping vanished.

Data Structures

Organizing large quantities of data so that records can be retrieved one-by-one requires the imposition of some type of structure upon the collection of individual records. Through the years a number of data structures have been proposed, but all fit into one of three major categories: arrays, lists, or trees.

An **array** arranges the records as a contiguous table, using the metaphor of a mathematical matrix. An index number identifies each record. This index number is the record's sequential position in the table and serves to retrieve the record on demand. Sequential storage locations, free of intervening data from other structures, form the array's identifying feature.

Unlike the array, a **list** contains individual records scattered throughout the possible storage space. A **pointer** or **link field** in each record chains to the next record in the structure. Data from other structures may be adjacent to any record. Random locations identified by link fields characterize the list.

A list-like structure that allows more than one other record to be connected to any record it contains is known as a **tree.** A tree, like a list, can be scattered throughout the storage space. However, it can also be stored in a tabular format like an array. The presence of multiple associated records for each specific record places a structure in the tree category, which has many variations.

Note that the type of physical storage used with any specific file may have significant effects on the types of data structures and search techniques permissible. For example, magnetic tape is inherently a sequential medium, and its use makes random access retrieval extremely inefficient. Because of this, the array is the only type of efficient data structure for tape files.

Arrays   An array uses the metaphor of a mathematical matrix, with each element assigned an index number. This index number serves to retrieve the record on demand. Use of the index number as the primary retrieval address for the record forces an array to be stored as a single contiguous structure within the storage space (see Figure 3.2). To keep all its elements together, the array must initially reserve space for all future records; the alternative requires creation of a new and larger structure each time a record is added, with all old records copied to the new one.

Figure 3.2   *An array always keeps its data together.*

1	First array element
2	Second element
3	and so on
	. . .
n	Until end of array

The array's rigid size limitations and extravagant use of storage resources make it unattractive for structuring large quantities of data, but this structure finds wide use for internal storage of small data packages. In Chapters 5, 6, and 7 of this book we see that Btrieve employs arrays to store many of its internal values. These include index segment specifications, page assignment tables, and so on. In fact, the other two types of data structures usually organize each individual record as an array in order to permit rapid access to the desired values.

So long as the size of an array remains within reasonable bounds, it's easy to search. Virtually all databases built upon magnetic tape storage used arrays as their primary data structure, since the sequential nature of tape storage and that of the array complemented each other.

Lists   To overcome the rigid space limitations of the array, Maurice V. Wilkes (one of the pioneers of computer science in Great Britain) added to each of the array's elements a **link field** containing the address of the next element. As a result, the elements no longer had to remain next to each other. Inserting a new element became a simple matter of putting it wherever space was available, setting its link field to the next element, and changing the link field of the previous element to point to the new item instead.

Wilkes called this new structure a list since it formed a list of items, rather than a single contiguous unit such as the array (see Figure 3.3). Almost immediately after he introduced it in the early 1950s, the list became immensely popular, not only for data structuring but for many other uses. AI pioneer John McCarthy created a language for list processing that he called LISP (*LIS*t *P*rocessor); it remains popular today.

The presence of the pointer or link field in each record, which chains to the next record in the structure, identifies the type of list. In the simple or singly linked list, each item contains only one such link field, and it points to the next item in the list as shown in the illustration. The last item in the list must either contain some reserved

Figure 3.3 *Lists made the array flexible.*

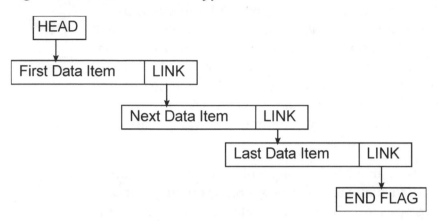

end-of-list value in its link field, or must point to a special flag record that identifies the end of the list.

The singly linked list is simple, but has a number of disadvantages. To back up to a previous item, it's necessary to go back to the head of the list and traverse all intervening material. If the list is small, not exceeding a few hundred items, this isn't serious. However, when millions of elements are involved, the work involved to move backward by just one item becomes prohibitive. One solution to this difficulty involved adding to each item a second link field that would point to the previous one. With this addition, it's as easy to move backward in the list as it is to move forward.

The doubly linked list has additional advantages: Adding an item at the end of the list no longer requires traversal of all records to locate the pointer field involved. The need for a special end-of-list link value or end flag record goes away; the last item simply chains to the **home item;** when a search reaches home it's recognized as end of list (see Figure 3.4).

The doubly linked variant's inventors seem to have been legion; apparently the idea occurred to many researchers independently. For instance, I came up with it independently in 1967 and was preparing a report on its advantages when I discovered it was already widely known!

Figure 3.4 *The doubly linked list is even more useful.*

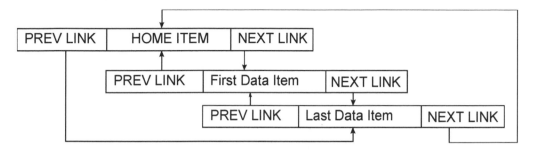

Btrieve keeps its internal lists of duplicate-keyed records and of available record locations as doubly linked lists, as we see in Chapters 6, 7, and 8.

Trees If just one pointer added to a singly linked list, turning it into a doubly linked one, can provide so much improvement, what can we expect if we add even more? In a word, much.

A list-like structure with multiple link fields that allow more than one other record to be connected forms a tree. The tree structure lends itself to direct study using mathematical graph theory. This constitutes a major advance, in comparison to the pragmatic development of its predecessors. Graph theory provides a solid foundation for prediction of results and suggests interesting avenues of development to explore.

Graph theory deals with two kinds of entities called **vertices** and **edges.** Each vertex can be represented by a point, and each edge by a line. A graph consists of two or more vertices connected by one or more edges (actually theory permits a single vertex, with no edges, to be called a graph but this null graph isn't useful in our applications).

The kind of mathematical graph we deal with in data processing has each vertex connected to one or more other vertices and is called a **connected** graph. A road map furnishes a simple example of such a graph; each city, town, or intersection forms a vertex and the roads form the edges.

Figure 3.5   *General tree structure has many nodes.*

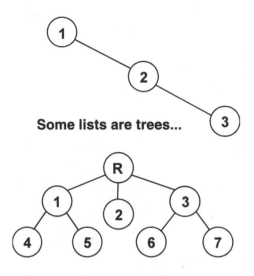

Some lists are trees...

But not all trees are lists

Tracing the movement along any edge of a connected graph from one vertex to another is called **traversing the edge.** If, while traversing the edges of a connected graph, one returns to any vertex previously visited, the graph contains a circuit, which consists of all the vertices and edges traversed since arriving at this vertex before.

The graph theory definition of a tree structure is "a connected graph that has no circuits." A tree begins at one vertex, called its **root,** and edges known as **branches** connect this vertex to other vertices. These other vertices can, in turn, connect to still more, and so on, permitting the tree's size to grow without limit.

Since no circuit is permitted in a tree, each branch is independent of all others. Each branch must eventually end at a **terminal vertex** from which no other branches sprout. Until that point is reached, each vertex can be considered the root of a subtree. The term **forest** describes the entire tree, including all subtrees. The analogy between this theory and a collection of records connected by multiple pointers is strong.

As the illustration shows, the graph theory definition includes the singly linked list itself as a primitive form of tree structure in which the first and last vertices (or nodes) are terminal, and in which each node had only one branch. Note, though, that the doubly linked list is *not* a tree, since it includes not one but two circuits because of the home record connected to the first and last items.

An empty tree, with no data records, consists of only one vertex, the root. Such a tree is said to have one **level** of depth. As soon as one record enters the tree a second level comes into existence. A level contains all nodes that branch from a **parent** on the next higher level. The circularity of this definition is difficult to avoid!

In Figure 3.6, the list has three levels, and in general such a single-edge tree has as many levels as it has nodes since each node can have only a single branch and as a result can have only one child.

Figure 3.6   *Levels within a tree structure indicate depth.*

Levels

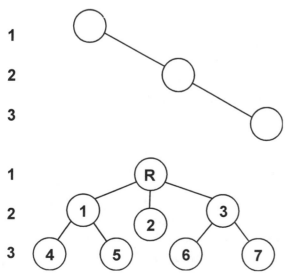

The full tree, however, exhibits three levels. The root itself, R, forms the first; nodes 1, 2, and 3, all of which branch from the root, forms the second. The third and final level contains all nodes that branch from any node on the second level, or nodes 4, 5, 6, and 7.

When a node is added to a tree, a choice becomes necessary: the new node may be inserted at the same level as its predecessors, or may create a new lower level. Which of these events occur depends on the criteria that define the connecting edges. In particular these criteria may limit the number of branches allowed from a single node.

This dependency permits creation of many different views for the same nodes, by varying the edge definition criteria. The possibility of such variations gives the tree structure its extreme flexibility. Later in this chapter, we examine two such variations in greater detail.

Search Techniques

Retrieval of data from any database always requires some type of search to locate the desired item. Thus, search technology has been at the forefront of the data processing industry since the first business applications were written. Despite nearly fifty years of development, all search techniques still fit into one of three major categories: linear searches, binary searching, or using indexes.

Linear Searches

The simplest and most familiar technique for searching is the linear method. To use the linear approach, you simply start at the beginning and examine each record in turn until either reaching the end or locating the desired information. One example of such a search is to locate one paragraph that you think occurs in a thousand-page reference book. If you can't use the index, you must start reading at page 1 and leaf through each page one after another to find the paragraph you want (see Figure 3.7).

Since the book isn't arranged with its paragraphs in any defined searchable sequence, such a hunt is tedious and lengthy. The example does show, however, that even unsorted input data allows linear searches.

Figure 3.7   *Linear searches go from front to back, like a book.*

The book example also illustrates the fact that a linear search becomes much simpler if it can be done in a sequential manner (for example, looking up a book title in a library card catalog). Maintaining the records in sorted sequence makes it possible to detect absence of the desired record and thus to stop searching when the first record past the target is found. This **sequential** linear search cuts the average access time in half.

The only processing overhead necessary for a computer-based sequential linear search is that required to traverse the file from its beginning until the end of the search, whether that's caused by finding the target record, or establishing that it doesn't exist. If the data structure being searched is an array, the overhead is merely the index variable and the comparison function. For a list or a tree it's only slightly greater.

Because it requires so little overhead processing, the sequential linear search is the fastest of all search techniques so long as the file being searched contains only a small number of records, though it can become unusably slow with the huge data collections found in modern databases. Most other search algorithms resort to linear search of a subset of the entire file, once that subset has been made small enough for effective processing in sequential fashion.

Binary Searching

The sequential linear search requires that the data being searched be arranged in a sorted order. Once that requirement is accepted, search speed can undergo dramatic improvement by using a split-the-difference technique instead of going through the records in strict linear fashion. This search method is almost instinctive for human beings. When we want to find Joe Smith's telephone number, we don't start at the front of the book. Instead we go directly to the last half, where all the names that start with S are located. If instead we're looking for Allen Adams, we start at the front of the directory because that's where the As are.

In practice, though, we normally use this technique only to get close to the desired entry, then fall back to linear search and read each name one after another until either finding the one we want, or finding one that's past it that indicates that our target's not there. To find the name while making the absolute minimum number of comparisons, we could do it a bit differently. First, we could go to the exact midpoint of the directory and look at the name found there. (If the exact midpoint were less than a full item, we would round up so that we could always examine a complete item of information.)

One of three cases must be true: the name we examine may be the name we're hunting, in which case we're instant winners. If not the target, this midpoint name must be either beyond the name we want (greater than), or before it (smaller than). If it's beyond, that tells us our target is in the front half; if it's before, the target is in the back.

Either way, we have just cut in half the number of pages left to search. We move to the exact midpoint of whichever half was indicated by the system and repeat the comparison. Again, we may be lucky, but if not, we know which half of that half to look in next.

Each time we repeat this procedure, we cut in half the number of items where our target may be found. Eventually we'll wind up with just one item (see Figure 3.8). It's either the one we're looking for, or our target's not in the directory. In the latter case, the before-beyond result tells us where the target should be inserted if we were able to add it.

This sounds like lots of trouble to go through, but a look at the numbers shows that it may be worth the effort. If we had 65,536 names in the directory, a sequential linear search could be expected to

Figure 3.8   *Splitting the difference each time creates the binary search.*

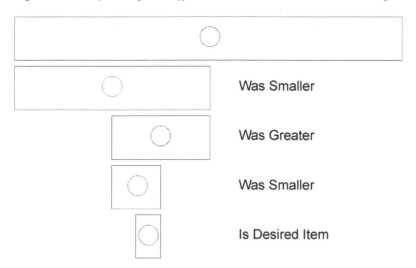

Was Smaller

Was Greater

Was Smaller

Is Desired Item

make half that many comparisons, or 32,768, on average to find any name picked at random. Using the binary search technique, only 16 comparisons suffice. Whenever a process can be sped up by more than 2,000 times, the technique that does so becomes interesting. This technique dates back at least to Isaac Newton and his algorithm for extracting square roots. It's also used by artillery fire observers to quickly zero in on their targets.

A computer program has no difficulty at all adjusting an address by either adding or subtracting half its value, and so the binary search is especially effective for dealing with array structures. Things get a bit trickier with lists, however.

Since the binary search method does require more processing overhead than a straight sequential linear search, it's best suited for larger collections of data. Each comparison cuts the search space in half, so using this method can rapidly reduce even the largest collection to a manageable size for applying sequential linear search if desired.

Using Indexes

The fastest technique of all for locating information within a file that's arbitrarily large depends on having an index, which keeps track of the location of each record and uses a key field. Within the index, either linear or binary search still must occur to find the key field. Since the key field is normally much shorter than the entire record, though, this search proceeds much faster than would a similar search of the full file. Once the search finds a key record that matches the target, an associated pointer provides the exact address from which to retrieve the full record.

Note that the data storage media may not permit random access of the information; in such a situation only sequential search may be useful. Indexing techniques require random access capability for best speed, although they will work after a fashion when nothing but sequential access methods are available.

Indexing Techniques

Use of an index implies two properties for the index: a **key,** and a **sort order.** The key may be of any data type: a character string, a number in either binary or BCD representation, or any other entity that can be sorted into a defined sequence. The sort order can be alphabetic, numeric, or a combination of the two, and can be either ascending or descending. Without these two properties, the index can only be searched linearly from one end to the other and loses most if not all of its advantages; their presence is assumed throughout this book.

Two major groups of indexing techniques worth studying are calculated-address indexing, with its descendant the hash table, and the family of methods based on binary tree structures. Although the calculated-address technique is seldom used in modern data processing, its study provides background helpful in comparing more recent methods.

Calculated-Address Indexing, a Mainframe Technique

Calculated-address indexing is a form of random access to data in which the record number assigned to any specific record is calculated from information contained in the record itself. When properly designed and applied to suitable data structures, this technique cannot be surpassed for speed of information retrieval. Unfortunately, any change in the data structure for a system based on this technique usually requires complete redesign of the address calculation mechanisms. Thus, the method has fallen from favor and been replaced by other approaches that trade small amounts of speed for large increases in system flexibility.

Direct Addressing   In the days before true operating systems and file structures, a single storage unit could contain just one file of data. By mapping functions of the search key directly to physical data addresses, little or no actual searching was necessary. For instance, with a twenty-six-surface disk drive containing a file indexed by Customer Name, each surface might correspond to the first letter of the Name key field. If each surface held 260 tracks, they could be divided into groups of ten and each group mapped to the second letter of the key. Similarly with 26 sectors per track (260 per group) each sector could be mapped to the third letter multiplied by ten.

With this direct addressing method, finding the sector for customer Jones would involve going directly to Surface J, Group O, and Sector N. For small keys and large drives, this technique found moderate acceptance in the 1960s, but it required too much custom programming for most MIS departments and never became a widespread technology.

As the sizes of databases increased—and more importantly, as the acceptance of complete operating systems took the place of specialized single-purpose programs that assumed total ownership of all storage resources—the direct addressing method went totally out of favor and today exists primarily as a footnote to history (see Figure 3.9).

Hash-Table Lookup   Before direct addressing vanished into the mists of history, however, it gave rise to a variation that's still in widespread use for special purposes. This variant uses a mathematical function of some sort, not necessarily related in any logical way to the data itself, to convert the key string into a smaller **hash** number. The name derives from a fanciful analogy to boarding-house hash: once the function has produced a number it's impossible to guess what went into it!

Figure 3.9   *Direct addressing ignored file-system needs.*

Surface J
 Track O
Sector N

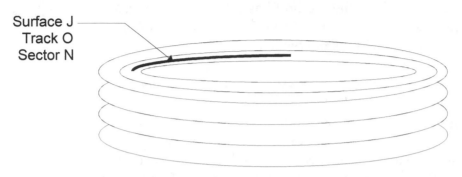

The **hash value** then indexes an array of physical pointers. This array, the **hash table,** contains the locations of the actual data (see Figure 3.10). Using the hash table technique is almost as fast as direct addressing, but sidesteps the custom programming requirements and can easily generalize to most needs.

Hashing, as the hash table technique is generally known, is often applied to small indexes when speed is essential. Examples of such use include both symbol table lookup in compilers or file access within an operating system. For large databases, however, the need for the hash table limits the usefulness of this method.

Figure 3.10   *The hash table contains locations of data.*

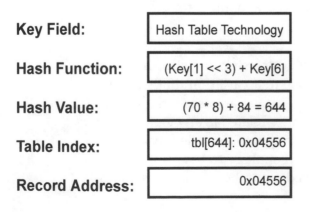

Key Field:	Hash Table Technology
Hash Function:	(Key[1] << 3) + Key[6]
Hash Value:	(70 * 8) + 84 = 644
Table Index:	tbl[644]: 0x04556
Record Address:	0x04556

Binary Tree Techniques

The hash table technique is one of the few remaining applications of pure array data structures for indexing. The size of the structures necessary to deal with a million-record (or larger) database has forced pure arrays out of wide use. They have been replaced by variants of the tree structure. Two such variations have been popular: the generic binary tree and an evolution from it known as the B-tree. The B-tree's advantages have made it essentially the industry standard today, but to better appreciate those benefits we examine the original binary tree first.

The Binary Tree   A fundamental binary tree is a classic tree in which each node has a limit of two branches (see Figure 3.11). In addition, each node contains the data for one record. One branch consists of all records for which the key field sorts to a lower or lesser position in the sequence than does that for this node's data, and the other branch contains all records that sort to a higher or greater position.

A binary tree of this fundamental design needs no index itself, yet if properly balanced will always result in binary-search speed when retrieving data. At each node, comparison of the current key field to the desired target's key shows which branch to follow, so that a minimum number of comparisons need be made to locate the data sought.

Unfortunately, random entry of data into such a binary tree more often than not results in the tree becoming unbalanced. The extreme case of unbalance occurs when a binary tree is loaded from input

Figure 3.11   *The fundamental binary tree*

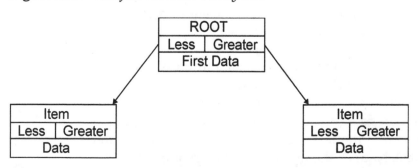

data that is already in key-sort sequence. When this happens, the resulting tree has only one branch from each node, turning it into a simple list. With such a tree, the search time is no better than that achieved by the sequential linear method.

Even if this worst case can be avoided, the tree is still likely to become unbalanced over time and evolve into a structure such as the seven-level tree shown in Figure 3.12. With such a structure, the search time for any specific record will vary widely: some targets will require going the full seven levels down; others may end the search after only the second level.

Figure 3.12   *An unbalanced binary tree seven levels deep*

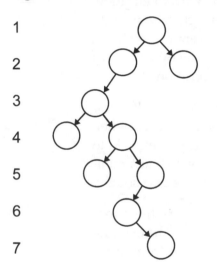

1
2
3
4
5
6
7

When we delete a node from a binary tree, this may force many other nodes to move to new positions in the tree. Figure 3.13 gives a sample of what can occur.

The illustration shows a nine-node tree that's initially six levels deep. The numbers at each node represent the sort order of that node's key and range from 1 to 9. Seven of the nine nodes are in the lesser branch from the root (node 8) and only one is in the greater branch. Of the seven in the lesser branch, five are in the greater branch from node 2. Node 3, the immediate successor of node 2 in

Figure 3.13   *Deleting a node from a binary tree can be tricky.*

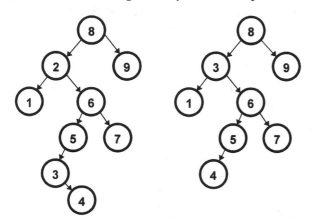

the sort sequence, is three levels down from it in the tree structure. If we delete node 2, then node 3 must move up to take its place. This, however, leaves node 4 disconnected, so it must replace node 2 as the lesser branch from node 5.

Similar rearrangement would be necessary for deletion of any other node, unless the one deleted was a terminal node having no branches. Three rules cover all situations: If the node being deleted is a terminal node, no rearrangement is required. If the node in question has only one branch, it can be deleted and its parent spliced to the sole child. Only if a node to be deleted has two branches do complications arise.

For this case, the immediate successor of the candidate must be located and removed from its position in the tree so that it can be moved into the place of the candidate. Removing the successor must follow the same three rules, so it's possible in a deep enough tree to find that many successors must move to new position.

Although the balance problem is one disadvantage of the funda-mental binary tree, an even more serious drawback is its limitation to only two branches at each level. It's true that this creates a struc-ture much more compact than that resulting from only one node per level, but consider how much more rapidly searches could proceed if each level were permitted four, ten, or even a hundred branches.

What was needed to make the binary tree really attractive for production database use were two new features: a good method for rebalancing the tree as necessary to keep the number of levels minimized and the capability to have many more branches at each level. The search for good methods gave us a variety of techniques. The one first providing the multiple-node capability as well was that known as the B-tree. As a direct result, the B-tree has become the industry standard for index organization. Virtually all commercial DBMSs are built around it; it's also the basis of the Btrieve microkernel engine.

No tree structure is capable of handling duplicate keys well, although a number of workarounds are possible. This creates a problem in the real world, where duplicates are likely to occur in many key fields. All production-quality DBMSs include special capabilities to handle this problem when it arises. See Chapters 5, 7, and 8 for a discussion of the methods by which Btrieve deals with the problem. Basically, Btrieve omits duplicates from the tree structure itself so that the problem does not arise. The system then accounts for the omitted keys by creating doubly linked lists in the data pages, allowing all duplicates to be found with only a single key shared among them.

The B-Tree Structure   Today's industry standard form for a database index is the B-tree, which was introduced in 1972 by Rudolph Bayer and E. M. McCreight. In the article that revealed the design to the world, the authors named their structure the B-tree, but offered no explanation for their choice of names. Some other writers have suggested that it derives from binary, but most appear to agree that the initial B stands for Bayer.

Some two years before the B-tree appeared on the scene, J. E. Hopcroft invented a precursor known as the 2-3 tree. According to *Introduction to Algorithms,* every internal node of this design had either two or three children, foreshadowing the B-tree's use of many children at each node.

A typical B-tree consists of a root, internal nodes, and leaf nodes (see Figure 3.14). The leaves are terminal nodes of the tree structure,

Figure 3.14   *B-tree organization*

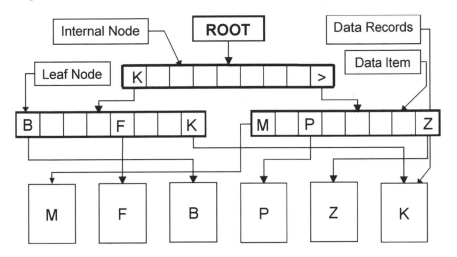

having no branches descending from them. Each node, including the root, may contain at least one data item. Such items normally consist of the key field and the record address of the full record to which the key applies.

The root may have the same form as either an internal node or a leaf node. It's distinguished from the other two types only by the fact that it forms the point of entry to the structure for each search. Until the tree contains enough data items to fill the node, the root uses the leaf-node format; when it fills, it is converted to an internal node with two leaf nodes, each holding half of the total count of data items.

The difference between an internal node and a leaf node is simple: a leaf has no children, but an internal node always has between n and $2n$ children where n is half the maximum number of data items that a node can hold. The requirement that an internal node have at least n children does not apply to the root, which can have any number of children up to $2n$.

Because of the way in which a B-tree automatically maintains its balance, all leaf nodes of the tree are always on the same level. That is, no branch of the forest is any deeper than any other branch. This assures that all branches have the shortest possible search-path length. For all data items except those located on internal nodes, this length is equal to the depth of the tree; the exceptions are all of shorter length.

Within all nodes of the B-tree, each data item contains a pointer to the next node (which is ignored if the data item is in a leaf node), the key data for comparison when searching, and a pointer to the associated data record. This organization is shown in Figure 3.15.

Figure 3.15 *Data item of a typical B-tree*

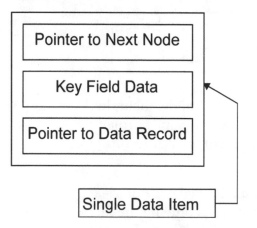

The number of data items that can fit into a node determines the order of the B-tree. If each node has room for sixteen data items, the tree is of order 16. The depth of the B-tree is determined directly by both the total number of data items it contains and the order of the tree.

You can calculate the maximum depth of the leaf level for each branch, *h*, as the base-*t* log of the quantity data-items-plus-one divided by two, where *t* is the order of the tree. The algebraic expression of this formula is

$$h \le \log_t \frac{n+1}{2}$$

Thus, with 131,071 data items and a tree of order 16, the depth of the tree would not exceed four levels: 131,072 / 2 is 65,536 and the log base-16 of 65,536 is 4. Adding one more level to the depth would increase the number of possible items by a factor of 16, to 2,097,151. You don't really need this formula to use a B-tree effectively, though.

This relationship brings out the major performance improvement achieved by the B-tree structure. By allowing more branches at each level, each one-level step within the tree multiplies the number of data items by the number of branches per node. With a tree of order 1,000 (easily achievable with moderate node sizes if the key is small enough), only two levels permit storage of a million data items, and every level deeper increases the possible number of records a thousandfold. Since access time for large disk-based indexes is determined almost exclusively by the time required to retrieve the next node from storage, reducing the number of levels required translates to significant improvement in performance.

Before leaving this topic, we'll explore the way in which a B-tree keeps its balance and how it deals with deletion of data items. First, though, let's pin the earlier descriptive definition of a B-tree's structure down to mathematical strictness.

In mathematical terms, a B-tree is defined strictly as a rooted tree having the following properties:

1. Every node contains a count of the keys it contains, the keys themselves, and a means to determine whether the node is a leaf node or an internal node. If an internal node, it also contains pointers to all its children; these pointers may be contained in a leaf node as well but are ignored in such a situation.

2. The number of keys a node can contain is constrained by both an upper and a lower bound expressed as its minimum degree *t*. The minimum number of keys is then expressed *t-1*, and the maximum as *2t-1*. The value *2t-1* is called the order of the tree. Every node except the root must contain at least the

minimum number of keys. Any node containing the maximum number is said to be full.

3. The keys divide the ranges of keys contained in each child subtree so that every key value within the entire tree is unique and can be reached by only one path.

4. Every leaf node has the same depth (level).

In the B-tree, balancing action occurs automatically when a new data item is inserted. As the search proceeds, beginning at the root, to determine which node should receive the new data item, any full node encountered is split by creating a new node at the same level.

Since the maximum number of items is defined as *2t-1*, which is always an odd number, the full node must yield two nodes each containing the minimum number of items, with one left over. The item in the middle position within the node becomes the leftover and moves to the parent of the node being split. There, it becomes the key separating the values in the resulting pair of nodes and contains the pointer to the new node added. The original node retains the lower-sequence group of its original items, and the higher-sequence group moves to the new node.

Because the search begins at the root and every full node found is split whether or not splitting is required, space is always available in the parent node to accept the data item that is moved up when a split occurs (see Figure 3.16). Because all new nodes are added at the same level as the full node, the depth of the tree never changes. The exception to both these rules occurs if the root itself becomes full, since the root has no parent.

Figure 3.16 *Splitting a full node when t = 4*

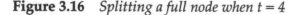
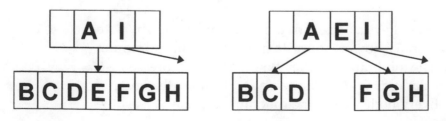

To split the root, two new nodes instead of one are added. The median-position data item from the full root remains in the root, and the other two groups of items move to the new, added nodes (see Figure 3.17). This increases the depth of the tree by one level. Since no other technique exists to increase the tree's depth, all leaf nodes are always at the same level.

Actual insertion of an item becomes trivial. The split, already completed whether it would have been needed or not, assures that a node can never overflow. The data item is merely inserted into the node at the point established by the search, which is in most situations a leaf node.

Just as in the binary tree, deleting a data item from a B-tree is more complicated than inserting a new one. A number of different situations can occur. Each requires different actions. Three general cases exist, but two of them contain multiple subcases. The following discussion makes no attempt to deal with all possible variations that can be encountered, but should give you solid understanding of the issues involved.

All three examples that follow assume a tree in which $t = 3$; consequently, the order of the tree is 7. Initially the tree contains twenty-three data items. One is at the root, five are at the next level down, and the remaining seventeen are in leaf nodes.

Figure 3.17   *Splitting the root when $t = 4$*

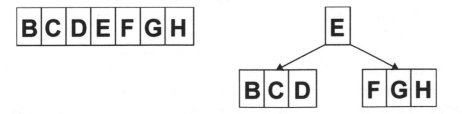

The simplest situation is that of deleting a data item from a leaf node when the leaf contains at least *t* items. Figure 3.18 shows what happens when data item 6 comes out of the tree: the item just vanishes, with no effect on any other node in the tree. Fortunately, this is the most frequent case, because most data items within any B-tree are located in the leaf nodes.

Figure 3.18   *This is the simplest item-delete situation.*

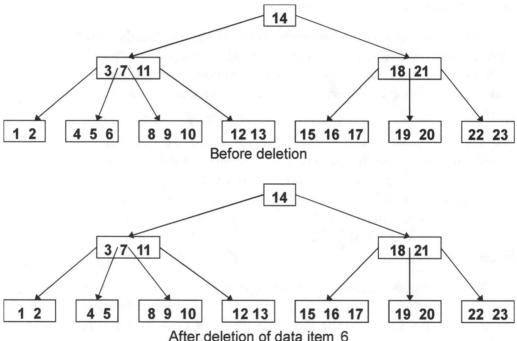

To delete a data item from an internal node, we must examine both branches adjacent to that item: that is, the one associated with the item itself and the one associated with the item immediately past the one to be deleted (see Figure 3.19). This second branch always exists; if the item to be deleted is the largest in the internal node (the situation shown in the second illustration), the branch for "greater than any key in the node" is used. If at least one of the nodes reached by the two branches has *t* or more items in it, then the appropriate item from that node moves up to replace the item being deleted. Node pointers are not affected by this move.

Figure 3.19   *Sometimes items must move to new nodes.*

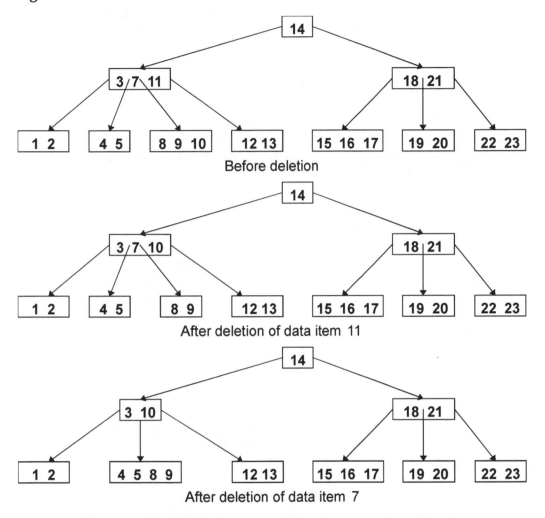

The second diagram in Figure 3.19 shows what happens when we delete data item 11 from the leftmost node on the middle level. This involves the same tree, in the condition in which our first example left it. Since the 8-9-10 node contains three items, we move item 10 up to replace item 11 and leave everything else unchanged.

How do we choose which item to move up from the lower level? If only one of the two nodes has at least *t* items, no choice is necessary; the node with the most items in it gives one up. Had both nodes associated with item 11 contained t or more items, we could have moved either the rightmost item of the left, or the leftmost item of the right node. In practice, the item from the first node encountered with more than t items is used.

Had neither of the two nodes associated with the item being deleted contained more than t items, the situation would have been a bit more complicated. The two nodes must be merged into one, and one of them released along with the pointer in the parent node. The remaining pointer in the parent provides the branch to the newly merged node. This is shown in Figure 3.19, in the third diagram where data item 7 has been removed.

To avoid excessive recursion, the B-tree algorithms check, during the search for an item to be deleted, for adjacent nodes that both have fewer than t data items. When such a pair of nodes is found, they are merged and one of the parent node's items is moved down to become the midpoint item of the single merged node. This action, called merge-at-half, is similar to that which occurred in our previous example, but takes place *before* any deletion rather than afterward.

In Figure 3.20, the merge-at-half takes place at the start of the search for item 4 and pulls the root (and item 14) down into the merged nodes. The newly formed node becomes the tree's new root. This process reduces the depth of the tree by one, and since it's the only way for the depth to decrease, maintains all leaves at the same level.

After the first merge, the search continues. When item 4 is found, it's on a leaf node that has more than the minimum number of items. The item goes away without any other node changes being necessary.

The third diagram in Figure 3.20 shows what happens when we delete an item from a leaf node that already contains the minimum t-1 number of items. We must move the appropriate data item from its parent down to the node, and this in turn requires pulling the leftmost item in the next higher leaf up to the parent. This is the single situation in which recursion might be necessary. The merge-at-half rule, however, assures us that no higher level of the tree can

Figure 3.20   *Examples of item deletion*

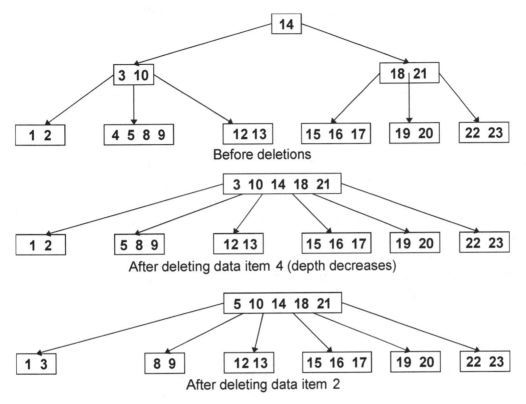

also contain the minimum *t-1* number of items; this prevents the addition from rippling back to the root.

While the merge-at-half algorithm described in the preceding paragraphs is an integral part of the B-tree algorithms presented by Bayer, researchers Ted Johnson and Dennis Shasha have raised questions as to its advisability in both academic and industry journals. They cite experimental evidence indicating improved performance with only slight wastage of space if, instead, nodes are left in the tree until they become completely empty.

Their reasoning is that premature merging of nodes to keep the number of items between half-full and full creates unnecessary processing loads when multiple deletions and insertions occur as they do in production systems. Nodes that may be merged by a deletion may soon afterward require splitting, where no split would have been necessary had they been left alone.

Both the theoretical and empirical publications by Johnson and Sasha are listed in the references at the end of this chapter. Btrieve uses the classic techniques, retaining index pages between half full and full, and shows no sign of degraded performance by doing so.

Note that when you use a commercial record manager such as Btrieve, you don't really need this theoretical background. The record manager's internal routines take care of everything, invisibly. Similarly, you don't have to know what goes on inside your automobile's engine to be able to drive. However, when the car suddenly refuses to start, it's helpful to have some idea of what happens under the hood. For the same reason, every database developer or system administrator needs to understand at least a little about the theory underlying the tools in use.

Additional Resources

Should your interest in the theoretical aspects of indexing have been aroused by this chapter, you can read more about it in the books and articles listed below. Meanwhile, in the next chapter of this book, we examine the Btrieve package itself, learn about the platforms it currently supports, and how to use it on each.

Magazine Articles

Many techniques were introduced by publication in professional journals; tutorials on their use are more commonly found in the popular industry press. The following list includes both types of references.

"A Data Structure for Dynamic Trees," by D. D. Sleator and R. E. Tarjan, in *Journal of Computer and System Sciences,* 1983, 26:3 pp. 362–391. Introduces dynamic trees.

"A Dichromatic Framework for Balanced Trees," by L. Guibas and R. Sedgewick, in *Proceedings of the 19th Symp Foundations of*

Computer Science, 1978, pp. 8–21. Gave name to red-black tree structure.

"Adaptable Concurrency Control for Atomic Data Types," by M. S. Atkins and M. Y. Coady, in *ACM Transactions on Computer Systems*, August 1992, 10:3 p. 190. Discusses need for an adaptable server, required for optimum performance. An atomic shared B-tree is used to outline a general design for implementing adaptable concurrency control in servers for atomic objects. Includes appendices on semiqueue implementation and type-specific deadlock detection.

"An Algorithm for the Organization of Information," by G.M. Adel'sin-Vel'skii and E. M. Landis, in *Soviet Mathematics Doklady*, 3, pp. 1259–1263, 1962. Introduces the structure now known as the AVL tree.

"Bit-tree: A Data Structure for Fast File Processing," by David E. Ferguson, in *Communications of the ACM*, 35:6 (June 1992), p. 114. Describes a variant of B-tree structure called a Bit-tree, intended to pack more information into leaf nodes, lower the height of the tree, and reduce the number of I/O operations required to search the tree.

"Concurrent Search Structure Algorithms," by N. Goodman and Dennis Shasha, in *ACM Transactions on Database Systems* (March 1988).

"Genetic Algorithms and Database Indexing," by Joe Celko, in *Dr. Dobb's Journal*, April 1993. Suggests use of AI techniques to optimize index structures.

"Improving DB2 index performance," by Mark M. Davydov, in *Database Programming & Design*, 5:9 (September 1992), p. 50. Discusses the concepts behind DB2 indexes, including B-trees. Describes index structures and use.

"Ingres Table Structures," by David Snellen, in *DBMS Magazine*, 5:8 (July 1992), p. 60. The Ingres RDBMS includes storage-structure options: balanced tree, hash, heap (random), heap sort, Indexed Sequential Access Method (ISAM), CBtree, CISAM,

CHeap, and CHeapsort. The Ingres ISAM, hash, B-tree, and heap storage structures are discussed in detail.

"On Random 2-3 Trees," by Andrew Yao, in *Acta Informatica 9*, (1978).

"Organization and Maintenance of Large Ordered Indexes," by Rudolph Bayer and E. McCreight. *Acta Informatica 1* (1972), p. 173. Introduces B-tree structure.

"PATRICIA—Practical Algorithm To Retrieve Information Coded In Alphanumeric," by D. Morrison, in *Journal of the ACM 15* (1968), pp. 514–534.

"Prefix B-Trees," by Rudolph Bayer and K. Unterauer, in *ACM Transactions on Database Systems* 2, (March 1977), pp. 11–26.

"Red-Black Trees," by Bruce Schneier, in *Dr. Dobb's Journal* 17:4 (April 1992), p. 42. Tutorial on this self-adjusting partially balanced structure.

"Reexamining B-trees," by Ted Johnson and Dennis Shasha, in *Dr. Dobb's Journal* (January 1992), 17:1 p. 44. Presents a guide to the use of B-tree data structures in searches.

"Self-adjusting Binary Search Trees," by D. D. Sleator and R. E. Tarjan, in *Journal of the ACM*. Introduces splay trees.

"Self-Adjusting Data Structures," by Andrew M. Liao, in *Dr. Dobb's Journal* 15:2 (February 1990), p. 44. Surveys several structures including splay trees.

"Symmetric Binary B-Trees: Data Structure and Maintenance Algorithms," by R. Bayer, in *Acta Informatica* 1 (1972), pp. 290–306. Introduces what later became known as red-black trees.

"The Ubiquitous B-Tree," by D. Comer, in *ACM Computing Surveys* (June 1979). A comprehensive survey of the subject.

"Tree Structures," by Atindra Chaturvedi, in *PC Tech Journal* (February and March 1985).

"Utilization of B-trees with Inserts, Deletes, and Modifies," by Ted Johnson and Dennis Shasha, in *ACM Symposium on Principles of Database Systems Conference* (1989).

Books

Most of the books listed in this section have a decidedly academic flavor, but a few are directed at professional software developers rather than at students.

Algorithms, by Robert Sedgewick, Addison-Wesley, 1988. Covers a wide range of subject matter in addition to its discussion of B-trees.

Algorithms + Data Structures = Programs, by Niklaus Wirth, Prentice Hall, 1976.

Computer Sorting, by Ivan Flores, Prentice Hall, 1969. Historical source for early search and sort techniques.

Data Structures and Network Algorithms, by R. E. Tarjan. Discusses both dynamic and splay trees.

Handbook of Algorithms and Data Structures, by G. H. Gonnet, Addison-Wesley, 1984. Discusses hash table techniques and other algorithms.

Introduction to Algorithms, by T. H. Cormen, C. E. Leiserson, and R. L. Rivest, The MIT Press, 1990. Updated discussion of many standard and advanced techniques aimed at both undergraduate and graduate students of computer science.

Sorting and Searching, Volume 3 of *The Art of Computer Programming*, by Donald E. Knuth, Addison-Wesley, 1973. The acknowledged authority on all techniques developed up to the time of publication.

The Design and Analysis of Computer Algorithms, by A. V. Aho, J. E. Hopcroft, and J. D. Ullman, Addison-Wesley, 1974.

Conclusion

In this chapter we've gone into the theory of index techniques, possibly to greater depth than you really wanted. Now we have all the background we need and can concentrate on Btrieve itself, how to use it, and how it works under the hood.

Chapter 4 describes the API and the platforms that Btrieve currently supports. Although you still need the full developer's kit in order to create applications that make full use of Btrieve's capabilities, I think that the descriptions here will be adequate to help you troubleshoot situations that may arise in practice.

4

Getting to Know Btrieve

We've now met the people who created Btrieve, some of those who use it, and have a clear overview of both database structure and indexing techniques. Now let's get better acquainted with Btrieve itself.

This chapter first examines the Btrieve application programming interface (API) and its use, then describes the platforms for which Btrieve is currently available (MS-DOS, Windows 3.x, and NetWare) and compares the capabilities and differences of each Btrieve version. It also catalogs the platforms expected to become available in the immediate future (Windows NT and OS/2) and the capabilities they may provide.

Note that this chapter makes no attempt to completely replace the official Btrieve manuals, which (unlike the original SoftCraft manuals or the Novell "red books") are replete with detailed examples and illustrations, not to mention special "hot tips" flags that call attention to important details likely to be overlooked. Instead, the purpose is to provide a complete introduction to this record manager, together with a somewhat different point of view than that of its originators. The additional perspective may thus help you more easily comprehend the official manuals.

Btrieve's Durable API

A feature to which Btrieve management points with great pride is the fact that Btrieve's API has remained essentially unchanged through the twelve years of the product's existence. Although new functions have appeared, the package retains virtually all backward compatibility. Only one function has been totally dropped, and it was not widely used. Thus, applications written to use the original 1982 version of Btrieve will run, unmodified, on the latest versions.

This total compatibility plays no small part in the wide acceptance of Btrieve by the developer community, and management has promised that it will be retained "for all time to come." While that may be a touch of hyperbole, it underscores the company commitment to the idea.

The following pages describe the standard interface methods for Btrieve, using position and parameter blocks, both at the machine-code level of detail and at the more abstract layer used by the high-level language interfaces furnished with the Software Developers' Kits.

This section then goes on to explain each of the forty-four functions defined in the Btrieve API. For most of these functions, more detail beyond what this chapter provides appears in the manuals in the Btrieve SDK. The main purpose of the discussion herein is to provide understanding of each function, but not to attempt to completely take the place of the official documentation.

The Parameter and Position Blocks

The Btrieve engines differ somewhat for the various supported platforms, but all use common interfacing techniques that remain essentially unchanged from one platform to another. At the lowest, or machine, level, the interface involves a 28-byte parameter block that contains pointers to other blocks of memory. The engine receives a far pointer to this parameter block and uses the content of the block to access all other data needed for performing the request operation.

The other memory blocks involved include a data buffer and a **position block** in which the engine keeps pointers to the current record, the next logical record, the next physical record, the previous logical record, and the previous physical record in addition to other data that identifies the file. The 90-byte position block is maintained by the Btrieve engine and should never be modified in any way by an application. Along with these two blocks, the system requires a 38-byte File Control block, a key buffer, and a 16-bit variable in which to return status information.

Content and size of the data buffer and the key buffer varies from one operation to another and is described later in this chapter in association with each individual operation. The File Control block is often combined with the position block into a single 128-byte entity, although the machine level parameter block treats them differently.

The logical and physical sequence information kept in the positioning block distinguishes between the physical sequence and a sequence specified by an index (logical). When a different index is used for a positioning operation, the logical sequence changes, but the physical sequence does not.

The information maintained in the positioning block, often called **currency,** is of utmost importance to understanding Btrieve's operation. Some examples may help distinguish the two kinds of currency and illustrate how one can change without affecting the other. Consider a file containing names of some famous photographers, as in Table 4.1. Note that Btrieve makes no use of a record number as such, but this is a concept that corresponds to the physical record address and simplifies the examples in Tables 4.1–4.5.

Assume that index keys exist for both the Last Name and First Name fields of this file and that the Last Name key is in use. The logical sequence of the file will be as shown in the following diagram, although the physical sequence has not changed.

Table 4.1 *Database Records in Physical Sequence*

Record Number (reference only)	Last Name	First Name
1	Bourke-White	Margaret
2	Steichen	Edward
3	Duncan	David D.
4	Adams	Ansel
5	Lee	Russ

If the record for David D. Duncan is retrieved and therefore becomes the current record in both logical and physical sequence, the next records and previous records are different for the two sequences (see Table 4.2).

Table 4.2 *Logical and Physical Sequence, Keyed on Last Name*

Record Number (reference only)	Using Key: Last Name	First Name	Logical	Physical
4	Adams	Ansel		Next
1	Bourke-White	Margaret	Previous	
3	Duncan	David D.	Current	Current
5	Lee	Russ	Next	
2	Steichen	Edward		Previous

If the index in use changes to that for the First Name field without changing the current record (this is done by means of the Get Direct/Record operation), the physical currency remains unchanged. The logical currency, however, turns inside out. The physical next record becomes the logical previous, and vice versa (see Table 4.3).

Table 4.3 *Logical and Physical Sequence, Keyed on First Name*

Record Number (reference only)	Last Name	Using Key: First Name	Logical	Physical
4	Adams	Ansel	Previous	Next
3	Duncan	David D.	Current	Current
2	Steichen	Edward	Next	Previous
1	Bourke-White	Margaret		
5	Lee	Russ		

Switching back to the Last Name key for the rest of the examples, we find that retrieving the record for Ansel Adams does away with the logical previous record entirely, since no other record comes before this one in the index although it's the fourth record in the file physically (see Table 4.4).

Table 4.4 *Situation in Which No Logical Previous Record Exists*

Record Number (reference only)	Using Key: Last Name	First Name	Logical (no prev)	Physical
4	Adams	Ansel	Current	Current
1	Bourke-White	Margaret	Next	
3	Duncan	David D.		Previous
5	Lee	Russ		Next
2	Steichen	Edward		

Similarly, performing a Get Next operation to make the record for Margaret Bourke-White the current one causes the physical previous entry to vanish since this is the first record in the file (see Table 4.5).

Table 4.5 *First Record Has No Physical Predecessor*

Record Number (reference only)	Using Key: Last Name	First Name	Logical	Physical (no prev)
4	Adams	Ansel	Previous	
1	Bourke-White	Margaret	Current	Current
3	Duncan	David D.	Next	
5	Lee	Russ		
2	Steichen	Edward		Next

The same conditions occur at the end of the file. In addition, some operations destroy all file currency information and restore only parts of it. Any special effects upon this essential data are noted in the discussions of individual Btrieve operations that follow in this chapter.

At Machine Level   The parameter block for use at the machine level uses the structure shown in Figure 4.1. First comes a 4-byte far pointer to the data buffer in standard segment:offset (or selector:offset if in protected mode) format. This pointer is followed by a 16-bit value giving the number of bytes available for use starting at the data buffer's address. Note that this length value may be larger than the actual byte count passed in the buffer, for any single operation.

Following the length value, at offset 6, is another far pointer to the position block associated with the current file. A far pointer to the

Figure 4.1   *Parameter block as passed to Btrieve engine at machine level*

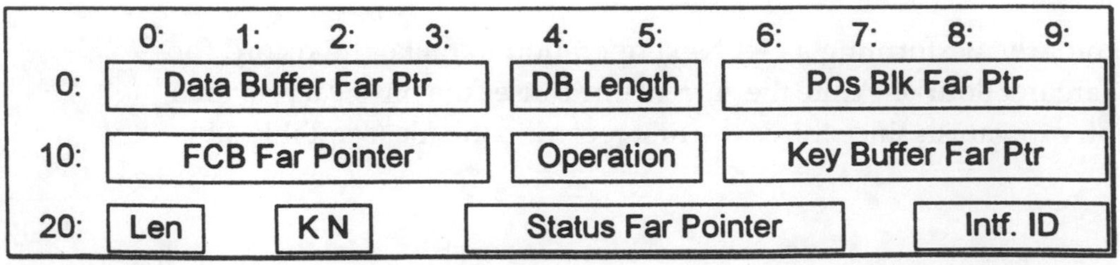

FCB is the next item; if both are combined into a single 128-byte block, the FCB pointer will have the same segment/selector value and an offset 90 bytes greater than that of the position block.

At offset 14 (0x0E) is the 16-bit operation code that specifies the exact function being requested. It's followed by a far pointer to the key buffer, which in turn is followed by a single byte holding the length of the key buffer. The following byte, indicated as KN in Figure 4.1, specifies the key number to be used; for some operations, this field has alternate meanings. The key specified here by number identifies the index that determines the logical next and logical previous records within the file.

The final two fields within the parameter block are a far pointer to the 16-bit variable that will receive the status code at completion of each operation and an interface ID code that tells whether the engine is capable of handling variable-length records. The interface ID field should always be set to 0x6176.

When using assembly language, your program must fill in all fields of the parameter block, then pass the block to the Btrieve engine using the method appropriate to your platform. For example, on the MS-DOS platform access to the engine is achieved via INT 7Bh, and the far pointer to the parameter block is passed in DS:DX. Before calling INT 7Bh, the application must verify that a Btrieve engine is indeed present; if not, it should return the appropriate error code.

Sample code to verify the presence of the Btrieve engine appears in the Developer SDK from BTI.

Using HLL Interfaces   When interfacing with the Btrieve engines from high-level languages, the wrapper routines furnished in the Btrieve Software Developer's Kit for each platform handle most of the small details and the application need only provide the most significant items.

For example, the C-language interface provided with the MS-DOS SDK uses a single function named BTRV() to communicate with the Btrieve engines. This function's prototype is

```
int BTRV( int Operation,        /* operation code */
          char far * PosBlk,     /* 128-byte array */
          char far * DataBuf,    /* as required */
          int far * DataLen,     /* as required */
          char far * KeyBuf,     /* as required */
          int KeyNbr );          /* 0 or as needed */
```

Note that neither the FCB pointer nor the status variable need be supplied by the C program. That's because this function expects a 128-byte array to be passed as the position block, and the last 38 bytes of that array become the FCB. Similarly, the function provides the status variable within itself and returns as the function's own value, whatever value the engine places in that internal location.

Typical declarations for a C program using this interface might be something like the following ones, which assume purely arbitrary values for the record structure and its key fields:

```
struct tagRecord {
  char Field1 [22];            /*arbitrary layout for data record*/
  long Binary4;
  char Field3 [18];
};

struct tagRecord DataBuf;
int DataLen = sizeof( DataBuf );
char KeyBuf[26];               /* assume Field1 and Binary4 as key */
char PosBlk[128];
int Stat;
```

Using these typical declarations and assuming that the file is named MYFILE.DAT in the current directory and has no owner-name assigned, here's how Btrieve could be called to open the file for read-only access and, if successful, read into the data buffer the first logical record listed in index 0:

```
Stat = BTRV( 0, PosBlk, ""   , &DataLen,  MYFILE.DAT , -2 );
if( Stat == 0 )
```

```
{DataLen = sizeof( DataBuf );
  Stat = BTRV(12, PosBlk, &DataBuf, &DataLen, KeyBuf, 0);
}
```

Note that the Open function (code 0) put the filename in the key buffer and the read-only open mode code in the key number position. Since no owner name existed, an empty string replaced the data buffer. If successful, the returned status was 0, so DataLen was set to tell the Btrieve engine how much space it could use to return data. The Get First function was then called using the actual data buffer and specifying key number 0.

The reason for using the & operator on some parameters but not on others is that C recognizes the names of arrays as being syntactically equal to pointers, but this rule doesn't apply to a struct such as DataBuf or to an integer such as DataLen.

The SDKs provide similar interface wrappers for other languages including BASIC, Pascal (both IBM and Turbo varieties), and COBOL. SDKs for other platforms supply different wrappers that fit the needs of the associated platforms, but all follow the same approach. Certain versions of BASIC require different, special treatment of the FCB block and the key buffer. Details appear in the appropriate SDK manuals.

The Primitive Operations

The forty-four primitive operations defined for Btrieve's API divide into eight major groups. These groups deal with file access, information, addition, retrieval, record change, transaction control, index control, and miscellaneous operations.

The File Access Group   The eight operations comprising the file access group permit creation of new files, access to existing ones, splitting a file across two drives (only in versions prior to 6.0), setting or clearing access restrictions, closing a file when all work of a session has been completed, closing all files with a single operation, and finally unloading of the Btrieve engine (see Table 4.6).

Table 4.6 *Eight Operations for File Access Group*

Operation	Name
00	Open
01	Close
14	Create
16	Extend
25	Stop
28	Reset
29	Set Owner
30	Clear Owner

Open (Code 0)   The Open operation makes a file available for use and initializes its position block (see Table 4.7). The file must exist, and a file handle for it must be available. If successful, the operation initializes the position block. Otherwise an appropriate error status reports the cause of failure.

Table 4.7 *Open Operation Parameters*

Operation:	OPEN (0)	
Position Block:	Required	Initialized
Data Buffer:	Owner Name if any	Unchanged
Data Buffer Length:	Length of name	Unchanged
Key Buffer:	PathSpec of file	Unchanged
Key Buffer Length:	PathSpec Length	Unchanged
Key Number:	Open Mode	Unchanged

The open mode specified in the Key Number field of the parameters can be any of the values in Table 4.8.

Table 4.8   *Open Mode Values*

0	Normal open mode
–1	Accelerated mode (obsolescent)
–2	Read-Only; file cannot be modified
–3	Verify write operations (local drives only)
–4	Exclusive access to file

The Open operation has no effect on file positioning. A GET or STEP operation is necessary to establish both logical and physical current, next, and previous record values before most operations are available.

Close (Code 1)   The Close operation makes the specified file unavailable (see Table 4.9). The position block is no longer valid upon return and may be reused or released. The file must be open, and no active transaction may involve the file. Any locks placed on the file are released by this operation.

Table 4.9   *Close Operation Parameters*

Operation:	CLOSE (1)	
Position Block:	Identifies file	No longer valid
Data Buffer:	Ignored	Unchanged
Data Buffer Length:	Ignored	Unchanged
Key Buffer:	Ignored	Unchanged
Key Buffer Length:	Ignored	Unchanged
Key Number:	Ignored	Unchanged

Closing a file destroys all information within the position block, including both logical and physical record pointers.

Create (Code 14)   The Create operation brings into existence a Btrieve file, using specifications placed in the data buffer and the path and filename contained in the key buffer (see Table 4.10). The

Table 4.10 *Create Operation Parameters*

Operation:	CREATE (14)	
Position Block:	Ignored	Unchanged
Data Buffer:	File specifications	Unchanged
Data Buffer Length:	Size of spec.	Unchanged
Key Buffer:	PathSpec of file	Unchanged
Key Buffer Length:	PathSpec Length	Unchanged
Key Number:	Overwrite Warn	Unchanged

Key Number parameter holds an Overwrite Warning flag, which is
–1 to prevent overwriting. A value of 0 causes Btrieve to create the
new file, replacing any existing file of the same name.

The file specifications passed to Create as its data buffer contain
three distinct structures. Only the first (16 bytes of attributes specifying record length, page size, how many indexes to create, a 16-bit
file-flags bitmap, the number of additional duplicate-key pointers to
include, and the number of pages to pre-allocate) is required. The
other two (an array of key-segment specifications and an array of
ACS tables) are optional.

Figure 4.2 shows how the data buffer information must be organized. Each empty rectangle represents one byte in the buffer. Values are numeric, expressed in standard Intel low-byte-high-byte
format for both 16-bit and 32-bit items. All bytes indicated as not
used must be set to 0.

The Record Length, Page Size, and Number of Indexes fields are all
straightforward. Record Length sets up the logical size for each data
record. Page Size establishes the unit that Btrieve will move to and
from storage. Note that best storage use occurs when Record Length
and Page Size fit each other with minimum waste space. Within the
required attributes structure's File Flags field, the bit flags shown in
Table 4.11 apply.

Figure 4.2   *Layout of data buffer for Create function*

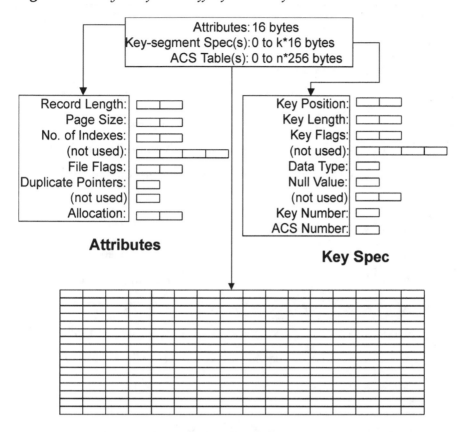

Details of the differences that result from flag bit settings appear latter in this book, in the discussion of the internal file structures.

For every index listed in the Number of indexes field of the attributes section, at least one key segment must be specified in the key-segment-specs array when using a version prior to 6.0. A key may have more than one segment, but older versions required that each key be specified at file creation time. The newer versions allow extra keys to be reserved without being defined.

Each key segment occupies 16 bytes in the segment-spec array, as shown in Figure 4.2. The Key Position field is the offset in bytes

Table 4.11 *Bits in File Flags Field*

15	14	13	12	11	10	9	8	7	6	5	4	3	2	1	0	Meaning
x	x	x	x	x	x	x	x	x	x	x	x	x	x	x	1	Variable-length records
x	x	x	x	x	x	x	x	x	x	x	x	x	x	1	x	Truncate trailing blanks
x	x	x	x	x	x	x	x	x	x	x	x	x	1	x	x	Pre-allocate pages
x	x	x	x	x	x	x	x	x	x	x	x	1	x	x	x	Compress the data
x	x	x	x	x	x	x	x	x	x	x	1	x	x	x	x	Key-only file, no data
x	x	x	x	x	x	x	x	x	x	1	x	x	x	x	x	Use index balancing
x	x	x	x	x	x	x	x	0	1	x	x	x	x	x	x	Keep 10% free on V-pages
x	x	x	x	x	x	x	x	1	0	x	x	x	x	x	x	Keep 20% free on V-pages
x	x	x	x	x	x	x	x	1	1	x	x	x	x	x	x	Keep 30% free on V-pages
x	x	x	x	x	x	x	1	x	x	x	x	x	x	x	x	Extra duplicate pointers
x	x	x	x	x	x	0	x	x	x	x	x	x	x	x	x	(future use, set to 0 now)
x	x	x	x	x	1	x	x	x	x	x	x	x	x	x	x	Preassign key numbers
x	x	x	x	1	x	x	x	x	x	x	x	x	x	x	x	Use VATs (6.0 and up)
0	0	0	0	x	x	x	x	x	x	x	x	x	x	x	x	(future use, set to 0 now)

from the beginning of the data record to the start of the key field, and the Key Length field is the length of the field, also in bytes. The Key Flags field is a bitmap in which the bits have the significance shown in Table 4.12.

The 4 bytes not used and the two noted later must be set to 0. The Data Type field contains the type code indicating how the field's content is to be interpreted. See Chapter 5 for a detailed description of the data types. The Null Value field contains the byte value that tells Btrieve to omit this record from the associated index. This is also the value with which the key field is padded if no value for it is specified when a record is added. The Key Number field specifies the ID number to be assigned this key if the file-flag bit for explicit assignment is set. Finally, the ACS Number field identifies which of several ACS tables applies to this key, if multiple ACS tables are present.

Table 4.12 *Bits in Key Flags Field*

15	14	13	12	11	10	9	8	7	6	5	4	3	2	1	0	Meaning
x	x	x	x	x	x	x	x	x	x	x	x	x	x	x	1	Duplicate values allowed
x	x	x	x	x	x	x	x	x	x	x	x	x	x	1	x	Value can be modified
x	x	x	x	x	x	x	0	x	x	x	x	x	1	x	x	Binary data
x	x	x	x	x	x	x	x	x	x	x	x	1	x	x	x	All-segment null key
x	x	x	x	x	x	x	x	x	x	x	1	x	x	x	x	Key has another segment
x	x	x	x	x	x	x	x	x	x	1	x	x	x	x	x	Key sorted using ACS
x	x	x	x	x	x	x	x	x	1	x	x	x	x	x	x	Descending sort sequence
x	x	x	x	x	x	x	x	1	x	x	x	x	x	x	x	Repeating Duplicatable
x	x	x	x	x	x	x	1	x	x	x	x	x	x	x	x	Extended data type
x	x	x	x	x	x	1	x	x	x	x	x	x	x	x	x	Any-segment null key
x	x	x	x	x	1	x	x	x	x	x	x	x	x	x	x	Ignore case when sorting
0	0	0	0	0	x	x	x	x	x	x	x	x	x	x	x	(future use, set to 0 now)

Each ACS table, if any, consists of 256 bytes holding the values that Btrieve uses for sort comparisons. If an ACS applies to a key, the byte value from the actual key field becomes an index into the applicable ACS table, and the value found at that location determines the sort sequence.

The Create operation has no effect on file positioning. An Open operation is still required to obtain access to the file.

Extend (Code 16)   The Extend operation, available only in Btrieve versions before 6.0, creates an extension file on another drive; the new file's absolute pathspec is written into the original file, thus requiring that all users have identical drive maps in order to access the file after this operation has been performed. The operation was dropped at version 6.0 since it is not compatible with logical page mapping.

To extend a file, the file must be open and not involved in an active transaction. The zero-terminated full path and name for the new file must be passed as the key buffer, while the key number contains an Immediacy flag (see Table 4.13). If this flag's value is –1 (0xFF), Btrieve begins storing data in the extension file immediately. Otherwise, Btrieve waits until the original file fills before storing anything in the extension.

Table 4.13   *Extend Operation Parameters*

Operation:	EXTEND (16)	
Position Block:	Required	Unchanged
Data Buffer:	Ignored	Unchanged
Data Buffer Length:	Ignored	Unchanged
Key Buffer:	Name for New File	Unchanged
Key Buffer Length:	Name Length	Unchanged
Key Number:	Immediacy Flag	Unchanged

Regardless of the Immediacy flag, your application must close the file and reopen it before becoming able to access the extension. In future sessions, the extension file must always be available before an Open operation on the original file can succeed.

This function came into existence primarily to overcome the limited storage capacity available with floppies and early hard disk systems. With modern storage units able to hold hundreds of megabytes in a single volume, the operation is no longer useful.

The Extend function has no effect on file positioning.

Stop (Code 25)   The Stop function performs all operations of a Reset function, then causes the Btrieve engine to unload from memory if no other client is using it. In an environment such as Windows or NetWare, the engine may not unload, but its reference count of active users will decrease by one. If that brings the count to zero, unloading occurs.

The Stop function invalidates all position blocks and thus destroys all file positioning information (see Table 4.14).

Table 4.14   *Stop Operation Parameters*

Operation:	STOP(25)	
Position Block:	Ignored	Unchanged
Data Buffer:	Ignored	Unchanged
Data Buffer Length:	Ignored	Unchanged
Key Buffer:	Ignored	Unchanged
Key Buffer Length:	Ignored	Unchanged
Key Number:	Ignored	Unchanged

Reset (Code 28)   The Reset function aborts all transactions, releases all locks, closes all files, and may release resources. Since all this is accomplished by a single call to the Btrieve engine, this function is now a recommended way to terminate an application.

In a Windows or similar environment, this function releases resources for the specific client issuing the request.

The Reset function invalidates all position blocks and thus destroys all file positioning information (see Table 4.15).

Table 4.15   *Reset Operation Parameters*

Operation:	RESET (28)	
Position Block:	Ignored	Unchanged
Data Buffer:	Ignored	Unchanged
Data Buffer Length:	Ignored	Unchanged
Key Buffer:	Ignored	Unchanged
Key Buffer Length:	Set to 0	Unchanged
Key Number:	Set to 0	Unchanged

Set Owner (Code 29)   The Set Owner function restricts access to the specified file and can also encrypt data stored in the file. The file must be open, no active transaction may involve the file, and no owner name can already exist.

If you specify encryption of data, Btrieve will complete the changes to all records before returning from this operation. For large files the delay may be significant (see Table 4.16).

Table 4.16   *Set Owner Operation Parameters*

Operation:	SET OWNER (29)	
Position Block:	Required	Returned
Data Buffer:	Owner name	Unchanged
Data Buffer Length:	Name length	Unchanged
Key Buffer:	Owner name	Unchanged
Key Buffer Length:	Name length	Unchanged
Key Number:	Option Code	Unchanged

The four option codes applicable to the Set Owner function are listed in Table 4.17.

Table 4.17   *Option Codes for Set Owner Functions*

0	Owner name required for any access, no data encryption
1	Read-only access without owner name but name required to modify file, no data encryption
2	Owner name required for any access, data encryption specified
3	Read-only access without owner name but name required to modify file, data encryption specified

The Set Owner function has no effect on file positioning.

Clear Owner (Code 30)   The Clear Owner function removes an existing owner name from a file and decrypts the data if it had been encrypted. The file must be open, which requires the user name. To identify the file to the Clear Owner function, its position block is passed in the request (see Table 4.18). If data was encrypted, Btrieve decrypts all records before returning from the operation. This may take significant time.

Table 4.18   *Clear Owner Operation Parameters*

Operation:	CLEAR OWNER (30)	
Position Block:	Required	Returned
Data Buffer:	Ignored	Unchanged
Data Buffer Length:	Ignored	Unchanged
Key Buffer:	Ignored	Unchanged
Key Buffer Length:	Ignored	Unchanged
Key Number:	Ignored	Unchanged

The Clear Owner function has no effect on file positioning.

The Information Group   The five operations in the Information group all return information concerning the current file, the Btrieve engines available to the application, or the operating environment (see Table 4.19).

Table 4.19   *Information Group Operations*

Operation	Name
15	Stat
18	Get Directory
22	Get Position
26	Version
45	Find By Percentage

Stat (Code 15)   The Stat function returns information about a specified file, placing most of the data in the data buffer and the rest in the key buffer. The file must be open and is identified to the Stat function by its position block (see Table 4.20).

Table 4.20   *Stat Operation Parameters*

Operation:	STAT (15)	
Position Block:	Required	Unchanged
Data Buffer:	Empty Block	File Attr
Data Buffer Length:	Block Size	Attr Length
Key Buffer:	Empty Block	Ext. Name
Key Buffer Length:	Block Size	Unchanged
Key Number:	Ignored	Unchanged

All characteristics that the Create function can specify are returned in the data buffer, plus counts of the number of records and the number of keys in the file. Adequate space must be provided in the buffer to accept the data. If the supplied data buffer is too small, Btrieve returns status code 22. For version 6.0 and later file formats, required size could be as large as 33,455 bytes but only if all structure sizes were at their maximum limits.

Information returned in the data buffer uses the same structure as does the Create function, except for the following differences.

1. The 4 bytes not used in the Create structure hold a 32-bit count of the number of records the file contains.

2. The Allocation field contains the number of unused pages in the file.

3. The 4 bytes not used in each key segment specification contain a 32-bit count of the number of keys in the file.

4. The ACS tables are omitted.

If the Extend function has split the file (possible only with versions before 6.0), the full path and name of the extension file are in the key buffer upon return from the Stat function. If no extension file exists, the first byte of the key buffer is set to zero indicating an empty string. The buffer must allow space for a maximum-sized path. This size may vary from one platform to another.

The Stat function has no effect on file positioning.

Get Directory (Code 18)   The Get Directory function returns the current directory path for a specified drive, in the key buffer. The Key Number field specifies the desired drive, using standard MS-DOS conventions of 0 for the current drive, 1 for A, 2 for B, 3 for C, and so on. Upon successful return, the key buffer contains the full path including an all-zero terminator byte in the count (see Table 4.21).

Table 4.21 *Get Directory Operation Parameters*

Operation:	GET DIRECTORY (18)	
Position Block:	Ignored	Unchanged
Data Buffer:	Ignored	Unchanged
Data Buffer Length:	Ignored	Unchanged
Key Buffer:	Ignored	Directory path
Key Buffer Length:	Ignored	Unchanged
Key Number:	Drive Code	Unchanged

The Get Directory function has no effect on file positioning.

Get Position (Code 22)   The Get Position function returns the physical position of the current record as a 4-byte address in the data buffer. The file must be open, and a current record must exist. Existence of a current record is established by any Get or Step retrieval operation, by an Insert operation, or by an Update operation (see Table 4.22).

Table 4.22   *Get Position Operation Parameters*

Operation:	GET POSITION (22)	
Position Block:	Required	Unchanged
Data Buffer:	Empty Block	4-byte value
Data Buffer Length:	Block Size	Set to 4
Key Buffer:	Ignored	Unchanged
Key Buffer Length:	Ignored	Unchanged
Key Number:	Ignored	Unchanged

The Get Position function has no effect on file positioning. No disk I/O occurs during this operation; the address is taken from the position block.

Once an application has the physical address of a record, the direct retrieval operations can access that record without regard to the index in use or the file positioning.

Version (Code 26)   The Version function returns version number(s) of all active engines. Before version 6, only one engine could be active at any time. Later versions permit both the client engine and a server engine at the same time, together with the requester; if all three are in use, the Version function returns version data for each. If insufficient room exists in the buffer to hold all three sets of data, Btrieve returns only that for the requester.

Because different engine versions react so differently in this area, be sure to comply with the requirements of the version you use, without regard to the needs of the current version.

Before version 6, the Version function required only the operation, data buffer address, and data buffer length. Newer versions also require, when requesting data concerning a server, either a position block for an open file on that server, or a valid pathname to the server in the key buffer. When one of these is furnished, the other is set to zero (see Table 4.23).

Table 4.23 *Version Operation Parameters*

Operation:	VERSION (26)	
Position Block:	Sometimes	Unchanged
Data Buffer:	Empty Block	Version Data
Data Buffer Length:	5 or 15	Data Length
Key Buffer:	Sometimes	Unchanged
Key Buffer Length:	Ignored	Unchanged
Key Number:	Ignored	Unchanged

Version data returns in the data buffer as one or more 5-byte sequences in the format shown in Table 4.24.

Table 4.24 *Version Data Structure*

2 bytes	Revision number as integer
1 byte	Engine code in ASCII:
	S=Server-based Btrieve
	N=Requester
	D=Btrieve for DOS
	P=Btrieve for OS/2
	W=Btrieve for Windows

The Version function has no effect on file positioning.

Find By Percentage (Code 45)   The Find By Percentage function, introduced at version 6.0, returns the position of a specified record within a file, as a percentage of total file size. The value returns as a 16-bit integer in the first two bytes of the data buffer, expressing the percentage in the range 0 to 10,000 (0.00 to 100.00 percent).

The file must be open and in version 6.0 format; its position block identifies the file to this function.

The Find By Percentage function may use either direct or key addressing. For direct addressing, the data buffer must contain the 4-byte physical address obtained by the Get Direct operation. Note that this buffer is overwritten with the percentage value on return. The key number must be set to 0xFF (-1) for direct addressing. In this case the engine ignores the key buffer and key buffer length.

For key addressing, no direct address is necessary. Instead, the key buffer contains the search target value, key buffer length contains the size of the target, and key number specifies the index to use (see Table 4.25).

Table 4.25   *Find By Percentage Operation Parameters*

Operation:	FIND BY PERCENTAGE(45)	
Position Block:	Required	Unchanged
Data Buffer:	Physical Address	Filled in
Data Buffer Length:	At least 4	Unchanged
Key Buffer:	Search Target	Unchanged
Key Buffer Length:	Target Length	Unchanged
Key Number:	Desired Key, or –1	Unchanged

The Find By Percentage function has no effect on file positioning.

The Addition Group   The two operations in the Addition group provide the only available methods for adding new records to a file. One inserts a single record, and the other inserts a group of records with a single call to the Btrieve engine (see Table 4.26).

Table 4.26   *Addition Group Operations*

Operation	Name
2	Insert
40	Insert Extended

Insert (Code 2)   The Insert function adds a new record to the specified file and updates all the file's indexes. The file must be open, and the new record (in the data buffer) must be the proper length for the file.

The Key Number field serves as a no currency change (NCC) switch. If the Key Number field value is zero or positive (and not greater than permitted by the page size), Btrieve uses the corresponding key to establish logical currency and returns its key field value in the key buffer.

If the Key Number field value is 0xFF (–1), both the logical currency and the key buffer remain unchanged. In this case a subsequent operation based on logical currency, such as Get Next, uses the values in effect before the Insert occurred (see Table 4.27).

Table 4.27   *Insert Operation Parameters*

Operation:	INSERT(2)	
Position Block:	Required	Updated
Data Buffer:	New Record	Unchanged
Data Buffer Length:	Record Length	Unchanged
Key Buffer:	Empty Block	May be filled
Key Buffer Length:	Block Length	Unchanged
Key Number:	NCC Switch	Unchanged

Regardless of the NCC switch, the inserted record becomes the physical current record.

Insert Extended (Code 40)   The Insert Extended function, introduced at version 5.1, adds an entire set of new records to the specified file and updates all the file's indexes, with a single call to the Btrieve engine. The file must be open, and each record in the structure passed in the data buffer must be the proper length for the file.

For the Insert Extended operation, the data buffer contains a 2-byte fixed portion consisting of the 16-bit binary count of records to be inserted, followed by a repeating portion. The reporting portion contains all the records to be inserted, each preceded by a 16-bit binary record length. This length must match the record length established for the file. Thus, to insert n records, each of length l, in a file, the structure passed as the data buffer must be $(2 + n * (2 + l))$ bytes long.

As with the single Insert operation, the key number field serves as a no currency change (NCC) switch. If the key number field value is zero or positive, Btrieve uses the corresponding key to establish logical currency and returns its key field value in the key buffer. The returned value is that for the last record inserted, which becomes the logical current record.

If the key number field value is 0xFF (–1), both the logical currency and the key buffer remain unchanged. In this case, a subsequent operation based on logical currency, such as Get Next, uses the values that were in effect before the Insert Extended function occurred (see Table 4.28).

Table 4.28   *Insert Extended Operation Parameters*

Operation:	INSERT EXTENDED(40)	
Position Block:	Required	Updated
Data Buffer:	New Records	Unchanged
Data Buffer Length:	Total Length	Unchanged
Key Buffer:	Empty Block	May be filled
Key Buffer Length:	Block Length	Unchanged
Key Number:	NCC Switch	Unchanged

Regardless of the NCC switch, the record last inserted becomes the physical current record.

The Retrieval Group   Btrieve offers nineteen retrieval operations, plus five **bias code** modifiers for basic Get and Step actions.

The retrieval operations separate naturally into two major subgroups: one gets the desired record using an index to establish logical sequence, and the other steps through the file in physical sequence. Within the get subgroup, an additional distinction divides the group into two parts: functions that search the index for a specified record and functions that step through the file in physical sequence.

Two operations fall outside both subgroups. These special-purpose retrieval functions are described separately.

Index Searching Functions   The searching subgroup contains five operations, identical in action except for the comparison criteria that specify the desired record. Each operation uses the index set by the Key Number field and retrieves the first record that satisfies the comparison criterion. The criterion used appears in the operation name (see Table 4.29).

Table 4.29   *Searching Subgroup Operations*

Operation	Name
5	Get Equal
8	Get Greater Than
9	Get Greater Than or Equal
10	Get Less Than
11	Get Less Than or Equal

The file involved in the search must be open and must have at least one index. The position block identifies the file and is modified if the search succeeds. The data buffer pointer must hold the address of an empty block that is large enough to hold the largest record in the file, and the data length variable must hold the size of this block. The key buffer contains the target for the search and its length is set into the Key Length field. These rules apply to all five operations in the group. The operation code specifies which of the five is desired (see Table 4.30).

Table 4.30 *Index Searching Operation Parameters*

Operations:	INDEX SEARCHING FUNCTIONS	
Position Block:	Required	Updated
Data Buffer:	Empty Block	Contains Record
Data Buffer Length:	Block Size	Record Size
Key Buffer:	Search Target	Unchanged
Key Buffer Length:	Target Size	Unchanged
Key Number:	Identifies Index	Unchanged

With file formats before version 6.0, the search is case sensitive but uses the specified ACS if one exists for the key. The new file format allows case-insensitive searches with no need for an ACS. This permits the ACS capability to serve other needs instead, if such exist.

If the search succeeds, Btrieve returns the record in the data buffer and sets the data buffer length variable to the number of bytes placed in the data buffer. This need not be equal to the size of the empty block passed to the function, since variable length records may be shorter than the buffer itself.

An unsuccessful search has no effect on file positioning. A successful search modifies all position records. The record returned becomes the current record in both logical and physical sense. The logical next and previous records depend on the index used for searching, and the physical next and previous records depend on the record's storage location.

Logical-Sequence Functions The logical-sequence subgroup includes six operations that retrieve a record based upon logical sequence (see Table 4.31). Four are identical in action except for the sequence involved. Each operation uses the index set by the Key

Table 4.31 *Operations in Logical-Sequence Subgroup*

Operation	Name
6	Get Next
7	Get Previous
12	Get First
13	Get Last
36	Get Next Extended
37	Get Previous Extended

Number field and retrieves the record that satisfies the desired sequence. This sequence (first, previous, next, or last) appears in the operation name.

Two other extended operations, introduced at version 5.1, perform similar actions, but upon an entire set of records rather than a single record.

The four basic logical-sequence functions (Get First, Get Next, Get Previous, Get Last) differ only in their direction of movement. Get First retrieves the first record appearing in the specified index. Get Last does the same for the last record. Get Previous returns the record that precedes the current record in the index, and Get Next retrieves the following record. All operate as follows: The file involved must be open and must have at least one index (see Table 4.32). The position block identifies the file and is modified if the search succeeds. The data buffer pointer must hold the address of an empty block that is large enough to hold the largest record in the file, and the data length variable must hold the size of this block. The key buffer contains the target for the search and its length is set into the key length field. The operation code specifies which operation is desired.

If the operation succeeds, Btrieve returns the record in the data buffer and sets the data buffer length variable to the number of bytes placed in the data buffer. This need not be equal to the size of the empty block passed to the function, since variable length records may be shorter than the buffer itself. Note that the first

Table 4.32 *Logical-Sequence Operation Parameters*

Operations:	LOGICAL-SEQUENCE FUNCTIONS	
Position Block:	Required	Updated
Data Buffer:	Empty Block	Contains Record
Data Buffer Length:	Block Size	Record Size
Key Buffer:	Ignored	Holds key field
Key Buffer Length:	Ignored	Unchanged
Key Number:	Identifies Index	Unchanged

record has no logical previous record; a Get Previous operation issued when the first record is current fails. The same is true of a Get Next issued when the last record is current.

An unsuccessful search has no effect on file positioning. A successful search modifies all position records. The record returned becomes the current record in both logical and physical sense. The logical next and previous records depend on the index used for searching, and the physical next and previous records depend on the record's storage location.

The two extended get functions (Get Next Extended and Get Previous Extended) allow retrieving an entire set of records in a single operation. Using an index that was previously established, these functions start at either the current record or at the logically adjacent record in the specified direction and search toward the end or the beginning of the file to obtain a set of records that satisfy desired criteria.

The file must be open and must have a logically adjacent record in the specified direction. The direction is established by the operation code.

The data buffer contains a search structure at call and a different return structure upon return. The search structure specifies a filter that selects records from the file according to a logic expression included in the filter and a descriptor that tells Btrieve which fields of the record to return. The filter includes a field specifying how many records may be skipped for failure to satisfy the filter, and the descriptor specifies how many records are expected. The operation returns successfully when the requested number of records have been retrieved and returns with a nonzero status code if the reject limit is exceeded, if the end of the file is reached, or if it becomes apparent that no subsequent record can satisfy the filter condition (see Table 4.33).

Table 4.33 *Extended Get Operation Parameters*

Operation:	EXTENDED GET FUNCTIONS	
Position Block:	Required	Updated
Data Buffer:	Search Structure	Return Structure
Data Buffer Length:	Structure Size	Structure Size
Key Buffer:	Ignored	Holds key field
Key Buffer Length:	Ignored	Unchanged
Key Number:	Must not change	Unchanged

The optional repeating portion of the filter specifies the logic expression, and Btrieve interprets terms in this expression in strict left-to-right order (that is, the same sequence in which they appear in the specification). No parentheses are available to modify the sequence of evaluation. That is, if the first part of the expression evaluates to TRUE and the next operator is OR, the record is accepted. If the next operator is AND, Btrieve evaluates the next part of the expression. If this evaluates as FALSE, the record is rejected. Otherwise, evaluation continues.

If the first part of the expression evaluates to FALSE and the next operator is AND, the record is rejected. If the next operator is OR, evaluation continues with the next part. This sequence of evaluation continues until the engine either accepts or rejects the record. If the evaluation is TRUE when the end of the logic expression is reached, Btrieve accepts the record; otherwise rejection occurs.

The search structure contains three sections, one fixed in length and the other two variable, in the format shown in Table 4.34.

Table 4.34 *Search Structure*

Section	Size	Description
Header	2 bytes	Total length of entire structure in bytes, as integer
	2 bytes	One of two signature codes in ASCII:
		EG means begin search with adjacent record.
		UC means begin search with current record.
Filter, Fixed part	2 bytes	Number of rejects allowed during search. 0 means use maximum, which defaults to 4,095 for version 6.15.
	2 bytes	Number of terms in filter expression that follows. 0 means no filtering and the repeating portion of the filter is omitted. Otherwise the repeating portion occurs the number of times specified by this field.
Filter, Repeating part	1 byte	Data type code for field
	2 bytes	Field's length
	2 bytes	Offset of field; first byte of record is offset 0.
	1 byte	Comparison code: 1=equal 2=greater than 3=less than 4=not equal 5=greater than or equal to 6=less than or equal to To compare strings using ACS, add 32 to this field. To compare to another field of the record rather than to a constant, add 64 to this field. To compare ignoring case, add 128 to this field.

Table 4.34 *Continued*

Section	Size	Description
	1 byte	Operator for combining terms:
		0=end of expression, no next term
		1=AND with next term
		2=OR with next term
	2 or *n* bytes	When comparing fields, 2-byte offset to second field being compared
		When comparing to constant, actual constant value; size *n* is determined by data type code
Descriptor,	2 bytes	Number of records to be retrieved, as integer
Fixed part	2 bytes	Number of fields to extract from each record. Repeating part occurs once for each field.
Descriptor,	2 bytes	Field's length
Repeating part	2 bytes	Offset of field; first byte of record is offset 0.

The return structure contains two sections, one fixed in length and the other variable, in the format shown in Table 4.35.

For fixed-length fields, the length values for each record will be identical. However, if the file permits varying-length fields, these values may vary from one record to another.

Table 4.35 *Return Structure*

Section	Size	Description
Header	2 bytes	Number of records actually returned
Records,	2 bytes	Length of returned fields for this record (*n* below)
Repeating part	4 bytes	Physical position of record in same format that Get Position returns
	n bytes	Returned field data (all fields combined)

The Get Extended functions establish complete logical and physical current, next, and previous record values, but these values are those of the last record examined, not those for the last record that was accepted. Because of this, the extended functions cannot be used to set currency values for other operations requiring them. Use the physical address data from the return structure and perform a Get Direct operation, after the extended operation, to establish currency for updating or deleting records.

Physical-Sequence Functions   The physical-sequence subgroup includes six operations that retrieve a record based upon physical sequence (see Table 4.36). Four are identical in action except for the sequence involved. Each operation uses physical currency information without regard to any index and retrieves the record that satisfies the desired sequence. This sequence (first, previous, next, or last) appears in the operation name. Before version 5.0, when the first, previous, and last operations were added, the operation now called Step Next was known as Step Direct.

Table 4.36   *Physical-Sequence Subgroup Operations*

Operation	Name
24	Step Next
33	Step First
34	Step Last
35	Step Previous
38	Step Next Extended
39	Step Previous Extended

Two other extended operations, introduced at version 5.1, perform similar actions, but upon an entire set of records rather than a single record.

The four basic physical-sequence functions (Step First, Step Next, Step Previous, Step Last) differ only in their direction of movement. Step First retrieves the first record in the file. Step Last does the same for the last record. Step Previous returns the record that physically precedes the current record, and Step Next retrieves the following record. All operate as follows: The file involved must be open. The position block identifies the file and is modified if the search succeeds. The data buffer pointer must hold the address of an empty block that is large enough to hold the largest record in the file, and the data length variable must hold the size of this block. The operation code specifies which operation is desired (see Table 4.37).

Table 4.37 *Physical-Sequence Operation Parameters*

Operations:	PHYSICAL-SEQUENCE FUNCTIONS	
Position Block:	Required	Updated
Data Buffer:	Empty Block	Contains Record
Data Buffer Length:	Block Size	Record Size
Key Buffer:	Ignored	Unchanged
Key Buffer Length:	Ignored	Unchanged
Key Number:	Ignored	Unchanged

If the operation succeeds, Btrieve returns the record in the data buffer and sets the data buffer length variable to the number of bytes placed in the data buffer. This need not be equal to the size of the empty block passed to the function, since variable length records may be shorter than the buffer itself. Note that the first record has no logical previous record; a Step Previous operation issued when the first record is current fails. The same is true of a Step Next issued when the last record is current.

An unsuccessful search has no effect on file positioning. A successful search modifies all position records. The record returned becomes the physical current record. The physical next and previous records depend on the record's storage location. The operation destroys all logical currency.

The basic Step functions prove quite useful for data recovery should an index become damaged. Although this is not a frequent happening, it's possible for many reasons. To recover, create an empty copy of the damaged file that has the same record layout and index structure but no content. Then use Step First to retrieve the first record of the damaged file, and write that record to the new copy using the Insert function. Use Step Next to retrieve the next record and write it also. Continue in this fashion until reaching the end of the file. If that happens, recovery is complete. The damaged file can be destroyed and the new one renamed to take its place.

If, however, an error occurs when trying to Step Next, back up to the last record successfully read, and note its physical address. Then use Step Last to go to the end of the file, and copy each record in turn (using Step Previous rather than Step Next) until either reaching the record already successfully copied, or encountering another error.

If a second error occurs, data located between the two points cannot be recovered by Btrieve itself. In Part 3 of this book, however, we'll examine a method of overcoming this problem using knowledge of the internal file format and getting back all the data that survives. Note that the non-Btrieve retrieval technique cannot guarantee that all data read back is actually valid. Any disaster that might require such measures can easily destroy several records beyond any hope of recovery. These methods can, however, earn their keep when disaster strikes.

The two extended step functions (Step Next Extended and Step Previous Extended) allow retrieving an entire set of records in a single operation. These functions start at the physically adjacent record in the specified direction and search toward the end or the beginning of the file to obtain a set of records that satisfy desired criteria.

The file must be open and must have a physically adjacent record in the specified direction. The direction is established by the operation code (see Table 4.38).

The data buffer contains a search structure at call and a different return structure upon return. These structures are identical to those used by the Extended Get functions except that only the EG signatures are valid. The UC option is not allowed. The operation returns

Table 4.38 *Extended Step Operation Parameters*

Operation:	EXTENDED STEP FUNCTIONS	
Position Block:	Required	Updated
Data Buffer:	Search Structure	Return Structure
Data Buffer Length:	Structure Size	Structure Size
Key Buffer:	Ignored	Unchanged
Key Buffer Length:	Ignored	Unchanged
Key Number:	Ignored	Unchanged

successfully when the requested number of records have been retrieved and returns with a non-zero status code if the reject limit is exceeded, if the end of the file is reached, or if it becomes apparent that no subsequent record can satisfy the filter condition.

The Step Extended functions establish physical current, next, and previous record values, but these values are those of the last record examined, not those for the last record that was accepted. Because of this, the extended functions cannot be used to set currency values for other operations requiring them. Use the physical address data from the return structure and perform a Get Direct operation, after the extended operation, to establish currency for updating or deleting records.

Special Retrieval Functions   The remaining two special retrieval functions, one added and the other greatly extended at version 6.0, fall outside both major subgroups (see Table 4.39).

Table 4.39 *Special Retrieval Operations*

Operation	Name
23	Get Direct/Chunk or Record
44	Get By Percentage

The Get Direct/Chunk or Record operations retrieve either a complete record or a chunk of one, using a physical address. Before version 6.0, only the record form of this operation existed. Chunk action is available only with newer versions and with files using the new format.

To retrieve a complete record using this operation, the file must be open. The physical address of the desired record, obtained through either the Get Position operation or through one of the Get/Step Extended operations, goes into the first 4 bytes of the data buffer. Set the data buffer length to the maximum size available for return of the record.

The key number field determines whether this operation will have any effect on logical currency. If the key number is zero or positive, it specifies the key for which Btrieve will establish logical currency. If set to 0xFF (–1), logical currency is destroyed and not replaced. If logical currency is specified, the key buffer contains the key fields from the addressed record when the operation completes (see Table 4.40).

Table 4.40 *Get Direct/Record Operation Parameters*

Operation:	Get Direct/Record(23)	
Position Block:	Required	Updated
Data Buffer:	Physical Address	Data Record
Data Buffer Length:	Size Available	Record Size
Key Buffer:	Empty Block	Key Fields
Key Buffer Length:	Block Length	Unchanged
Key Number:	0xFF(-1) or key number	Unchanged

The Get Direct/Record operation always erases the logical current, previous, and next record information from the position block. If a non-negative key number is used, they will be set from the specified key and the record's key fields returned in the key buffer. In all cases, the physical current, previous, and next record values are set from physical locations in the file.

The Get Direct / Chunk variation introduced at version 6.0 allows retrieval of data from records longer than the 65,536-byte limit (imposed by the Intel CPU design) on the other retrieval operations. It does so by retrieving one or more portions of a record, rather than retrieving the complete record.

Like fields, the chunks within a record use offset and length as their identifying features. Providing all needed information requires a descriptor structure along with the 4-byte physical address of the record, however. This structure follows the physical address in the data buffer. Data buffer length should be set to the larger of either the structure size plus address bytes, or the size of all chunks to be returned by the operation. Note that in both Btrieve for DOS and Btrieve for Windows the data buffer's size is limited to 64,512 bytes maximum (see Table 4.41).

Table 4.41   *Get Direct/Chunk Operation Parameters*

Operation:	Get Direct/Chunk (23)	
Position Block:	Required	Updated
Data Buffer:	Descriptor Data	Chunk data
Data Buffer Length:	Max of Sizes	Chunk Size
Key Buffer:	Ignored	Unchanged
Key Buffer Length:	Ignored	Unchanged
Key Number:	0xFE(−2)	Unchanged

The descriptor data has four variations, two groups of two members each. In all four, the first 4 bytes of the data buffer must be the physical address of the record that contains the desired chunk, and the next 4 bytes form a descriptor "subfunction" code. The high 3 bytes of this subfunction are 0x800000 and the low byte is 00, 01, 02, or 03 to distinguish among the four variations.

We can group the variations in either of two ways: by dividing them between direct and indirect storage specification, or by drawing the major division between random and rectangular placement of chunks in the physical record. The Btrieve manuals follow the second choice, discussing direct random and indirect random chunk descriptors together. Since the structures differ greatly between the random and the rectangular groups, but hardly at all between direct and indirect addressing, we follow that choice also.

In this grouping, the distinction between direct and indirect storage address is common to both structures. Direct addressing tells Btrieve to return the requested chunks in the data buffer, overwriting the descriptor structure. The data buffer length must be set to a value high enough to allow all requested chunks to be stored. No delimiters or count fields separate the chunks from each other in the buffer; the program must know how to distinguish them if necessary. With direct addressing, the Storage Address field(s) in the chunk descriptors must be set to 0.

Indirect addressing tells Btrieve to return the chunks at the specified storage address(es) rather than in the data buffer itself. Each specified address must have enough space available to contain the data. This technique allows the program to place random chunks at individually specified locations, or rectangular chunks in a single regular array structure anywhere in memory.

A random arrangement of chunks, unlike a rectangular collection, has no regularity in its layout within the record. Each chunk may be a different length from all others, and spacing between adjacent chunks may vary.

A low descriptor byte of 00 specifies a direct random descriptor, and 01 specifies an indirect random descriptor. In both cases the 4 bytes that follow the descriptor specify how many chunks are being requested. That many groups of 12-byte chunk specifiers then follow. The data buffer length for these descriptors must be at least $(n + 1)*$ 12 bytes where n is the number of chunks the descriptor requests; the 12 added bytes resulting from the "+ 1" allow for the physical address, the descriptor itself, and the chunk count.

The complete data buffer layout for the random chunk descriptors is shown in Table 4.42.

Table 4.42   *Data Buffer Layout for Random Chunk Descriptors*

Portion	Field Size	Description
Fixed Part	4 bytes	Physical record address
	4 bytes	Random chunk descriptor: 0x80000000 = direct random chunk 0x80000001 = indirect random chunk
	4 bytes	Number of chunk specifiers that follow
Repeating Part: Chunk Specifier	4 bytes	Chunk offset from start of record, 0-based (from first byte past last chunk read, if 0x40000000 is ORed into descriptor)
	4 bytes	Chunk length in bytes, range 1 to 64,512 under DOS or Windows, or 1 to 65,535 otherwise
	4 bytes	Storage Address. Must be 0 for direct descriptor, or operating-system compatible 32-bit pointer for indirect. DOS uses 16-bit segment:offset convention, Windows and OS/2 are 16-bit selector:offset pair, and NetWare uses 32-bit flat addressing.

A rectangular arrangement of chunks differs from a random collection in that each chunk in the group has the same number of bytes, and all the chunks are the same distance apart.

A low descriptor byte of 02 specifies a direct rectangular descriptor, and 03 specifies an indirect rectangular descriptor. In both cases, the following six 4-byte values completely describe the desired group of chunks. Total size of such a descriptor is always 32 bytes.

The complete data buffer layout for the rectangular chunk descriptors is shown in Table 4.43.

Table 4.43 *Data Buffer Layout for Rectangular Chunk Descriptors*

Field Size	Description
4 bytes	Physical record address

4 bytes	Rectangular chunk descriptor:
	
	    0x80000002 = direct rectangular chunk
	
	    0x80000003 = indirect rectangular chunk

4 bytes	Number of rows requested
4 bytes	Offset from start of record, 0-based, for first chunk (from first byte past last chunk read, if 0x40000000 is ORed into descriptor)
4 bytes	Number of bytes per row, from 0 to 65,535
4 bytes	Number of bytes from start of one chunk to start of next in Btrieve file
4 bytes	Storage Address for first byte of first chunk. Must be 0 for direct descriptor, or operating-system compatible 32-bit pointer for indirect. DOS uses 16-bit segment:offset convention, Windows and OS/2 are 16-bit selector:offset air, and NetWare uses 32-bit flat addressing.
4 bytes	Number of bytes from start of one chunk to start of next in Storage Address area.

The Get Direct/Chunk operations have no effect on logical currency, but set physical currency to that for the specified record.

It's essential, when using Get Direct/Chunk in any of its variations, to verify that all requested chunks were actually read. In some situations, the operation may terminate before all chunks have been read, without returning any indication of error. To verify that all data has been read, check the returned data buffer length value, comparing it to the expected total length for all chunks requested. Even when indirect storage is specified, the data buffer length variable contains the count of bytes retrieved by the operation.

The Get By Percentage operation (code 44) retrieves a data record based on its position in the file, specified as a percentage of the total file size. The percentage may apply to any index path, or to physical location, depending on the key number passed to the operation. The file must be open, and must be in version 6.0 or later format to use physical positioning. If a key path is to be used, the index for that key must exist (see Table 4.44).

Table 4.44 *Get By Percentage Operation Parameters*

Operation:	GET BY PERCENTAGE(44)	
Position Block:	Required	Updated
Data Buffer:	Percentage Value	Record Data
Data Buffer Length:	Enough for Record	Data Length
Key Buffer:	Empty Block	Key Fields
Key Buffer Length:	Block Size	Unchanged
Key Number:	Specifies Option	Unchanged

To retrieve a record by percentage position, store the percentage as a value from 0 to 10,000 (0.00% to 100.00% with implied decimal point) in binary integer format as the first 2 bytes of the data buffer. Set the data buffer length to a size equal to or larger than the desired record. In the key number field, place either the number of the key to be used, or 0xFF (–1) to specify use of the physical percentage instead of any index.

If successful, the function returns the specified record in the data buffer and sets the data buffer length variable to the count of bytes actually returned. If positioning via a key is specified and the key permits duplicate values, Btrieve always returns the first record in the chain of duplicates.

This function, together with Find Percentage, assumes a uniform distribution of records within the data files and of keys within the index pages. The assumption will be false if many records within a narrow range of keys have been deleted, if many records within a narrow physical address range have been deleted, or if the key specified permits duplicates and many duplicates exist. However even when the assumption fails, accuracy of the operation is adequate to achieve acceptable results when using Windows scroll bars to position the current location within a data file.

Like other related operations, Get By Percentage returns, in the key buffer, the key fields of the returned record when using a key path. When using a physical path, the key buffer remains unchanged.

When using a key path, a successful Get By Percentage operation establishes both logical and physical current, previous, and next records in the position block. If using physical percentage, a successful operation erases all logical currency but establishes physical currency. An operation that does not succeed changes nothing in the position block.

Bias Codes   Btrieve provides five bias codes that allow most GET operations to check for existence of a record without moving its data, or to specify one of four different locking options (Table 4.45). The four codes that deal with locking also apply to most STEP operations. These bias codes cannot be used with any other operations.

Table 4.45   *Bias Codes*

Bias	Name	Action	Comments
+ 50	Get Key	Same as basic GET but does not bring data into buffer	Same as basic GET
+100	Lock Single Wait	Same as basic GET but locks record; waits if already locked	Same as basic GET; used on STEP also
+200	Lock Single No-Wait	Same as basic GET but locks record; fails if already locked	Same as basic GET; used on STEP also
+300	Lock Multiple Wait	Same as basic GET but locks record; waits if already locked	Same as basic GET; used on STEP also
+400	Lock Multiple No-Wait	Same as basic GET but locks record; fails if already locked	Same as basic GET: used on STEP also

To use any of the five bias codes, just add it to the basic operation code for the GET or STEP function. The Get Key bias prevents the function from actually transferring data, but all other actions, including establishing currency, are performed. The most common use for this bias is to verify a record's existence when that's all a program needs to know. Since the Get Key operations do no imaging, operations that modify a record cannot use Get Key to establish positioning within the file. Chapter 7 deals with this restriction in more detail.

The four bias codes dealing with locking differ in two respects: two of them (100 and 200) allow locking only a single record while the other two (300 and 400) permit locking multiple records at the same time. Different operations must be used for each record when locking more than one, however. The distinction between wait and no-wait operation is significant only when the requested record is already locked. In that case, Btrieve will wait indefinitely for it to become available when a "wait" bias code is in effect. If a "no-wait" is requested, however, the request will fail with a status code indicating that the record is locked.

Choice between the wait and no-wait options depends on many factors. The wait options can always obtain the record more rapidly, if they can get it at all. Using no-wait requires the program to test the status code, and loop back to issue the request again, while using wait needs only a single call to the engine.

However in practice, it's possible for two users to ask for the same pair of records, but in different sequence. If the timing overlaps in exactly the right way, User 1 can achieve a lock on Record A and immediately afterward User 2 locks Record B. Now when User 1 attempts to lock Record B, it's already locked. Similarly when User 2 attempts to lock Record A, it's unavailable.

Such a situation is known as "deadlock" or by an even more picturesque term, "the deadly embrace." If both users request wait style locks, neither can go forward. Btrieve does exactly what was requested: waits for the record to become available. The only way to escape is drastic: one of the users must disconnect and the other must wait for Btrieve to clean up the locks. This may result in data corruption, and is almost certain to do so if an operator becomes impatient and reboots the system in a misguided effort to speed recovery.

If, however, the user requests the no-wait option, and the loops for re-trying the request include limits on the number of retry attempts, the programs can notify either or both of the users of the deadlock, and ask them to cancel their operations. Therefore any time there's a chance of a deadly embrace situation developing, it's best to use no-wait locks and build limits into the retry loops of programs.

Under Windows, the wait and no-wait options produce almost identical results. No wait occurs; Windows does not permit it. The difference is that a wait operation that encounters an already locked record may return a status code of 78, "deadlock detected," rather than 84 or 85, indicating record/page lock or file lock respectively. The Btrieve engine for Windows explicitly checks for a deadlock situation in order to report such status; no other engine does so.

The explicit locks applied to records by successful use of a bias code vanish automatically under certain circumstances. Deleting a locked record removes any associated locks. Closing the file, either explicitly or through a Reset operation, also releases all locks on that file. These automatic releases apply to all types of locks. Additionally, a specific Unlock operation (code 27) permits release of locks under program control with no need for any data change.

Other automatic release circumstances vary, depending upon whether the lock is single-record or multi-record. A single-record lock releases automatically when another single-record lock request occurs, permitting records to be locked when browsing with no need to release each individually. Single-record locks also release automatically when the record is updated.

Multi-record locks remain in effect when additional locks are requested, and also when a locked record is updated.

Initiating a transaction also automatically releases any locks, whether single- or multi-record, that may be in effect then. More detail of this appears with discussion of the Transaction group of operations later in this chapter.

The Record Change Group   The three functions within the Record Change group include two for updating records, and one for deleting a record (Table 4.46). For all three, the record involved must be the "current record" as indicated by the file's position block. Since the extended operations set file currency to the last record examined, rather than the last record satisfying filter requirements, the functions of the Record Change group are not allowed when an extended operation has been the last to modify the file's position block.

Table 4.46   *Record Change Group Operations*

Operation	Name
3	Update
53	Update Chunk
4	Delete

Update (Code 3)   The Update operation writes a complete record from the data buffer back to the data file at the physical current-record position. The file must be open, and physical currency must exist. If issued within the limits of a transaction, the record's retrieval must also have happened inside the transaction boundary. Any modifiable indexes associated with the file are updated to reflect changes in key fields of the record. Any change to a key field for an index not tagged as modifiable results in failure of the operation.

The data buffer must contain a complete record; thus neither the Get Key options nor any of the extended operations are suitable methods to establish currency. Normally one of the standard Get or Step functions retrieves the record, the program makes appropriate changes, and then requests the Update operation.

The key number field specifies the index upon which logical currency is to be established. When set to 0xFF (-1), a "no currency change"

(NCC) update occurs. Successful non-NCC update operations modify the key buffer to contain the key fields for the specified index. NCC updates have no effect upon the key buffer. See Table 4.47.

Table 4.47 *Update Operation Parameters*

Operation:	UPDATE(3)	
Position Block:	Required	May Be Modified
Data Buffer:	Changed Record	Unchanged
Data Buffer Length:	Record Size	Unchanged
Key Buffer:	Empty Block	Key Fields
Key Buffer Length:	Block Size	Unchanged
Key Number:	Option Switch	Unchanged

The Update operation leaves physical currency unchanged, but (if key fields change) can modify logical currency for the file to that for the specified key number unless the operation is flagged as NCC. For an NCC Update operation the position block remains unchanged in all respects, allowing use of the original key sequence to get the original next record even though the key was modified by the update.

Update Chunk (Code 53)   The Update Chunk operation writes one or more partial records (chunks) back to the data file. This operation can append data to an existing record, making it longer, or can truncate an existing record to reduce its length.

The file must be open, must have established logical or physical currency, and must use version 6.0 and later format. If the operation request is inside a transaction, the retrieval operation that established currency must also be within the same transaction.

This operation's complex options require that the data buffer contain a chunk descriptor, which in turn provides details of the action requested, and full specification of the chunk or chunks involved. Five types of chunk descriptors exist; four of them are identical to the chunk descriptors described in detail for the Get Direct/Chunk operation, except that the direct-address descriptors are followed immediately by the data for all chunks. The fifth specifies truncation of a record. (See Table 4.48.)

Table 4.48   *Update Chunk Operation Parameters*

Operation:	Update Chunk(53)	
Position Block:	Required	Updated
Data Buffer:	Chunk Descriptor	Unchanged
Data Buffer Length:	Total Length	Unchanged
Key Buffer:	As left by Get	Key Fields
Key Buffer Length:	As left by Get	Unchanged
Key Number:	As left by Get	Unchanged

For the two direct descriptor types, the data buffer layout is shown in Table 4.49.

Table 4.49   *Data Buffer Layout for First Four*
                 Update Chunk Variations

Chunk Descriptor (see Get Direct/Chunk)
Data for Chunk 1
Data for Chunk 2
Data for Chunk 3
. . .
Data for Chunk *n*

The fifth chunk descriptor subfunction, Truncate, has the simplest layout: this descriptor contains only two 4-byte fields. The first identifies the subfunction and is 0x800004 for the truncate action. The other identifies the offset from the front of the record at which truncation occurs. The byte at that position and all following bytes vanish. Minimum value for this field is 4 and maximum is the record length minus 1 (since offset values are zero-based).

The last-chunk bias code, 0x40000000, described for Get Direct/Chunk descriptors applies also to descriptors for Update Chunk and causes Btrieve to measure the offset from the current position in the record rather than from the start of the record. Current position is the first byte beyond the last byte read or written in the same record, and is reset to 0 each time a new record is accessed.

An additional bias code, 0x20000000, applies only to Update Chunk descriptors and specifies that the current position is to be one byte past the end of the record. This appends the chunks listed in the descriptor to the record instead of overwriting existing data. This code cannot be used with the last-chunk bias code nor with the Truncate subfunction.

For all forms of chunk descriptor, set the data buffer length value to the total size of the descriptor plus all associated data. This can range from a minimum of 8 (for the Truncate subfunction) to a maximum of approximately 64K. Exact maximum value depends on the platform in use.

Successful completion of an Update Chunk operation may modify key indexes if any key fields were involved. Key fields for the index specified by the key number return, in the key buffer, whether modified or not. The NCC option switch is not available for this operation, but the operation has no effect upon either logical or physical currency of the file. The key number passed to the operation must be the same used to retrieve the record originally.

Delete (Code 4)   The Delete operation removes the complete current record from file, updates all indexes to account for the deletion, and makes the space formerly occupied by the record available for reuse. The file must be open, and a physical current record must exist. The currency requirement can be met by use of a valid Get or Step (except Get Key or extended operations), Insert, or Update operation. If inside a transaction, the read or write operation that established currency must also be within the transaction.

Although the Delete operation itself ignores the key number, this field should not be changed from the value left there by the preceding read operation. Otherwise Btrieve may report an error on the next subsequent read operation although the delete succeeds.

The Delete operation destroys all physical currency information together with the logical current record position, but logical next and previous record values remain valid and can be used for retrieval of an adjacent record in the file. See Table 4.50.

Table 4.50   *Delete Operation Parameters*

Operation:	DELETE(4)	
Position Block:	Required	Destroyed
Data Buffer:	Ignored	Unchanged
Data Buffer Length:	Ignored	Unchanged
Key Buffer:	Ignored	Unchanged
Key Buffer Length:	Ignored	Unchanged
Key Number:	See Text	Unchanged

The Transaction Control Group   Earlier in this chapter we met the concept of record locking to prevent one user's actions from corrupting records being updated by another user. Sometimes locking is inadequate to prevent data corruption; it's necessary to make certain that an entire group of operations be done on an all-or-none basis. That is, failure of any single action must cause all previous operations in the group to be undone, restoring the integrity of the database. The Transaction Control group provides this capability and contains the four operations in Table 4.51.

Table 4.51   *Transaction Control Group Operations*

Operation	Name
19	Begin Transaction
20	End Transaction
21	Abort Transaction
27	Unlock

Three operations in the Transaction Control group allow a program to restrict a group of actions to an all-or-none basis. These capabilities were added to Btrieve at version 4.1.

Such a group of related actions, called a **transaction,** can involve multiple files. The transaction begins with execution of a Begin Transaction operation. If successful, the End Transaction operation can terminate the sequence. If something goes wrong, the Abort Transaction operation cancels everything done, back to the Begin Operation point.

Only one transaction can be active within any application at one time. Nesting of transactions within other transactions is not allowed as of version 6.15, but has been mentioned as a possible future enhancement to Btrieve's capabilities.

The fourth operation in this group unlocks any explicit locks placed on records, either inside of or outside of transactions, should automatic unlock action not occur.

Begin Transaction (Code 19)   The Begin Transaction operation marks the start of a sequence of operations to be done all-or-none. Btrieve versions 6.0 and later allow an operation code of 1019 to specify a concurrent user transaction. Before version 6.0, only exclusive transactions existed. Using operation code 19 with newer versions requests that the user transaction be exclusive, also.

In a concurrent transaction, only those pages containing records being modified are locked for the duration of the transaction or until explicit Unlock requests occur. In an exclusive transaction, the engine locks all pages of each file involved, rather than locking only specific records or pages. The adjective "user" applied to a transaction distinguishes it from a "system transaction," which is outside user or program control. Part 2 of this book describes system transactions. Within this chapter, "transaction" implies "user transaction."

Files and records involved in either concurrent or exclusive transactions are available to other users but only for data retrieval; insert, update, or delete operations on locked files or records are prohibited to other users during the transaction. This restriction preserves the integrity of imaging data should the transaction have to be aborted. See Table 4.52.

Table 4.52 *Begin Transaction Operation Parameters*

Operation:	BEGIN TRANSACTION(19)	
Position Block:	Required	Unchanged
Data Buffer:	Ignored	Unchanged
Data Buffer Length:	Ignored	Unchanged
Key Buffer:	Ignored	Unchanged
Key Buffer Length:	Ignored	Unchanged
Key Number:	Ignored	Unchanged

To begin a transaction involving a file, the file must be open and no existing exclusive transaction may be active. Any existing locks on the file unlock automatically when a transaction begins.

While a transaction is active (uncommitted), Btrieve logs all operations to a separate transaction control file, so that they can be undone by a subsequent Abort Transaction if necessary. Implicit locks occur for all pages and records involved, preventing other users from invalidating the saved images.

No action taken within a transaction becomes permanent until an End Transaction operation occurs, committing the transaction.

When using Btrieve version 6.0 and later on files in the new format, uncommitted concurrent transactions *are not* visible to other users. When using older Btrieve versions, exclusive transactions, or a pre-6.0-format file, uncommitted changes *are* visible to others.

The Begin Transaction operation does not affect either physical or logical currency of the file.

End Transaction (Code 20)   The End Transaction operation terminates the currently active transaction and makes all file modifications effective, thus committing the transaction. A transaction must be active; if not, Btrieve returns a status code indicating a transaction control file error. All fields of the parameter block, except the operation code itself, should be set to zero for compatibility with possible future versions of Btrieve. See Table 4.53.

Table 4.53   *End Transaction Operation Parameters*

Operation:	END TRANSACTION(20)	
Position Block:	0	Unchanged
Data Buffer:	0	Unchanged
Data Buffer Length:	0	Unchanged
Key Buffer:	0	Unchanged
Key Buffer Length:	0	Unchanged
Key Number:	0	Unchanged

If successful, this operation commits all changes made to all files and unlocks all files or records that were locked during the transaction. End Transaction has no effect on either physical or logical currency data for any file.

Abort Transaction (Code 21)   The Abort Transaction operation terminates the currently active transaction and undoes all operations performed since the Begin Transaction operation that initiated it. A transaction must be active; if not, Btrieve returns a status code indicating a transaction control file error. All fields of the parameter block, except the operation code itself, should be set to zero for compatibility with possible future versions of Btrieve. See Table 4.54.

Table 4.54 *Abort Transaction Operation Parameters*

Operation:	ABORT TRANSACTION(21)	
Position Block:	0	Unchanged
Data Buffer:	0	Unchanged
Data Buffer Length:	0	Unchanged
Key Buffer:	0	Unchanged
Key Buffer Length:	0	Unchanged
Key Number:	0	Unchanged

If successful, all changes made to all files by Insert, Update, or Delete operations during the transaction are undone and the files are restored to their condition at the time the transaction began. All files locked by the transaction are unlocked. The Abort Transaction operation has no effect on either physical or logical currency data for any file.

Unlock (Code 27)   The Unlock operation removes explicit record locks set in a single file by use of a bias code on a Get or Step operation. The file must be open and at least one record must be locked. Three options, distinguished by the key number field of the parameter block, define the type of lock or locks to remove.

To remove a single-record lock, set the key number to any value from 0 to 127. To unlock just one record when multiple-record locks are in effect, set the data buffer to the record's physical address as returned by Get Position, set data buffer length to 4, and set the key number to 0xFF (–1). To unlock all multiple-record locks for a file, set the key number to 0xFE (–2). See Table 4.55.

Table 4.55 *Unlock Operation Parameters*

Operation:	UNLOCK(27)	
Position Block:	Required	Unchanged
Data Buffer:	Record Address or Ignored	Unchanged
Data Buffer Length:	4 or Ignored	Unchanged
Key Buffer:	Ignored	Unchanged
Key Buffer Length:	Ignored	Unchanged
Key Number:	Option Switch	Unchanged

The Unlock operation has no effect on either logical or physical currency for the file.

The Index Control Group   Two operations of the Index Control group share four names; before version 6.0 these operations worked to create and destroy only supplemental indexes and could not affect indexes defined at file creation time. As of version 6.0, the restriction vanished. The operations now create and destroy any indexes, so long as the total number of segments does not exceed the limit established by the file's page size (see Table 4.56).

Create Index (Code 31)   The Create Index operation, in version 6.0 and later, adds an index to an already existing Btrieve file, using

Table 4.56 *Index Control Group Operation Parameters*

Operation	Name
31	Create Index
31	Create Supplemental Index
32	Drop Index
32	Drop Supplemental Index

key-segment specifications set into the data buffer. The new index cannot be distinguished from an original. Before version 6.0, this operation tagged the new index to indicate that it was supplemental in nature. The supplemental identifier was dropped when the enhancement appeared at version 6.0.

To add an index, the file must be open and the total number of segments (those already existing plus those to be added by the operation) must not exceed the limit set by the file's page size (see Table 4.57).

Table 4.57 *Index Segment Limits*

Page Size	Number of Segments	
	6.0 format	old format
512	8	8
1,024	23	24
1,536	24	24
2,048–3,584	54	24
4,096	119	24

Additionally, no transactions can be active when an index is created, although a file that has been opened by more than one Btrieve engine will permit other clients to retrieve records while one client adds a new index. If no autoincrement key is specified for the new index, the other clients can even lock records while the index is being added, although they cannot write to the file until index creation is complete.

The key segment specifications placed into the data buffer are identical to those used when creating a file and are fully described under the Create operation earlier in this chapter. Since each segment specification is 16 bytes long, Btrieve determines the total number of segments to add from the data buffer length. Following the segment definitions may be an ACS table for use by the new index. To use an ACS bit 5 of the key flags field in the segment specification must be set; if this bit is set but no ACS follows the specification, the first ACS defined for the file is used. Note that this operation cannot specify any other ACS to be used, unlike indexes defined at file creation time. To assign a specific key number to the new index (version 6.0 format files only), add the desired number to 0x80 and place the result in the key number field of the parameter block (see Table 4.58).

Table 4.58   *Create Index Operation Parameters*

Operation:	CREATE INDEX(31)	
Position Block:	Required	Unchanged
Data Buffer:	Key Specifications	Unchanged
Data Buffer Length:	Spec Length	Unchanged
Key Buffer:	Ignored	Unchanged
Key Buffer Length:	Ignored	Unchanged
Key Number:	Number to Use	Unchanged

If no key number is specified, Btrieve will assign the lowest unused number to the added index. This always occurs with old-version files and with older versions of the Btrieve engines.

Btrieve updates the newly created index before returning from this operation. For a file containing many records, the required time can be long. Exact duration of the operation cannot be predicted easily since it depends upon the total number of records in the file, the size of the file, and the size of the combined key field, not to mention the platform in use and the specific system's hardware.

If the system fails for any reason (power failure or a system reset are prime examples) during creation of a new index, the file remains fully usable with all other indexes but any attempt to use the incomplete index returns an error status. To correct this situation, use the Drop Index operation to remove the incomplete index, then add it back.

The Create Index operation has no effect on either logical or physical currency of the file.

Drop Index (Code 32)   The Drop Index operation, in version 6.0 and later, removes any index from an already existing Btrieve file and releases all pages used by that index for reuse. Before version 6.0, this operation could be used only on supplemental indexes. The word *supplemental* vanished from the operation name at version 6.0 to reflect the enhanced capability.

To drop an index from a file, the file must be open, the index must exist, and no transactions can be active. Additionally, dropping an index that was created at file creation time requires that the file use the new format; old-format files retain the pre-version-6 restriction that allows only added indexes to be dropped.

Pass the position block for the file to identify the file to the engine and the key number for the index to drop. To prevent the numbers for other indexes from being automatically renumbered, add a bias of 0x80 (128) to the key number. Without this bias, all key numbers above the one being dropped will decrease by one to close the gap. Btrieve ignores all other fields of the parameter block (see Table 4.59).

Table 4.59   *Drop Index Operation Parameters*

Operation:	DROP INDEX(32)	
Position Block:	Required	Updated
Data Buffer:	Ignored	Unchanged
Data Buffer Length:	Ignored	Unchanged
Key Buffer:	Ignored	Unchanged
Key Buffer Length:	Ignored	Unchanged
Key Number:	Index to Drop	Unchanged

Should the system fail while dropping an index, the file remains usable but any attempt to use the incomplete index will return an error status. To correct the situation, repeat the Drop Index operation with the same parameters.

The Drop Index operation has no effect upon physical currency of the file, nor upon logical currency if the index dropped is not the one that established logical currency. If the index that established logical currency is dropped, all logical currency for the file is destroyed.

The Miscellaneous Group   The single operation within the Miscellaneous group permits an application to change the current directory of a specified logical drive (see Table 4.60).

Table 4.60   *Miscellaneous Group Operation*

Operation	Name
17	Set Directory

Set Directory (Code 17)   The Set Directory operation establishes a possibly new current directory for a specified logical drive. The drive is specified as part of the directory path. If no drive letter is included in the path supplied in the key buffer, Btrieve performs the operation using the current default drive. Both the drive and the directory specified must be accessible (see Table 4.61).

Table 4.61   *Set Directory Operation Parameters*

Operation:	SET DIRECTORY(17)	
Position Block:	Ignored	Unchanged
Data Buffer:	Ignored	Unchanged
Data Buffer Length:	Ignored	Unchanged
Key Buffer:	New Directory Path	Unchanged
Key Buffer Length:	Path Length	Unchanged
Key Number:	Ignored	Unchanged

If the Set Directory operation cannot be performed, Btrieve returns a nonzero status code. The operation has no effect on either physical or logical currency of any file.

Available Platforms

Since its introduction in 1982 Btrieve has been a key-indexed record management system created to meet two primary goals: high performance when handling data and improved productivity for software developers. Through the years, each new version of Btrieve has added operations or features to better reach those goals.

The original version ran only on a standalone MS-DOS system. As the product has evolved, it has expanded to many additional platforms, and even more are expected in the very near future. For all versions and on all platforms, though, Btrieve has been implemented as a self-contained executable program that serves client applications by means of the API described earlier in this chapter. In one sense of the phrase, it has always been a **client-server** system. However, popular interpretation of the term client-server includes an implication that the client and the server are two separate computers, and Btrieve conforms to this interpretation by providing two different implementations called client and server engines for platforms other than single-computer systems, such as NetWare or Windows NTAS. These client-server systems consist of one or more central servers, to which multiple workstations connect.

The Btrieve client engine performs all processing at the workstation itself. This engine accesses all files through operating system calls, which may (if on a network) be redirected to the network server to access remote files. However, the engine remains unaware of other network activity, and all data to or from remote files must pass through the network connections.

The server engine, on the other hand, runs at the central file server and does its processing there, in response to requests it receives from workstation-based requester programs. These programs recognize the same API as the client engine. Applications need never know whether they are dealing with a client engine directly, or a server engine through a requester. For high-volume network use, the server offers many advantages.

For example, only the results of a filtered extended operation must be passed from a server back to the requester, whereas a client engine must obtain all data over the connection even though half or more may be discarded by the filter. Multiuser access to the same records also becomes much simpler when handled at a central location. Other advantages include the following:

1. A smaller quantity of data need be transferred across the network, which reduces network traffic.

2. Fewer network requests occur, which uses the file server more efficiently.

3. The centralized processing at the server allows more effective multiuser controls.

Before version 6.0, the major server-based version of Btrieve was that for the Novell NetWare file server. Both it and the MS-DOS-based client version were bundled as part of the NetWare system offering, together with the single software development kit. Only one SDK was needed because applications written for the client-based version could run unchanged on the server-based version, and vice versa.

Although only the NetWare server engine was widely available, client-based engines existed for several operating systems including MS-DOS, OS/2, and Windows. For a time, Xenix was also supported.

With the emergence of Btrieve Technologies Inc. as an independent company separate from Novell, the distinction between client engines and server engines became much more explicit than it had been under the Novell banner. Server engines and client engines are now sold as totally separate products, and separate engines exist for each of the supported platforms. The rest of this chapter offers brief introductions to the engines currently available, segregated by platform.

Each platform discussion includes summarized descriptions, where applicable, explaining how that platform's special interface requirements differ from the basic Btrieve API.

Btrieve for DOS

Since DOS has never provided built-in networking or multitasking operations, only the client engine version of Btrieve is available for this platform. Workstations using DOS as part of a network can run either the Btrieve for DOS client engine, or one of the requesters from a server engine package; with version 6.0 and later, both engines can run at the same time on the same workstation.

Before version 6.0, the standard MS-DOS client engine ran as a TSR that required a significant fraction of the conventional RAM space below 640K. Because of the engine's appetite for RAM, many if not most applications loaded Btrieve, did what they needed to do, then automatically unloaded the engine before returning to DOS.

Although this technique added a noticeable delay to the starting time for the application, it did free the RAM when Btrieve was not in use. It also made possible customizing the Btrieve configuration for each different application, through the command-line option switches that control the number of buffers available, maximum page size, and so on.

During the redesign that became version 6.0, the DOS client engine became an extended-DOS application to obtain access to all available memory even above the 1-MB mark. Because of this, hardware requirements for version 6.0 and later begin at the 80386 level, with at least 2 MB of extended memory being necessary.

If these hardware needs are met, Btrieve for DOS version 6.0 and later runs with Novell DOS 7, PC-DOS 3.1 or later (from IBM), and MS-DOS 3.1 or later. However, operation with MS-DOS version 4.x does not work with XMAEM.SYS, which fails to provide the necessary extended memory. Along with the true DOS operating systems, this client engine runs with the OS/2 Virtual DOS Machine.

Instead of the command-line option switches used with earlier versions, the current versions of Btrieve for DOS employ a BTI.CFG file to establish configuration values. They also require access to PMSWITCH.EXE, the DOS extended package, when loading.

Btrieve for Windows

The original Windows package for Btrieve contained separate DLLs for communication with a local Btrieve engine or with a requester for server-based operation, plus a copy of the local engine. To load the local engine or to connect to the requester, an application had to call a special function. These functions differed depending on whether the local engine or the requester was the target. To disconnect at the end of the application, a call to `btrvstop()` or `wbtrvstop()`

was necessary. Failure to do so would cause the engine or requester to remain loaded, taking up resources unnecessarily.

The current version still provides one DLL for communicating only with the local engine (WBTRLOCL.DLL), another (WBTRCALL.DLL) for loading the local engine and dealing with the requester, and a copy of the local engine (WBTR32.EXE). The local engine for Windows, however, now loads automatically at the first call to any function within WBTRCALL.DLL. This makes the special initialization functions obsolete, though they still exist as empty dummy calls to retain compatibility with source code in older Windows applications. The same is true of the `btrvstop()` functions; the Windows client engines detect the fact that an application has ended. They automatically unload themselves when no more Btrieve clients exist.

Within a Windows-based Btrieve application, several special functions are usable for communicating with the appropriate Btrieve engine. BTI, however, recommends only four of these for general use. Of the four, two are platform-independent and thus fully portable; the other two are Windows-specific.

1. BTRV. Platform independent, handles all API functions. Interface modules provided in the development kits for DOS, Windows, OS/2, and NetWare all support this function and all require the same set of parameters to it. These are the parameters described with the API, earlier in this chapter. Using this call makes an application's source code fully portable between supported platforms.

2. BTRVID. Platform independent, handles all API functions and adds client ID capability so that one application can support multiple Btrieve client entities. The application itself defines these clients, in a manner analogous to the Windows Multiple Document Interface with its independent child windows. Each such client has a unique ID. The application handles all communication with Btrieve on behalf of the clients, using the ID to properly route requests and responses. The BTRVID function appears in the development kits for Windows and for NetWare only at this time.

3. BTRCALL. Windows specific, exported as ordinal @1, provides actual interface to Btrieve engines. BTRV simply passes its parameters to BTRCALL for action.

4. BTRCALLID. Windows specific, exported as ordinal @7, provides the interface for Btrieve client ID calls. BTRVID passes its parameters to BTRCALLIN for action.

The Windows DLLs permit shared access to files by different applications running at the same time. If the BTI.CFG file configuration allows, applications may use both the local and requester engines at the same time.

Windows applications that use Btrieve-based files together with Microsoft's ODBC approach to connectivity may uncover serious shortcomings in ODBC drivers currently available. Stated in its simplest terms, one major problem is that ODBC is based upon use of SQL; Btrieve files prior to version 6.0 were not totally SQL-compatible since the older engines had no mechanism to enforce referential integrity. As a result, existing ODBC drivers make no use of the indexes within Btrieve files and thus discard one of the major advantages of the system. By forcing all data retrieval to use the slow linear search method, these drivers limit system speed to that of a glacier's travel.

The newer file format and microkernel architecture make it possible to create an ODBC driver that retains Btrieve's speed advantages. Doing so has become a high priority goal at BTI. Until such a driver is available, however, developers are well-advised to avoid ODBC entirely when working with Btrieve files and instead use other tools that access the data directly through the Btrieve engines. See Chapter 9 for several such tools.

Btrieve for OS/2

The current Btrieve for OS/2 client engine, Btrieve for OS/2 version 5.10a, is similar to that for Windows. A pre-release of Btrieve for OS/2 client engine version 6.15, which includes no requesters, has been made available to registered Btrieve developers and may be in distribution by the time this book appears.

The new version is for use only with native OS/2 Btrieve applications, not for OS/2 DOS boxes or WIN/OS2 sessions. It requires 2MB of extended memory, as do all version 6.0 and later client engines.

The version 6.0 and later OS/2 engine features true multi-threaded operation, with at least thirteen permanent threads in the standard engine plus several more used only for logging, durability, startup, or shutdown. The thirteen standard threads include one main controller, four doing background I/O in parallel, six serving as workers for whatever operation is available, one coordinator, and one pipe/queue responder. The number of I/O and worker threads can be changed by system configuration. The multi-threaded architecture permits all processes to operate in parallel with each other, rather than serially as required by single-threaded operation.

Like the Windows product, the Btrieve for OS/2 client engine loads automatically when an application first calls it. However, the Btrieve engine can also be forced to load even before an application by adding it to the Startup folder so that OS/2 starts it automatically. A Settings option allows Btrieve's resources to be allocated at startup, rather than when the first client process requests an operation.

When Btrieve loads automatically, it can be forced to start minimized by changing the icon's default desktop settings. Doing so, however, requires a little trick, since OS/2 version 2.x Session pages are disabled by default for native PM applications.

To force Btrieve to start minimized, first go to the Program page. There, change the Btrieve executable name to something that does not exist, such as BTRIEVEX.EXE. This enables the Session page, allowing you to set the Start Minimized option. Once the option is set, go back to the Program page and restore the Btrieve executable name.

NetWare Server Usage

The original NetWare Btrieve implementation consisted of three separate programs: BSERVER ran at the file server, BREQUEST ran at each workstation, and BROUTER provided interconnection between multiple servers in the same network.

The BSERVER Program   Every file server holding Btrieve files requires its own copy of the Btrieve record manager, BSERVER, to act as the server engine. First implemented as BSERVER.VAP, the current version is a network loadable module (BTRIEVE.NLM) that must be configured into the file server. BSERVER here refers to both versions. BSERVER is the record manager program that handles specific Btrieve requests involving any file on the server.

BSERVER performs these four major functions.

1. It handles all disk I/O for Btrieve files stored on the same server.

2. It issues and releases all locks (at record, page, or file level) on the server.

3. It parses and, if necessary, repackages all processed Btrieve requests for transmittal either to the Btrieve requester at a workstation, or to BROUTER at another server.

4. Finally, if logging is required for any file, it maintains the necessary log of all Btrieve requests that change that file.

The Btrieve Requester Program   The Btrieve requester program (BREQUEST.EXE) must run at each workstation to communicate with BSERVER. The requester acts as a client engine and provides two basic actions.

1. The requester accepts operation requests from an application, using the standard Btrieve API, and relays them to BSERVER at the proper file server.

2. When BSERVER responds to the requests, the requester returns the results to the application.

When using Windows at a workstation, it's necessary to load the DOS requester before starting Windows so that its functions will be available to all instances of all applications. The Windows client engine then communicates through the requester for all actions involving network drives. If local drives also contain Btrieve files, the Windows client engine deals with them. Before version 6.0, only one of the two engines could be used in a single Windows session. Current versions allow both, and automatically route requests through the appropriate one.

The BROUTER Program   BROUTER is a server-based application that provides communication between other server-based applications and BSERVER. If a system requires none of the following four functions, BROUTER need not be loaded at the server; in most cases, however, the functions are required. BROUTER performs these four major functions.

1. handles interprocess communication between BSERVER and other server-based applications on the same file server

2. provides conventional SPX-based access to applications on other file servers in the network

3. coordinates locks, transactions, and other access control mechanisms so they work without conflict across the entire network

4. enables server-based applications to use BSERVER without conflict

Bundling With NetWare   When Novell owned Btrieve, the company bundled the package as part of the complete NetWare product since much internal NetWare processing depends upon Btrieve being present. As part of the agreement that allowed Btrieve Technologies Inc. to spin off, Novell retained a perpetual license to continue this practice.

The license, however, was for versions of Btrieve in existence at that time. It included provisions permitting, but not requiring, Novell to include future upgrades. Since that time, several products (including the NetWare server engine itself) have undergone upgrades, but at this writing Novell still distributes only the older versions that were current when the agreement was signed. The newer versions may be purchased directly from BTI but are not included with NetWare.

System administrators who upgrade their network software must thus choose between using an older version of Btrieve (6.10c as of this writing) at no extra cost, or buying the latest version (6.15.1 at this time) directly from BTI. In many cases, the differences between versions may be insignificant for a specific system, but in other cases the effects could be critical.

The need to face this choice is expected to continue into the foreseeable future. While Novell is quite likely to upgrade the version of Btrieve included with the next subsequent upgrade of NetWare itself, it's unlikely that any immediate free upgrade path will exist. Thus a window during which the bundled version is one or more revision levels behind the current version can always be expected.

Coming Platforms

At the time this book was written, a server engine for the Windows NT platform was under development and a new server engine for OS/2 was under review, as were both server and client engines for Unix, a client engine for the Macintosh, and a server engine for the PowerPC.

Since none of these has yet made it out of the labs, little detail is available. This section simply attempts to summarize what can be expected from Btrieve both in the near future and over the long haul.

The Windows NT Platform

Btrieve's client engines for DOS and for Windows are currently usable with Windows NT version 3.5, the final release of Daytona. BTI has tested Btrieve for DOS version 6.15 under a DOS box on this version of NT, and reports that it works nicely. Users also report that using the Btrieve for Windows package works well under NT, although limited to 16-bit operation. Similar success has been reported by Windows 95 Beta testers.

To use either of these as a network client, load BREQUEST.EXE from the AUTOEXEC.NT file. The normal step of loading the requester from DOS before starting Windows is impossible with NT.

On another front, the Btrieve for Windows NT server engine is scheduled to become available early in 1995. This release will feature a special bundled offer. Each Windows NT box from Microsoft is to include a coupon that enables purchase of a ten-seat Btrieve for Windows NT server engine for $99. This offer will be valid for twelve months after release of the engine.

The Btrieve for Windows NT server will support DOS, Windows, OS/2, and Windows NTAS workstations. Since NT is a multi-threading operating system, its Btrieve engines can use true multi-threading to achieve fully parallel operation, rather than emulating such action by time-slicing as is required by single-thread operating systems such as DOS or Windows.

Multithread operation is already part of the new OS/2 client engine, and the Windows NT server will evolve from that tested design. The new server, though, will be a major step forward and will earn a new revision number. Besides multithreading, it's expected to allow nested transactions, files larger than 4 GB, transparent two-phase commit capability, and significantly enhanced logging capa-bilities. It's also expected to implement requesters as DLLs to support other platforms such as the IPX protocol.

Btrieve for OS/2

The OS/2 server product is expected to be similar in many ways to the Windows NT engine. Both will be based on the existing OS/2 version 6.0 and later client engine, with significant additions. Little more can be said about features at this time.

Conclusion

In this chapter you've seen, in detail, the Btrieve application pro-gram interface. This concludes Part 1 of this book.

Next, we look at the previously undocumented file organization that Btrieve uses. Chapter 5 starts at the beginning, with the data types and internal structures; it also introduces the data definition files (DDF), which form the link between Btrieve and more familiar DBMS inter-faces. Chapter 6 then describes header pages, Chapter 7 the index page structures, and Chapter 8 the different formats for data pages.

5

The (Undocumented) File Layout

It's not absolutely necessary to know all about the internal file structures to make effective use of Btrieve, but the more knowledge you have, the better your results can be. For example, when you know how records are placed within data pages, you can avoid excessive waste space by selecting a page size best suited to your record size and the number of duplicate keys you use.

Although the Btrieve manuals provide you with the formula for calculating this optimum page size, they don't tell you why it's important and consequently many beginning developers don't bother with it. Instead, they simply allow "enough" room or, worse yet, choose a page size that's already in use for some other file. The result is that their applications may require nearly twice as much file space and take twice as long to access the data as they should have.

Before we get into any specific discussion of the various kinds of pages found in a Btrieve file, let's first examine the elements used within the system to define pages and to refer to pages and to records.

Btrieve's File Elements

This section introduces and defines concepts that are common to all parts of Btrieve files. Btrieve operates at the file level, although systems built atop the Btrieve engine can and frequently do contain many different files. Each Btrieve file normally contains both the data itself and the indexes by which the data is retrieved. This contrasts with many other systems in which data and indexes are maintained in separate files.

From the very first version of Btrieve that was distributed in 1982, through the widely-used version 5.10c, no significant change was made to the file format. This meant that files written with the original system could still be read and maintained with all newer versions. With the advent of version 6.0 in 1992, however, a complete redesign was unveiled in order to allow the microkernel architecture to be implemented. This redesign also makes it possible to grow past the traditional 4-GB file-size limit and improves the already excellent reliability of the system.

The original file format can still be read and maintained by the newer versions of the software, but to gain full advantage of the features added in versions 6.0 and 6.15, it's necessary to convert files to the new format. In this and the following chapters dealing with internal file structures, the new formats are described first, and the older ones then described in terms of their differences.

Pages in Btrieve Files

Every Btrieve file consists of a number of pages, and the entire Btrieve file structure is defined in terms of the page. A **page** is the unit of data that moves between memory and external storage during each I/O operation. For this reason, the selection of appropriate page size must be a tradeoff between operating speed and space requirements.

In the current (version 6.0 and later) structure, seven different kinds of pages (FCR, PAT, ACS, Index, Data, VarData, and Extra) are used. The older structure, prior to version 6.0, defined only three types of page: FCR, Index, and Data (see Figure 5.1). Although the size of a page can and does vary from one file to another, all pages within a single file are the same size. No file's page size can be less than 512 bytes.

Every Btrieve file begins with at least one File Control Record (FCR) page, and one of the first fields found on that page specifies the page size in bytes for the file. This permits Btrieve to read the first 512 bytes of a file without prior knowledge of its page size and to determine the size to be used for all dealings with that file. See Chapter 6 for full layout of the FCR for both current and older file formats.

Prior to version 6.0, Btrieve used only physical pages in its addressing. When a file required updating, pre-image copies were made of the page (in another file) and the changes were then written out to the file, replacing the original data. If for any reason the update could not be successfully completed, the pre-image copy of the data was written back to erase the effect of the incomplete update. The security and data integrity provided by this technique were significant factors in establishing Btrieve's reputation for reliability.

Figure 5.1   *The different kinds of pages*

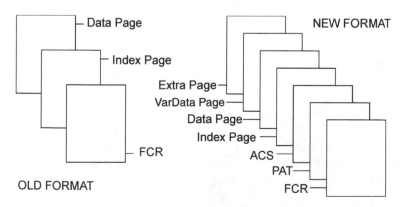

However, a tiny window remained (because of the multiple file access involved) in which data could still become corrupted. At version 6.0 when the entire Btrieve package was redesigned into its current microkernel architecture, the handling of pages was drastically modified. Instead of using separate pre-image copying, the system now works with **logical pages** rather than directly with physical pages and simply allocates a new physical page whenever an update is necessary. If the update succeeds, the logical page is remapped to the new physical address; if not, the new physical address is added to the list of Extra (available) pages.

This technique reduces to the absolute minimum the window in which error can occur; this is the time required by the data storage hardware to complete a single write operation.

The logical pages are mapped into physical pages by a pair of Page Allocation Tables (PATs), which are themselves physical pages at defined locations within each file. See "The Header Pages (FCRs, PATs, and ACSs)" section later in this chapter for a summary of PAT structures and their location in the file; see Chapter 6 for a detailed description of both.

In the new file format, each page (except for FCR and PAT pages) is identified by a page type code that forms part of its page pointer and which appears in the PAT entry for that page. This permits the Btrieve engine to access only the kinds of pages it needs at any specific instant. In the older format, only data pages are distinguished by any kind of header tag. The FCR page is identified by its position in the file, and an Alternate Collating Sequence is identified by a signature word as the first item in the data area of the page.

The minimum page size allowed by Btrieve is 512 bytes. The maximum is 4,096 bytes, which most applications find adequate. All pages must be a multiple of 512 bytes in length; best performance is usually achieved by using a power of 2 such as 512, 1024, 2048, or 4096.

Many of the other size limits applicable to a Btrieve file are determined by the size of its pages. For instance, the number of logical page pointers that can be stored in a single PAT is determined by subtracting 8 bytes from the page size (to allow for the PAT header and usage count) and dividing the remainder by the size of a page pointer (4 bytes). Thus, each PAT in a 512-byte-sized file can map 126 logical pages; a PAT in a file with 4096-byte pages can handle 1,022 mappings.

Pointers

In both the old and the new file formats, Btrieve files depend heavily on pointers to relate data records and the corresponding index key entries. In the new format, four different kinds of pointers exist: the Null pointer (indicating that no such record or page exists), the page pointer (which may point to either a physical page or a logical page, depending on the context in which it is found), the record pointer (always indicating a physical byte offset within a logical page of the file), and the Vrecord pointer (pointing to a fragment of a variable-length record).

All pointers are 32-bit quantities, stored as 4 consecutive bytes within the file, and all of them follow the same rather unusual word-swapped format. In this format, the 32-bit value consists of two 16-bit words, each arranged in standard Intel low-byte high-byte sequence, but the two words themselves are in high-word low-word sequence.

This word sequence is the exact opposite of that normally used for C-language 32-bit values and differs from the sequence used when storing 32-bit data values also. Presumably the sequence was established before any widespread standard existed for representing 32-bit numbers, and, once in use, was preserved to maintain full compatibility of new versions with existing software.

The Null pointer always consists of 32 1-bits, which is the usual representation of –1. When found in a location normally used to chain to another record, it indicates that no more records exist in the chain (see Figure 5.2).

The page pointer consists of a single-byte Page Type Code, followed by a 3-byte page number, which may refer to either a physical page or a logical page depending on the context in which the

Figure 5.2   *Null pointer format*

Byte 0	Byte 1	Byte 2	Byte 3
1 1 1 1 1 1 1 1	1 1 1 1 1 1 1 1	1 1 1 1 1 1 1 1	1 1 1 1 1 1 1 1

pointer occurs (see Figure 5.3). Within a Page Allocation Table, page pointers refer to physical pages. Everywhere else in the file, page pointers refer to logical pages and must be mapped to actual physical-page offsets by way of the corresponding PAT entry.

Figure 5.3   *New format page pointer*

Byte 0	Byte 1	Byte 2	Byte 3
Hi Byte Page	Type Code	Lo Byte Page	Mid Byte Page

Valid Page Type Codes include **A** for Alternate Collating Sequence pages, **D** for fixed-length data pages, **E** for Extra pages, and **V** for variable-length data pages. Index pages are identified by the high bit of the Page Type Code being set; the remaining bits of the code byte are set to the number of the key to which the index applies. That is, 0x80 identifies an index page for Key 0, and 0x84 means an index page for Key 4. Keys are always numbered beginning at zero, although logical page numbering begins at one.

The record pointer is a 32-bit offset into the file, in which the low-order bits represent physical offset within the page and the high-order bits indicate the physical page number (see Figure 5.4). These are the remainder and the quotient, respectively, when a record pointer is divided by the file's page size. In C, they can be calculated by these expressions:

```
Logical_Page = Record_Pointer / Page_Size;
Physical_Offset = Record_Pointer % Page_Size;
```

Figure 5.4 *New format record pointer*

Byte 0	Byte 1	Byte 2	Byte 3
High Word of Record Offset		Low Word of Record Offset	

The Vrecord pointer is similar to the record pointer, but rather than specifying a physical record offset in its low-order bits, it specifies a **fragment number** that indirectly locates the next part of a variable-length record within a V-page. Unlike the record pointer, the logical page portion of a Vrecord pointer always occupies the first 3 bytes, and the fragment number is in the final byte (see Figure 5.5).

Figure 5.5 *Vrecord pointer, both formats*

Byte 0	Byte 1	Byte 2	Byte 3
Hi Byte Pg. #	Lo Byte Pg. #	M. Byte Pg. #	Fragment #

In the old format, the same kinds of pointers are used but most are arranged rather differently. Logical pages do not exist; physical page pointers are multiplied by the page size of the file to determine the physical offset from the beginning of the file at which the page pointed to begins (see Figure 5.6).

Figure 5.6 *Old format page pointer*

Byte 0	Byte 1	Byte 2	Byte 3
High Word of Page Offset		Low Word of Page Offset	

Page pointers for the old format are simply 32-bit values, in the word-swapped Btrieve format. Record pointers, however, are absolute offsets into the file (again, in the word-swapped format) rather than containing any sort of page number as such (see Figure 5.7).

Figure 5.7   *Old format record pointer*

Byte 0	Byte 1	Byte 2	Byte 3
High Word of Record Offset		Low Word of Record Offset	

Data Types

In its earliest version, Btrieve dealt with only two types of data: string and integer. Subsequently, the list of data types has been extended frequently; as of version 6.15, the system defines seventeen different data types (see Table 5.1). In addition, files in the new format introduced at version 6.0 can deal with arbitrarily large chunk data, called binary large object (BLOB) in other systems. Such an entity can provide image storage within a database, as an example. Three of the seventeen types of data are defined only for XQL and Scalable SQL and are omitted from Btrieve manuals.

The fourteen data types defined by the Btrieve manual are used only when processing key segments. The Btrieve engine is not concerned in any way with the type of data in any record outside of the defined key segments, although the chunk operations introduced at Version 6.1 do permit partial records to be read or written.

The original type definitions included only string and integer and are indicated by the extended type flag bit (Bit 8) in the key-segment flag word being "0" and distinguished by the binary flag bit in this same word. If the binary bit (Bit 2) is 0, the data type is string; if the bit is 1, the type is binary. Any binary data is sorted as unsigned integers. String data is sorted by the ASCII sequence unless an Alternate Collating Sequence is defined for the key segment concerned.

One of the earliest enhancements of Btrieve added extended types. If the extended type flag bit is 1, then the binary flag bit is ignored

Table 5.1   *The Seventeen Data Types*
Defined by Btrieve Version 6.15[1]

Type Code	Type Name
0	String
1	Integer
2	Float
3	Date
4	Time
5	Decimal
6	Money
7	Logical
8	Numeric
9	Bfloat
10	Lstring
11	Zstring
12	Note*
13	Lvar*
14	Unsigned Binary
15	AutoIncrement
16	Bit*
17	Sign Trailing Separate

[1]The three data types (note, lvar, and bit) defined only for XQL and Scalable SQL usage are indicated by "*".

by Btrieve and instead the data type code from the segment definition is used.

In Figures 5.8–5.15, bytes are shown in the same sequence in which they appear in a file. In general, data is stored in Intel LowByte-HighByte format, and data items longer than 16 bits have the least significant 16 bits stored first and the most significant 16 bits stored last. All binary data items (as opposed to logical, numeric (BCD), or string data items) occupy an even number of bytes, except those of length 1.

AutoIncrement   The autoincrement extended data type, added to the list with version 5.0, is an unsigned binary value of either 16 or 32 bits (2 or 4 bytes). Btrieve itself assigns the value of any key segment defined as this data type when a record is added to the file. Each new record is assigned a value that is one higher than the highest value previously used in the file.

Several restrictions apply to this data type. Duplicate keys cannot be allowed, nor can an autoincrement key segment be combined with any other key segment to form a composite key. Finally, an autoincrement key cannot overlap any other key field; overlap is permitted for other data types.

You can specify a desired value for this key when a record is added; if you do, Btrieve will verify that the value does not already exist in some other record. If duplication would not result, the record is added with your specified value. If the operation would result in a duplicate value, Btrieve returns an error status and does not insert the record.

To obtain autoincrementing action, you must specify a value of 0 when the new record is inserted. The Btrieve engine will then determine the appropriate actual value and assign it. Versions prior to 6.0 had certain problems in dealing with this data type: when initially loading data the system returned a duplicates error if the input file contained more than one record with 0 in this key. To prevent this, you can omit definition of the key segment for autoincrement, then add it using CREATE INDEX after the file has been loaded.

Bit   The bit SQL data type consists of a single bit that can have either 0 or 1 value and is used in the same manner as the logical extended data type. However, the bit data type cannot be used as a key segment. The advantage of this data type over the logical type is that adjacent fields declared as type bit will be packed, right-justified, into bytes and occupy less space in the data record.

Bfloat   The bfloat extended data type is a single (32-bit) or double (64 bit) precision floating point value stored in a format compatible with that used by Microsoft's BASIC.

The single-precision format is shown in Figure 5.8.

Figure 5.8   *Single-precision format for the bfloat extended data type*

0 0 0 0 0 0 0 0 7 6 5 4 3 2 1 0	1 1 1 1 1 1 0 0 5 4 3 2 1 0 9 8	3 3 2 2 2 2 2 2 1 0 9 8 7 6 5 4	2 2 2 2 1 1 1 1 3 2 1 0 9 8 7 6
LOW WORD OF MANTISSA		EXPONENT	S HI MANT.

The double-precision format is the same except that it contains another 32 bits of lower significance. These bits precede those mapped in Figure 5.8 and are arranged in the same sequence: the first byte is lowest significance and the third byte is highest significance, as shown in Figure 5.9.

Figure 5.9   *Double-precision format for the bfloat extended data type*

0 0 0 0 0 0 0 0 7 6 5 4 3 2 1 0	1 1 1 1 1 1 0 0 5 4 3 2 1 0 9 8	3 3 2 2 2 2 2 2 1 0 9 8 7 6 5 4	2 2 2 2 1 1 1 1 3 2 1 0 9 8 7 6
LOW WORD OF MANTISSA		MIDDLE OF MANTISSA	

3 3 3 3 3 3 3 3 9 8 7 6 5 4 3 2	4 4 4 4 4 4 4 4 7 6 5 4 3 2 1 0	6 6 6 6 5 5 5 5 3 2 1 0 9 8 7 6	5 5 5 5 5 5 4 4 5 4 3 2 1 0 9 8
HI WORD OF MANTISSA		EXPONENT	S TOP MANT.

Date   The date extended data type is a 4-byte value separated into bytes for day and month and a 2-byte field for the year. All are stored in binary form, as shown in Figure 5.10.

Figure 5.10   *The date extended data type*

00000000 76543210	11111100 54321098	33222222 10987654	22221111 32109876
DAY	MONTH	\multicolumn{2}{c}{YEAR}

00000000 76543210	11111100 54321098	33222222 10987654	22221111 32109876
DAY	MONTH	YEAR	

This data type can be described in the C language by the following structure type definition.

```
typedef struct {
BYTE Day
BYTE Month;
WORD Year;
} BT_DATE;
```

The year is represented by the actual value rather than by some off-set from an arbitrary point such as those used by MS-DOS and Unix system time formats.

Decimal   The decimal extended data type is consistent with the COMP-3 type defined for ANSI-74 standard COBOL and is usually known as BCD representation. The internal storage format is packed decimal, two decimal digits to each byte. The decimal point is implied, not stored, and the high 4 bits of the final byte contain the sign, which is either 0xF or 0xC for positive numbers, or 0xD for negative numbers. Leading zeroes must be supplied to pad the field to an integral number of bytes, including the sign.

Float   The float extended data type conforms to the IEEE standard for single- and double-precision real numbers. The single precision 4-byte float has 23 bits of mantissa, an 8-bit exponent biased by 127, and a sign bit, arranged as shown in Figure 5.11.

Figure 5.11 *The single-precision 4-byte float extended data type*

00000000 76543210	11111100 54321098	33222222 10987654	22221111 32109876
LOW BYTE OF MANTISSA	S EXPONENT		HI MANT.

The double-precision 8-byte float has 52 bits of mantissa, an 11-bit exponent biased by 1023, and a single sign bit. Its layout is shown in Figure 5.12.

Figure 5.12 *The double-precision 8-byte float extended data type*

00000000 76543210	11111100 54321098	33222222 10987654	22221111 32109876
LOW WORD OF MANTISSA		MIDDLE OF MANTISSA	

33333333 98765432	44444444 76543210	66665555 32109876	55555544 54321098
HI WORD OF MANTISSA	S EXPONENT		TOP MANT.

Integer   The integer data type is a signed whole number with no fractional part and must use an even number of bytes. Each 16-bit word is stored in Intel's binary format (least significant byte first), and the words are also sequenced in order of low-to-high significance. Btrieve evaluates the key from right to left, a word at a time, when sorting or comparing values of this data type.

Internally this data type is stored in the format shown in Figure 5.13.

Figure 5.13 *The integer data type*

00000000 76543210	11111100 54321098	33222222 10987654	22221111 32109876
LOW ORDER WORD		HIGH ORDER WORD	

Logical   The logical extended data type can have a length of either 1 or 2 bytes. Logical data types are collated as if they were strings, allowing the application to determine which stored value(s) represent TRUE and which represent FALSE.

Lstring   The lstring extended data type corresponds to the Pascal string, having its length stored as the first byte, followed by ASCII characters. Since only 1 byte is available for the length value, this data type is limited to a maximum size of 256 bytes (one for length followed by 255 characters). Btrieve ignores all data in the field past the specified length. Refer also to the zstring data type for an alternate representation.

Lvar   The lvar SQL data type is a variable-length field, which uses both a 16-bit length subfield at the start and a 16-bit all-zero delimiter at the end of the field. The maximum size of a field of this data type is declared when the field is defined in the data dictionary and cannot exceed 4,092 bytes including the 2 bytes required at each end. Any length from 5 bytes up to the maximum size declared for the field may be stored in the data record. More than one lvar field may be declared within a record, but all must follow the last fixed-length field in the record. This data type cannot be used if the record also uses a field of type note.

Money   The money extended data type is simply a special case of the decimal data type, which always has two decimal places.

Note   The note SQL data type is a variable-length field, which uses a 1-byte delimiter to denote the end of both the field and the record. The delimiter, which must be specified separately, can be any value that does not appear within the field itself. Two special codes permit CR/LF or LF/CR pairs to be used as the delimiter byte: 0x8D indicates CR/LF, and 0x8A indicates LF/CR. This data type cannot be used if the record also uses a field of type lvar.

Numeric   The numeric extended data type is stored as an ASCII string of decimal digits, right-justified with leading zeros, and with the sign embedded in the rightmost digit. If the value is positive, no sign indication need be stored. If explicit indication of the positive sign is desired, 1 through 9 are represented as A through I and 0 is indicated by a {. Negative signs are indicated by J through R (for –1 through –9) and a } for zero.

Sign Trailing Separate   The sign trailing separate (sometimes referred to as numeric STS or simply STS) data type, introduced at version 6.1, is similar to the numeric data type except that the sign character, either "+" or "-", follows the least significant byte of the value as the rightmost byte of the field, rather than being encoded into the least significant byte of the value.

String   The string data type is a sequence of ASCII characters ordered from left to right. Each character occupies a single byte. All bytes within the defined field size are significant to selection and sorting. The fact that every byte within the field affects selection makes it essential that any unused space be explicitly set to a predefined value such as binary 0 or the ASCII blank (0x20) each time a record is stored or updated. Doing so eliminates any possibility that the record may subsequently be unrecoverable because of unknown random values within the field. Refer to the lstring and zstring extended data types for alternate methods of dealing with this potential problem.

Time   The time extended data type is similar to the date field, except that it contains 4 bytes that allow time to be specified to one one-hundredth of a second if desired.

The structure layout of the time extended data type is shown in Figure 5.14.

Figure 5.14   *The time-extended data type*

0 0 0 0 0 0 0 0	1 1 1 1 1 1 0 0	3 3 2 2 2 2 2 2	2 2 2 2 1 1 1 1
7 6 5 4 3 2 1 0	5 4 3 2 1 0 9 8	1 0 9 8 7 6 5 4	3 2 1 0 9 8 7 6
SEC/100	SECOND	MINUTE	HOUR

This structure can be represented in the C language by the following type definition:

```
typedef struct {
BYTE Sec100;
BYTE Second;
BYTE Minute;
BYTE Hour;
} BT_TIME;
```

Each of the 4 bytes in the \ field contains a binary value, in the range 0–99 for the Sec100 field, 0–59 for the Second and Minute fields, and 0–23 for the Hour field. The 24-hour time standard distinguishes between a.m. and p.m.; if display in a 12-hour format is desired, the application must explicitly convert the stored value.

Unsigned Binary   The unsigned binary extended data type is represented in the same manner as the integer data type and similarly must contain an even number of bytes. Btrieve compares this data type one word at a time starting with the rightmost word of the field.

Storage format for the unsigned binary data type is the same as for integers, as shown in Figure 5.15.

Figure 5.15   *The unsigned binary extended data type*

00000000	11111100	33222222	22221111
76543210	54321098	10987654	32109876
LOW ORDER WORD		HIGH ORDER WORD	

Zstring   The zstring extended data type corresponds to a standard C-language string (an array of characters terminated by an all-zero byte). This data type is treated exactly the same as the standard string type, except that comparison stops when the zero end-of-string terminator byte is encountered. Refer also to the lstring data type for an alternate representation.

The Header Pages (FCRs, PATs, and ACSs)

As mentioned earlier in this chapter, every Btrieve file begins with a page containing a File Control Record (FCR). In the new file format, two FCR pages exist, as the first two physical pages of every file. The old format has only one FCR, which is always physical page 0 located at the beginning of the file.

The PAT, introduced at version 6.0, immediately follows the two FCR pages as physical pages 2 and 3 of the file. The PAT occurs only in the new file format. Its predecessor, the pre-image file, was a totally separate file. It had the same base name as the Btrieve file to which it applied, but the extension "PRE" to identify it as a pre-image file.

Following each pair of PATs are a variable number of other types of pages and then another pair of PATs. The number of logical pages between PAT pairs is determined by the number of logical pages that can be mapped by a single PAT, although there may be no relation between any logical page and the one or two PAT pairs nearest to it. See "The Page Allocation Table (PAT) and the PRE File" section later in this chapter for more detail.

Another kind of header page is the Alternate Collating Sequence page. In the new file format, multiple ACS pages are allowed and can be added or removed after the file has been created. In the old format, only one ACS can be used for any one file; it must be specified at file creation time and cannot be removed subsequently.

The final variety of page we meet in this section is the Extra page, which is found only in the new file format. Since the old format never reused pages after they were initially allocated, this type had no purpose there.

The following four sections are intended only to introduce these four page types. See Chapter 6 for full details, including internal structures, of these four types of pages.

The File Control Record (FCR)

As its name implies, the File Control Record of a Btrieve file contains a variety of information essential to proper control of the system's actions for that file. This information includes such statistics as the number of records, the number of pages in current use, and the number of keys by which the file can be accessed. It also includes constants such as the file's page size; the length of the data portion of each record and also the total length of each record; the location, size, and type of the various key fields within each data record; and the presence or absence of variable-length records and data compression. Finally, the FCR retains variable information such as the next record available for reuse.

One of the most essential items of information provided by the FCR is the page size used by the file. This makes it possible to access the rest of the file. Another essential item, in the new file format, is a 32-bit value known as the Usage Count field. This field determines which of the two FCR pages is currently valid. Each time an operation is performed on the file, the system increments the usage count in the memory image of the FCR. When the operation completes successfully, that memory image is written back to the physical FCR page in the file that has the lowest usage count value.

Thus, the FCR page in the file that has the highest usage count is always the most recent copy; the other FCR represents the state of the file after the last previous successful operation. This history record improves system reliability and assists the implementation of concurrent operations. Version 6.0 used a 32-bit Main Bit Map field in the FCR to supplement the usage-count tests, but this was abandoned with version 6.15 when it proved to have no significant benefit to system performance.

In the older file format, the usage count field in the FCR was only 16 bits and was much less significant, although it did serve essential purposes in identifying pre-image page copies and in processing transactions.

The Page Allocation Table (PAT) and the PRE File

In the new file format only, the second FCR is followed immediately by a pair of page allocation tables, each filling one physical page. Like the FCRs, the PAT is maintained as a pair of pages with the currently valid copy being identified by its usage count.

Each PAT is filled with physical page pointers that map logical pages to physical pages and permit transactions to be hidden while in process through a technique called **shadow paging.** This technique was a major reason for the change in format, since it is far less complicated than the older transaction tracking process and consequently has less margin in which failure could occur.

When the file is initially created, the first pair of PATs at physical pages 2 and 3 are filled with page pointers to the following physical pages, even though those pages have not yet been allocated to the file. That is, the first pointer in the PAT, to logical page 1 by virtue of its position as the first pointer, contains the physical page number 4 since the next physical page in the file is page 4. The following pointers similarly point to pages 5 through n, where n is the number of pointers plus four.

In each of these page pointers, the page type code is set to zero to indicate that the corresponding physical page has not been allocated. When the page is actually allocated to the file, the code of zero is replaced by one of the other page type codes to indicate the usage of that page.

The number of pointers contained by each PAT is determined by the page size. After subtracting the page's header field size (8 bytes) from the page size, the remainder is divided by the size of a page pointer (4 bytes). The result is the number of pointers the PAT can contain.

For the minimum page size of 512 bytes each PAT can hold 126 pointers. As page size increases, so does the number of pointers per PAT page, as shown in Table 5.2.

Table 5.2 *Pointers Per Page Size*

Page Size	Pointers	Page Size	Pointers
512	126	1,024	254
1,536	382	2,048	510
2,560	638	3,072	766
3,584	894	4,096	1,022

As the file grows, eventually the last physical page mapped by the first PAT will be used, and at that time a new PAT pair is created (see Figure 5.16) to map the next n pages. Thus, in a large Btrieve file, each PAT pair is followed, physically, by n pages of other types (where n is the number of PAT entries permitted by the page size). As operations on the file cause the logical-to-physical page mappings to change, a physical page's mapping may move from one PAT pair to another. A file that has been in active use for some time may show no discernible relationship between the physical pages mapped by any PAT pair and those pages adjacent to that pair.

After the thirtieth such sequence of PAT pair followed by n logical pages (if the file grows that large), version 6.0 and later created a one-time-only 4,096-byte "extended bitmap." This block is unique and occurs only once, if at all. It is followed by more PAT-pair-plus-logical-group sequences until the file size limit is reached. See Chapter 6 for a discussion of the purpose of this extended bitmap.

Because of the shadow paging method used to hide page changes or more extensive transactions until they are complete, most files have more physical pages allocated than are in active use at any time. These pages, known as Extra pages and identified in version 6.0 by page type code E, are reused before any new space is allocated.

Prior to version 6.0 (and even with the newer versions of Btrieve, if the system is configured to create files only in the old format), shadow paging did not exist. Instead, Btrieve creates a pre-image file before making any changes, by copying the existing page from

Figure 5.16   *Interleaving of PAT pages and logical pages*

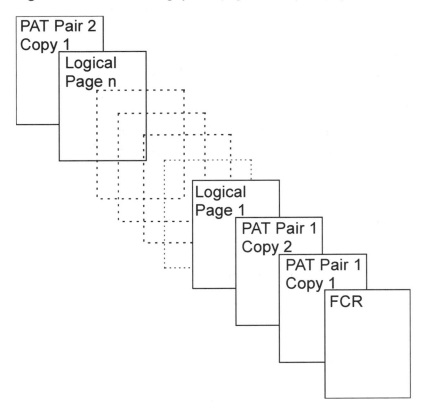

the actual file into a temporary file. The system also writes information into the FCR that permits the copy to be located if recovery becomes necessary.

With a safe copy of the original data stored in the pre-image file, the operation is performed in place on the original file. If successful, Btrieve then deletes the pre-image copy. If the operation fails for any reason, Btrieve copies the original page back from the pre-image file to the original file to remove all traces of the incomplete action, then deletes the pre-image copy. In either case, the pre-image copy vanishes; finding PRE files in the system indicates some failure to recover completely and is cause for diagnostic action to discover what may be wrong. Note that presence of PRE files upon initial restart is normal if the system failed during an operation. Their existence flags Btrieve to restore the original at the next file open action.

Alternate Collating Sequence (ACS) Pages

Alternate Collating Sequence pages are identified by the Page Type code A and are distinguished by the logical page number they occupy. The new file format allows for multiple ACS pages and for them to be attached or detached at any time; the old format permits only one ACS page that must be attached when the file is created and that cannot be changed for the life of the file.

The purpose of an ACS is to provide a sort sequence to be used for index searches and comparisons that differs from the standard ASCII character values. For instance, in many cases it's desirable that upper-case and lower-case letters sort and compare identically, although the ASCII values of "A" and "a" differ by 32. In ASCII, "a" follows "Z", rather than being treated the same as "A".

Extra (Unused) Pages

In the shadow-paging technique, a copy of the existing logical page is made before any change occurs, using another available page (either freshly allocated, or from a pool of available pages). Once the change (or in the case of a transaction, the series of changes) has been completed successfully, the mapping of the original logical page is changed from the physical page containing the original copy to the physical page containing the changed copy, retaining the logical page number unchanged. Since all references to data or other information on the page are made in terms of the logical page number rather than the physical location, they remain unaffected. The physical page containing the original copy then becomes available for reuse, and is mapped to the logical page number originally belonging to the new copy's location.

This pool of available pages carries the name Extra pages and each of them bore the Page Type code E in version 6.0. Version 6.15 zeroes the page code for Extra pages. The distinctive code makes it easy for Btrieve to locate such pages by scanning the PAT, but to make things even faster, all information past the first 10 bytes of each Extra page is zeroed out when the page becomes available. The first 4 bytes of the data area of the page then get a logical page pointer to the next Extra page, or a Null pointer if this is the last Extra page in the file, so as to form a chain of available pages. A pointer to the head of the chain is kept in the FCR and updated as necessary.

Index Pages

Although the main reason for Btrieve's superlative record of reliability and performance is undoubtedly the close attention to detail paid by its creators, a significant supporting factor is its B-tree index structure. As described in Chapter 3, the B-tree provides rapid initial access to a desired record and also allows quick movement to adjacent records, in either direction. Here we present only an overview of the index page structures. See Chapter 7 for more detail.

Tree Organization

The B-tree arrangement used by Btrieve builds a separate tree (see Figure 5.17) for each index and places each level of each tree on its own index page or pages. The root page for each tree is specified in the FCR's index-spec area.

Until data is actually placed in the file, no index pages exist in the tree (except for an empty root page for each key). The pages are allocated as the need arises, which means that a key with relatively short data length may use far fewer pages than would a key based on a long field or on a number of moderate-length segments. Because of this, index and data pages are intermixed in the file in an unpredictable manner.

In the new file format, an index can be defined at the time a file is created or can be added subsequently, so long as adequate space remains in the FCR to accept the necessary segment specification. Existing indexes can also be removed from the file. In the old format, modification of any embedded segment specification is not allowed after a file has been created. However, supplemental indexes can be created and dropped at will.

Figure 5.17   *Btrieve's B-tree arrangement*

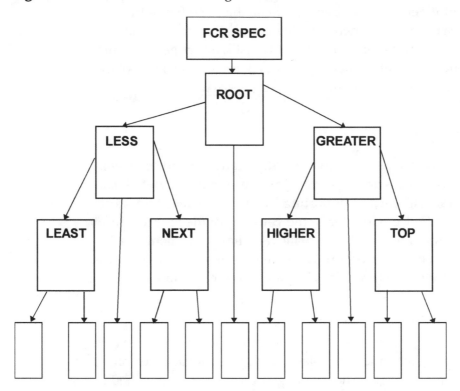

The number of possible key segments, like the number of logical pages mapped by a single PAT page, depends upon the page size of the file, but the relationship is not at all linear. The limits for the new format are shown in Table 5.3.

Table 5.3   *Segment Limits in the New File Format*

Page Size	Max. Segments
512	8
1,024	23
1,536	24
2,048 through 3,584	54
4,096	119

For the old format the limits are simpler: 8 segments are the limit when page size is 512 bytes; all other page sizes are limited to 24 segments.

In both formats, the limit applies to segments rather than to keys. One key composed of 8 segments uses the same space in the FCR as 8 different single-segment keys, although its index page requirements might be much smaller.

Index Pages

Each index page is identified by a Page Type code in the range 0x80 through 0xF6. The high bit of the code being set identifies the page as an index page, and the remaining 7 bits are interpreted as a binary number specify to which key this page applies.

In the simplest situation, that of a key having a single segment and no duplication of its values allowed, each entry on an index page will be just 8 bytes longer than the length of the key itself. Four of these bytes are for the lesser-node page pointer that precedes the actual key data, and the other 4 bytes contain a record pointer to the referenced data record. In addition, each index page contains a greater-node page pointer to an adjacent index page at the same level of the tree, which is used when the key value being sought is greater than any key data on the current page.

The header of each index page contains, following the 16-bit usage count, a 16-bit field that specifies the number of valid items on the page. Thus, the maximum space available for entries on any index page is equal to the page size, minus 8 bytes for the header and an additional 4 bytes for the greater-node page pointer.

When the file is created, Btrieve calculates the maximum number of entries that an index page can contain and stores that value in one field of the index-spec area of the file's FCR. Note that this value may vary from one key to another within the same file because of differences in the length of the key data involved.

Btrieve also calculates a minimum number of entries, which is simply the maximum number shifted to the right by one place (that is, halved and rounded down). As entries are made in the index trees, the system continually compares the number of entries on each page with these minimum and maximum values.

When addition of a key would cause the maximum number to be exceeded, another index page is added and the minimum number of entries is copied from the latter half of the old page into the new one. This always leaves at least the minimum number on the old page also. Then the new key is added to the appropriate one of the two pages resulting from the split.

When a record is deleted, resulting in removal of its associated key data from the indexes, the number of entries on an index page may fall below the minimum. When this occurs, that page is merged with an adjacent page in such a way as to either bring both to counts between the minimum and maximum values or to combine all entries from both into a single page and release the other for reuse. This action, and the splitting described previously, act to maintain the indexes in proper balance.

The minimum count does not apply to the root page of any tree; in fact, root pages quite often contain only a single entry to balance the remainder of the tree as closely as possible.

Duplicate-Key Handling

When a key's definition permits duplicate values, both the index pages for that key and the data pages for all records become much more complicated. In the new format, two different ways of dealing with duplicate key values are available. In the old format, duplicates are treated differently for supplemental indexes than they are for original indexes defined at file creation time.

The different techniques for dealing with duplicates are known as **linked duplicates** and **repeating duplicates.** Although these names were not established until the new file format came into use at version 6.0, the techniques themselves were already in use. The linked technique is that used for original indexes in the old format, and the repeating method is that used for supplemental indexes.

In the linked technique, the record pointers on each index page are replaced by a pair of record pointers that indicate the first and last links in the chain of records that duplicate that key's value. Intermediate links in this chain are dealt with on the data pages. The record pointer immediately following the key data indicates the first record for that key value that was added to the file, and the second record pointer immediately after the first indicates the last duplicate record added (see Figure 5.18).

After the first record is written but before any additional ones have been added, both pointers have the same value: the address of that first record. Subsequent records cause the second pointer to be changed to point to each record as it is added. This permits the record pointer for the last record to be used as the previous-record link of the chain built in the data page when the record is added and also to be used to locate that previous record and modify its next-record pointer.

Figure 5.18   *Linked duplicate key chains*

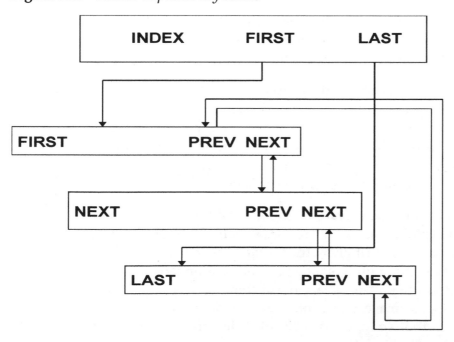

In the repeating duplicates method, each duplicate record gets its own index page entry, and the key value is made unique by adding the record's own record pointer to the true key as an additional 4 bytes. This method requires no chaining within the data records, but causes significant increase in the size of the indexes affected.

The differences have practical implications: a linked-duplicate index retrieves duplicates in the order in which they were inserted, and a repeating-duplicate index retrieves them in order of location.

Data Pages

The primary purpose of a Btrieve file is storing data, and that's done by its data pages. The other page types we've met serve no purpose other than supporting the data pages themselves. Here, we take a first look at the various kinds of data pages that Btrieve can use. See Chapter 8 for more detail and examples of how these different types relate to each other.

Simple Data Pages

Page type D (for data) stores the fixed-length portions of the file's records. If no compressed or variable-length records exist in the file, this is the only type of data page the file contains.

Following its 6-byte header and usage count, this type of page contains a sequence of records. In the new file format, each record includes several subfields; the simplest record has just two of them. The first is a record usage count, which may range from 1–32,767 and is 0 if the record has been deleted or has not yet been used. The data image itself forms the remaining subfield.

Other subfields include **private data** (specified but not yet implemented), a Vrecord pointer (if the file has variable length records), a blank-truncation count (if blank truncation is active), and pairs of duplicate-key record pointers (one pair for each linked-duplicate key in the file). The Private Data subfield comes between the usage count and the data image, if present. The remaining fields follow the data image in the sequence listed. In the old format, the record usage count and Private Data subfields are absent. The remaining subfields are present if applicable.

When duplicate-key record pointers are present in the record, they always occur in pairs and form a linked list of all records that share the duplicated key. The pointer nearest the data image points to the previous duplicate, and the other points to the next. Each key that allows linked duplicates has its own pair of pointers. The pointer sets occur in the same sequence that the keys appear in the FCR.

In the new format, sets of duplicate-key pointers may be reserved without using them; such pointer pairs follow those defined by index segment specifications. Also in the new format, keys may be deleted. If this happens, the pointers to which they apply become invalid. Neither of these situations can occur in a file using the old format.

Each deleted record contains as its first 4 bytes (following the usage count if using new format) a record pointer to the next deleted record. This forms a singly-linked list of all deleted records in the file. A null pointer appears in the first 4 bytes of the last record in the list. A record pointer in the FCR indicates the first record in the list, when any records are available for reuse. If none exist, the FCR field contains a null pointer.

Two other fields within the FCR hold the data record size. One indicates the size of the data image itself, and the other holds the total record length including all record pointers. For compatibility with the old file format, the data image count includes the 2-byte usage count subfield and the (currently 0-byte) private data area as part of the data image. The physical length count includes all subfields that are present for each record. This count serves as the increment for stepping from one record to the next while traversing data pages by the direct operations.

Variable-Length Pages

The presence of variable-length records significantly increases the complexity of a Btrieve file's structure. The system splits each record across at least two pages, placing its fixed-length portion on a Page Type D page and the variable-length portion on one or more type V (variable) pages. This provides the only exception to the rule that a record cannot span a page boundary.

Each type V page can contain multiple variable-length portions called **fragments.** Each fragment contains either all or part of a variable-length record. No more than one fragment of any specific record appears on a single V-page; other fragments of the record reside on different pages. The total number of fragments on a page depends on the data itself, but cannot exceed 256 because the fragment is identified by an 8-bit value.

Structure for the V-page includes several elements not found on other page types. The first item following the usage count is a Vrecord pointer to the next V page having free space. A 16-bit field follows, containing the count of fragments the page contains. This is followed, starting at the 12th byte of the page, with the first byte of the first fragment.

A table of 16-bit offsets appears at the end of the page, allowing access to each fragment and to any available unused space. At the final 16-bit location on the page is the offset of fragment 0, normally 0x0C. The immediately preceding 16 bits hold the offset of fragment 1, and this pattern is repeated for all the fragments included in the count at the top of the page.

The first offset after that pointing to the last fragment is the available space pointer (ASP) and indicates the first usable space within the record. When adding a fragment to a new-format page, a pointer to the next fragment (initially set as a NULL pointer) is written at this offset, followed by the first byte of data. If using original format, no pointer appears. The fragment count at the top of the page then increases by one, and an internal pointer to the ASP is backed up by two to indicate the new ASP location. The offset to the first unused byte then goes into the new ASP.

The remaining bytes of the fragment are written in sequence, incrementing the ASP value by one each time. When the ASP holds its own address, the page is full. If more bytes remain in the fragment, they must go on another V-page. If the final byte is written before the page fills, the ASP automatically has the correct address.

When a fragment continues to another V-page, a pointer to the new record replaces the NULL pointer at the start of this fragment. In the original file format, a pointer is added and all data moves down by 4 bytes. Then the high bit of the offset pointer is set to indicate that more bytes exist in the record. The next-record pointer at the start of the fragment exists only if this bit is set. The length of any fragment is determined by subtracting its offset from the offset immediately ahead of it in the offset table, ignoring Bit 15 in this action. Deleting a fragment from a V-page causes all following fragments to move up and close the gap. Their offsets are adjusted automatically when this occurs. See Chapter 8 for additional description of these actions and examples to illustrate each variation.

Compressed Data Pages

When a Btrieve file uses compressed data, its data pages consist of both fixed-length records and variable-length records. Only the variable-length pages hold actual record image data. The fixed-length portions of each record provide housekeeping information required by the system.

In the new format, the fixed-length records are 7 bytes long (plus any duplicate-key record pointers that may be required). Old-format records are 5 bytes in length.

In both formats, the first 4 bytes hold a Vrecord pointer to the actual compressed data image. The following byte indicates both the active/deleted state of the record and the compression algorithm used. For new-format files, the remaining 2 bytes hold the usage count for the record, but this field has little significance at present. Future developments are expected to provide improved concurrency by taking advantage of record usage counts.

If byte 5 of a record is zero, the record has been deleted and the Vrecord pointer indicates the next deleted record in a single-linked chain of variable-length records. If the value of byte 5 is 1, the record was compressed using the current run-length algorithm (see

Chapter 8). Btrieve reserves all other values for this byte to use with any possible future algorithms.

The Data Dictionary Files

Although the Btrieve engine itself is completely unconcerned with the content of the data records apart from the key fields, it's often necessary to have complete information about the schema of any database. For instance, provision of referential integrity or access via SQL requires knowledge of the schema. Having such data available usually makes it much simpler to apply such utilities as report generators or ad-hoc query programs to the files.

The standard method for defining the schema of most relational database systems uses a file or set of files called a **data dictionary,** which contains all the particulars. Btrieve files use a series of data dictionary files (DDF), named for the extension assigned to them.

DDF files came into existence when Xtrieve was introduced and have since become a key part of the XQL and Scalable SQL products. They are also essential when interfacing Btrieve files to Microsoft's open database connectivity (ODBC) specification since all ODBC drivers use them to obtain required field information. This chapter introduces DDF files and their usage. See Chapters 6, 7, and 8 for further details.

Btrieve deals with files, pages, records, and fields; the relational database model upon which SQL is built deals with tables containing columns of rows. To use Btrieve as a foundation for a relational interface, a separate file is created for each table. Within that file, each record becomes a row and each field becomes a column.

Although at least seven different DDF files have been officially specified and documented by the developers of Btrieve and Scalable SQL, only three are necessary in virtually every situation. These are FILE.DDF, defining the files that comprise the database; FIELD.DDF, defining the fields used within each file; and INDEX.DDF, defining the indexes associated with the various files and fields. Even INDEX.DDF is ignored by Visual Basic's Btrieve support.

The DDF files themselves are organized along the relational model, the relations being specified by means of primary and foreign keys. Each data dictionary created begins by defining its own files, fields, and indexes, but these definitions are flagged to make them invisible to normal DDF editing tools. In addition, all true DDF files have an owner name to prevent unauthorized changes, and Btrieve Technologies Inc. keeps that owner name proprietary. Third-party DDF editors (which we meet in Chapter 9) bypass this problem by licensing the critical part of the DDF-maintenance facility and using it to make their changes to the files. (A pair of Data Description Language, DDL, interfaces were released after this book was written.)

The DDF approach permits multiple data dictionaries so long as each set of DDF files resides in a separate subdirectory. Distributing dictionaries in this manner increases flexibility and security at the cost of a slight increase in original effort. Any single table file can appear in multiple dictionaries, but all field and index definitions for that file must be compatible between one dictionary and all others.

The FILE.DDF File

Fields within FILE.DDF identify the name used within the data dictionary for each different table and associate this table name with a path specification and filename used by the operating system to open, read, write, and close that file. See Chapter 6 for more detail.

The FIELD.DDF File

Fields within FIELD.DDF identify the names, data types, and sizes of each column within each table to which the data dictionary applies and also specify any supplementary index names associated with the database. Each row of this table is related to FILE.DDF by means of foreign keys. See Chapter 8 for more detail.

The INDEX.DDF File

Fields within INDEX.DDF identify all attributes of each index used with the database and associate each with a file and one or more fields by means of foreign keys into the other two DDF files. See Chapter 7 for more detail.

Other DDF Files

In addition to the FILE, FIELD, and INDEX dictionary files, Btrieve Technologies Inc. has specified four more DDF files: ATTRIB.DDF, VIEW.DDF, USER.DDF, and RIGHTS.DDF. All of these files are optional and none of them are generally found in ordinary Btrieve applications; the first two listed deal with functions of Xtrieve, and the last two apply only when security features are invoked.

The ATTRIB.DDF file contains field attributes and masks that can be used by Xtrieve and Xtrieve Plus for validating input data and editing output data into a desired display format.

VIEW.DDF defines SQL views that may collect information from a number of different tables, allowing permanent storage of often-used views and subsequent use of them with no need to define them afresh each time. USER.DDF identifies specific users and their passwords to the system, and RIGHTS.DDF defines the access rights assigned to each user.

Since these files are not normally used with non-Xtrieve installations, they are not discussed at greater length in this book. Layouts and file structures for them are published in the Xtrieve, Xtrieve Plus, and Scalable SQL manuals.

Conclusion

In this chapter you've encountered all the internal data types defined for both Btrieve and SSQL, and have met the DDF organization. Chapter 6 describes the header pages that Btrieve uses to keep track of each file.

6

Header Page Content

In Chapter 5, we met the internals of Btrieve files, but didn't go into great detail about any of them. This chapter explores the header pages in much greater detail. Much, if not most, of the material presented here has in the past been impossible for Btrieve developers to locate.

Page types discussed in this chapter include the FCR, the PAT, and the ACS. The discussion covers in detail layouts both of the current version and of versions prior to 6.0. Following the header-page material, we detail the FILES.DDF file's layout and usage.

The FCR contains such information as the file's page size, the size of each data record, the number of index keys, and specifications for each index key segment. The PAT, introduced at version 6.0, replaces the older pre-imaging technique with a new approach known as shadow imaging. Shadow imaging improves system reliability but introduces an additional layer of complication involving logical pages and physical pages. The PAT description brings out the differences between logical pages and physical pages, and examples illustrate how the new technique operates. The final header-page descriptions cover the Alternate Collating Sequence pages for both versions.

In this and subsequent chapters, C-language data declarations provide specific format and file layout information. A complete header file (BTRIEVE.H) incorporating these declarations appears at the end of this chapter and on the accompanying companion diskette.

The BTRIEVE.H header file uses three variable aliases extensively to cut down excessive verbiage. These aliases are BYTE for unsigned char, WORD for unsigned short (16-bit), and DWORD for unsigned long (32-bit). All declarations appearing in this and subsequent chapters employ these aliases without additional explanation.

In addition, a number of pointers that we met in Chapter 5 are defined through typedef statements. These include:

```
typedef struct {
  union {
    struct {
     WORD hi;       // ( u1.v5.hi << 16 ) + lo = page number
    } v5;
    struct {
      BYTE hi;     // ( u1.v6.hi << 16 ) + lo = page number
      BYTE code;
    } v6;
  } u1;
  WORD lo;
} PGPTR;
```

This PGPTR definition permits compiler type-checking in our file layout declarations. The necessary byte or word swapping to arrange the bits properly can be done using the appropriate one of these macro operations:

```
#define PageNo5( x )(long)(((long)(x).u1.v5.hi << 16)+(x).lo)
#define PageNo6( x )(long)(((long)(x).u1.v6.hi << 16)+(x).lo)
#define PageID( x )    (BYTE)((x).v6.code)
```

The RECPTR definition merely identifies a record pointer, since this pointer requires no swapping of bytes or words:

```
typedef struct {
  long wl;
} RECPTR;
```

The VRECPTR variable-length record pointer is a bit more complicated than the simple RECPTR, although it's the same size:

```
typedef struct {
BYTE hi;
  BYTE lo;
  BYTE mid;
  BYTE frag;
} VRECPTR;
```

The following two macros help extract the appropriate sections of a VRECPTR from the variable:

```
#define VRFrag(x) (BYTE)((x).frag)
#define VRPage(x) (long)(((long)(x).hi<<16)| ((x).mid<<8)|(x).lo)
```

The final typedef creates a set of pointers that tracks free space in a new-format file. Each FSPSET is 12 bytes long, consisting of a PGPTR, a RECPTR, and a VRECPTR:

```
typedef struct {
  PGPTR   nxpg;       // next free page
  RECPTR nxrec;       // next free record
  VRECPTR nxvrec;     // next free vrecord
} FSPSET;             // v 6+ only
```

All of these data types appear in subsequent discussions, without additional definition.

In nine specific areas of the FCR, meanings of individual variables differ widely from one format to the other. These areas appear in BTRIEVE.H as C-language unions, named with the symbols r1 through r9. Within each union, the different formats appear as structs named v5 and v6. In some cases, one version or the other may have only one variable and in such cases the struct is omitted. Instead the variable name begins with v5 or v6.

File Attributes

The FCR page supplies several groups of information. Possibly the most important of these is the group listing file attributes. This provides full information about the format in use, the Btrieve version necessary to support the file, the page size, the record size, and security considerations (who can read the file and who can edit it). Other groups include statistical data such as the number of records the file contains and the number of times it has been modified, specifications that define all key fields of the file, and a collection of free-space pointers that permit reuse of space within the file.

The first thing we must determine about any Btrieve file (before we can read it) is which file format it uses, since all other information depends on the format. The second thing we must know is the file's page size, since all Btrieve files are organized in terms of their pages. Fortunately, both questions can be answered just by reading the first 10 bytes of the file. In all Btrieve files, the very first page is a File Control Record, and this is what those first 10 bytes contain (as declared in BTRIEVE.H):

```
typedef struct {
  union {
    struct {
      PGPTR  PgSeq;      // 00 - page number, always 0x0L
      int    Usage;      // 04 - match with usage count
      int    Version;    // 06 - version code, <0 if owned
```

```
  } v5;
  struct {
    int    RecSig;      // 00 - 'FC'
    int    SeqNbr;      // 02 - always binary zeroes
    long   Usage;       // 04 - usage count
  } v6;
} r1;
int    PagSize;         // 08 - in bytes
```

If the first 2 bytes of the 10-byte sample are both zero, the file uses a version prior to 6.0 (old) format, and the v5 struct defines the applicable portion of the format-dependent union r1. If these bytes are 0x4346 (ASCII "FC" in Intel sequence), the file uses the new format and the v6 struct applies. If the two bytes have any other value, the file is either not a valid Btrieve file or has been corrupted.

Regardless of the format in use, the 16-bit value at offset 0x08 (the last two bytes of the 10-byte sample) specifies the page size in bytes. Minimum page size is 512 and maximum is 4,096 bytes. Although any multiple of 512 within that range can be used, best performance occurs when the page size is a power of 2 such as 1,024 or 2,048 bytes.

For new-format files, once the page size has been determined, the program should save the usage count read from r1.v6.Usage. It should then seek to the second page of the file and again read the first 10 bytes of that page. If the current value of r1.v6.Usage is greater than the saved value, the second page is the valid copy of the FCR and should be used. If less, the first page contains the valid FCR. Maintaining dual copies, with the valid one selected on the basis of having the higher usage count, allows program modification of one copy while other applications work with the other unmodified one; this is the basis of the new and faster shadow imaging technology.

The Version item located at offset 0x06 in the old format and at 0x4A in the new format contains a code that indicates version compatibility. This isn't necessarily the same as the version of Btrieve that wrote the file. Instead, this code indicates the oldest version that can read the file successfully. The codes and their meanings are listed in Table 6.1.

Table 6.1   *Codes for Version Compatibility*

Code	Meaning
3	Uses only features of 4.0 and before.
4	Requires at least version 4.1.
5	Requires at least version 5.0.
6	Requires at least version 6.0

If the `Version` code is negative, that indicates the file has an Owner and is subject to security restrictions. In such a case, subtract the code from 0 (that is, reverse its sign) to recover the version information itself.

If an Owner Name exists for the file, then an encrypted version of that name occupies the 9-byte buffer starting at offset 0x2E in the FCR (although the owner name is only 8 bytes), and a single byte at offset 0x37 contains flags that determine who can read the file, who can edit the file, and whether the data is encrypted (Table 6.2).

Table 6.2   *Codes for File Ownership*

Code	Encrypted?	Who Can Read	Who Can Edit
0	No	Owner only	Owner only
1	No	Anyone	Owner only
2	Yes	Owner only	Owner only
3	Yes	Anyone	Owner only

The declaration of `Owner` name and `OwnerFlags` appears in BTRIEVE.H as follows:

```
BYTE  Owner[9];     // 2E - encoded owner name
char  OwnerFlags;   // 37 - flags byte
```

Note that these lines do not immediately follow the `PagSize` variable. The two or three characters immediately to the right of the `//` comment delimiters indicate the byte offset at which each variable of the FCR begins.

Other file-attribute variables located between `PagSize` and `Owner` include the following:

```
int AccelFlags; // 0A open, firstupdate, cleared on close
int Nkeys;      // 14 - number of keys defined
int RecLen;     // 16 - data rec length excl pointers
int PhyLen;     // 18 - physical rec length incl ptrs
```

The `AccelFlags` variable has no meaning for Btrieve files in the new file format, since the accelerated mode Open option vanished at version 6.0 at the same time the new format came into being. In older versions, applications could use accelerated mode to bypass the normal safety features achieved by pre-image files, at the risk of possible data corruption. This variable contains bitflags used while the file is open in accelerated mode to help control actions of the Btrieve engine. When the file is not actually open in accelerated mode, the value should always be zero.

The `Nkeys` variable tells the total number of distinct keys (not segments) defined for the file.

The two record-length variables (`RecLen` and `PhyLen`) tell the Btrieve engine how to find any duplicate-key pointers associated with a specific record. The `RecLen` variable contains the byte count of the data record itself, exclusive of any pointers. The `PhyLen` variable's value is equal to `RecLen` plus the number of bytes of pointer data associated with each record (and, in new version files, two more bytes for the record usage count). If no duplicate-key pointers exist (or, in versions 6.0 and later, have been reserved) for the file, the values of these two variables are identical in the original format, or differ by two in the new.

A 16-bit variable at offset 0x24 of the FCB, ExtFile, identifies extended files, possible only for the old format. ExtFile has a value of 1 for normal files and 2 if the file has been extended to a second drive. In new-format files, this variable is always zero. Since it's closely associated with other variables that hold statistical and free-space information, the declaration appears in a subsequent section of this chapter.

Extfile isn't the only variable involved with extended files. Another variable, r6.v5.Extended, at offset 0x44, is set to 0xFFFF when a file is extended, or to 0 otherwise. In the new format files, this variable is always set to 0.

```
union {
  struct {
    int    Extended;    // 44 - 0xFFFF if extended, else 0
    int    v5vac2;      // 46 - unused
  } v5;
  struct {
    int    v6vac5;      // 44 - always 0 for v6.0+
    int    v6vac6;      // 46 - unused
  } v6;
} r6;
```

The EXTEND command no longer exists as of Btrieve version 6.0; its original purpose was to double the storage capacity of floppy-disk-only systems by allowing a single logical file to span two drives. It worked by creating a new file on the second drive, then setting the FCR variables to indicate extension and copying the full pathname for the new file into the FCR at offset 0x98 (within union r9's v5 struct):

```
BYTE  Path[64];     // 98 - EXTEND filepath,
                    //      also holds PRE path
```

Btrieve copies the data from `r9.v5.Path` to an internal buffer when opening the file the first time and is then free to reuse the FCR space to record the path for any pre-imaging files that are needed. For this reason, it's not safe to assume that any pathname found at this location is actually that of an extend file.

Additional variables associated with the extended files include `r8.v5.ResFCB` and `r8.v5.ExtFirst`:

```
int    ResFCB[3];  // 66 - used with extended FCB
PGPTR ExtFirst;    // 6C - first page number of
                   //  extended file
```

The `r8.v5.ResFCB` array provides a 6-byte area used with the extended FCB for the extension file; `r8.v5.ExtFirst` records the first page number in the extension file and thus defines the point at which data is divided.

The next file-attribute item (after the `Owner` and `OwnerFlags` variables) is a single byte that specifies presence or absence of variable-length data:

```
char   VRecsOkay;  // 38 FF = ok, FD = trunc blanks
```

VRecsOkay, at offset 0x38, is zero if the file's records are fixed length, 0xFF if records contain a variable-length field, and 0xFD if truncation of trailing blanks was specified at file creation time. If variable-length records exist in a file, the variation must all occur at the end of each record so that each record contains a fixed-length front part and a variable-length trailing portion.

Btrieve permits preallocation of pages when creating a file. If this option applied when a file was created, the following variable (present in both the old and the new formats) contains the number of pages that were preallocated:

```
int PreAlloc; // 48 - number of pages preallocated
              //       at create time
```

Immediately following `PreAlloc` is an 8-byte area that is unused in the older format; in the newer format it contains the `version` code followed by four values used in the Page Allocation techniques:

```
union {
 int  v5vac3[4];    // 4A - unused
 struct {
  int Version;      // 4A - version number,
                    //      3 for 4.0 and before
  int PaPage;       // 4C - PAT pair number for
                    //      first unalloc phys page
  int PaOffset;     // 4E - offset in PaPage for
                    //      first unalloc phys page
    int PaLast;     // 50 - last PAT page in page array
 } v6;
} r7;               // end of version-specific union
```

The next file-attribute variables in the FCR deal with duplicate-key pointers. These variables, present in both file formats, are zeroed if no duplicate keys exist for the file:

```
int  DupOffset; // 72 - offset of first dup-key
                //      ptr from rec start
char NumDupes;  // 74 - Number of dupe ptrs on record
char NumUnused; // 75 - Number of unused dupe ptrs
```

`DupOffset` specifies the offset, in bytes from the start of the record, of the first duplicate key pointer associated with the record. `NumDupes` tells how many such keys exist for each record (each pointer is four bytes long). `NumUnused` has no meaning for the older file formats since unused duplicate-key pointers could not be reserved in anticipation of future needs.

In union `r9`'s `v6` struct appear several file-attribute variables:

```
VRECPTR Ridata;      // 94 - special RI definition pointer
char    DupeRes;     // D8 - number of dupe-key ptrs
                     //      reserved at create time
```

```
char      PrivDataSz;  // D9 - size of private data field
                       //          in data records
```

The `r9.v6.Ridata` pointer, never modified by Btrieve itself, is created by SSQL when full enforcement of relational integrity is specified at file create time. This pointer directs the Btrieve engine to a special data record within the file that specifies all restrictions that the engine should enforce to assure integrity of relations when processing the file.

Variable `r9.v6.DupeRes` specifies the number of duplicate-key pointers that were reserved when the file was created; `r9.v6.PrivDataSz` specifies the size in bytes of the Private Data field within each data record. Since this field is an enhancement planned for future implementation and does not yet exist within a Btrieve file at version 6.15, `r9.v6.PrivDataSz` always contains zero.

The final group of file-attribute variables appears (for both formats) just before the Key Segment Specification area begins:

```
int     UsrFlgs;     //106 - user-specified flags
                     //          (CREATE bitmap)
int     VarThresh;   //108 - variable space threshold
PGPTR   ACSpage;     //10A - allows ACS to be added
                     //          after creation of file
int     ComprLen;    //10E - record length if file
                     //          is compressed
```

Variable `UsrFlgs` contains bitmapped flags that specify various attributes of the file, as listed in Table 6.3.

The `VarThresh` value indicates the threshold to be maintained when working with variable-length records. When the amount of free space within a page falls below this value, a new page is allocated for the next record.

Table 6.3 *Flags for File Attributes*

Flag Bits(s)	Meaning
0x0001	File contains variable-length records.
0x0002	Trailing blanks are truncated from file.
0x0004	Pages were preallocated.
0x0008	Data in file is compressed.
0x0010	File contains keys only, no data.
0x0020	Index balancing is in effect.
0x0040	Free space threshold is 10 percent.
0x0080	Free space threshold is 20 percent.
0x00C0	Free space threshold is 30 percent.
0x0100	File has reserved space for duplicate pointers.
0x0200	Reserved for future use.
0x0400	Specific key number was assigned.
0x0800	File contains VATs (version 6.1+ only).

Normally, an ACS page specified when a file is created appears immediately following the FCR (or, in the new format, after the first PAT pair). If an ACS is added later it might appear at any page of the file, so the `ACSpage` page pointer records the actual location of the ACS. In the new format, Page Type Code data stored in the PAT serves this purpose.

Finally, `ComprLen` specifies the record length, when compression reduces the actual record size below the original physical character count.

Using only the information contained in this part of the FCR, it's possible to create a program that duplicates the action of the STAT command within Btrieve or the BUTIL -STAT utility, yet does not require Btrieve's presence to run. Such a program can be quite useful as part of a database diagnostic toolkit. In Chapter 10, we present just such a package.

Statistical Data

Along with the essential data concerning attributes of the file, the FCR contains a number of important statistical items. One that directly impacts every action of the Btrieve engine is the usage count, kept in the first 10 bytes of the FCR record as part of union r1. In the v5 struct, this count is an integer (16 bits), but in the v6 struct, it's a long (32-bit) value. In either case, the value is initialized to zero when a file is created; after that, every Btrieve operation that makes any change to the file causes the count to increase.

Besides the "official" value kept in the FCR, the usage count also appears as part of the header on each and every page of the file. It's written there when the page is modified, which means that almost every page's usage-count value will be different. The exception is that we may find the same usage value on the FCR, one of the PATs, one index page, and one data page. This will happen if an operation modifies all three pages; each modified page gets the current usage value.

In the new file format, the usage count automatically indicates which of the two copies of the FCR and which of the two PAT pages in each pair are the valid ones. In every case, the valid copy's usage count will be a higher number than the invalid one. We've already discussed the use of this capability to determine from which of the two FCR copies to retrieve information.

The record count, Nrecs, is a 32-bit variable defined as a long in BTRIEVE.H but actually consisting of word-swapped values exactly like the original-version PGPTR. When used in a program, the high and low words must be swapped to create the proper values. In the declaration the word-swapped comment identifies this requirement:

```
Long   Nrecs;   // 1A - number of records in file
                //      (word-swapped)
```

For versions prior to 6.1, the possibility existed that some kinds of internal inconsistency might result should the system crash during small but critical timing windows. To guard against this possibility, the consistency flag Consistent is set to 0xFFFF at the start of such a window and cleared back to zero when the danger is past. Should the system crash during that window, the flag indicates this fact the next time Btrieve attempts to open the file:

```
int   Consistent;   // 22 - 0xFFFF = need recovery
```

Any time that Btrieve versions earlier than 6.1 find Consistent set at open time, they attempt to restore consistency automatically. For version 6.0, this involves verifying all logical page mappings and rebuilding the MainBitMap variable we'll be meeting in a later section of this chapter. For older versions, the actions may include restoring entire pages from existing pre-imaging (PRE) files.

Btrieve maintains a second word-swapped variable, the page count of the file, as Npages:

```
long   Npages;    // 26 number of pages in file
                  //          (word-swapped)
```

In the original file format, Npages increments the count of pages each time Btrieve physically allocates a new page to the file. In the newer file format, this count contains only active pages. Pages physically allocated but not in current use are omitted.

Besides these statistical counts applicable to the entire file, Btrieve maintains counts of the total number of unique index values, for each index, in the Segment Specification tables we'll examine in a later section. Like Nrecs and Npages, these are 32-bit counts kept in word-swapped format. A simple C routine to convert the word-swapped values to "normal" long integers is:

```
long swap( long n )     // undoes word swapping
{ return ((n >> 16) & 0xFFFFL) | (n << 16);
}
```

We use this routine quite often in the sample programs that appear later in the book. Forgetting it leads to quite unbelievable figures for the counts!

Other Content

Btrieve, in all versions, uses a number of variables in the FCR to track its space allocation activities. Although some of these remain in the same locations for both file formats, most of them differ. The introduction of shadow imaging and the Page Allocation Table significantly changed the way in which Btrieve manages its internal resources.

With both the old format and the new, Btrieve maintains chains of freespace pointers to keep track of deleted records and pages. New data goes into these records and pages so long as reusable space remains available; Btrieve does not allocate new pages while old space remains for reuse.

In the new format, struct **v6** in union **r9** provides an array of 12-byte pointer sets that support concurrent operations by various clients in the same file at the same time:

```
FSPSET Free[5];  // 98 - allows concurrent operations
```

Each of the five FSPSET structures in this array deals only with a single one of the five possible concurrent operations, tracking the next free page, the next free record, and the next free variable-length record available for each of the operations. Since any operation on a page locks the entire page for the duration of the operation, Btrieve can maintain these values consistently even though the operations remain asynchronous to each other. When only a single user is active, the set at **Free[0]** tracks reusable space.

Freespace pointers maintained by the original file formats include:

```
PGPTR  NxtReusePag;   // 0C - available deleted page
RECPTR NxtReuseRec;   // 10 - available deleted record
```

The PGPTR at `r9v6.Free[0].nxpg` of a new-format file, or at `NxtReusePag` for the old format indicates the first page within the chain of available pages. The RECPTR at `r9v6.Free[0].nxrec` of a new-format file, or at `NxtReuseRec` for the old format, indicates the first reusable record area. See the "Extra Pages" section later in this chapter for more information about the available-page chain; see Chapter 8 for information regarding the available-record chain (it appears part of the organization of data pages).

The old file format tracks, in `r2.v5LastAlloc,` the number of the last page allocated:

```
union {
  PGPTR v5LastAlloc;    // 1E - last alloc page
  long v6vac1;          // 1E - unused
} r2;
```

When no more pages are available for reuse and a new page is needed, Btrieve versions prior to 6.0 increment `r2.v5LastAlloc` and add a new blank page to the end of the file, writing appropriate page header information to it depending on the purpose that the page will serve. Newer versions use the PAT instead as described in Chapter 5.

Two major variables maintained by the old file format appear in struct `v5` of union `r4`:

```
union {
   struct {
    int     FreeBytes;  // 2A - free bytes on last page
    int     PrePages;   // 2B - indicates preimage
                        //      pages used
   } v5;
   struct {
    int    v6vac3;    // 2A - unused
    int    v6vac4;    // 2B - unused
   } v6;
  } r4;
```

The r4.v5.FreeBytes variable tracks the amount of space remaining on the last page allocated. When this value drops below the number of bytes required to write a record (or an index entry, as appropriate for the page), allocation of additional space is necessary. The r4.v5.PrePages variable records the number of pre-image pages stored in the PREfile; this becomes significant only when a system failure requires restoration of pages from the pre-image information. As indicated in the declaration, the newer file format uses neither of these variables.

In the new file format, most space allocation is handled by the Page Allocation Table mappings, but three values stored in struct v6 of union r7 track the PAT itself:

```
int    PaPage;        // 4C - PAT pair number for
                      //       first unalloc phys page
int    PaOffset;      // 4E - offset in PaPage for
                      //       first unalloc phys page
int    PaLast;        // 50 - last PAT page in page array
```

The first two of these, r7.v6.PaPage and r7.v6.PaOffset, identify the last logical page that has been allocated in the file. The third, r7.v6.PaLast, identifies the last PAT pair defined for the file. It's quite possible to have many more PAT pairs defined than are being used at any time. Once a PAT pair is added to the file, it remains there so long as the file exists, although all records to which it points may subsequently be deleted.

When the new file format showed up in version 6.0, a 32-bit variable called the main bitmap and declared in BTRIEVE.H as r8.v6.MainBitMap appeared to help track physical page allocation:

```
union {
   struct {
     long    v5vac4[4]; // 56 - unused
     int     ResFCB[3]; // 66 - used with reserved ext FCB
     PGPTR   ExtFirst;  // 6C - first page number of
                        //      extended file
     int     PREPgs;    // 70 - total page count of PRE file
   } v5;
   struct {
     long    MainBitMap; // 56 - identifies active FCR and PATs
     FSPSET  Backup;     // 5A - backup free pool
     int     v6vac7[6];  // 66 - unused
   } v6;
  } r8;
```

The idea behind this bitmap was to retain a compact indication of which FCR and PAT was the currently valid copy, formatted to reduce RAM requirements. The least significant bit represented the FCR, and the next least significant the first PAT pair. Other bits applied to later PAT pairs if any exist. After a total of thirty PAT pairs accumulated in a file, the next time a PAT pair became necessary an entire 4,096-byte bitmap was to be added at the end of the file, just before the new PAT pair, and all the bitmap functions then transferred to this new larger version. The most significant bit of the original 32-bit value was then set to 1 to indicate existence of the auxiliary bitmap.

As experience with the shadow-imaging technique accumulated, it became apparent that the MainBitMap idea wasn't as good as its developers had thought. Keeping the bitmap updated simply created additional overhead, since it was still necessary to update both the PAT and the FCR when usage counts changed. The bitmaps served no useful purpose. Instead of saving RAM space, the extra code increased the drain on resources and slowed the system slightly.

Therefore, at version 6.10 this technique quietly dropped from use. The variable remains to support version 6.0 engines that require it, but is not updated by newer engines. Since this can pose problems when a file that has been edited via version 6.1 or later is subsequently read by a 6.0 engine, these newer versions also set the consistency flag Consistent to 0xFFFF to indicate a need for rebuilding of the bitmap and verification of PAT data. Since versions 6.1 and later ignore the Consistent flag, this causes no harm and closes off the possibility of problems.

The Index Specifications

The new file format of version 6.0 and later uses a Key Allocation Table (KAT) in the FCR to locate its key segment specifications. The original file format depended on fixed locations for this data.

By going through the KAT, the new format allows keys to be added to or removed from the file at any time, so long as room remains in the FCR to accommodate the specifications. Also, the key's identification number becomes independent of the physical location of its specification in the FCR.

The KAT is an array of 16-bit values, stored in normal Intel format. Location of the KAT itself varies with the file's page size. Essential data about it appears in three variables (KATSize, KATUsed, and KATOffset) declared in the r9.v6 area in BTRIEVE.H:

```
union {
  struct {
    WORD  v5vac5[10];  // 76 - unused
          ... other variables omitted here ...
  } v5;
  struct {
    char  KATSize;     // 76 - Number of keys
    char  KATUsed;     // 77 - Number of segments
    WORD  KATOffset;   // 78 - offset from FCR start
                       //      to KAT data
    WORD  KAT512[8];   // 7A - KAT for 512-byte page files
          ... other variables omitted here ...
  } v6;
} r9;
```

In this excerpt, other variables within union r9 that are not associated with the KAT have been omitted.

For page sizes larger than 512 bytes, the KAT occupies the last available space on the FCR page. It begins just far enough back from the end of the page to allow room for the maximum number of key segments allowed for that page size. For instance, a 1,024-byte page's KAT starts at offset 0x03D0 within the FCR, allowing it to hold 24 key-specification pointers before reaching the end of the page.

For a 512-byte page, the KAT appears at offset 0x007A (r9.v6.KAT512), leaving the last part of the FCR page available to hold up to eight key-segment specifications.

Regardless, the offset of the first word of the KAT appears in r9.v6.KATOffset. Variable r9.v6.KATSize holds the number of different keys (not key segments), and r9.v6.KATUsed holds the total number of segment specifications, which may be different.

Within the table, each 16-bit item stores the offset to the first byte of the first segment of the associated key. The KAT does not contain pointers to subsequent segments of the key, since the segment specifications for any key must always be contiguous with each other. Never-used entries of the table contain the value 0000 while erased-key entries contain 0xFFFF.

Figure 6.1 shows the relationships between the three KAT pointers, the KAT itself, and the segment specifications. In this example, the file has 1,024-byte pages and contains five different keys. The first three of these keys (key 0, key 1, and key 2; key and segment numbers always start at zero) are all single-segment keys. Each segment occupies 0x1E (30) bytes, so the starting addresses in the KAT increase by 0x1E from one key to the next. Key 3 has two segments and thus occupies 0x3C (60) bytes instead of 0x1E. Key 4 thus starts at 0x016A + 0x003C, or 0x01A6. This final key has three segments.

Both 8-bit pointer values can be thought of as indexes to the first free space in the respective tables: r9.v6.KATSize points to the first

Figure 6.1 *This diagram shows how Btrieve navigates the Key Alloca-*
tion Table of the new file format to locate its key segment
specifications for any specific key. Using the index and
pointer values permits a new set of segment specs to easily
be inserted between existing keys, at any time, without
changing any key ID numbers.

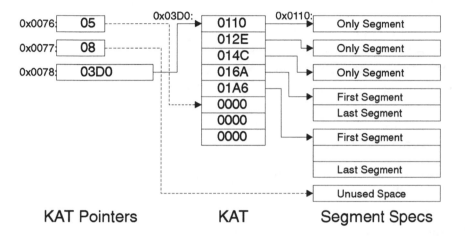

free element of the KAT, and r9.v6.KATUsed points to the first
unused segment spec area. If you consider the segment spec area to
be a linear array of 30-byte structures, with each structure containing
a single segment's specification, everything falls into place.

This whole idea of segments within keys may not be familiar to you,
if your previous experience has been limited to less powerful database packages such as the popular xBase applications. A segment is
simply one field of the record that becomes part of a key index. In
the xBase approach, you would define an **index expression** that
might combine several fields into one key. In more advanced systems, keys consist of one or more segments. For Btrieve, the advantage of the segment specification is simply that it operates entirely
on the basis of data location within a record, and is independent of
any field names assigned. While Btrieve allows this freedom, other
systems that may attempt access by way of the DDF files can run
into problems if index key segments don't match defined fields
exactly.

Key segments allow more flexibility when defining record layout. For instance, you can define a record containing two fields, with multiple duplicate values allowed for each field; however, by combining both fields into a single key (with each field defined as a different segment of that key), you can force the combination of the two to be unique in your file.

In both Btrieve file formats, the first key segment specification always appears at location 0x110. All other segment specifications follow this one, and all are contiguous. When you delete a key, any segment specifications following it move up to close the gap. When you insert a key, however, it can simply be added to the end of the existing specifications because in the new file format each key's specification contains the ID number embedded within its PGPTR element.

The original format did not embed the ID numbers and consequently could not allow addition or deletion of keys except at the end of the segment-spec area. Even these supplemental keys weren't available during the first several years of Btrieve's existence.

Except for its use of the KAT and associated pointers, the segment specification structure for the new file format differs in only one field from that originally used. The first 8 bytes of each specification and bytes 0x0A through 0x13 define values that apply to the entire key; the remaining 12 bytes define only one segment of the key.

In the BTRIEVE.H declaration for the SEGSPEC structure, the elements that apply to the entire key are

```
PGPTR  Entry;      // 00 - 0 if continuation segment (old
                   //      only), else root page number
long   Total;      // 04 - count of unique entries for
                   //      this key (word-swapped)
int    Kflags;     // 08 - key definition flags (will
                   //      vary with each segment)
int    Siz;        // 0A - total length all segments
int    Klen;       // 0C - full size including dup ptrs
int    PgMax;      // 0E - max number of items per page
```

```
int     PgMin;      // 10 - min number of items per page
int     DupOffset;  // 12 - offset to dupes from start
                    //      of data record
```

The **Entry** PGPTR identifies the root page for the index associated with this key, and in the new file format contains the key's ID code embedded within it. In the original format, this value was simply a physical page offset from the front of the file.

The **Total** value is, like the statistical values discussed earlier in this chapter, word-swapped and provides the count of the number of unique values contained for this key.

Kflags is a bitmap of 16 flags that define characteristics for the current segment of the key; only one bit is unique to each segment and the others must all be identical to those in other segments of the same key. Meanings of the bits are listed in Table 6.4. In this table, the letter x indicates that the bit's value has no meaning for the specific characteristic. Note that meanings for some bits depend on the format in use, and others may depend on other bits.

The **Siz** and **Klen** values define the number of bytes each key requires on its index pages. **Siz** is simply the sum of all the segment-length values for the key, and **Klen** is the sum of **Siz** and the byte count of all duplicate-key pointers associated with each key. Btrieve calculates these values when it creates the file initially, and they remain unchanged for the life of the key.

The **PgMax** and **PgMin** values tell Btrieve when it's necessary to split or compress an index page. Btrieve calculates these values from the page size and the value of **Klen** when creating the file.

Finally, **DupOffset** records the location within each data record at which any duplicate-key pointers begin.

Table 6.4 *Bit Significance for Key Segment*

1 1 1 1 1 1 0 0 0 0 0 0 0 0 0 0 5 4 3 2 1 0 9 8 7 6 5 4 3 2 1 0	Bit Significance
x x x x x x x x x x x x x x x 0	No duplicate keys allowed.
x x x x x x x x x x x x x x x 1	Duplicates permitted.
x x x x x x x x x x x x x x 0 x	Key is not modifiable.
x x x x x x x x x x x x x x 1 x	Key is modifiable.
x x x x x x x 0 x x x x x 0 x x	Data type is ASCII.
x x x x x x x 0 x x x x x 1 x x	Data type is Binary.
x x x x x x x x x x x x 0 x x x	Null values prohibited.
x x x x x x x x x x x x 1 x x x	Null values allowed; for version 6.0 and later, all segments must be null to be treated as null key.
x x x x x x x x x x x 0 x x x x	This is last segment.
x x x x x x x x x x x 1 x x x x	This is not last segment.
x x x x x x x x x x 0 x x x x x	No ACS used.
x x x x x x x x x x 1 x x x x x	ACS used.
x x x x x x x x x 0 x x x x x x	Ascending sort sequence.
x x x x x x x x x 1 x x x x x x	Descending sort sequence.
x x x x x x x x 1 x x x x x x x	Supplemental Index (v5 only).
x x x x x x x x 1 x x x x x x 0	Linked duplicate key values (6.0 and later only).
x x x x x x x x 1 x x x x x x 1	Repeated duplicate key values (6.0 and later only).
x x x x x x x 0 x x x x x x x x	Data type determined by Bit 2.
x x x x x x x 1 x x x x x x x x	Segment uses extended data type codes (Chapter 5).
x x x x x x 1 x x x x x x x x x	For Version 6.0 and later, if any segment is null, entire key is treated as null key.
x x x x x 1 x x x x 0 x x x x x	Insensitive to case (6.0 and later only).
x x x x x 1 x x x x 1 x x x x x	Multiple ACS used (6.1 and later only).

The remaining 10 bytes that define each segment individually are

```
int   Beg;              // 14 - offset of first byte of key
int   Len;              // 16 - length in bytes, this segment
union {
  char v5empty[4];      // 18 - unused in older format
  struct{
    char KeyID;         // 18 - 6+ only, assigned
                        //      key ID value
    char ACSPage[3];    // 19 - 6.1+ only, unused previously;
                        //      ACS ID
  } v6;
} r1;
char ExTyp;             // 1C - data type code for segment
char NulVal;            // 1D - null value for this segment
```

Beg and Len specify the segment's location within each data record. Beg is the offset in bytes from the start of the record, and Len is the segment's length.

The next 4 bytes remain unused in the original format, but identify the ID number to be assigned to the key at file-creation time (for all new-format files) and also the applicable Alternate Collating Sequence for the segment, if one has been specified (only for version 6.1 and later).

The ExTyp variable identifies the segment's data type (if extended types were specified in the Kflags bitmap for the key). NulVal specifies the value to be inserted automatically for this segment, if the data record is empty at the specified locations. Normally NulVal is set to 0x20 (ASCII blank space) for character or string data types, or to 0x00 for any other data type; many systems, however, leave the null value at 0x00 for all types of data.

Page Allocation Tables

The Page Allocation Tables (PAT) are the backbone of the shadow-imaging technique that did away with pre-image files for version 6.0 and later. These tables map logical page numbers (used by all

Btrieve internal page references) to the corresponding physical page numbers (byte offset to start of page, divided by page size) required for access to the page. As discussed in Chapter 5, physical page pointers in the PAT, like logical page numbers elsewhere in the new Btrieve format, use the PGPTR variable type that includes a page type ID code as its most significant byte.

PATs always occur in pairs; in each pair, one copy is the currently valid PAT, and the other is a working copy used during modification of the file. The valid copy carries a higher usage count than does the working copy. When an operation that modifies the file completes, its usage count value goes into the header of the working PAT, causing that copy to become the current valid copy and making all changes effective in one near-instantaneous action. Before this happens, while the changes are still going on, all other users of the file see only the pages mapped by the original current copy, thus protecting them from partially written changes.

Each PAT carries an 8-byte identifying page header as shown in Figure 6.2. The first 2 bytes contain ASCII P characters as a signature, and the next 2 bytes contain the sequence number of the PAT pair. The remaining 4 bytes hold the usage count, which tells Btrieve which copy is the valid one in the pair at any moment.

Figure 6.2   *The PAT page header. Both pages of a PAT pair contain the same PAT number.*

P	P	PAT Nbr.		Usage Count		
0	1	2	3	4	5	6	7

To achieve the shadow imaging, Btrieve first locates a currently unused page, from the extra or unallocated pages in the current PAT and copies the content of the page to be changed into that page. The engine then swaps the physical page values of the page being changed with the extra page on the working copy of the PAT. This maps the original logical page to the new copy and makes the original physical page an unused extra, but the changes won't take effect until this PAT copy becomes valid.

The same thing happens for data pages and for index pages; any page that will be affected by this operation gets a shadow image built on an extra page, and its logical-to-physical mapping swapped.

Any necessary file changes then take place on the hidden, new pages. When all are complete and the file is again totally consistent, the operation's usage count goes into the header of the PAT working copy. When that copy is written to the file, all changes take effect at once and any new operations see the new versions of the affected pages.

Because of the 8 bytes used by the PAT page header information, the number of logical pages a PAT can hold is two less than the value resulting when you divide the page size by four (the size of a physical page pointer). Thus, a 512-byte PAT can hold 126 logical page mappings, a 1,024-byte PAT can hold 254, and so on.

When Btrieve creates a file, it builds only the first PAT pair (at physical page addresses 2 and 3, immediately following the FCR pair created on physical pages 0 and 1). Then the system initializes all entries in the table even though physical pages for those entries do not yet exist. The first physical page assigned (as logical page 1) is page 4, as shown in Figure 6.3. Subsequent page assignments follow in increasing sequence. Btrieve sets the page type code for each of these nonexistent pages to 0; when a new page becomes necessary and no type E (extra, existing, but unused) pages exist, Btrieve uses the first type 0 page found on the PAT. Version 6.1 and later omit the E code and instead use 0 just as for pages never before used. The PaPage and PaOffset pointers suffice to distinguish between used and unused pages.

As pages are physically added later, the appropriate type code for each goes into both its page header and its PAT entry. Keeping type codes in the PAT greatly speeds Btrieve's search for pages in normal operation.

Figure 6.3 *Each Page Allocation Table contains an array of 4-byte physical page pointers; logical pages map to these physical addresses as shown here, using the logical page number as a subscript into the array. Note that in most cases the physical page number bears no fixed relation to its logical page number, except that created by the PAT.*

Logical Page	Page Type	Physical Page
1	Key 0	4
2	Key 1	5
3	Data	7
4	Extra	6
5	Unused	8
6	Unused	9
. . .	. . .	. . .
125	Unused	128
126	Unused	129

PaOffset (arrow pointing to row between 4 and 5)

Index   In Array

Once all the pages that the first PAT pair can hold are physically allocated, Btrieve adds another PAT pair as the next two physical pages. Because the number of logical pages per PAT remains constant for any specific page size, Btrieve can calculate the physical addresses of each PAT pair throughout the file and does not need to store pointers to any of them. By holding all PATs in memory whenever possible, search time to locate available space is cut to the minimum.

Earlier in this chapter we discussed how variables r7.v6.PaPage and r7.v6.PaOffset in the FCRTOP structure identify the last logical page allocated in the file. For the example shown in Figure 6.3, the value of r7.v6.PaPage would be 1 since the first (and only) PAT pair contains the boundary offset. The value of r7.v6.PaLast would also be 1 since only one PAT pair exists at this point, and the value of r7.v6.PaOffset would be 0x1C (indicated by the arrow in the illustration).

Alternate Collating Sequences

Before version 6.1, Btrieve required use of an Alternate Collating Sequence (ACS) in order to achieve a case-insensitive sort sequence. This ACS provided a 256-byte lookup table to map any ASCII character to its desired sort position. Btrieve used the original character value as an index into the ACS table, and the resulting value read from the indexed location as the comparison criterion when establishing sort sequence.

The software development kit includes a sample ACS file named UPPER that eliminates case sensitivity. Although introduction of the case-insensitive key option at version 5.1 made use of this file unnecessary, many older files still contain copies of it, and the need for an ACS remains valid.

When creating a new-format file that uses an ACS, Btrieve copies the ACS data into the file at logical page 4, immediately following the first PAT pair. The ACS page header (Figure 6.4) includes the Page Type Code A (0x41) at offset 1 and also the signature byte 0xAC at offset 6. A 2-byte usage count (always zero since ACS creation occurs before any operation is possible) separates the PGPTR from the 0xAC signature byte. The 8-byte name of the ACS begins at offset 7. The table itself begins at offset 0x00F and extends through offset 0x10E. Btrieve makes no use of the remaining bytes on the ACS page for any reason.

Version 6.1 of Btrieve introduced the capability of using multiple ACS tables. The three page-number bytes of the PGPTR in the PAT header provide unique identifiers for each. Normally all ACS tables

Figure 6.4 *Page layout for the new-format ACS page(s)*

00	41	04	00	AC	ACS Name (9)
0	1	2	3	4	5 through F

.......User-defined collating sequence (256).......
10   10F

are defined at file creation time; in this case the ACS pages will use sequential pages in the file. However, using the logical page number to identify the ACS makes it possible to add more special sequences after the file is in use.

The original-format ACS page layout is almost, but not quite, identical to that of the new format. Figure 6.5 shows the differences: The first 4 bytes of the page header always contain the values shown. Definition of the ACS takes place when creating the file, so the ACS page will always immediately follow the FCR. From offset 0x004 on, the two formats are identical to each other.

Figure 6.5   *Page layout for the original-format ACS page*

00	00	01	00	00	00	AC	Name (9)
0	1	2	3	4	5	6	7 - F

.......User-defined collating sequence (256).......
10   10F

When any key uses an ACS, the ALT bit (Bit 5, 0x20) in its **Kflags** specification must be 1. If multiple ACSs are in use, Bit 11 (0x800) must also be 1 (Bit 11 has totally different significance if Bit 5 is "0" though). In addition, the **r1.v6.ACSPage** field of the appropriate key segment(s) must contain a valid ACS logical page number in PGPTR format less the Page ID code.

Extra Pages

When Btrieve needs a new page, it takes any existing available pages before physically adding an additional new page to the file. This both conserves storage space and speeds the system action.

In the file format introduced with version 6.0, entire pages that become available for reuse were known as **extra pages.** A page code of E in both the page header and the PAT entry for that page identified each extra page.

With the release of version 6.1, however, the same 0 code that flags never-used pages replaced the E code. The `PaPage` and `PaOffset` pointers maintained in the FCR suffice to distinguish released pages that remain physically part of the file from never-used pages that do not physically exist. Whether the Page Type code assigned to reusable pages is "E" or "0", the available page chain works the same way.

Btrieve tracks the pages that are available for reuse by placing them in a singly-linked chain. The PGPTR at `r9v6.Free[0].nxpg` of a new-format file, or at `NxtReusePag` for the old format, points to the first page of the chain. Another PGPTR, at offset 0x06 within each reusable page, points to the next link in the chain.

When Btrieve releases a page for reuse, it copies the value from `r9v6.Free[0].nxpg` or `NxtReusePag` into the page being released, at offset 0x06. The engine then writes the pointer to the released page into `r9v6.Free[0].nxpg` or `NxtReusePag`. Since the value initially placed into `r9v6.Free[0].nxpg` or `NxtReusePag` at file creation time is –1 (Btrieve's NULL-pointer value, indicating that the chain is empty), this automatically inserts an End-of-Chain marker into the first page released.

When Btrieve needs a page and the value at `r9v6.Free[0].nxpg` or `NxtReusePag` is not equal to –1, the engine takes the PGPTR from `r9v6.Free[0].nxpg` or `NxtReusePag` and replaces it with the one from the page that it addresses. When the last page in the chain is taken, the –1 marker automatically returns to `r9v6.Free[0].nxpg` or `NxtReusePag`, indicating that no more reusable pages are available. Btrieve then physically allocates a new page to the file.

FILE.DDF Layout and Usage

In Chapter 5 we met the data dictionary files that allow Xtrieve, XQL, and Scalable SQL to implement fully relational databases using the Btrieve engine as their foundation. Here, we examine the FILE.DDF dictionary file in more detail.

In the data dictionary, each table within the relational database described by the data dictionary is in a distinct Btrieve file. FILE.DDF, also known within the data dictionary as the X$File table, correlates each table name in the data dictionary with the corresponding Btrieve file.

FILE.DDF contains five fields (or, in relational terms, columns). All are named, and all names begin with the three characters Xf$ to identify them as dictionary-defined fields within the File table. Layout of these fields within each row or record is shown in Table 6.5 (subsequent discussion drops the initial three characters except when necessary to eliminate any ambiguity).

Table 6.5   *Fields in FILE.DDF*

Field Name	Description	Data Type	Position	Length
Xf$ID	File ID number (assigned automatically)	Integer	1	2
Xf$Name	Table name	String	3	20
Xf$Loc	Table location (path)	String	23	64
Xf$Flags	File flags	Integer	87	1
Xf$Reserved	Reserved	String	88	10

The ID field contains a numeric identifier assigned by the data dictionary programs when creating a new table. This value is unique within the data dictionary and serves as the primary key when defining relations with other tables.

The Name field contains the name by which the table is known within the data dictionary. This name may be up to twenty characters long, and Btrieve fills unused positions at the right of the field with blanks.

The Loc field contains the path and filename that Btrieve uses to access the file. Length may be up to sixty-four) characters, and the path specification may be either absolute (including drive letter, a complete path from the root of the drive, or both) or relative (beginning with something other than a drive letter or directory delimiting "\" character). If relative, Btrieve assumes that the path is relative to the current working directory. When possible, leave this field relative to permit easy transfer of applications from one drive to another.

The Flags field consists of a single byte, capable of holding up to eight individual flag bits. Only one bit of the field seems to be in use: Bit 4 (0x10) indicates a dictionary file if set (1), and a user-defined file if clear (0). The other seven bits appear unused and are always 0.

Although defined as a String data type, the 10-byte Reserved field contains raw binary data. Usage of this field has not been released for publication.

FILE.DDF contains two indexes, as shown in Table 6.6.

Table 6.6   *Indexes in FILE.DDF*

Index	Segment	Field	Description
0	0	Xf$ID	File ID
1	0	Xf$Name	Table Name

Neither index allows duplicate key values, both are single-segment keys, and the Name key uses the UPPER ACS to achieve case-insensitive sort sequence.

The default content of this table, normally not visible to users, consists of the three required data dictionary files. These entries are shown in Table 6.7.

Table 6.7   *The Three Files Needed for Full Data Dictionary Capabilities*

ID	Name	File	Flags
1	X$File	file.ddf	16
2	X$Field	field.ddf	16
3	X$Index	index.ddf	16

Like all data dictionary files created by Btrieve's own utilities or accessories, FILE.DDF carries an owner name to make it read-only for normal usage. BTI does not make this owner name public; the company considers the name a form of security against random meddling with data dictionary files. The XQLP library (from the XQL product) provides routines that can open DDF files for modification, which have the correct owner name built in. Most third-party utilities for editing DDF files use this library, under license from BTI, to be sure of creating fully compatible files.

In later chapters we explore the Field and Index tables. All three must be used together to provide full data dictionary capabilities. All other DDF files serve only special purposes, and most programs such as ODBC ignore them.

The BTRIEVE.H File

Throughout this chapter we've shown snippets and extracts from the BTRIEVE.H file, which is not an official BTI file but was created by the author to document header-page information. The file appears on the companion diskette, but a full listing follows for ready reference:

```
/* * * * * * * * * * * * * * * * * * * * * * * * * * * *\
 *                                                      *
 *        BTRIEVE.H - Jim Kyle December, 1994           *
 *                                                      *
 *        Defines data structures for Btrieve files,    *
 *        all versions                                  *
 *                                                      *
 * * * * * * * * * * * * * * * * * * * * * * * * * * * */
#ifndef BYTE
#define BYTE unsigned char
#endif
#ifndef WORD
#define WORD unsigned short
#endif
#ifndef DWORD
```

```
#define DWORD unsigned long
#endif

#define MAXBTRPG 4096

static int PgShift;        // set for new-format record pointers
static int CurFmt;         // indicates whether old or new format

typedef struct {
  union {
    struct {
      WORD hi;             // ( u1.v5.hi << 16 ) + lo = page number
    } v5;
    struct {
      BYTE hi;             // ( u1.v6.hi << 16 ) + lo = page number
      BYTE code;
    } v6;
  } u1;
 WORD lo;
} PGTR;

#define PageNo5( x )(long)(((long)(x).u1.v5.hi << 16)+(x).lo)
#define PageNo6( x )(long)(((long)(x).u1.v6.hi << 16)+(x).lo)
#define PageID( x )    (BYTE)((x).v6.code)

typedef struct {
  long wl;
} RECPTR;

typedef struct {
  BYTE lo;
  BYTE mid;
  BYTE frag;
} VRECPTR;

#define VRFrag( x ) (BYTE)((x).frag
#define VRPage( x )
               (long)(((long)(x).hi<<16)|((x).mid<<8)|(x).lo

typedef struct {
  PGPTR  nxpg;          // next free page
  RECPTR nxrec;         // next free record
  VRECPTR nxvrec;       // next free vrecord
```

```
} FSPSET;                   // v 6+ only

/********
        FCR Header Layout
        uses 9 unions (r1 ... r9) for pre/post 6.0 variations
                                within each, structs v5 and v6
                                hold differences
 */
typedef struct {
  union {
  struct {
    PGPTR  PgSeq;           // 00 - page number
    int    Usage;           // 04 - match with usage count
    int    Version;         // 06 - version code, <0 if owned
  } v5;
    struct {
    int    RecSig;          // 00 - 'FC'
    int    SeqNbr;          // 02 - always binary zeroes
    long   Usage;           // 04 - usage count
  } v6;
} r1;
int    PagSize;             // 08 - in bytes
int    AccelFlags;          // 0A - open, firstupdate, cleared on
                            //      close
PGPTR  NxtReusePag;         // 0C - available deleted page
RECPTR NxtReuseRec;         // 10 - available deleted record
int    Nkeys;               // 14 - number of keys defined
int    RecLen;              // 16 - data rec length excl
                            //      pointers
int    PhyLen;              // 18 - physical rec length incl ptrs
long   Nrecs;               // 1A - number of records in file
                            //      (word-swapped)
union {
  PGPTR v5LastAlloc;        // 1E - last alloc page
  long  v6vac1;             //  1E - unused
} r2;
int      Consistent;        // 22 - 0xFFFF = need recovery
union {
    int    v5ExtFile;       // 24 - number of files (1 normal,
                            //      2 extended)
    int    v6vac2;          // 24 - unused
```

```
} r3;
long    Npages;            // 26 - number of pages in file
                           //       (word-swapped)
union {
  struct {
    int   FreeBytes;       // 2A - free bytes on last page
    int   PrePages;        // 2B - indicates preimage pages used
  } v5;
  struct {
    int   v6vac3;          // 2A - unused
    int   v6vac4;          // 2B - unused
  } v6;
} r4;
BYTE   Owner[9];           // 2E - encoded owner name
char   OwnerFlags;         // 37 - flags byte
char   VRecsOkay;          // 38 - FF = ok, FD = trunc blanks
union {
  char v5vac1[3];          // 39 - unused
  char v6VFree[3];         // 39 - 3-byte PGPTR to first V
                           //       page with free space
} r5;
char   ACSName[8];          // 3C - 8-byte ACS identifier
union {
  struct {
    int   Extended;        // 44 - 0xFFFF if file extended,
                           //       else 0
    int   v5vac2;          // 46 - unused
  } v5;
  struct {
    int   v6vac5;          // 44 - always 0 for v6.0
    int   v6vac6;          // 46 - unused
  } v6;
} r6;
int   PreAlloc;            // 48 - number of pages preallocated
                           //       at create time
union {
  int v5vac3[4];           // 4A - unused
  struct {
    int   Version;         // 4A - version number,
                           //       3 for 4.0 and before
```

```
    int    PaPage;           // 4C - PAT pair number for
                             //       first unalloc phys page
    int    PaOffset;         // 4E - offset in PaPage for
                             //       first unalloc phys page
    int    PaLast;           // 50 - last PAT page in page array
  } v6;
} r7;
int    LastOp;               // 52 - last operation performed
                             //       including bias
int    res1;                 // 54 - reserved for future development
union {
  struct {
    long   v5vac4[4];        // 56 - unused
    int    ResFCB[3];        // 66 - used with reserved
                             //       extended FCB
    PGPTR  ExtFirst;         // 6C - first page number of
                             //       extended file
    int    PREPgs;           // 70 - total page count of
                             //       PRE file
  } v5;
  struct {
    long   MainBitMap;       // 56 - identifies active FCR and PATs
    FSPSET Backup;           // 5A - backup free pool
    int    v6vac7[6];        // 66 - unused
  } v6;
} r8;
int    DupOffset;            // 72 - offset of first dup-key ptr
                             //       from rec start
char   NumDupes;             // 74 - Number of dupe ptrs on record
char   NumUnused;            // 75 - Number of unused dupe ptrs
union {
  struct {
    WORD   v5vac5[10];       // 76 - unused
    char   PreFCB[10];       // 8A - used with PRE FCB
    long   v5vac6;           // 94 - unused
    BYTE   Path[64];         // 98 - EXTEND filepath,
                             //       also holds PRE path
    char   v5vac7[46];       // D8 - unused
  } v5;
```

```
  struct {
    char   KATSize;              // 76 - Number of keys
    char   KATUsed;              // 77 - Number of segments
    WORD   KATOffset;            // 78 - offset from FCR start
                                 //       to KAT data
    WORD   KAT512[8];            // 7A - KAT for 512-byte page files
    char   v6vac8[10];           // 8A - unused
    VRECPTR Ridata;              // 94 - special RI definition pointer
    FSPSET  Free[5];             // 98 - allows concurrent operations
    long   v6vac9;               // D4 - unused
    char   DupeRes;              // D8 - number of dupe-key ptrs
                                 //       reserved at create time
    char   PrivDataSz;           // D9 - size of private data field
                                 //       in data records
    char   v6vac10[44];          //DA - unused
  } v6;
} r9;
int    UsrFlgs;                  //106 - user-specified flags
                                 //       (CREATE bitmap)
int    VarThresh;                //108 - variable space threshold
PGPTR  ACSpage;                  //10A - allows ACS to be added
                                 //       after creation of file
int    ComprLen;                 //10E - record length if file
                                 //       is compressed

} FCRTOP;

/********
 Key-segment Specification

    */
typedef struct {
 PGPTR Entry;                    // 00 - 0 if continuation segment
                                 //       (old only), else root page
                                 //        number
 long  Total;                    // 04 - count of unique entries for
                                 //       this key (word-swapped)
 int   Kflags;                   // 08 - key definition flags
                                 //       (will vary with each
                                 //       segment)
 int   Siz;                      // 0A - total length all segments
```

```
  int   Klen;                    // 0C - full size  including dup ptrs
  int   PgMax;                   // 0E - max number of items per page
  int   PgMin;                   // 10 - min number of items per page
  int   DupOffset;               // 12 - offset to dupes from
                                 //      start of data record
// preceding info (except Kflags) used only once  per key,
            not per segment
  int   Beg;                     // 14 - offset of first byte of key
  int   Len;                     // 16 - length in bytes, this
                                 //      segment
  union {
    char v5empty[4];             // 18 - unused in older format
    struct{
      char KeyID;                // 18 - 6+ only, assigned key
                                 //      ID value
      char ACSPage[3];           // 19 - 6.1+ only, unused
                                 //   previously; ACS ID
    } v6;
  } r1;
  char ExTyp;                    // 1C - data type code for segment
char NulVal;                     // 1D - null value for this segment
} SEGSPEC;

/********
   Page Field definition for all pages
   except new FC and PP types
*/
typedef struct {
  PGPTR PgSeq;                   // differs between formats!
  WORD  Usage;                   // high bit set if this is data
                                 //   page pre-6
} PAGHDR;

/********
        PAT Header definition (v6+ only)
*/
    typedef struct {
  int sig;                       // always  'PP'
  int pair;                      // 0-based ID of PAT pair
  long Usage;
    } PATHDR;
```

Conclusion

In this chapter we examined all details of the Btrieve file header page, PAT, extra pages, and the FILE.DDF data dictionary file. Chapter 7 continues our journey with similar exploration of the key pages that make Btrieve's rapid data access possible.

7

Index Page Details

This chapter explains both the identification and page layout for
index pages and the way in which the Btrieve engine traverses the
index tree. This chapter also describes layout and use of the
INDEX.DDF file, part of the XQL/SSQL/ODBC data dictionary for
Btrieve. Although this chapter is brief, its content is essential to fully
comprehend the way Btrieve achieves its goals.

The heart of Btrieve's speed and effectiveness is the B-tree structure
that the index pages implement. Little change has taken place in
this structure from one version of Btrieve to another. Even the
change of file formats at version 6.0 had minimal impact on the
index structure.

The use of logical pages rather than physical pages is the most significant difference between the index pages for the original file format and those used in the new format. Since the logical page pointer
in each page header includes a Page Type Code, every new-format

page carries a type identifier. In the original format, the only distinction made in the header was between data and non-data pages. The high bit of the usage count was always zero in non-data pages such as indexes and 1 for all data pages.

Threading Through the Tree

The starting point for navigating the B-tree for any index of a file is that index's segment specification within the file's FCR (see Chapter 5). The first segment specification for each key includes the starting page pointer (`Entry` in the SEGSPEC structure of BTRIEVE.H), which points to the root of that tree. The same segment specification also includes the size of the key's data area in bytes (`Siz` in SEGSPEC) and the total length (including all associated pointers) of each key on an index page (`Klen` in SEGSPEC). In addition, the specification lists the maximum number of key items allowed on each page (`PgMax` in SEGSPEC) and the minimum number (`PgMin` in SEGSPEC).

As noted in Chapter 3, the B-tree algorithms automatically split a page when adding a key could take it over the maximum, and they merge pages when deleting a key could reduce a page item count below the minimum. Without deletions, the number of index pages for each key of a Btrieve file will always be odd because the B-tree grows only by splitting pages, and each page split adds two new pages to keep the index in balance.

The **key data** area for any key consists of the fields for each of that key's segments, arranged from left to right in the same sequence as the segment specifications. (This rule does not apply to key-only files, which are discussed in the "Key-Only Files" section later in this chapter.) Sort order for each segment depends on the data type, presence or absence of an ACS, and the ascending/descending sequence flag. Key fields must always lie completely within the fixed-length portion of a data record, with a single exception: compressed data files may have keys, even though the data compression technique treats the data records as variable-length.

Layout of the index pages varies slightly between indexes that allow only unique key values and those that permit duplicate values in key fields. Figure 7.1 shows the simplest layout, that for unique keys and without data compression.

In this situation, the Klen value is 8 bytes larger than Siz: 4 bytes for the page pointer to the index page that contains the next smaller key value and 4 bytes for the record pointer to the record that matches the key data of this item. If the page pointer value is null (0x00FFFFFF in the new file format), no smaller key exists in the file.

Figure 7.1   *Key pages for new-format file, when index requires unique key values*

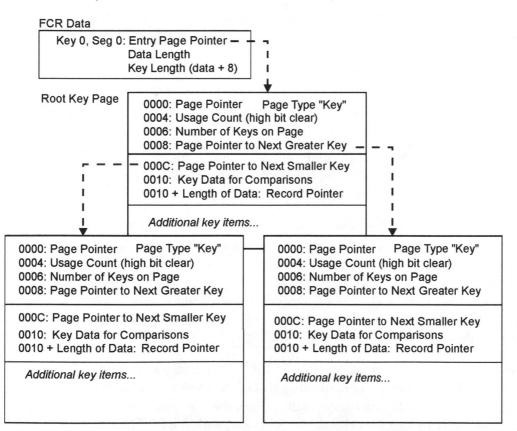

The header of each index page contains the page pointer, the usage count, the number of keys the page contains, and finally a page pointer to the index page containing the first key value greater than the largest value on this page.

The page type code in the page pointer always has the high bit set for an index page; the remaining 7 bits contain the key number. For example, the type code byte for Key 0 has the value 0x80.

The high bit of the 16-bit usage count value is always zero for an index page; this allows certain functions to distinguish between index and data pages when stepping through a file in physical sequence rather than following any index. The remaining 15 bits of this field contain the FCR usage count value in effect when this page was last changed. In the new file format, this value currently has little significance, but it is expected to be used more in the future when Btrieve develops a true distributed cache. In the interim, retaining the field precludes any need for still another format change in the future.

The key count field tells Btrieve when to stop getting key items from the page; it also distinguishes between active index pages and those that are empty and consequently available for reuse. Available pages carry a count of zero.

The Next Greater page pointer identifies the end of the tree; when it contains a null pointer, the last key on the current page is the highest value in the file for this index.

Differences between the new file format and the original format are minimal (see Figure 7.2). The most significant difference is that the page pointers, both in the header and within the page, are physical rather than logical page pointers, and that the value of a null pointer is –1L rather than 0x00FFFFFF. Placement of all fields within the page is identical between the formats, as is treatment of the usage count high bit.

In the original file format, the low 15 bits of the usage count field found extensive use for concurrency and for recovery with the pre-image files. By matching usage count values, the system could select the correct copy from several that might exist within a PRE file.

Figure 7.2   *Key pages for original-format file, when index requires*
unique key values

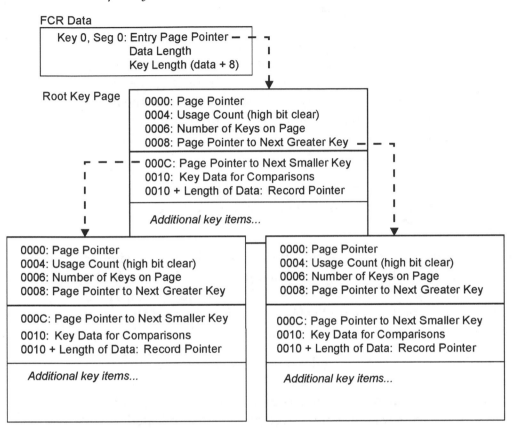

Both formats use a layout that combines the leaves and the nodes of
the classic theoretical B-tree into a single index page structure, used
recursively. To locate any record, the system uses the page pointer in
the FCR key specification to find the root page. Next, the engine
compares the data portion of each item on that page, in turn, to the
target key value being sought.

Whenever the target is smaller than the current key item and the
Next Smaller page pointer's value in the item is null, the search has

ended in failure. Otherwise, the search moves to the index page indicated by the Next Smaller page pointer and continues comparing until either finding a match or failing.

When the target is larger than the current key item, the engine compares the next item on the page. If the last item on the page is still too small and the Next Greater page pointer in the page header is null, the search has failed. Otherwise, the search moves to the index page indicated by that pointer and continues, until either finding a match or failing.

The page pointers in the Btrieve index pages provide the function of the nodes in the classic theoretical structure. Key items with which null-valued pointers are associated provide the function of the leaves.

When a file uses data compression, the index page layout is similar but the content of the key data area within each index item is not compressed. Instead, it remains in its fully expanded form. Thus, from the viewpoint of an application, no difference exists between compressed and uncompressed data files in the index page layouts.

Since indexes using the page layout we've discussed so far are restricted to unique values for each key, no more than a single record can ever match any target. Thus, only one record pointer is necessary in each key item. Things get a bit more complicated, however, when an index specification allows duplicate key values to exist within the file.

Dealing with Duplicate Key Values

When we allow more than one record to carry a key value that duplicates that in any other record, we've opened the door to the possibility of an unlimited number of records all carrying the same duplicated key value. Thus, it's necessary to keep track of the duplicated records by some technique that's totally open-ended regarding the number of records involved. One of the simplest such techniques involves the data structure known as a **list** or **chain,** in which each record in the group connects to its neighbors by means of some kind of pointer value. In the case of Btrieve, the record pointer necessary anyway for data access provides the necessary pointer.

When a key specification permits duplicate values, Btrieve adds an extra record pointer to each index item and changes the interpretation of the original single record pointer. Figure 7.3 shows the modification.

When duplicate keys are involved, the first record pointer holds the address of the first or oldest record stored, and the second pointer holds the address of the most recent or newest one. If no duplicate exists (always true the first time the key appears in a record), the oldest-record address goes into both pointers. Subsequent additions modify only the second pointer.

The new file format permits you, when creating a file, to reserve space for duplicate pointers that may occur in keys not yet defined. Until you define the keys, this space simply goes to waste. The original file format (see Figure 7.4) treated duplicate keys defined at file creation time just as described for the new format but didn't permit reservation of pointers for future needs.

This made necessary an alternate method for dealing with duplicate key values in supplemental indexes (those added after file creation). This method forces each duplicate to a unique value by appending its record pointer to the end of the actual key value. Since no two records can share the identical record address, each such repeated duplicate key value becomes unique; the system ignores the appended record pointer when searching, giving the effect of true duplicate values without requiring a duplicate chain to be built.

The new file format permits you to specify whether keys that permit duplicate values are to use linked or repeated values. The linked method is shown in Figures 7.3 and 7.4, and the repeated method appends the record pointer invisibly as part of the data field in each item. So long as duplicate-pointer space remains available, the default method is linked. When no more such space remains, the default becomes repeated.

Figure 7.3   *Key pages for new-format file, when index permits duplicated key values*

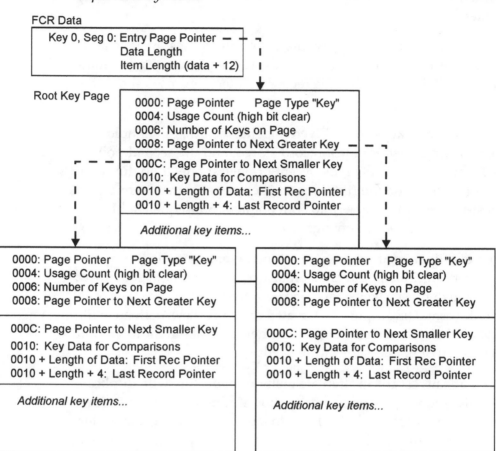

When a file permits duplicate values for some keys and restricts others to unique values, that file will contain both kinds of index pages. Those for the keys permitting linked duplicates will follow the layout of Figures 7.3 (new format) or 7.4 (original format); those for unique or repeated-duplicate keys follow Figures 7.1 (new format) or 7.2 (original format).

Having both the oldest and the newest record pointers stored in the index page permits the Btrieve engine to traverse the duplicate-key chain in either direction when retrieving records. See Chapter 8 for

Figure 7.4 *Key pages for original-format file, when index permits duplicated key values*

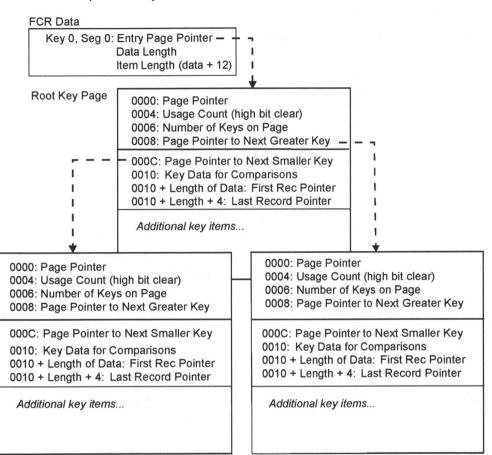

more details about how Btrieve deals with the chain of records for duplicated key values.

One point requiring attention here, though, is the matter of what happens to the index key entry when you delete either the newest or the oldest record in a duplicate-key chain. This could corrupt the record pointer stored in the index item. However, the Btrieve engine checks for this possibility when deleting records and replaces the affected record pointer with the new, correct value. The record chosen to replace a deleted oldest record will be the next oldest; similarly, the next newest will replace the newest, as the two ends of the chain.

And if the chain has only one record (that is, duplicate keys are permitted but none actually exist) then deleting that record also deletes the index item, which may in turn trigger a merge of index pages if the number of items on a page falls below `PgMin` for the index.

The Reusable Page Chain

In Chapter 6 we met the pointers kept in the FCR to permit Btrieve to reuse pages and records that have become empty through deletion of material. Of the three reusability chains that Btrieve maintains, only one affects index pages—the `NxtReusePage` chain of reusable pages, at offset 0x0C in the FCR for both the old and the new file formats.

In version 6.15, Btrieve does not use the pointer; instead, the engine uses element `Free[n].nxpg` in one of the five FSPSET structures in array `Free` that starts at offset 0x98 of the FCR. In a single-user system, the value of n is always zero; up to five concurrent operations can occur within the file at one time, however, and each will have its own FSPSET data. Throughout this discussion, all references to `NxtReusePage` apply to `Free[n].nxpg` when using version 6.15.

Initially when Btrieve creates a file, the value set into `NxtReuse-Page` is 0xFFFFFFFF (the null value for a page pointer). This tells the engine that no reusable pages exist in the chain. Any time an index page's item count drops to zero, the page type code for that page changes from the 0x8X key-number indicator to 0x00, and Btrieve links the page into the reusable page chain.

As activity continues in a file, eventually an index page becomes empty. Then Btrieve copies the current value of `NxtReusePage` into the page being freed, at offset 0x008, and zeroes out the rest of the page except for the page header (first 6 bytes). The engine then copies the page pointer for the page being freed into `NxtReuse-Page`, creating the first link in the chain. After several repetitions of this action, the reusable page chain resembles Figure 7.5.

Figure 7.5 *Reusable Page chain for new-format file*

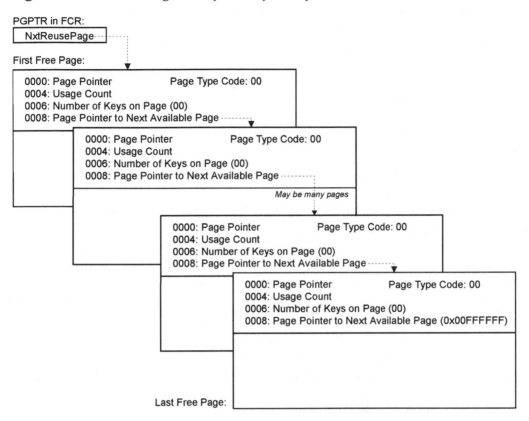

When Btrieve later needs a new index page, the engine takes the page pointed to by **NxtReusePage** (unless the value of **NxtReusePage** is 0xFFFFFFFF, indicating that no reusable pages exist), then copies the page pointer from offset 0x008 in that page back into **NxtReusePage**. When Btrieve takes the last page, this action automatically copies the end-of-chain flag into **NxtReuse-Page** so that the next time a page is needed, a brand new one will be allocated.

One exception exists to the rule that an index page moves onto the reusable page chain when its item count is zero: When Btrieve initially creates a file, the engine assigns empty index pages for each of its specified keys, and one empty page for data. This happens both for the original format and for the new format. Creating these empty pages prevents any "boundary-condition" problems that might arise from attempting to create the very first root page for any index. Similarly, when you delete the very last record from a Btrieve file, the index item counts for all keys drop to zero, but those pages remain in the file to duplicate the situation of having a newly created empty file. Btrieve uses the record count in the FCR to trigger this special-case action; only when the record count exceeds zero are index pages released to the reusable page chain.

The only significant differences between the chains maintained in the new file format (Figure 7.5) and those of the original format (Figure 7.6) are the presence of page type codes in the new format, which are changed for the new format but (not being there) require no action for the old.

Figure 7.6   *Reusable Page chain for original-format file*

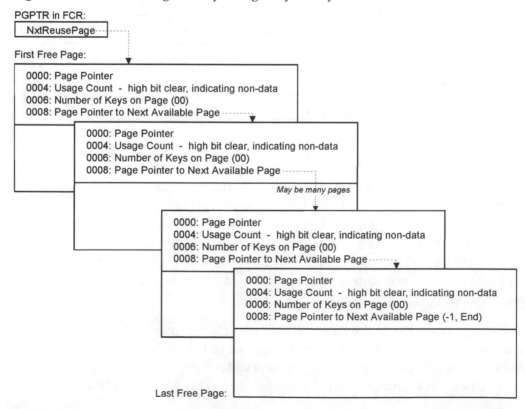

Supplemental Indexes

Before version 6.0 introduced the new file format, Btrieve did not permit any index defined at file creation time to be dropped later. New indexes, however, could be added. These indexes defined after file creation were called **supplemental indexes.** Unlike the original indexes, Btrieve permitted you to drop a supplemental index.

In the new file format, no distinction exists between original and supplemental indexes; any index can be dropped, and so long as the segment-count limit imposed by the file's page size allows, new indexes can be added. The only distinction that remains between original and later indexes is that an added index may be forced to use the repeated method of dealing with duplicate key values, when no reserved pointer space exists to allow use of the linked method.

In the original file format, supplemental key pages carry a key identifier in the high-order byte of their page number (the byte at offset 0x01 of each page), and normal index pages always have a value of 0x00 in this byte. No such distinction exists in the new format, for which this byte is always a page type code.

Key-Only Files

Btrieve permits creation of key-only files that contain no separate data records in themselves but serve as indexes to other Btrieve files. You may also find such files useful when records have just one key and that key consists of most of the record (such as a name table, for example). In a key-only file, the entire record becomes the Key Data field within each index item.

Key-only files have a number of restrictions: They may have only one key and may not use data compression. The maximum record size allowed is 253 bytes in the new format, or 255 for the original format (the 2-byte difference is the record-usage flag). However, if SSQL has specified referential-integrity constraints, the file may contain one or more variable-length pages. To create a key-only file, Bit 4 of the file's flag word must be set when the file is created.

To use a key-only file as an index for another Btrieve file, you must write a program that obtains the record address for each record of the file being indexed and inserts that address as part of the data field for the key-only file. Btrieve will not automatically maintain such external index files. Therefore, their use cannot be recommended as a generic practice.

INDEX.DDF Layout and Usage

In Chapter 5 we met the data dictionary files (FILE.DDF, INDEX.DDF, and FIELD.DDF) that allow Xtrieve, XQL, and Scalable SQL to implement fully relational databases using Btrieve as their foundation. In Chapter 6 we looked at FILE.DDF. Here, we examine INDEX.DDF in more detail.

In the data dictionary, each table within the relational database described by the data dictionary is in a distinct Btrieve file. INDEX.DDF, also known within the data dictionary as the X$Index table, holds all necessary information that relates index fields to files for all tables that the data dictionary defines.

INDEX.DDF contains five fields (or, in relational terms, columns). All are named, and all names begin with the three characters "Xi$" to identify them as dictionary-defined fields within the Index table. Layout of these fields within each row or record is shown in Table 7.1 (subsequent discussion drops the initial three characters except when necessary to eliminate any ambiguity).

The File and Field fields contain numeric values that identify the File and Field to which this segment definition applies. Chapter 6 listed the numeric values for the three DDF files, and in Chapter 8 we will meet the field identifiers. The Number field contains the index number within the file, starting with 0 for the first key in each file. Similarly, the Part field contains the segment number within each key, also starting at 0. Single-segment keys contain only segment 0. The Flags field contains key attribute flags that match those listed in Chapter 6

Table 7.1 *Fields in INDEX.DDF*

Field Name	Description	Data Type	Position	Length
Xi$File	Foreign key to File table	Integer	0	2
Xi$Field	Foreign key to Field table	Integer	2	2
Xi$Number	Index ID number within file	Integer	4	2
Xi$Part	Segment ID number within index	Integer	6	2
Xi$Flags	Key attribute flags (Kflags, in Chapter 6)	Integer	8	2

for K f l a g s. The value for this field is the decimal sum of all the individual key attribute values for the segment being specified.

INDEX.DDF contains two indexes as shown in Table 7.2.

Table 7.2 *Indexes in INDEX.DDF*

Index	Segment	Field	Description
0	0	Xi$File	Link to File table
1	0	Xi$Field	Link to Field table

Both indexes allow duplicate key values, and both are single-segment keys.

The default content of this table, normally not visible to users, defines all indexes associated with the three required data dictionary files. Table 7.3 shows these entries.

File 1 is FILE.DDF, File 2 is FIELD.DDF, and File 3 is INDEX.DDF. The two entries here for File 3 show that Key 0 uses Xi$File as its key field, and Key 1 uses Xi$Field.

Like all data dictionary files created by Btrieve's own utilities or accessories, INDEX.DDF carries an unpublicized owner name to

Table 7.3   *Default Values in INDEX.DDF Describe*
All Three DDF Files

File	Field	Number	Part	Flags
1	1	0	0	4
1	2	1	0	34
2	5	0	0	4
2	6	1	0	5
2	6	3	0	22
2	7	3	1	34
3	13	0	0	5
3	14	1	0	5

make it read-only for normal usage. The XQLP library (from the XQL product) provides routines that have the correct owner name built in.

In Chapter 8 we complete our examination of the data dictionary by looking at the Field table. All three must be used together to provide full data dictionary capabilities. All other DDF files serve only special purposes, and most programs such as ODBC ignore them.

Conclusion

In this chapter we examined details of Btrieve's key pages and of the INDEX.DDF data dictionary file. Chapter 8 concludes our study of the Btrieve file formats, with similar exploration of the many kinds of data pages that make Btrieve so versatile and of the FIELD.DDF data dictionary file.

8

Data Page Details

This chapter discusses in detail how to identify data pages and specific data records. It also explains the duplicate-key access chain that is embedded in each data record when linked duplicate keys (see Chapter 7) are specified. Btrieve reuses space that was occupied by deleted records, and this chapter describes how it's done. Layout and use of the FIELD.DDF file round out the information contained here.

Btrieve stores three distinct kinds of data records: those of fixed length, those of variable length, and those in which repeating characters are compressed to save space. All records include a fixed-length portion, and (except in the special case of data compression) all key segments must appear within this portion. This permits Btrieve to locate the key segments rapidly and effectively when a record is added or updated.

When dealing with compressed data, Btrieve uses the expanded data in the application's data buffer to create index key data items, but stores the address of the fixed-length (7 bytes in new format, 5 in the original) compressed-data descriptors in the index as the data record location. When a file contains variable length records, you can specify at creation time that Btrieve is to truncate trailing blanks from each record. In many cases doing so can achieve significant space reduction. However, since the blank-truncation mechanism is in effect a limited special case of data compression, it may be more effective to specify that the data be compressed, rather than using variable length records and truncation.

All access to data normally goes through the index mechanism. However, the Step functions (see Chapter 4) allow Btrieve to retrieve data in the physical sequence of the file. To make these functions possible, all fixed-length data pages have the high bit of their usage counts (the byte at offset 0x05 of each page, in all formats) set to 1. All other kinds of pages keep this bit clear. Btrieve can locate the first data record in any file by searching the pages sequentially from Page 1 and examining the byte at offset 5; the first one found with its high bit set is the first data page. Although the Page Type codes embedded in each page header make the usage-count flag redundant for the new file format, the convention continues in the interests of backward compatibility with older Btrieve versions and to minimize the amount of change necessary to the code that implements the Step functions.

Of the several kinds of data records possible, the simplest and possibly the most often used is the fixed-length data record. We examine such records first for the case in which every index key must be unique. Then we look at the way in which the record layout differs, when a file permits duplicate values in one or more of its key fields. Once we've examined these two situations (for both file formats), the remaining types of records become much simpler to comprehend. We next explore how Btrieve handles variable-length records, since a similar technique applies for data compression. We defer study of the special case of blank truncation within variable-length records until we've examined the compression algorithm, since truncation uses the same algorithm. Finally, we explore the FIELDS.DDF file from the data dictionary group.

Fixed-Length Records

For the new file format, fixed-length record pages in files that permit only unique key values follow the layout shown in Figure 8.1. Each such page contains only fixed-length records, and the Page Type Code D in the header identifies these pages. The high bit of the usage counter field is set, identifying these pages for the Step functions.

Within the page, every record begins with a 2-byte Record Usage field (Ruse in Figure 8.1) that indicates whether the record is currently valid. Every such record in the file is the same size (the explicit meaning of fixed-length). Because of the Record Usage field, this length is 2 bytes more than the value of RecLen maintained in the FCR. The PhyLen field of the FCR contains the total physical length of each record, in bytes. Many Btrieve functions use these two values to navigate through the files.

Figure 8.1   *Fixed-Length Data Storage in new format when all keys are unique*

FCR:

```
RecLen: 48 bytes (typical example)
PhyLen: 50 bytes
NumDupes: 0
```

```
0000: Page Pointer       Fixed-length "D" page 4
0004: Usage Count        (high bit set)
         Ruse   Data
0006: 1
0008:          48 bytes of data here, filling out field
0038: 1
003A:          Second valid record on page . . .
006A: 0        00 00089C   next free at 4:009C
009C: 0        00 0008CE   next free at 4:00CE
00CE: 0        00 000900   next free at 4:0100
0100: 0        00 000932   next free at 4:0132
0132: 0        00 000964   next free at 4:0164
0164: 0        00 000996   next free at 4:0196
0196: 0        00 0009C8   next free at 4:01C8
01C8: 0        00 FFFFFF   end of record chain
```

Each page contains as many records as can fit, and no record extends past the end of a page. The page header occupies the first 6 bytes of each page, so the first record begins at offset 0x006 within the page and continues for **PhyLen** bytes.

For the 50-byte **PhyLen** shown in Figure 8.1 and a page size of 512 bytes, each page can hold just ten records: the 512-byte page, minus 6 for the header, leaves 506 bytes for record storage. Dividing 506 by 50 gives us 10, with 6 bytes left over.

One of the essential factors, when laying out a Btrieve file's structure, is to balance its page size with the sizes of its data records to minimize waste space. For instance, using 2,048-byte pages with a record size of 1,024 bytes would waste nearly half the space the file would occupy. Since only 2,042 bytes of each page would be available for data, the file could hold just one record on each page, with 1,018 bytes wasted! I'm aware of at least one commercial product that does just this.

Since the maximum page size for a Btrieve file is 4,096 bytes, the largest fixed-length record possible is 4,090 bytes. Btrieve can store longer records, but only as variable-length data in which all index information appears in the first 4,000 bytes, or in compressed format.

Each time Btrieve allocates a fresh page to store fixed-length data records, the engine builds a complete set of record pointers that identifies each possible record location on that page. Part of this chain appears in Figure 8.1, as the next free data in every record with a record usage count of 0.

In the illustration, the final record space on the field holds the NULL indicator rather than a record pointer, indicating that the file contains no more fixed-length records space for reuse. When Btrieve finds this flag at the end of the free record chain, the engine allocates a fresh page and initializes all pointers on that page. We'll look at the free chains in more detail a bit later in this chapter and see how deleted records affect them.

The requirement that each fixed-length record be able to hold both the 2-byte record usage count and a 4-byte pointer to the next available record sets 6 bytes as the minimum possible size for a Btrieve data record in the new file format. In practice, nearly all actual record lengths are well above this minimum value.

The original file format uses a similar layout for its fixed-length data record pages, but they have neither a Page Type Code nor a Record Usage field (see Figure 8.2). This makes the values for RecLen and PhyLen the same in such files, and reduces the minimum record size to 4 rather than 6 bytes. No internal distinction exists between an unused record and a valid record that just by chance matches the format of an unused record: all zeroes except for the first 4 bytes and those 4 bytes appear to contain a valid record pointer. This (admittedly extremely unlikely) possibility makes the original format slightly more susceptible to accidental data corruption and was one of the reasons for adding the Record Usage field to the new format.

All the other rules of the new-format page layout apply; the waste space at the end of our example would increase from the 6 bytes of

Figure 8.2   *Fixed-Length Data Storage in original format when all keys are unique*

FCR:

```
RecLen: 48 bytes (typical example)
PhyLen: 48 bytes
NumDupes: 0
```

```
0000: Page Pointer        Fixed-length data page 4
0004: Usage Count         (high bit set to indicate data)

              Data
0006:      48 bytes of data here, filling out field
0036:      Second valid record on page . . .
0066:      0000896    next free at 4:096
0096:      00008C6    next free at 4:0C6
00C6:      00008F6    next free at 4:0F6
00F6:      0000926    next free at 4:126
0126:      0000956    next free at 4:156
0156:      0000986    next free at 4:186
0186:      00009B6    next free at 4:1B6
01B6:      FFFFFFFF End of Chain
```

the new format to 26 because there are no record usage fields. By increasing page size from 512 to 1,024 bytes, the waste could be almost entirely eliminated, since each page could then hold 21 records. Simply tailoring the page size to the data requirements yields a gain of 5 percent in the number of records possible, with no increase in file size.

One more difference between the original file format and the new one introduced at version 6.0 lies in the way Btrieve tracks its free space. In the original format, the engine maintains three pointers in the FCR: one (NxtReusePag) tracks available pages (see Chapter 7), the second (NxtReuseRec) tracks fixed-length records, and the last (VFree) tracks variable-length record space. The record pointers each contain the address of the corresponding kind of record that most recently became available for use, whether by a record deletion, or by creation of a new data page.

Each time Btrieve takes a record from the chain, the engine copies the address of the next free record from the first 4 bytes of the record itself into the appropriate pointer. When Btrieve takes the last record of a chain, its first 4 bytes contain the NULL value that signifies End of Chain, and this automatically tells the engine to create a new page next time it needs a record.

Similar actions occur for new-format files; however, instead of using the three pointers, the engine uses one of five FSPSET structures. Each such structure contains a page pointer, a record pointer, and a variable-record pointer. The five constitute an array that starts at off-set 0x098 in the FCR of the file. By having five sets of pointers rather than just one, the new format allows several users to work on a file concurrently without interfering with each other.

Duplicate-Key Access Chains

When a file permits duplicate values to exist in any of its keys, Btrieve adds two record pointers to the record for each such key. These pointers follow the data portion of the record. Thus, a file that allows duplicated values for two of its keys will have four record pointers appended to each data record as shown in Figure 8.3 for the new file format and Figure 8.4 for the original format. Since each pointer occupies 4 bytes, the value of PhyLen for this file is 16 bytes larger than it would be if no duplicate keys existed.

Each pair of pointers becomes part of a doubly linked chain that connects all records having duplicate values for the associated key. The association is by sequence of key numbers. For example, the page shown in Figure 8.3 (new format) or Figure 8.4 (original format) could be from a file having five different defined keys. Of the five, Keys 0, 2, and 3 require that values be unique, and Key 1 and Key 4 allow duplicated values. Only Key 1 and Key 4 add pointer pairs to each data record. The first pair associates with Key 1 since it's the first key (in the specifications contained in the FCR) that permits duplicates. The second pair associates with Key 4 since it's the next for which duplicates are valid.

Figure 8.3   *Data Storage, new format, when duplicate key values are permitted*

FCR:

```
RecLen: 48 bytes (typical example)
PhyLen: 66 bytes
NumDupes: 2
```

```
0000: Page Pointer        Fixed-length "D" page 4
0004: Usage Count         (high bit set)

       Ruse  Data          Duplicate Key Pointers
0006: 1
0008:               48 bytes of data here, filling out field
0038:                      prev rec for first dupl key
003C:                      next rec for first dupl key
0040:                      prev, 2nd dupl key
0044:                      next, 2nd dupl key

0048: 1
004A:               Second valid record on page . . .
007A:                      prev rec for first dupl key
007E:                      next rec for first dupl key
0082:                      prev, 2nd dupl key
0086:                      next, 2nd dupl key
008A: 0     next record, and so on
```

Figure 8.4 *Data Storage, original format, when duplicate key values are permitted*

FCR:

```
RecLen: 48 bytes (typical example)
PhyLen: 64 bytes
NumDupes: 2
```

```
0000: Page Pointer        Fixed-length page 4
0004: Usage Count         (high bit set to indicate data)

              Data        Duplicate Key Pointers
0006:         48 bytes of data here, filling out field
0036:                     prev rec for first dupl key
003A:                     next rec for first dupl key
003E:                     prev, 2nd dupl key
0042:                     next, 2nd dupl key

0046:         Second valid record on page . . .
0076:                     prev rec for first dupl key
007A:                     next rec for first dupl key
007E:                     prev, 2nd dupl key
0082:                     next, 2nd dupl key

0086:         next record, and so on
```

In each pointer pair, the first pointer addresses the previous record and the second pointer addresses the next in the chain. Both chains are circular. That is, neither has a beginning or an end. To determine when to stop, Btrieve remembers the record address at which it begins traversing the chain and stops upon reaching that record the second time.

This rule allows the system to traverse the entire chain without regard to any starting or ending point, no matter which data record is retrieved first. Since Btrieve permits you to change keys during an application without losing track of the current record, it's impossible to guarantee that any such chain will always be reached by means of an index lookup.

The meanings of previous and next regarding the duplicate-key chains can be confusing: The terms usually refer to the chronological age of the record. To illustrate how the chain is built while clarifying the definitions, consider a sequence in which we add three records to a file that permits duplicate keys in at least one field.

When we add the first record, no existing record in the entire file shares the duplicate key value and so Btrieve creates an index item for the new record (which we assume goes into the file at Offset 6 of Page 4). Since the file permits duplicate values for the key, the index entry includes record pointers for the First and Last record added. The data record includes record pointers for the previous and next records. However, this is the only record in the chain, so all four pointers (two in the index entry and two in the data record) contain the record's own address of Page 4, Offset 6, as shown in Figure 8.5.

Figure 8.5   *Duplicate key chain, first record entered for key*

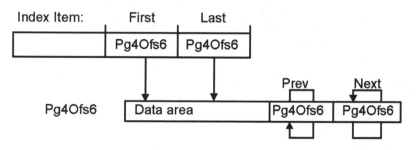

A front-to-back search, using this key as the current key for traversing the file, will begin at the record pointed to by the First pointer in the index item. A back-to-front search will use the record pointed to by the Last pointer. Since there's only one record, either direction retrieves it.

When Btrieve attempts to move through the file, the rule for ending a chain assures that the engine retrieves this record only once. Regardless of the direction of travel (from front to back, using Next, or from back to front, using Prev) the pointer contains the record's address, thus signaling Btrieve that it has reached the end of this chain.

Adding a second record with the same key to the file creates the situation shown in Figure 8.6. Btrieve stores the new record's address (assumed to be Offset 48 of Page 7) in the Last record pointer within

Figure 8.6   *Duplicate key chain, two records entered for same key*

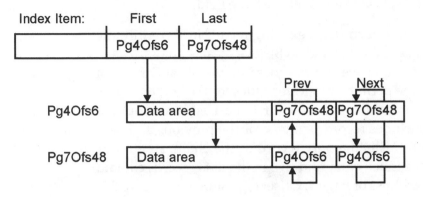

the index record but leaves the First pointer unaltered. In the original data record at Page 4 Offset 6, the engine stores the new record address as both the previous and the next records. Finally, when adding the new record at Page 7 Offset 48, Btrieve stores the address of the original record in both pointers.

Now, a front-to-back movement through the file, based on this key, will first retrieve the record at Page 4 Offset 6, which was the first of the two to be stored. The Next pointer in that record takes the engine to the second record, at Page 7 Offset 48. From this record, the Next pointer would go back to Page 4 Offset 6, but Btrieve recognizes this as its starting location and quits tracing through the duplicate-key chain. When we add one more record to the chain, as shown in Figure 8.7, we reach the completely generic representation of the way Btrieve handles linked duplicate-key values. (The other method of dealing with duplicate values that we met in Chapter 7 becomes, to the data record, the same situation as for unique keys.) When we add the new record at Page 9 Offset 6, both records addressed by the index item require change. The first record at Page 4 Offset 6 gets a new previous value, pointing to the new record at Page 9 Offset 6. The last record at Page 7 Offset 48 gets a new next value, also the address of the new record. The index item's pointer to the last record changes, holding the address of the new record. The new record shows the old last record as its previous link, and the first record as its next, keeping the chain intact in both directions.

Figure 8.7   *Duplicate key chain, three records entered for same key*

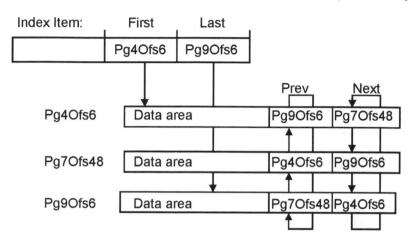

Additional records go into the file in the same way. Each new record becomes the previous record to the first data record, the next record for the last data record, and points back to the last and forward to the first. Its address goes into the index item as last so that reverse-direction movement becomes possible. The only limit to growth of these chains is that imposed by the 4-GB file-size; in practice, physical storage capacity usually cuts the figure down.

Variable-Length Records

When you define the records within a Btrieve file as being of variable length, Btrieve divides them into a fixed-length portion and a variable-length portion. As always in Btrieve, only one kind of record appears on any page, so the data in a file that has variable-length records spreads over at least two pages. The fixed-length part of the record can occupy any number of bytes (up to the maximum that will fit on the page) and must contain all index key fields.

The example shown in Figure 8.8, based on the ATTRIBUTES.DDF file provided as part of the Xtrieve Plus tutorial, has only 5 bytes of fixed-length data: the first 2 bytes are a 16-bit autoincrement field holding the ID field used as a primary key, the next byte holds an attribute code of "H", "M", or "V" and the final 2 bytes are a 16-bit binary field

Figure 8.8   *Variable-Length Record Layout, new format*

```
0000: Page Pointer       Fixed-length "D" page 4
0004: Usage Count        (high bit set)
     Ruse       Atr              Variable-Length Record
                ID          Length   Page        Record
0006: 1 1B 00  H          0A 00    00 05       00 00
0011: 1 1E 00  H          05 00    00 05       00 01
001C: 1 21 00  M          0A 00    00 05       00 02
0027: 1 1F 00  V          15 00    00 05       00 03
0032: 0 00 00 3D 04       next free at 4:003D
003D: 0
0048: 0        0000: Page Pointer           Variable-length "V" page 5
0053: 0        0004: Usage Count
               0006: Vrecord pointer to next variable page
               000A: Number of fragments on page
                          Next Frag   Data
01EA: 0        000C: FFFF FFFF Patient ID
01F5: 0        001A: FFFF FFFF AM/PM
               0023: FFFF FFFF $ZZ,ZZZ.99
               0031: FFFF FFFF Benbrook.Farlow.Drake
               004A: 0000 0000 (space not yet used on page)


               01F6: 3A 00     offset, free space
               01F8: 25 00     offset, fragment 3
               01FA: 1B 00     offset, fragment 2
               01FC: 16 00     offset, fragment 1
               01FE: 0C 00     offset, fragment 0
```

holding the length of the variable data. For each record, a variable-length record pointer follows the fixed-length portion of the record, indicating where the variable-length portion of the record begins.

Unlike the normal record pointer, which gives logical page number and offset within that page, the variable-length record pointer always uses 3 bytes for the logical page number and 1 byte as a fragment number. This limits the maximum number of fragments on a Type V (variable-length record) page to 255. Normally, a page fills with data well before approaching this limit.

Variable-length record pages use a double-pointer technique to identify each fragment of a record (see Figure 8.8). Every variable-length record page begins at offset 0x006, with a variable-length record pointer to the next page in the V chain. The last page of the chain has a NULL pointer in this location (page 0xFFFFFF). Following this link pointer is a 16-bit binary field holding the number of fragments the page contains. In our example, it's 4. The first offset available within the page for storing a fragment is at 0x00C. However, fragments are addressed by number (starting at zero), and the fragment number is an index into a reverse-sequenced array that occupies the last few words of the page. In the example shown, page size is 512 (0x200) and the five-word array (one for each fragment plus one for free space) starts 10 bytes before the end, at offset 0x1F6.

Fragment 0's entry in this table is the final word on the page, at offset 0x01FE. Fragment 1 gets the entry immediately before that one, and so on. These entries hold the actual offset on the page at which the data for that fragment begins. It's more accurate to say "at which that fragment begins," because the first 4 bytes at that address are a pointer to the next link for the fragment. A valid fragment has a nonzero value in this count, and free space holds all zeroes. Following the pointer are the bytes of the fragment.

The first entry in this table (that is, the one at the lowest address, immediately before the entry for the final fragment of the page) holds the offset of the first space on the page that's available for storing data. As more and more fragments occupy the page, the data itself grows toward the end of the page while the pointer table grows toward the beginning. Eventually, the two may meet. At this point the free-space offset entry of the pointer table will hold its own address. This signals Btrieve that no more space remains on the page.

Since the length of variable-length data may change from one record to the next, it's possible that the free space on the page may be less than the 5 bytes necessary to hold any valid fragment but still be greater than zero. Btrieve detects this condition and interprets it just as if the pointer held its own address: the page is out of room.

If a variable-length record is too large to fit onto a single page, Btrieve splits it into multiple fragments, chaining each to the next in the same way that the fixed-length portion of the record chains to the first fragment. The pointer at the start of each fragment is the variable-length record pointer to the next fragment. The final fragment holds a NULL pointer (0xFFFFFFFF); this is the case in our example since no fragment extends to an additional page.

Each variable-length data page can hold at most a single fragment of a specific record. Any other fragments must be on other pages. Since Btrieve locks pages, rather than records, when operating in a multiuser environment, this requirement reduces the length of time that any page remains locked when editing large records. When deleting data from variable-length pages, fragment renumbering never occurs. Instead, the offset value for any deleted fragment becomes 0xFFFF. The data itself, though, closes up to fill the gap. This causes all offsets to change and may make space available on pages that had been full. The ability to close up gaps without changing the variable-length record pointers associated with the fragment is the reason for the complicated double-pointer technique.

In the original file format, variable-length record pages are much the same (see Figure 8.9). They have no page type codes, record usage counters, or VATs, but follow the same rules for dividing

Figure 8.9   *Variable-Length Record Layout, original format*

0000: Page Pointer		Fixed-length data page 2			
0004: Usage Count		(high bit set to indicate data)			
ID	Atr	Len	Vrec Pg	Vrec Rec	
0006: 1B 00	H	0A 00	00 03	00 00	
000F: 1E 00	H	05 00	00 03	00 01	
0018: 21 00	M	0A 00	00 03	00 02	
0021: 1F 00	V	15 00	00 03	00 03	
002A: (available space on page)					

0000: Page Pointer	Variable-length record page 3
0004: Usage Count	
0006: Vrecord pointer to next variable page	
000A: Number of fragments on page	

000C: Patient ID
0016: AM/PM
001B: $ZZ,ZZZ.99
0025: Benbrook.Farlow.Drake
003A: (space not yet used on page)

01F6: 3A 00	offset, free space
01F8: 25 00	offset, fragment 3
01FA: 1B 00	offset, fragment 2
01FC: 16 00	offset, fragment 1
01FE: 0C 00	offset, fragment 0

fixed-length and variable-length portions of each record between pages. Note that the next-fragment pointer at the start of each fragment exists only if needed; for the final fragment of any chain, this pointer isn't there. If the pointer exists, the high bit of the offset pointer table entry for the fragment is set to 1. Since all the records in this example needed only one fragment, none of them have any next-fragment pointer.

The Variable-Tail Allocation Table

If a file contains very large records, the number of fragments may grow accordingly. For instance, if the file has the maximum page size of 4,096 bytes and includes records of 409,600 bytes each (not an impossible size for some kinds of data), then each record must be spread over at least 100 different pages. The problem didn't exist before version 6.0 because older versions of Btrieve required that the entire record fit within a data buffer at one time, and the data buffer size parameter in the control block had only 16 bits. Consequently maximum record size was only 64K (less in a network environment, where network constraints applied).

The pure linked-list approach works, regardless of the number of fragments involved, but Btrieve may well spend a large part of its time sequentially reading through that list to locate a relatively small chunk of data that's near the end of each record. To reduce the overhead necessary in such nonsequential access to parts of very large records, Btrieve introduced a new file structure at version 6.1 called the Variable-Tail Allocation Table (VAT).

In a file containing VATs, each record that has a variable-length portion has its own VAT, stored on variable pages associated with that record. Btrieve divides the variable-length portion of the record into smaller sections according to an internal formula based on page size, then stores each of those sections in a number of variable tails. By reversing the calculation when it's time to retrieve part of the record, Btrieve can determine which of the intermediate variable tails contains the desired portion; by using the VAT, it can immediately locate that area without having to traverse all the intermediate fragments involved. In version 6.1, each intermediate variable tail's length is eight times the page size (except, of course, for the last). This formula, however, may change in future versions.

To use the VAT technique, you must specify it when creating the file. Unless you are using the new chunk operations on records that are more than eight times your file's page size, you'll gain little or nothing from using VATs. If you use only whole-record operations, VATs waste only a little space since Btrieve uses them only during chunk operations.

Compressed Records

If your file will contain records that include many repeated strings of characters, you may find significant resource savings possible by using data compression in the file. Btrieve's data compression algorithm is quite primitive when compared to such compression techniques as the LZW technique, but is also quite effective within its limitations. When you tell Btrieve to compress data in a file, the records become variable-length even though you specifically request fixed-length data. The reason for this is that the length of a record after compression depends entirely on its content. It may be 2 bytes longer than it would have been uncompressed, or it may be reduced to just 3 bytes regardless of original length. These, of course, represent extreme cases and most records will be somewhere in between; reduction in size to between 50 and 75 percent of the uncompressed size is a realistic expectation for the usual business data.

Btrieve's handling of a compressed-data file differs from that of a variable-length record file in only two major respects: The Insert and Update operations cannot produce a record longer than the specified fixed record length when compression is used, and a compressed-data file may include key fields. In a variable-length record file, all key fields must occur only in the fixed-length portion of the records.

Btrieve uses only one compression algorithm at this time, although the file format specification allows up to 255 algorithms. This algorithm, identified as Algorithm 1, is a simple run-length encoding of the original data string. Figure 8.10 shows how it works.

Figure 8.10 *Data compression algorithm 1*

Original string:

ABCDEFGHIJ	KKKKKKKKKKKKKK	LMNOPQR	SSSSSSSSSSSS
10 chars	14 chars	7 chars	12 chars

Total string length = 43 bytes

Compressed using Algorithm 1:

10	ABCDEFGHIJ	14	K	7	LMNOPQR	12	S	*net savings*
2	10	2	1	2	7	2	1	16

Total string length = 27 bytes

In this example, the original string contains a sequence of ten characters ("ABCDEFGHIJ"), followed by fourteen repetitions of the character "K." Next is a seven-character sequence ("LMNOPQR") followed by twelve repetitions of "S" that fill the 43-byte record to capacity.

The compression algorithm detects the repeating groups and replaces each with a count followed by a single copy of the repeated character. A length count also precedes each of the non-repeating sequences. Btrieve always writes a compressed file's data using a four-item repeating pattern: count-copy-count-repeat. The example in Figure 8.10 follows this pattern. If the first string hadn't been there, the encoding would have been "0 14 'K' 7 'LMNOPQR' 12 'S'" instead.

This fixed pattern is the secret to determining whether a count indicates the number of times to repeat the next byte or the number of bytes to literally copy to the output. Any time a count of zero occurs, its associated string isn't there. This can happen only for strings to be copied because absence of a byte to be repeated simply merges two copy-strings into one.

The example in Figure 8.10 is somewhat contrived, but shows a net savings of 16 bytes for the compressed version when compared to the original input. In practice, many files contain entire fields that are often left blank. Such fields can compress to just 3 bytes: a 16-bit length value followed by the single blank. If two or more such fields adjoin each other, savings can be even greater, since Btrieve ignores field boundaries within a record when compressing it.

When breaking the compressed data stream into fragments, Btrieve may split the stream in any of four places. The break can occur inside a copy string, immediately before a count word, between the two bytes of a copy word, or between a count word and its associated data. Only the break immediately before a count word corresponds to what's considered the normal case. The other three situations require special treatment when rebuilding the stream to retrieve the record. This is the reason that Btrieve requires the compression buffer to be at least twice the size of the largest fully expanded record. When a file contains compressed data, a 16-bit field in the FCR (`ComprLen` at offset 0x10E for all formats) holds the fully expanded length of each data record. The `RecLen` and `PhyLen` fields differ from what one might expect, though, as we are about to see.

Like a variable-length record file, a compressed file has data pages. These pages, which carry Page Type Code D, establish the record address for indexing, for Step and Get operations, and for duplicate key chains. In the new file format, each fixed-length data page contains 7 bytes of information about each record (see Figure 8.11). The first 4 bytes are a variable-length record pointer to the actual data. The next byte contains the algorithm number (0 for unused records, 1 for the only current algorithm, with 2 through 255 reserved for possible future expansion). The final 2 bytes are a 16-bit binary record usage count, nonzero for valid records and zero for those not in use.

Since none of the record's actual data appears on the data page, the value of `RecLen` in the FCR for such a file is zero. The value of `PhyLen`, however, is 7 (if no duplicate-key pointer pairs exist; if they do, `PhyLen's` value increases accordingly). The data itself, in compressed form, appears on the variable-length V page to which the variable-length record pointer takes us.

Figure 8.11 also shows how Btrieve maintains its free space chains for all types of index and data operations. The page shown originally contained a third data record, at offset 0006 of the data page. This record used Fragment 0 of variable-length Page 7 for its data. After deleting that record, the record pointer at offset 0006 of data page 2 changed from a variable-length pointer to become a record pointer addressing the second free record on the page, at offset 0x001B. The n x r e c element of the F r e e array in the FCR points to Page 2 Offset 6, indicating that this is the first candidate for reuse when another record is added to the file.

Figure 8.11 *Compressed data record, new format*

FCR freespace pointers:

```
Free[0].nxpg    = NULL
Free[0].nxrec   = Page 2 Offset 6
Free[0].nxvrec  = Page 5 Fragment 0
```

```
0000: Page Pointer        Fixed-length "D" page 2
0004: Usage Count         (high bit set)
        VRecPtr                    Dupl-Key Ptrs (if any)
                    Algo.   Ruse
        Page Frag                   Prev     Next
0006:  0002 001B   0       0        deleted record
000D:  0005 0001   1       1     xxxxxxxx xxxxxxxx
0014:  0005 0002   1       1     xxxxxxxx xxxxxxxx
001B:  0002 0022   0       0        unused record
0022:
0029:
0030:
0037:
```

```
0000: Page Pointer            Variable-length "V" page 5
0004: Usage Count
0006: Page pointer to next variable page (NULL here)
000A: Number of fragments on page (3 in example)

000C:  FF FF FF FF 0A 00 "1223334444" 05 00 "5" 00 00
       06 00 "6" 00 00 07 00 "7" 00 00 08 00 "8" 00 00 09
       00 "9" 00 00 0A 00 "0" 1A 00 "this is the leftover ar
       ea." 13 00 00
0057:  similar second record . . .
00A2:  free space . . .

01F8: A2 00   offset, free space
01FA: 57 00   offset, fragment 2
01FC: 0C 00   offset, fragment 1
01FE: FF FF   fragment 0 deleted
```

In the variable-length page, Btrieve moved all data up to close the gap and fixed the offset pointers for the remaining fragments and for free space to reflect the resulting new addresses. The offset pointer for Fragment 0 became 0xFFFF, indicating availability for reuse of that fragment number. The next time a record is added to this page, it will become Fragment 0, since that's what `Free[0].nxrec` contains as the next free variable-length record.

Except for the absence of record usage fields in the fixed-length data pages and the different locations for the free space pointers in the FCR, compressed records in the original file format are essentially identical to those in the new (see Figure 8.12).

Note that in both examples Btrieve treats any sequence of four or fewer repetitions of a character as a unique sequence. The reason for this is to avoid excessive overhead. It takes 2 bytes to hold the repetition count, 1 for the byte itself, and 2 more for the following copy count word. Nothing could be gained by attempting to compress runs of fewer than five characters; doing so would actually increase the string length.

Blank Truncation

When you define a file that uses variable-length records, you can also specify that Btrieve is to truncate any trailing blanks from the variable-length portion of each record. If you do so, Btrieve writes a modified form of a compression record as the last 2 or 4 bytes of each record, instead of any trailing blanks. Btrieve truncates only those blanks that appear in the variable-length portion of the record. Any in the fixed-length portion of the record remain unchanged. If you specify this option for a fixed-length file, Btrieve sets the flag bit but pays no attention at all to it. The resulting file is indistinguishable from a normal fixed-length file.

In most situations, using data compression will be far more effective than specifying blank truncation, since compression applies not

Figure 8.12 *Compressed data record, original format*

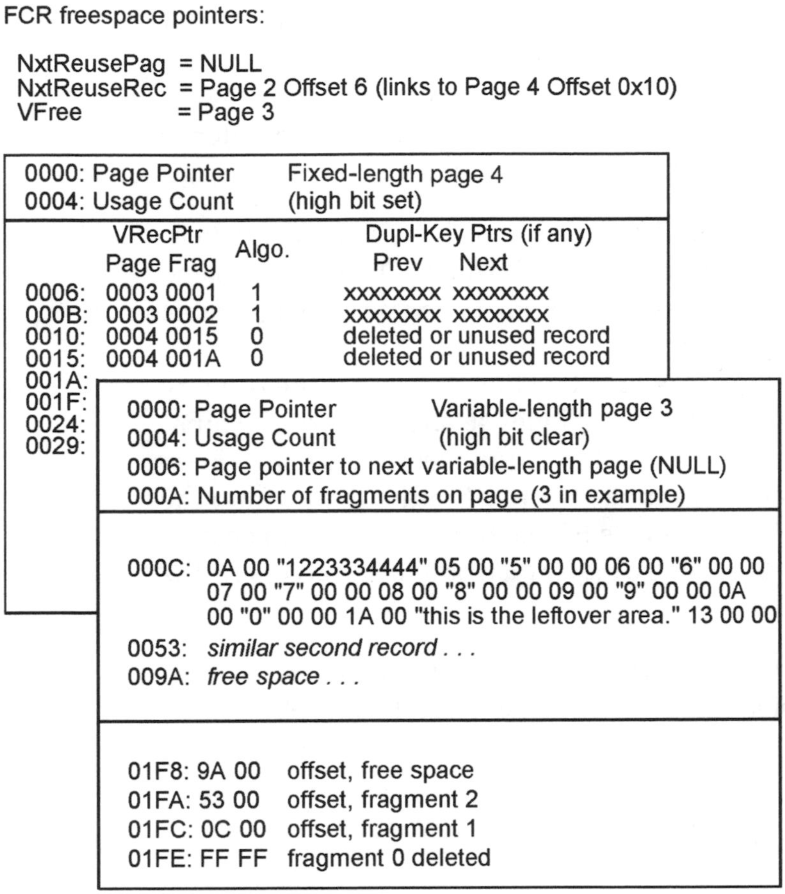

FCR freespace pointers:

```
NxtReusePag = NULL
NxtReuseRec = Page 2 Offset 6 (links to Page 4 Offset 0x10)
VFree       = Page 3
```

```
0000: Page Pointer         Fixed-length page 4
0004: Usage Count          (high bit set)
```

	VRecPtr Page Frag	Algo.	Dupl-Key Ptrs (if any) Prev Next
0006:	0003 0001	1	xxxxxxxx xxxxxxxx
000B:	0003 0002	1	xxxxxxxx xxxxxxxx
0010:	0004 0015	0	deleted or unused record
0015:	0004 001A	0	deleted or unused record
001A:			
001F:			
0024:			
0029:			

```
0000: Page Pointer         Variable-length page 3
0004: Usage Count          (high bit clear)
0006: Page pointer to next variable-length page (NULL)
000A: Number of fragments on page (3 in example)
```

```
000C:  0A 00 "1223334444" 05 00 "5" 00 00 06 00 "6" 00 00
       07 00 "7" 00 00 08 00 "8" 00 00 09 00 "9" 00 00 0A
       00 "0" 00 00 1A 00 "this is the leftover area." 13 00 00
0053:  similar second record . . .
009A:  free space . . .
```

```
01F8: 9A 00    offset, free space
01FA: 53 00    offset, fragment 2
01FC: 0C 00    offset, fragment 1
01FE: FF FF    fragment 0 deleted
```

only to trailing blanks but to any other sequences of repeating characters longer than 5 bytes.

When you request blank truncation, Btrieve adds a 2-byte blank count value to the end of the variable portion of the record unless VATs are in use. If VATs are present in the file, the count field becomes 4 bytes long. Upon retrieving a record, Btrieve reconstitutes (in the data buffer) any blanks that were truncated from it at storage time.

Relational Integrity Records

If you create a Btrieve file using SSQL and a version 6.0 or later engine, the engine will store information necessary to maintain relational integrity (RI) within your file automatically when creating the file. The FCR contains a special variable-length record pointer to such data, and the data itself goes onto a variable-length record page.

The format of such special RI records includes the signature pattern 00 00 00 01 as the first 4 bytes, followed by the SQL database name in bytes 4 through 23. Bytes 24 through 43 contain the SQL table name while the 16-bit binary value at bytes 44 and 45 holds the number of relationships to which this file contributes the primary key. Finally, another 16-bit value at bytes 46 and 47 holds the number of relationships to which this file contributes a foreign key. Having this data available within the file itself rather than within the data dictionary makes it possible for the Btrieve engines to enforce referential integrity at all times, rather than only when accessing the file by relational methods.

So long as the file was originally created using SSQL, the Btrieve engine's latest versions enforce RI even when not using SSQL.

Encrypted Data

One feature of Btrieve is, quite deliberately, omitted from discussion in this book. That's the subject of precisely how Btrieve encrypts data when you specify an owner name and specifically request data encryption. Any publication of the methods that implement this feature could serve no useful purpose and would dilute any security offered by encryption. Usefulness of this feature is, itself, open to serious question. To achieve real protection of the data stored in a file requires far more sophisticated encryption algorithms, which would in turn be counterproductive to Btrieve's capabilities both in resource efficiency and in operating speed.

If you decide to encrypt your data, remember that it will be essentially impossible to recover any of it should your files become corrupted for any reason. Recovery of data from files that are not encrypted is a simple matter, and frequently every record can be restored even though indexes may have been destroyed by a hardware malfunction. When data is encrypted, however, recovering any data becomes doubtful at best.

Thus, if you choose encryption, be certain you have good backups of every critical file, and keep them current. The data you save will be your own, should disaster strike your system.

FIELD.DDF Layout and Use

In Chapter 5 we met the data dictionary files (FILE.DDF, INDEX.DDF, and FIELD.DDF) that allow Xtrieve, XQL, and Scalable SQL to implement fully relational databases using Btrieve as their foundation. In Chapter 6 we looked at FILE.DDF. In Chapter 7 we explored INDEX.DDF. Here, we complete our data dictionary study with a look at FIELD.DDF in more detail.

Btrieve limits its concern with the idea of fields within a record to the specification of key segments. Only the record size, in bytes, appears in the FCR of any Btrieve file. Applications remain free to define fields within each record, or even to define multiple record layouts, with no restrictions from the record manager. However, since most database organization refers to fields or columns of data, XQL, Xtrieve, SSQL, and ODBC applications use the data dictionary composed of the DDF files. In the data dictionary, each table of the relational database described by the data dictionary is a distinct Btrieve file. Within that file, each column of the table is a distinct field of each record.

FIELD.DDF (also known in the data dictionary as the X$Field table) defines fields within each file's records (or, in relational terms, columns within each table). FIELD.DDF contains eight fields. All are named, and all names begin with the three characters Xe$ to identify them as dictionary-defined fields within the Field table. Layout of these fields within each row or record is shown in Table 8.1 (subsequent discussion drops the initial three characters except when necessary to eliminate any ambiguity).

Table 8.1   *Fields in FIELD.DDF*

Field Name	Description	Data Type	Position	Length
Xe$ID	File ID number (assigned automatically)	Integer	1	2
Xe$File	Foreign key to File table	Integer	2	2
Xe$Name	Field name used within data dictionary	String	4	20
Xe$DataType	Data type code, or 0xFF if supp index	Integer	24	1
Xe$Offset	Start of field in record, or index ID number if this is supplemental index	Integer	25	2
Xe$Size	Length of field in bytes	Integer	27	2
Xe$Dec	Number of decimal places	Integer	29	1
Xe$Flags	Reserved; 0xFF00 in data dictionary fields	Integer	30	2

The ID field contains a numeric identifier assigned by the data dictionary programs when creating a new field. This value is unique within the data dictionary and serves as the primary key when defining relations with other tables. The File field contains the value of Xf$Id (Chapter 6) for the file containing this field. This associates the field record with the file of which the field is a part. The Name field contains the field name. The data dictionary (and all utilities that use it) refers to the field by name, rather than by offset and length. The DataType field identifies the type of data that the field contains. Chapter 5 discusses data types in detail. If this field contains the value 0xFF, the record refers to a supplemental index rather than to a data field. The Offset field specifies the location within a data record at which the field begins (if this record refers to a data field). If this record refers to a supplemental index, the Offset field contains the Index ID number for the index. The Size field specifies the length, in bytes, of the field. The Dec field applies to the

Decimal, Numeric, and STS data types and specifies the location of the implied decimal point within the field. The Flags field content has not been released for publication. All data dictionary field entries contain the value 0xFF00 in this field.

FIELD.DDF contains four indexes (see Table 8.2).

Table 8.2   *Indexes in FIELD.DDF*

Index	Segment	Field	Description
0	0	Xe$Id	Primary Key
1	0	Xe$File	Link to File
2	0	Xe$Name	Sort by name
3	0	Xe$File	Link by file and name
	1	Xe$Name	

Index 1 allows duplicate key values but the other three do not. Indexes 0, 1, and 2 are single-segment keys. Both Name segments use the UPPER ACS to achieve case-insensitive sort sequence.

The default content of this table, normally not visible to users, consists of the 17 fields defined for the three required data dictionary files (four for FILE.DDF, eight for FIELD.DDF, and five for INDEX.DDF). These entries appear in Table 8.3.

Like all data dictionary files created by Btrieve's utilities or accessories, FIELD.DDF carries an unpublicized owner name to make it read-only for normal usage. The XQLP library (from the XQL product) provides routines that have the correct owner name built in.

This completes our examination of the data dictionary. All three files (FILE.DDF, FIELD.DDF, and INDEX.DDF) must be used together to provide full data dictionary capabilities. All other DDF files serve only special purposes, and most programs such as ODBC ignore them.

Table 8.3   *Default Values in FIELD.DDF*

ID	File	Name	Data Type	Offset	Size	Dec	Flags
1	1	Xf$Id	Integer	0	2	0	-256
2	1	Xf$Name	String	2	20	0	-256
3	1	Xf$Loc	String	22	64	0	-256
4	1	Xf$Flags	Integer	86	1	0	-256
5	2	Xe$Id	Integer	0	2	0	-256
6	2	Xe$File	Integer	2	2	0	-256
7	2	Xe$Name	String	4	20	0	-256
8	2	Xe$DataType	Integer	24	1	0	-256
9	2	Xe$Offset	Integer	25	2	0	-256
10	2	Xe$Size	Integer	27	3	0	-256
11	2	Xe$Dec	Integer	29	1	0	-256
12	2	Xe$Flags	Integer	30	2	0	-256
13	3	Xi$File	Integer	0	2	0	-256
14	3	Xi$Field	Integer	2	2	0	-256
15	3	Xi$Number	Integer	4	2	0	-256
16	3	Xi$Part	Integer	6	2	0	-256
17	3	Xi$Flags	Integer	8	2	0	-256

Conclusion

We've now completed our examination both of Btrieve's file formats for each kind of page the system uses and of the essential parts of the data dictionary files. This brings us to the end of Part II of this book.

In Chapters 9 through 12 we explore the kinds of utilities available to help support Btrieve developers and users, create some utility programs of our own, then spend one chapter each on the subjects of achieving optimum performance and recovering from disasters.

9

Related Programs and Utilities

This chapter lists and briefly describes programs and utilities for use with Btrieve. It begins with the packages that BTI furnishes as part of the Btrieve engine kits. The listings and descriptions continue for those utilities available from third-party vendors, with conventional commercial packages and shareware offerings listed separately. Not all the interesting utilities available carry a price tag; some are available on BBS systems as freeware. Finally, CD-ROM publishers provide a relatively new means of obtaining utilities that might otherwise be unavailable to you.

We have attempted to make these listings as accurate as possible at the time of publication, but both the commercial and shareware marketplaces exhibit rapid change. New products appear without prior warning, and existing products may disappear overnight. Therefore, it's not possible to guarantee that the information in this chapter will remain accurate over the passage of time. Always verify a vendor's situation before sending a prepaid order.

BTI Utilities

Each of the Btrieve client engines comes with a suite of utility programs that between them provide full support for file creation, editing, and maintenance. Separate program suites exist for each platform supported.

In the DOS Engine Kits

Each Btrieve for DOS client engine, whether the restricted one shipped in the Developer Kit or the unrestricted version sold separately, includes the following utilities as part of the package. Standard installation places these files in the \BTI\DOS\BIN directory.

BREBUILD.EXE   This program converts original-format files to the new format and creates a log of its actions. It need be run only once for most systems.

BREQUEST.EXE   This file is the DOS requester for network use with the server engine. It must be loaded, instead of BTRIEVE.EXE, to access the server engine. With version 6.0 and later engines, both the local and the server engines may be in use at the same time. With older engines, only one of the two could be loaded. Having both loaded often resulted in data file corruption.

BROLLFWD.EXE   This command-line driven utility allows recovery of logged changes to file from the time of the last backup to the time of system failure. Logging must be in use for this utility to do any good.

BSETUP.EXE   This interactive utility creates and maintains the BTI.CFG file (system configuration).

BTREXEC.EXE   This is an interactive function executor that replaces the older B.EXE program. Its purpose is to allow you to issue single Btrieve function calls when testing or troubleshooting.

BUTIL.EXE   This command-line driven File Manager utility can create, save, restore, or load files. It also permits checking the version of Btrieve that is loaded and can unload both the local Btrieve engine and the server requester from memory.

PMSWITCH.EXE   This DOS Extender automatically loads the client engine when you issue the command "BTRIEVE" at the command line.

RMINFO.EXE   This Phar-Lap utility reports information about the current RAM configuration.

In the Windows Engine Kits

The Btrieve for Windows engine kits include a different set of support utilities. During installation, these all go into the \BTI\WIN \BIN directory by default. The setup program creates a Btrieve Tools group in Program Manager and adds to it icons for the four interactive applications together with applicable information files as shown in Figure 9.1.

BGBMNG.EXE   This program, never executed directly, is the File Manager's background processor.

Figure 9.1   *Btrieve Tools group in Windows Program Manager*

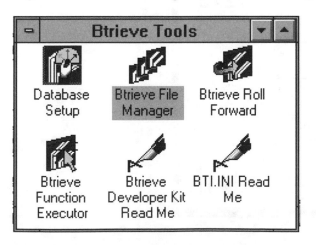

BREQUEST.EXE   This DOS requester must be used in NetWare applications to access the server engine. You must load BREQUEST before you load Windows.

BREQUTIL.EXE   This DOS program allows unloading of BREQUEST from memory; it also reports version information. The program is actually a limited version of BUTIL.EXE, with only the -VER and -STOP options enabled.

DBSETUP.EXE   This interactive application configures the BTI.INI file that controls all options of the Btrieve engine when running through the Windows DLL interface. Figure 9.2 shows the editing screen of this program.

WBEXEC.EXE   This is an interactive Btrieve function executor, similar to the DOS B.EXE utility.

Figure 9.2   *Btrieve Windows Setup utility in action*

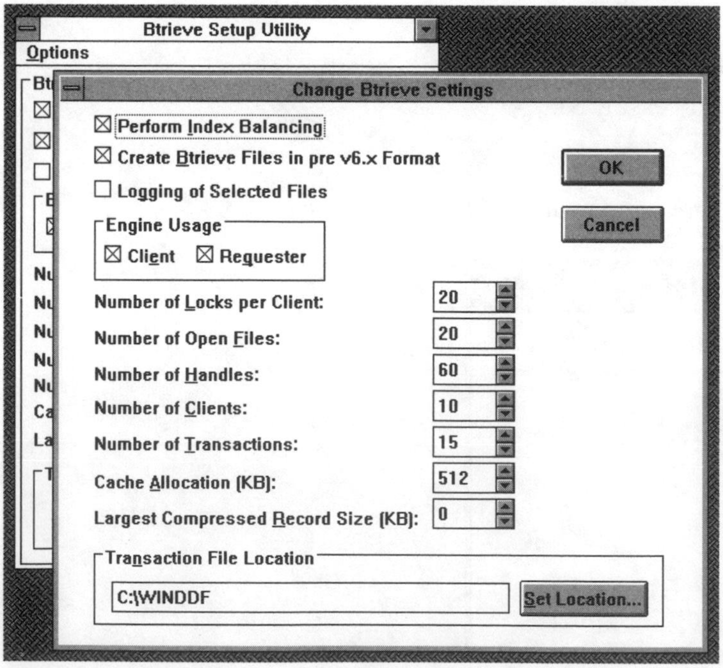

WBMANAGE.EXE   This program is an interactive File Manager workstation application, functionally similar to the DOS utility BUTIL.EXE, that enables you to create and edit Btrieve data files. Figure 9.3 shows the main screen of this program.

WBROLL.EXE   This interactive workstation utility allows you to recover changes made to a Btrieve file between the last backup and a system failure, provided that you have a log file. It's functionally equivalent to the DOS utility BROLLFWD.EXE.

WBTR32.EXE   This file is the actual client engine, for 32-bit operation under Windows DPMI server. It's never run directly, but instead is called by the Windows DLL when needed.

In the OS/2 Engine Kits

The Btrieve for OS/2 kits include still a different set of support utilities. During installation, these all go into the \BTI\OS2\BIN directory by default. The setup program creates a Btrieve Tools group

Figure 9.3   *Btrieve Windows File Manager in action*

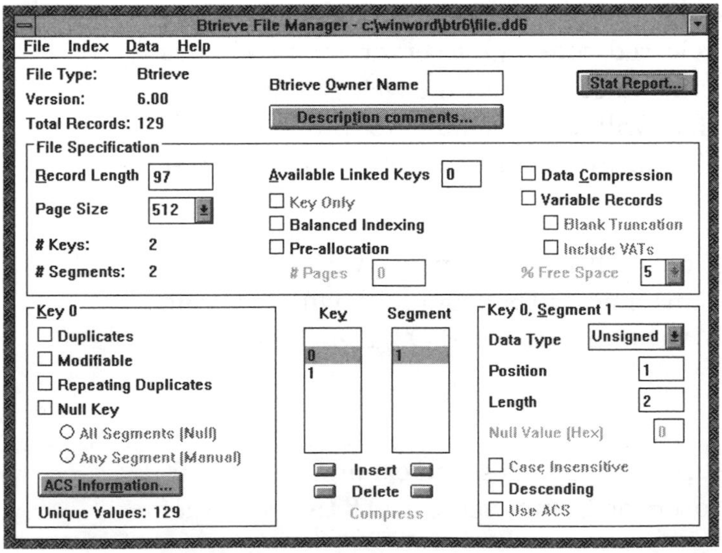

and adds to it icons for the four interactive applications together with applicable information files.

OS2MKDE.EXE   This is the Microkernel Database Engine, never invoked directly. Applications call it by using the WBTRCALL.DLL functions.

OS2FEXEC.EXE   This is an interactive Btrieve function executor, similar to the DOS B.EXE or Windows WBEXEC.EXE utilities.

OS2FMAN.EXE   This program is an interactive File Manager workstation application, functionally similar to the DOS utility BUTIL.EXE or the Windows WBMANAGE.EXE, which enables you to create and edit Btrieve data files.

PBROLL.EXE   This interactive workstation utility allows you to recover changes made to a Btrieve file between the last backup and a system failure, provided that you have a log file. It's functionally equivalent to the DOS utility BROLLFWD.EXE and the Windows version WBROLL.EXE.

In the Windows NT Engine Kits

At the time of writing, neither a server engine nor a client engine for Windows NT had been released, although a server engine kit was undergoing beta test. Its scheduled release date was first quarter of 1995. This is the kit that will be available to purchasers of Microsoft's NTAS for $99 during the first twelve months after release.

Filenames for the utilities that will accompany the WinNT kits have not been made public at this time, but functionality will duplicate that available with the DOS, Windows16, and OS/2 engines.

Available Separately

Many additional utilities, patches, updates, and examples are available from BTI's support forum on CompuServe. GO BTRIEVE to get there, and browse through the libraries. Only a sampling of the tools you'll find there are listed here. Note, too, that files that were in any specific library at the time of writing this chapter may be elsewhere by the time you visit.

Many of the following packages apply primarily to the original file formats; these still represent the majority of Btrieve applications in use and consequently most support material addresses only this format.

BTOOLS.EXE   This file, located in LIB 5 of the BTRIEVE CompuServe forum, contains Btrieve and XQL debugging utility programs. These utility programs are not products of BTI nor are they supported by BTI. The BSIM utility is a Btrieve function executor, BCLEAN is a utility to recover corrupted Btrieve files, BDEBUG intercepts calls to Btrieve from application programs, POSCHECK checks for position block corruption, RECPLAY records Btrieve NLM operations, and XTRAP intercepts calls to XQL. This collection also appears on Novell's developer CD-ROM. This self-extracting archive file contains the utilities shown in Table 9.1.

BTR610.EXE   This self-extracting archive, located in LIB 3 of the BTRIEVE forum, contains version 6.10c of the NetWare Btrieve NLM. It also provides installation and upgrade information, together with descriptions of the NetWare Btrieve program files. Support files included are NWSNUT, CLIB and AFTER311 NLMs.

BTRREQ.EXE   This self-extracting archive, located in LIB 3 of the BTRIEVE forum, contains the latest Btrieve requesters for use with the 5.x versions of the Btrieve VAP and NLM and the 6.0 and later versions of the Btrieve NLM. Included are requesters for DOS (BREQUEST 6.10e), Windows, OS/2, and UnixWare workstations.

BUNXEX.EXE   BUNXEX.EXE, a self-extracting archive located in LIB 4 of the BTRIEVE forum, contains an example C application, for use with the Btrieve UnixWare Requester available in BTRREQ.EXE.

Table 9.1   *Utilities within BTOOLS.EXE*

Utility	Description
BCLEAN.EXE	BCLEAN, written by David Harris, recovers corrupted Btrieve files. According to its documentation, it works only with version 5.10a files.
BDEBUG.COM	BDEBUG, written by Jacob Gafny in 1987, intercepts calls to Btrieve from application programs and displays all parameters in a special window on the CRT.
RECPLAY package	RECPLAY contains four separate tools: BRECORD.NLM, DUMPTR.EXE, CRDUMP.EXE, and BREPLAY.NLM. Together they can record and play back Btrieve NLM operations.
BSIM.EXE	BSIM, a $15 shareware program from Craig's Software, 902 East Live Oak, Austin, TX 78704, allows you to execute most of the Btrieve operations directly without having to write your own program.
POSCHECK.EXE	POSCHECK, created by Novell in 1992, is a TSR that checks for corrupted Btrieve position blocks and provides a trace log of Btrieve calls.
XTRAP.EXE	XTRAP is a TSR that will trap API calls between a front-end application and SSQL or XQL. The user may specify specific API functions to trap, or may trap them all.

REALBT.EXE   This self-extracting archive, located in LIB 4 of the BTRIEVE forum, contains an interface to Btrieve for Realia COBOL v4.0. The interface, written by Realia, replaces REAXBTRV.OBJ that originally shipped with Btrieve.

UPPER.ALT   The UPPER.ALT file, a self-extracting archive located in LIB 3 of the BTRIEVE forum, contains the alternate collating sequence for Btrieve. This file was not shipped with Btrieve for Windows or the OS/2 developer's kit v5.10, but the file is needed to create keys that are not case sensitive.

Commercial Offerings

The following list of commercial programs available to support Btrieve developers and users makes no pretense of being exhaustive. Based, with permission, on the Btrieve SourceBook published by Smithware, Inc. and distributed with Btrieve, it has been augmented from a number of other sources. It's intended primarily to show the types of utilities available to you and to let you know about resources of which you might otherwise not be aware.

@Trieve

@Trieve is a general purpose interface to Btrieve files from inside Lotus 1-2-3(2.x), Lotus 1-2-3 (Windows) and Excel. With menu commands, function commands, and macro commands, it allows users to dynamically pull up-to-date, accurate information from any number of Btrieve databases and to create reports based on that information. $395. **Contact:** Duane Laird, Synex Systems Corp. **Address:** 800-1188 West Georgia St., Vancouver, BC, V6E 4A2, Canada. **Phone:** (604) 688-8271 Ext 330. **FAX:** (604) 688-1286. **CompuServe:** 74431, 1123.

AutoTester Inc.

AutoTester Inc. offers a suite of automated testing solutions that test sophisticated distributed applications with either character-based or Graphical User Interfaces on virtually any platform, including client server. **Contact:** Holly Garner. **Address:** 8150 N. Central Expressway, Suite 1300, Dallas, TX 75206. **Phone:** (214) 368-1196, (800) 326-1196. **FAX:** (214) 750-9668.

Banalyze™ 2.0

The Btrieve specialists present in Banalyze a complete line of cross-platform Btrieve utilities that debug applications, view files, or recover/ edit/ export data. Use the tools that really work on all Btrieve-based products including the newest version 6.1. $99. **Contact:** Richard Bogard. **Address:** 3130 Pine Tree Road, Lansing, MI

48911. **Phone:** (517) 887-8000, (800) 359-2721. **FAX:** (517) 887-2366. **CompuServe:** 76317, 1056. **BBS:** (517) 887-8018.

BBUG.ZIP

bBUG is a task-specific memory resident monitor / debugger targeted to the needs of software developers using the Btrieve. A limited demonstration version of bBUG is available from CompuServe's BCPPDOS forum, Library 5. A more recently updated version appears on the companion diskette for this book. **Contact:** Access Technology Corporation. **Address:** Box 8121, Main Terminal, Ottawa, Ontario, CANADA. **Phone:** (613) 769-3775. **CompuServe:** 71630, 1053.

Btrieve Development Library (BDL)

A C-Language interface for Btrieve that supports all Btrieve operations, including extended calls. $200. With source code, $375. **Contact:** Michael Delaet, Intrepid Technology. **Address:** 9801 Hempstead Station Drive, Kettering, OH 45429. **Phone:** (513) 438-7435, (800) 398-8383. **FAX:** (513) 438-2207. **CompuServe:** 75730, 147.

Btrv++

C and C++ class libraries for Btrieve under Windows, Win32, DOS, and OS/2. Implements all Btrieve operations as member functions as well as many value added functions. **Contact:** Ed Moran, Classic Software, Inc. **Address:** 3542 Pheasant Run Circle #8, Ann Arbor, MI 48108. **Phone:** (313) 677-0732, (800) 677-2952. **FAX:** (313) 971-3287.

Btrvgen++

Database designer and C++ code generator for Btrieve. Integrated Btrieve DDF file editor. Generated Code supports Windows, Win32, DOS, and OS/2. Requires Btrv++. **Contact:** Ed Moran, Classic Software, Inc. **Address:** 3542 Pheasant Run Circle #8, Ann Arbor, MI 48108. **Phone:** (313) 677-0732, (800) 677-2952. **FAX:** (313) 971-3287.

BUtility

This package is a full-featured file editor and maintenance tool that can create, load, copy, and recover files. It's especially useful for helping you determine the internal structure of a file you must maintain but did not create. $129.95. **Contact:** Scott Smith, Smithware, Inc. **Address:** 2416 Hillsboro Road, Suite 201, Nashville, TN 37212. **Phone:** (615) 386-3100, (800) 8-Btriev (800-828-7438). **FAX:** (615) 386-3135. **CompuServe:** 75470,546. **Internet:** info@smithware.com.

CA-ACCPAC®/2000

Powerful GUI client/server reporting, query, and data analysis tools that access multiple databases including Btrieve and NetWare SQL. **Contact:** Dana Williams, Computer Associates Int'l Inc. **Address:** One Computer Associates Plaza, Islandia, NY 11788. **Phone:** (516) 342-5224, (800) 225-5224. **FAX:** (516) 342-5734.

CA-EASYTRIEVE®/Workstation

Powerful GUI client/server reporting, query, and data analysis tools that access multiple databases including Btrieve and NetWare SQL. **Contact:** Dana Williams, Computer Associates Int'l Inc. **Address:** One Computer Associates Plaza, Islandia, NY 11788. **Phone:** (516) 342-5224, (800) 225-5224. **FAX:** (516) 342-5734.

CA-Realia® CICS

Powerful GUI client/server reporting, query, and data analysis tools that access multiple databases including Btrieve and NetWare SQL. **Contact:** Dana Williams, Computer Associates Int'l Inc. **Address:** One Computer Associates Plaza, Islandia, NY 11788. **Phone:** (516) 342-5224, (800) 225-5224. **FAX:** (516) 342-5734.

CA-TELON® PWS

Powerful GUI client/server reporting, query, and data analysis tools that access multiple databases including Btrieve and NetWare SQL. **Contact:** Dana Williams, Computer Associates Int'l Inc.

Address: One Computer Associates Plaza, Islandia, NY 11788. **Phone:** (516) 342-5224, (800) 225-5224. **FAX:** (516) 342-5734.

CA-Visual Express™

Powerful GUI client/server reporting, query, and data analysis tools that access multiple databases including Btrieve and NetWare SQL. **Contact:** Dana Williams, Computer Associates Int'l Inc. **Address:** One Computer Associates Plaza, Islandia, NY 11788. **Phone:** (516) 342-5224, (800) 225-5224. **FAX:** (516) 342-5734.

CA-Visual Objects™

Powerful GUI client/server reporting, query, and data analysis tools that access multiple databases including Btrieve and NetWare SQL. **Contact:** Dana Williams, Computer Associates Int'l Inc. **Address:** One Computer Associates Plaza, Islandia, NY 11788. **Phone:** (516) 342-5224, (800) 225-5224. **FAX:** (516) 342-5734.

Clear Access for Windows

Clear Access for Windows is a graphical query and reporting tool that can access Btrieve data. Build queries with a simple drag and drop, then produce professional reports with full control over fonts, sizes, styles, breaks and more. **Contact:** Ridley Hutchinson, KnowledgeWare, Inc. **Address:** 200 West Lowe Ave., Fairfield, IA 52556. **Phone:** (515) 472-7077, (800) 522-4252. **FAX:** (515) 472-7198.

CommonBase

CommonBase is a C++ class interface to ISAM & SQL databases. Developers can build portable database applications across multiple database platforms and operating systems. **Contact:** Joshua Allen, ImageSoft, Inc. **Address:** 2 Haven Avenue, Port Washington, NY 11050. **Phone:** (516) 767-2233, (800) 245-8840. **FAX:** (718) 767-4307. **Internet:** CMNBASE@IMAGE.LINET.ORG.

Crystal Reports Pro 3.0

Crystal Reports Professional Edition 3.0 is an advanced data access and reporting tool with two components: a full-featured, easy-to-use Report Designer for creation of quality reports, and a Report Engine DLL for rapid addition of reports to Windows applications. Crystal Reports Pro supports PC, SQL, and ODBC compliant databases including Btrieve and NetWare SQL. Includes report compiler with FREE run-time, plus VB custom control, data dictionary builder, SQL editor, and extensible architecture. $395 single user, $1195 5-user LANpack. **Contact:** Ed Stein, Crystal Services. **Address:** Suite 2200, 1050 West Pender, Vancouver, BC, Canada. **Phone:** (410) 576-2040. **FAX:** (410) 576-1182.

Crystal Reports Server

Crystal Reports Server provides automatic report scheduling and production over networks, using the Crystal Report Manager. Each copy of Crystal Reports Server includes five Report Managers. Additional copies are available in blocks of five. $1195, each five-pak of additional managers $495. **Contact:** Ed Stein, Crystal Services. **Address:** Suite 2200, 1050 West Pender, Vancouver, BC, Canada. **Phone:** (410)576-2040. **FAX:** (410)576-1182.

Crystal Reports Standard 3.0

Crystal Reports Standard Edition 3.0 is an advanced data access and reporting tool with two components: a full-featured, easy-to-use Report Designer for creation of quality reports, and a Report Engine DLL for rapid addition of reports to Windows applications. Crystal Reports Pro supports PC compliant databases including Btrieve and NetWare SQL. Includes report compiler with FREE run-time. Does not include VB custom control, data dictionary builder, SQL or ODBC support, or extensible architecture of Pro edition. $195 single user, $495 5-user LANpack. **Contact:** Ed Stein, Crystal Services. **Address:** Suite 2200, 1050 West Pender, Vancouver, BC, Canada. **Phone:** (410) 576-2040. **FAX:** (410) 576-1182.

DataFlex for Btrieve

DataFlex for Btrieve is an enhanced version of the DataFlex for DOS version that supports Novell's Btrieve file manager. This version allows applications to read and write data stored in Btrieve using any flavor of Btrieve. **Contact:** Scott Bryan, Data Access Corporation. **Address:** 14000 S.W. 119 Avenue, Miami, FL 33186. **Phone:** (305) 238-0012, (800) 451-3539. **FAX:** (305) 238-0017. **CompuServe:** 74431, 1537.

DDF Builder

This utility allows you to create DDF files that describe the complete structure of your Btrieve files, whether the files already exist or will be part of a newly created database. Figure 9.4 shows one of the data entry screens for the program. $129.95, or $199 when bundled with Butility. **Contact:** Scott Smith, Smithware, Inc. **Address:** 2416 Hillsboro Road, Suite 201, Nashville, TN 37212. **Phone:** (615)

Figure 9.4   *Smithware's DDF Builder table-editing screen*

386-3100, (800) 8-Btriev (800-828-7438). **FAX:** (615) 386-3135. **CompuServe:** 75470,546. **Internet:** info@smithware.com.

DDF Maker

DDF Maker is a Windows-hosted editor for Btrieve DDF files. With it, you can define your tables, columns, and keys with a simple point-and-click interface. The program can merge multiple DDF files into one new DDF, create subsets of existing DDF Files, or create your Btrieve files. $129. **Contact:** Ed Moran, Classic Software, Inc. **Address:** 3542 Pheasant Run Circle #8 Ann Arbor, MI 48108. **Phone:** (313) 677-0732, (800) 677-2952. **FAX:** (313) 971-3287.

DDF Sniffer

This utility is an automated analyzer for Btrieve files that creates scripts that can, in turn, drive DDF Builder in creating DDF files. DDF Sniffer leads you through a series of questions designed to help it analyze the file, then creates the script file. DDF Builder is necessary. $199.95. **Contact:** Scott Smith, Smithware, Inc. **Address:** 2416 Hillsboro Road, Suite 201, Nashville, TN 37212. **Phone:** (615) 386-3100, (800) 8-Btriev (800-828-7438). **FAX:** (615) 386-3135. **CompuServe:** 75470,546. **Internet:** info@smithware.com.

DDTrieve for Windows

Use DDTrieve for Windows to create standard Btrieve DDF files for Microsoft Access, Visual Basic, Crystal Reports, and so on. DDTrieve also includes the client Btrieve WBTRCALL.DLL, $99.00. **Contact:** Mike Rogers, Ztech. **Address:** 1800 Lavaca, Suite 209E, P.O. Box 981, Austin, TX 78701. **Phone:** (512) 495-9101. **FAX:** (512) 495-1803. **CompuServe:** 72724,1263.

F9, The Financial Reporter Windows Edition

F9, The Financial Reporter Windows Edition, is an advanced General Ledger reporter for Btrieve-based accounting systems, including Great Plains, Macola, Platinum, Melson Technologies, Solomon,

DAC Easy, and Real World. F9 provides a hot-link to G/L data from Excel, Lotus (Windows), and Quattro Pro (Windows). Custom development available. **Contact:** Duane Laird, Synex Systems Corp. **Address:** 800-1188 West Georgia St., Vancouver, BC, V6E 4A2, Canada. **Phone:** (604) 688-8271 Ext. 330. **FAX:** (604) 688-1286. **CompuServe:** 74431,1123.

GENERAL COUNCEL

GENERAL COUNCEL is a software development tool that combines advanced document assembly technology with a relational database. **Contact:** Kenneth B. Frank, The Technology Group, Inc. **Address:** 36 S. Charles Street, Suite 2200, Baltimore, MD 21201. **Phone:** (410) 576-2040. **FAX:** (410) 576-1182.

Heaven Nodes

Heaven Nodes is a series of network management utilities. **Contact:** Harvey Diez, The dTech Group. **Address:** Fifteen West Sixth Street, Fifteenth Floor, Tulsa, OK 74119-5455. **Phone:** (918) 583-7447, (800) 800-4278. **FAX:** (918) 583-0560.

IVIS International

IVIS has developed a transparent API for the porting of mainframe COBOL CICS and Batch systems to Novell LANs deploying the Btrieve NLM. At link time the API translates the typical native VSAM calls to Btrieve Operation calls. Because this API interface was implemented to be utilized at the application link layer, the source code does not change and the application runs exactly as it did on the mainframe; it just executes on a less expensive platform. **Contact:** Jeff Zajac. **Address:** 5400 Glenwood Ave., Raleigh, NC 27612. **Phone:** (919) 781-7778. **FAX:** (919) 781-4847. **CompuServe:** 71421, 260.

Magic

Magic is a Rapid Application Development tool designed specifically for client-server environments. Magic is heterogeneous across multiple platforms including DOS, OVIX, VAX, VMS, and CTOS.

Magic also supports multiple databases including Drack, Sybase, Rollo and Informix. **Contact:** Lisa Parkhurst, Magic Software Enterprises. **Address:** 1200 Main Street, Irvine, CA 92714. **Phone:** (714) 250-1718, (800) 345-6244. **FAX:** (714) 250-7404.

MicroSTEP

MicroSTEP is the Visual Programming Tool that's ten times faster than Programming. You just (1) "draw" applications using icons and a mouse, (2) automatically generate 100% of the C Code, and (3) run the application stand-alone or on a LAN. Current version is for DOS only, but a Windows version is promised for early 1995. **Contact:** Mark Flanigan, Syscorp International. **Address:** 9430 Research Blvd., Bldg. 4, Suite 300, Austin, TX 78759. **Phone:** (512) 338-5800. **FAX:** (512) 338-5810.

NIVB–NetWare Interface for Visual Basic SDK

Develop NetWare applications using the NIVB–NetWare Interface for SDK, $49. **Contact:** Mike Rogers, Ztech. **Address:** 1800 Lavaca, Suite 209E, P.O. Box 981, Austin, TX 78701. **Phone:** (512) 495-9101. **FAX:** (512) 495-1803. **CompuServe:** 72724, 1263.

OEDEMO.EXE

OpenExchange for Windows allows you to easily convert, update, format, and transfer your database and spreadsheet data. Featuring an easy-to-use graphical user interface, this utility can link or map fields, using drag and drop; can update records in existing databases; can build and modify table, database, index structures including Btrieve DDF files; and much more. Formats supported include MS-Access 1 & 2, Paradox 3.x & 4.x, Btrieve 5.1x & 6.x, ASCII fixed & delimited, FoxPro 2.0 & 2.5, dBase III & IV, Excel 3 & 4. A free demonstration and ordering information can be found in the NOVUSER forum on CompuServe, in LIB 1.

OMNIS 7 (to the 3rd power)

Blyth Software's OMNIS 7 (to the 3rd power) is the application development environment for developing and deploying enterprise-wide client server applications. Designed to provide true portability, OMNIS 7 (to the 3rd power) enables developers to create an application once (on the platform of their choice) and then deploy that same application in native GUI across the widest range of platforms offered in the industry. **Contact:** Linda Cyganek, Blyth Software. **Address:** 989 E. Hillsdale Blvd., Suite #400, Foster City, CA 94404-2113. **Phone:** (415) 571-0222, (800) 346-6647. **FAX:** (415) 571-1132. **CompuServe:** 71333,2525. **Internet:** Support@blyth.com.

Parts Workbench

Digitalk's Parts Workbench is a visual development tool that is available for Windows and OS/2 and comes with over seventy pre-built components including Btrieve and report writing. **Contact:** Tom Murphy, Digitalk, Inc. **Address:** 5 Hutton Center Santa Ana, CA 92707. **Phone:** (714) 513-3000, (800) 944-8827. **FAX:** (714) 513-3100. **Internet:** Info@digitalk.com.

PP.ZIP

ProPrint Report Generator is a powerful report writer and data conversion utility. This package supports Btrieve, Paradox, xBase, ASCII, fixed record file formats, and many data types. It includes an optional C code generator to create standalone executables for any report created with the report writer, together with a file view/definition utility, a standalone sort utility, and DDF extraction utilities. A functional demonstration package with ordering information is available in the NOVUSER forum of CompuServe, in LIB 12.

R&R Report Writer, SQL Edition

Access the data from your client/server databases and present it in comprehensive, easy-to-understand reports. This utility includes desktop publishing style text control, graphic import, line/box drawing and shading, plain-English querying, WYSIWYG print preview with zoom, over eighty-five pre-defined functions, and royalty-free runtime. **Contact:** Deborah Boire, Concentric Data Systems, Inc. **Address:** 110 Turnpike Road, Westborough, MA 01581. **Phone:** (508) 366-1122, (800) 325-9035, ext. 8219. **FAX:** (508) 366-2954.

Relativity

Relativity for RM/COBOL and Micro Focus COBOL is a database engine that interfaces ODBC-enabled tools and existing COBOL application files (C-ISAM and Btrieve). This tool can help software developers transition data and commercial applications to open client/server systems. Pricing includes the Data Designer for $4995 and Database Engine for a single seat at $495. Volume pricing is available for multiseat installations. **Contact:** Gaylia Kelley, Liant Software Corporation. **Address:** 8911 N. Capital of Texas Highway, Austin, TX 78759. **Phone:** (800) RMCOBOL. **FAX:** (512) 343-9487. **Internet:** Gaylia@rmc.liant.com.

RM/COBOL v6.0

RM/COBOL v6.0 is a client/server COBOL application development tool-set. The RM/COBOL program I/O supports the Btrieve file system. Pricing includes DOS Development System at $1295 (single) and Runtime System at $155 (single). Other pricing includes WINDOWS Development System at $1495 and Runtime System at $245. Multiseat pricing is available. **Contact:** Gaylia Kelley, Liant Software Corporation. **Address:** 8911 N. Capital of TX Hwy, Austin, TX 78759. **Phone:** (800) RMCOBOL. **FAX:** (512) 343-9487. **Internet:** Gaylia@rmc.liant.com.

SBPRES.ZIP

SansBtrv, from Soft Recovery Technology, is a set of routines that allow access to Btrieve files from PowerBASIC (versions 2 and 3) without requiring the Btrieve record manager to be loaded. It is written in assembler for speed and compactness. This package can be used either for Btrieve data file recovery or for ad hoc querying of files. A press announcement of the product including two sample programs written in PB showing use of the routines is available for download from LIB 10 of the NOVUSER forum on CompuServe.

Smithware Class Library for Btrieve

Smithware's Class Library for Btrieve provides a comprehensive and powerful C++ object interface to Btrieve data. For Microsoft, Borland, and other popular C++ compilers, using object, library, or DLL format. Royalty-free distribution. $279.95. **Contact:** Scott Smith, Smithware, Inc. **Address:** 2416 Hillsboro Road, Suite 201, Nashville, TN 37212. **Phone:** (615) 386-3100, (800) 8-Btriev (800-828-7438). **FAX:** (615) 386-3135. **CompuServe:** 75470,546. **Internet:** info@smithware.com.

Smithware Controls for Btrieve

The Controls for Btrieve package includes a set of VBX custom controls for Visual Basic that provides full access to Btrieve files with no need for ODBC interfacing. Royalty-free distribution. Includes DDF Builder also, plus *The Illustrated Guide to Btrieve* from MIDI America. Complete package $249.95. **Contact:** Scott Smith, Smithware, Inc. **Address:** 2416 Hillsboro Road, Suite 201, Nashville, TN 37212. **Phone:** (615) 386-3100, (800) 8-Btriev (800-828-7438). **FAX:** (615) 386-3135. **CompuServe:** 75470,546. **Internet:** info@smithware.com.

Snow Report Writer

The Snow Report Writer, supporting all Btrieve data types, is the easiest way to lay out any kind of report, form, letter, or label and link up desired Btrieve data in a high-performance manner. **Contact:** Brian Rakestraw, Snow Software. **Address:** 2360 Congress Ave., Clearwater, FL 34623. **Phone:** (813)784-8899. **FAX:** (813)787-1904.

Sunbelt Databus MS-DOS Compilers

Sunbelt Databus MS-DOS compilers support Sequential, Random, Direct, Indexed Sequential, Associative, and Btrieve access methods and can read files in both forward and reverse order via any access method! **Contact:** Michael Potter, Sunbelt Computer Systems. **Address:** 1517 WSW Loop 323, Tyler, TX 75701. **Phone:** (903) 561-6005, (800) 359-5907. **FAX:** (903) 561-6007. **CompuServe:** 76020, 2146.

TAS Professional 4.0

This complete 4GL application development system includes screen painter, report writer, program editor, code generator, and utilities like import/export. Produces extremely fast, compact, compiled code. **Contact:** Clif McCormick, Business Tools Software. **Address:** 1507 E. Franklin Street, Suite 212, Chapel Hill, NC 27515. **Phone:** (919) 932-3068, (800) 648-6258. **FAX:** (919) 932-3069.

Tools & Techniques Inc.

Converts NetWare SQL, Xtrieve, and Btrieve files. Reads, modifies, and creates data dictionaries. Converts databases, spreadsheets, ASCII, binary/EBCDIC, accounting and statistical packages, and other apps. Edits and filters while converting: without programming, but is fully automatable. **Contact:** Mike Hoskins. **Address:** 2201 Northland Dr., Austin, TX 78756. **Phone:** (512) 459-1308, (800) 444-1945. **FAX:** (512) 459-1309. **CompuServe:** 76440, 3346. **Internet:** Tnt.com.

True DDF

Creates Btrieve DDF files without using Xtrieve. Allows documentation of table, field, and key. Imports and exports from Btrieve DDF files. Creates Btrieve files from DDF and can specify null or manual key. Allows Access, VB3, or DataFlex to access Btrieve file. $50. **Contact:** True Ware. **Address:** 1510 Wellwood Way, Edmonton, Alberta. **CompuServe:** 72133, 635.

True Query

Allows you to query Access-compatible files including Btrieve. **Contact:** True Ware. **Address:** 1510 Wellwood Way, Edmonton, Alberta. **CompuServe:** 72133, 635.

VBtrv for DOS

Function-call interface to Btrieve under MS Visual Basic for DOS. Supports full Btrieve functionality. $149, or $299 bundled with Vbtrv for Windows. **Contact:** Ed Moran, Classic Software, Inc.

Address: 3542 Pheasant Run Circle #8, Ann Arbor, MI 48108. **Phone:** (313) 677-0732, (800) 677-2952. **FAX:** (313) 971-3287.

VBtrv for Windows

Combines nine Custom VBX Controls, DDF Maker (a Windows-hosted Btrieve DDF file editor), Function call library (DLL), and a third party reference book called *The Illustrated Guide to Btrieve*. A demonstration package, VBTRV.ZIP, that contains the custom controls and function call library, is available in CompuServe's BTRIEVE forum in LIB 10. $249, or $349 with source code. **Contact:** Ed Moran, Classic Software, Inc. **Address:** 3542 Pheasant Run Circle #8, Ann Arbor, MI 48108. **Phone:** (313) 677-0732, (800) 677-2952. **FAX:** (313) 971-3287.

VBtrv/C++

Combines the nine VBX custom controls, DDF Maker, Function call library (DLL), and the binaries to BTRV++ product all in one package. Record and field Based access including SQL query support. $249, $349 with either source or Btrvgen++, or $449 with both source and Btrvgen++. **Contact:** Ed Moran, Classic Software, Inc. **Address:** 3542 Pheasant Run Circle #8, Ann Arbor, MI 48108. **Phone:** (313) 677-0732, (800) 677-2952. **FAX:** (313) 971-3287.

Visual Basic Programmers Guide to NetWare

This is a 600-page book covering all NetWare services needed to do Visual Basic development. $49. **Contact:** Mike Rogers, Ztech. **Address:** 1800 Lavaca, Suite 209E, P.O. Box 981, Austin, TX 78701. **Phone:** (512) 495-9101. **FAX:** (512) 495-1803. **CompuServe:** 72724, 1263.

Shareware Offerings

In the past several years, shareware has become a popular marketing technique. Unlike pure commercial distributed products, shareware packages offer you a chance to try the software before parting with any money. Shareware is a distribution method, not a type of software. You should select all your software on the basis of its fit to your needs and to your pocketbook, without regard to whether it's commercial or shareware.

Many in the computer industry confuse shareware and freeware, and others tend to assume that both types of programs are always amateurish and unprofessional. Both are misconceptions.

If you try a shareware program and continue to use it, you are expected to register and pay its price. When you do so, some program publishers provide a bonus. This often consists of an updated program with printed manual. Others give only the right to continue using the program.

Many of the programs listed in this section provide a more professional level of operation than do many of the shrink-wrapped commercial packages, and almost all shareware authors far outperform their commercial brethren when it comes to supporting the product. Technical support from shareware authors seldom involves hour-long waits just to get to a human at the other end of the line, which happens far too frequently when you call a commercial firm's support numbers.

BTCL22.ZIP

One problem with the standard Btrieve interface is that it consists of one function call (BTRV) with various meanings attached to the parameters depending on the exact operation being performed. This is both difficult to learn and quite error prone.

The classes provided in BTCLASS version 2.2 have abstracted various roles (such as keyed access path), from the many Btrieve operations. Since these concepts are much closer to how one thinks about databases, a programmer is freed from the need to constantly translate the required action into one or more of the many op-codes.

The zipped file available in LIB 6 of the BCPPDOS forum on CompuServe contains small model libraries for Borland 3.0 and Microsoft 7.0. Source and additional documentation is available with registration. $55, Texas residents must add sales tax. **Contact:**

Object Resource Corp. **Address:** 4323 Brown, Suite 249, Dallas, TX 75219.

BTEDXT.EXE

BTedit is designed for software developers who use Btrieve as the database manager. In addition, BTedit is extremely helpful to QA and support staffs. Its primary uses are to look at Btrieve records and to search for a specific record for analysis. If editing is required, it is easy to look at a record in detail format (HEX and ASCII) and to apply a change, using either format.

BTedit features include command line file argument, binary and ASCII key search, ASCII search and replace, marking of records for copying/moving to ASCII or Btrieve files, importing records from BUTIL ASCII format text file, resolution of binary data, file owner change, file statistics, and so on.

BTedit can be downloaded as a self-extracting file from BCPPDOS forum of CompuServe, in LIB 5 and is also on the companion diskette for this book. Registration of one to ten copies is $55 each. Contact C-Soft for larger licenses. **Contact:** C-Soft, Inc. **Address:** 4131 Wash Lee Court, Lilburn, GA 30247. **Phone:** (404) 279-9493. **CompuServe:** 75037,1605.

BTFILER

BTFILER version 1.45 (Figure 9.5) allows you to browse, edit, delete, and add records, pack, copy, clone, create, test, and rebuild Btrieve files, perform advanced data recovery, obtain information on Btrieve error codes, use a page-size calculator, view statistics, and use keystroke files to automate for use in batch files. The program includes supplemental index and transaction support and handles most status 30 and status 2 errors.

BTFILER is included on the companion diskette with this book; the latest version can be downloaded as BTFL*.ZIP, from either of these CompuServe forums: BCPPDOS, in LIB 1, or BTRIEVE, in LIB 10. The package can be registered through CompuServe's SWREG,

Figure 9.5   *BTFILER record editing screen, with Field Definition
dialog open*

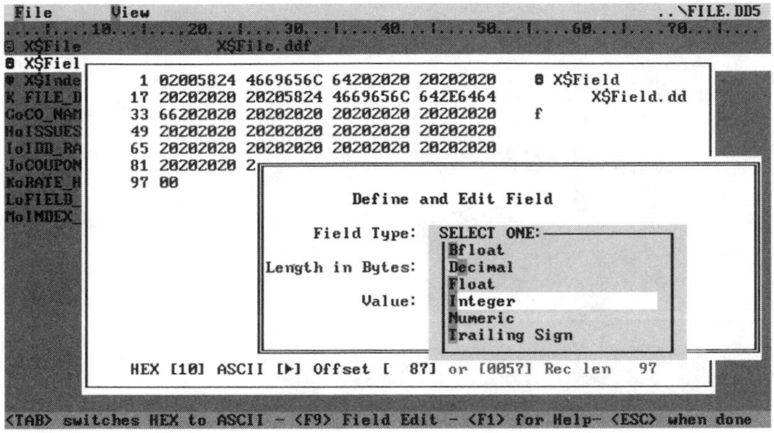

```
File     View                                      ..\FILE.DD5
....!...10...!....20...!....30...!....40...!....50...!....60...!....70...!....
0 X$File           X$File.ddf
0 X$Fiel
  X$Inde       1 02005824 4669656C 64202020 20202020    0 X$Field
K FILE_D      17 20202020 20205824 4669656C 642E6464        X$Field.dd
GoCO_NAM      33 66202020 20202020 20202020 20202020    f
HoISSUES      49 20202020 20202020 20202020 20202020
IoIDD_RA      65 20202020 20202020 20202020 20202020
JoCOUPON      81 20202020 2
KoRATE_H      97 00              Define and Edit Field
LoFIELD_
MoINDEX_          Field Type:    SELECT ONE:
                                 Bfloat
                  Length in Bytes: Decimal
                                 Float
                       Value:    Integer
                                 Numeric
                                 Trailing Sign

         HEX [10] ASCII [▶] Offset [  87] or [0057] Rec len   97

<TAB> switches HEX to ASCII - <F9> Field Edit - <F1> for Help- <ESC> when done
```

using ID #1. **Contact:** Douglas Reilly, Access Microsystems Inc.
Address: 404 Midstream Rd., Brick, NJ 08724. **Phone:** (908) 892-
2683. **FAX:** (908) 892-3737. **CompuServe:** 74040, 607.

BTP.ZIP

This file contains version 2 of a TP7 unit for handling Btrieve files.
The package includes source, documentation, examples, and several useful utilities. It also contains source for a total replacement for
BUTIL -STAT, freely distributable with your apps (if you register).
Newer features include easier file creation, simpler handling of creating supplemental indexes, handling of owner names. Available
for downloading in NOVUSER forum on CompuServe, in LIB 12.

BTRUTI.ZIP

BTRUTIL (Figure 9.6) prints out the contents of a DDF-file (data definition for Btrieve). Besides that, it can also calculate the optimal
page length for a Btrieve file, based on manual input or the file definitions (DDF-file). Available for downloading in NOVUSER forum
on CompuServe, in LIB 12. Registration fee $10 US. **Contact:** Rudolf
Ziegaus Software. **Address:** Adalbert-Stifter-Str. 4, 85098 Gross-
mehring, Germany.

Figure 9.6   *BTRUTIL.EXE screen to open a database*

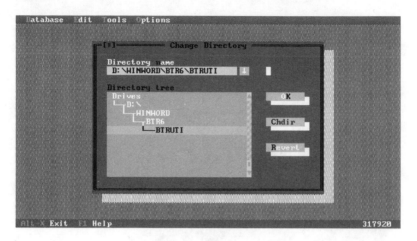

BTRV.ZIP

BTRV is a program for maintaining and creating files with Btrieve. BTRV was created primarily as an aid for programmers developing Btrieve applications, but can be invaluable to anyone who uses or maintains Btrieve files. All registrations are $50 plus $5 shipping and handling. Registered users receive the latest version and printed documentation.

To register using CompuServe's on-line registration service, GO SWREG and follow the prompts. The registration ID is 1169. This program can be found in the NOVUSER forum of CompuServe, in LIB 12. It's also available from Public Software Library at (800) 242-4PSL (from overseas, (713) 524-6394). **Contact:** Richard Hansen. **Address:** P.O. Box 18571, Saint Paul, MN 55118-0571, USA. **CompuServe:** 70242,3367. **Internet:** 70242.3367 @compuserve.com.

BTUTIL

BTUTIL version 1.20 is a command line Btrieve file utility. With it you can -SAVE, -LOAD, -RECOVER, -CLONE, -COPY, and -CREATE and create supplemental indexes in existing Btrieve files. It also includes an INDEXCOMP option to compare a BTB style description file with an existing Btrieve file. You may also use -XLOAD and -XSAVE, which use extended operations to speed up loading or saving a file. BTUTIL reports Btrieve error status as ERRORLEVEL.

Unlike BTI's utility BUTIL, BTUTIL recovers records from the damaged file directly to another Btrieve file that is a clone of the damaged file. Registration, $15. Available for downloading in NOVUSER forum on CompuServe, in LIB 12 as BTUTIL.ZIP. **Contact:** Douglas Reilly, Access Microsystems Inc. **Address:** 404 Midstream Rd., Brick, NJ 08724. **Phone:** (908) 892-2683. **FAX:** (908) 892-3737. **CompuServe:** 74040, 607.

BTV200.ZIP

BTV.PAS version 2.0 is a Turbo Pascal 6.0, 7.0 object-oriented interface to the Btrieve Record Manager. It implements Btrieve file, error handling and error display objects, and now supports the extended Btrieve operations. BTV.PAS, with over forty functions, greatly simplifies the interface to Btrieve. BTV.PAS is distributed as shareware, $50 + $5 shipping and handling. To use CompuServe's on-line registration facility, GO SWREG and follow the prompts. The CIS registration ID is 759. Available for downloading in NOVUSER forum on CompuServe, in LIB 12 as BTV200.ZIP. **Contact:** Richard Hansen. **Address:** P.O. Box 18571, Saint Paul, MN 55118-0571. **CompuServe:** 70242,3367.

BTVIEW.ZIP

BTVIEWER version 1.21 Query/Edit tool for Btrieve allows you to use your DDF files (INDEX.DDF, FIELD.DDF, FILE.DDF) to query, edit, import, export, and modify your Btrieve database. BTVIEWER is a more sophisticated tool than its companion utility BTFILER for viewing and querying Btrieve files that have .DDF description files. It allows SQL-like access to the data.

You can export to delimited ASCII as well as to dBase format. Use Restricts (=, !=, >, <, LIKE, CONTAINS) to select a subset of records (or a VIEW). Views may be batch modified or deleted. Shareware, $79 + $4 shipping and handling. Available for downloading in NOVUSER forum on CompuServe, in LIB 10.

To use CompuServe's on-line registration facility, GO SWREG. BTVIEWER's Registration ID is 135. **Contact:** Douglas Reilly, Access Microsystems Inc. **Address:** 404 Midstream Rd., Brick, NJ 08724. **Phone:** (908) 892-2683. **FAX:** (908) 892-3737. **CompuServe:** 74040, 607.

DDFMAKER

DDFMAKER.EXE is a self-extracting archive that unarchives an installation set of files for two utilities (DDFFILE.EXE and DDFFIELD.EXE) that you can use to create FILE.DDF and FIELD.DDF files. Registration, $20. Available for downloading in NOVUSER forum on CompuServe, in LIB 12 as DDFMAK.EXE. **Contact:** Bart W. Jenkins. **Address:** 4899 S. Dudley St., Littleton, CO 80123. **CompuServe:** 76276,305.

TYPCON.ZIP

TypConst is a utility for Visual Basic programmers to help manage Type element offsets for Btrieve keys, sorting, and so on. TypConst creates CONST declarations that name each element in each Type, giving its offset value. It requires VBRUN200.DLL. $10 registration, source code available to registered users for extra fee. Available for downloading in BTRIEVE forum on CompuServe, in LIB 10.

WBTRV.ZIP

This file contains the Wheaton Btrieve C++ Class interface Btrieve class, which is part of the Wheaton Libraries. Registration of this product is $50. Visa and MC are accepted. Registration provides all the following: The most recent copy of the Wheaton Libraries (WLIB); the most recent copy of the Wheaton Windows (WW); the most recent copy of a Source Parser (WPARSE) that will break up your large OBJ files so that your executable programs are much smaller and faster, with source; and support. Available for downloading in BCPPDOS forum on CompuServe, in LIB 6 as WBTRV.ZIP. **Contact:** Paul Wheaton. **Address:** 1916 Brooks #205, Missoula, MT 59801. **Phone:** (406) 543-1928. **CompuServe:** 72707,207. **Internet:** 72707.207@CompuServe.com.

WOODPECKER

Woodpecker is a debugging utility for programs that use Btrieve Record Manager version 5.11 for MS-Windows. Woodpecker allows the programmer to see details of Btrieve calls, in dialogs specifically formatted for each operation. The programmer can use these dialogs to modify data both before and after the call. The Woodpecker Control Panel allows the programmer to select the set of calls to break on.

Registration, $40. Available for downloading in NOVUSER forum on CompuServe, in LIB 12 as WOODPE.ZIP. **Contact:** Shawn Cannon, Adairiann Development Ltd. **Address:** 13522 W. 107th Street, Lenexa, KS 66215. **CompuServe:** 76366,531.

ZAQUERY

ZaQuery is a Btrieve utility and programmer's tool written by Zak. It allows the user to perform SQL type queries and operations from the command line without the overhead of DDFs. It may be useful for file purging and updating file formats as well as queries.

Available for downloading, as ZAQUER.ZIP, in LIB 12 of the NOVUSER forum on CompuServe. Registration, $35. **Contact:** ZaQuery. **Address:** P.O. Box 1237, Freehold, NJ 07728. **Internet:** ZacharyG@Delphi.COM.

Freeware Offerings

Unlike shareware, which requires that you pay for programs that you use, freeware is exactly what its name implies: software that costs you nothing other than, in some cases, the connect time required to download it from a commercial service.

Freeware exists for many reasons. Some programmers feel that it's more bother to try to sell a small utility than it's worth, so they release the package to the public domain for free use by anyone. Others simply want to share their work with the world without any effort to profit from their efforts. Finally, much current freeware comes from shareware and commercial program publishers who want wider exposure for their products and so post limited freeware versions to arouse industry interest.

As is true both for commercial products and for shareware, the quality of freeware packages ranges from one extreme to the other. Some products outperform the best commercial programs, within their limited range, while others aren't worth the connect time required to download them. Since in many cases, the perception of a program's quality is totally subjective, I've made no effort to rate the programs listed here. Rather, the intent is to provide a cross-section of available freeware programs. All were found on the CompuServe network at the time of writing; many are also available through other services and BBS facilities. When downloading any program, be cautious of the potential for virus infection of your system. Every file made public on CompuServe is first tested for all known virus strains, but not all systems perform this essential check. Better be safe than sorry.

BDUMP.ZIP

Bdump gives you the user name, network address, time and date of access to the file, along with a full dump of data if desired. Released to the public domain by Hans Wieser, CompuServe UserID 75730,2354. Available for download in LIB 12 of NOVUSER forum on CompuServe.

BERR.ZIP

BERR translates, displays (see Figure 9.7), and prints BTRIEVE error codes. Written by developers at Thompson Software because "we got tired of always looking for the Btrieve manuals to look up errors." Given the error code, the program displays a brief error

Figure 9.7   *BERR display resulting from DOS command-line entry
BERR 2*

```
2 - I/O ERROR
    An error occurred during a disk read/write.  This status code indicates
    that the file has been damaged and must be recreated, or that the file
    specified on the open call was not created.  This status code also occurs
    if the application passed an invalid position block.
TS - This is a general I/O error and does not necessary mean the file must
    be recreated.

    Press any key to exit...
```

description, and will not flash off the screen if run from Windows. An option prints a one-page Btrieve error code summary for Quick Reference, and a four-page error code description list. This free program is available for download in the NOVUSER form of CompuServe, in LIB 12.

BFILE

BFILE C++ Btrieve Class, this version of BFILE, available for download in LIB 6 of BCPPDOS forum on CompuServe as BFILE2.ZIP, adds support that makes it work better with variable length records, as well as a single cloning function. Public domain. **Contact:** Douglas Reilly, Access Microsystems Inc. **Address:** 404 Midstream Rd., Brick, NJ 08724. **Phone:** (908) 892-2683. **FAX:** (908) 892-3737. **CompuServe:** 74040, 607.

BLDBTB.ZIP

BLDBTB is a program that reads a Btrieve file and creates a .BTB file (that is, a Btrieve Build description file in a format used by the shareware packages BTFILER, BTVIEWER, and BTUTIL described earlier in this chapter). You can use this file as is, recreate a file later, or modify it slightly when you wish to create a "near clone" of a file. Freeware, but really useless without BTFILER, BTVIEWER, or BTUTIL. Available for download in LIB 12 of NOVUSER forum on CompuServe. **Contact:** Douglas Reilly, Access Microsystems Inc. **Address:** 404 Midstream Rd., Brick, NJ 08724. **Phone:** (908) 892-2683. **FAX:** (908) 892-3737. **CompuServe:** 74040, 607.

BRESET.ZIP

BRESET is a flexible utility for resetting Netware workstation connections to the Btrieve NLM. You can reset your own station, a single station, all stations, or all stations *not* in a predefined list of users. C++ source is included. Recompilation requires Borland C++ 3.1 and the Netware C Interface for DOS. Available for download in LIB 12 of NOVUSER forum on CompuServe. **Contact:** John C. Leon. **Address:** 3807 Wood Gardens Court, Kingwood, TX 77339. **Phone:**

713-216-4007. **Fax:** 713-216-2052. **CompuServe:** 72426,2077. **Internet:** 72426.2077 @compuserve.com.

BTR32.ZIP

BTR32 includes a small 16-bit server application with source and some details in READ.ME. The server, BLOGIN.EXE, is a tiny 16-bit Btrieve application. The BTRCALL function in the 32-bit application looks for BLOGIN, after which communication takes place using SendMessage and the clipboard. Available for download in LIB 12 of NOVUSER forum on CompuServe. **Contact:** Markus Bosshard. **CompuServe:** 100022,3131.

BTRVSM.C

This is a small, fast interface for BASIC PDS 7.0 near strings and for C/C++ in medium model. It handles the position blocks in the interface, thus freeing near memory and reducing the amount of data passed on the stack. Its author says, "I have been using it for 2 years now and it seems about 20 percent faster than the standard version." Available for download in LIB 17 of CompuServe's BTRIEVE forum. **Contact:** Clifford Wetherall. **CompuServe:** 100433,3363.

BU

BU, a Btrieve command line utility program, is a partial replacement for BUTIL. It implements the -STOP, -RESET, -CLONE, -LOAD, and -VER commands of BUTIL. BU is available for download in LIB 12 of NOVUSER forum on CompuServe, as BU2.ZIP. **Contact:** Douglas Reilly, Access Microsystems Inc. **Address:** 404 Midstream Rd., Brick, NJ 08724. **Phone:** (908) 892-2683. **FAX:** (908) 892-3737. **CompuServe:** 74040, 607.

DBLIB.ZIP

DBLIB is a data dictionary module for Btrieve, for use with BORLAND C++ (versions 3.1 and 4.0). The module provides a basic framework for inserting and for look-up of data dictionary entries. It has been tested with Xtrieve and third party query tools.

DBLIB allows for the creation of tables, fields, and keys. Available for download in LIB 12 of NOVUSER forum on CompuServe. Public domain, but please acknowledge author if used commercially. **Contact:** Australian Software Developments. **Address:** 249 Auburn Rd, Hawthorn, Melbourne 3142, Australia. **Phone:** (613) 882-8363. **Fax:** (613) 438-5129. **CompuServe:** 100250,777.

ERR.EXE

This simple freeware utility provides abbreviated text for Btrieve DOS error codes. Usage is simply "err x", where x is the decimal error code. Available for download in LIB 12 of NOVUSER forum on CompuServe.

EXTBTR.ZIP

Btrieve interfaces for use with Ergo OS/286 Extender (may work with OS/386 or their new DPMI extender but not tested) and with the Phar Lap 286 | DOS Extender (may also work with Phar Lap 386 | DOS Extender but, again, not tested). Microsoft source is included. Available for download in LIB 12 of NOVUSER forum on CompuServe. **Contact:** Jeff Gottschalk. **CompuServe:** 71530,2273.

MBTRV.ARC

This file contains interface routines for Btrieve. These are simple routines to create, open, add to, find, and close Btrieve files. These routines use Btrieve version 4.11b. These routines are strictly for the purpose of demonstrating how to call Btrieve from Turbo C. Available for download in LIB 6 of BCPPDOS forum on CompuServe.

PB-BTR.ZIP

This is an interface for Power Basic and Btrieve. You can now call BTRV as a function the way you would in C or Pascal, with no more need to use VARSEG and VARPTR() to your data buffer. Supports USERTYPE Variables, STRING, and FLEX data types. Files included: BT.BI, BT.OBJ, and BT.ASM. Available for download in LIB 12 of NOVUSER forum on CompuServe.

SIXTOFIV

SIXTOFIV.EXE was born out of the frustration of accidentally converting Btrieve files from a 5.x format to 6.x. This handy utility can downgrade Btrieve files from 6.x format to 5.x format. It's particularly useful for converting network files for access in a standalone DOS environment. Available for download, as SIXTOF.ZIP, in LIB 12 of NOVUSER forum on CompuServe. **Contacts:** Terry Willingham, Ray Crowther, Selven Ltd. 48 Collingwood Road, Witham, Essex, CM8 2DZ, England. **CompuServe:** 100012,432.

TMDT.ZIP

This zipped archive contains time and date classes developed for Borland C++ version 3.1 (which should work with 4.0). They are derived from Borland's classlib, so Borland C++ is required to use them. They will accept Btrieve date/time in the constructor (along with several other formats) and are able to return same. Date math is also supported. Available for download in LIB 12 of NOVUSER forum on CompuServe.

UNLDBT.EXE

This small program by Small Business Systems will unload Btrieve or Brequest. Available for download in LIB 12 of NOVUSER forum on CompuServe.

Other Possibilities

A relatively new source for utility programs is the CD-ROM collection. One widely available collection is the SimTel CD-ROM, updated regularly, from Walnut Creek CDROM in Walnut Creek, CA. I paid $19.50 for my most recent copy, a two-disk set containing more than 1 GB of assorted programs, source code, and reference material. The price varies over a 2:1 margin, depending on where you buy it.

The set contained just one Btrieve-related utility, but that one might be worth the cost in itself: It's BFAST11.ZIP, located in the CPLUS-PLS subdirectory on Disk 2. This package, written in September

1992, by Australia's Chao Lin Chang, is a freeware class library for Borland C++ that totally encapsulates the Btrieve interface. It revolves around a class named Btrieve. The constructor automatically opens a file, and the destructor closes it. Full instructions and sample code come in the ZIPfile.

Conclusion

In this chapter, we've seen a representative cross-section of the utilities available to support Btrieve, both from BTI and from other sources. In Chapter 10, we'll take the knowledge we gained from Chapters 5 through 8 and create some utilities of our own that can help us analyze Btrieve files and recover data should a file become corrupted.

10

Applying the Internal Details

This chapter applies the details described in Chapters 5 through 8 to provide programs that can be useful additions to your diagnostic toolkit. Unlike most of the utilities described in Chapter 9, none of these programs require the Btrieve engine's presence in order to run.

All the programs described in this chapter run under conventional text-mode DOS from the command line. In this era of Windows and GUI-oriented program development, you might think this a bit unusual. My purpose in doing this was to make the program structure as easy as possible for you to see, without confusing any issue by including the additional code needed to exist within a GUI environment.

When you understand the structure involved, the programs become simple to translate into Windows applications. The major differences you'll deal with in doing so (besides addition of the housekeeping code) will be in the disk and CRT interface techniques. Most of the disk activity translates directly, since all Btrieve files read a page at a time and a Btrieve page always contains an integral number of physical sectors. Replace all references to the `FILE*` variable type with int file descriptors, change `fopen()` calls to `lopen()`, `fread` to `lread`, and `fclose` to `lclose`.

Handling the output display is a bit more complicated since you have no direct equivalent to the printf statement in the Windows API. One way to meet this challenge is to create static controls for each displayed variable as child windows of your main application, and then use SetText API calls to place values into each such control. Another technique is to use a carefully crafted procedure when dealing with the WM_PAINT message, as described by Charles Petzold in his *Windows Programming* for most of his examples.

The programs I present in this chapter follow a consistent architecture, chosen to maximize the reuse of modules from one example to the next. I describe each such reusable module in the context of the first program that uses it, then say little or nothing about it for any subsequent instance. In some cases, modules of the same name may differ in internal details. When this happens, the description makes a point of noting the differences. All examples were developed using Borland's C++ compiler version 3.1, but have been tested with the newer version 4.5 and with Microsoft Visual C++ version 1.51. They should compile equally well under any other ANSI-compliant compiler for MS-DOS systems.

These programs were created and included here especially for your use. As the banner of each program indicates, you're free to use them in any way. The copyright notice is intended only to restrict anyone's direct resale of the unmodified utilities; I have no intent to restrict consultants from furnishing individual copies to their clients in order to simplify the tasks of maintaining client data files. You may also extract any portions of the source code that you need and use in your own programs, whether those programs are intended for private use or for resale, so long as the existing copyright notice becomes part of the final program (this is necessary to protect the copyright; you need not make it visible to your users).

Retrieving File Attributes

One of the most frequent needs faced by either a developer or a system administrator is finding out just what's inside a file. Our first sample program (BTATR) extracts all pertinent detail concerning a file's attributes from the FCR record of any Btrieve file.

As Figure 10.1 shows, this includes the file format in use (original or new), the version of Btrieve that's necessary to read the file, the record and page sizes, the number of indexes, read-write access restrictions if any exist, and the status of Btrieve's various special flags. This information is all displayed by the BUTIL -STAT option if using BTI's utilities (see Chapter 9) and can also be seen via several of the third-party utilities, but I believe that BTATR is unique in displaying the amount of space wasted on each data page. This information can be useful when you are designing a new file layout.

BTATR provides additional detail when reporting attributes for a new-format file, as Figure 10.2 shows. Duplicate-key pointer

Figure 10.1   *This screen capture shows the output from BTATR when it's run on an original-format DDF file (while testing, I renamed two sets of DDF files to indicate clearly which file format they used; they became DD5 and DD6 files instead). Note the wastage report midway down the screen.*

```
C:\SAMPLES>btatr file.dd5

            BTATR - from "Btrieve Complete" by Jim Kyle
            Copyright 1995 by Jim Kyle - All Rights Reserved
            Use freely, but do not distribute commercially.

Attributes for file FILE.DD5:
Format: Original             Requires Btrieve version 4.0 (or later) engine.

Sizes: Record:    97 bytes, Page:  512 bytes.    Has 2 indexes.
       Wastage:   21 bytes (per page)    Item size:    97 bytes.

Access: Can be read by anyone, edited only by owner.    Data is not encrypted.

Attributes: Record length is fixed
            Data is not compressed
            No pages were preallocated for the file
            File is not Key-Only
            Index-balancing flag is not set

File currently contains 11 records, on 7 pages.
```

Figure 10.2   *When BTATR analyzes a new-format file, two additional*
lines appear in the Attributes section of the display. When
a file uses variable-length records, the display shows the
threshold level and the blank-truncation status also. These
values don't show up on the fixed-length file display since
they apply only when record length can vary.

```
C:\SAMPLES>btatr folder.btr

          BTATR - from "Btrieve Complete" by Jim Kyle
          Copyright 1995 by Jim Kyle - All Rights Reserved
          Use freely, but do not distribute commercially.

Attributes for file FOLDER.BTR:
Format: New 6.+ version      Requires Btrieve version 6.0 (or later) engine.

Sizes: Record:   314 bytes, Page: 2048 bytes.    Has 2 indexes, prenumbered.
       Wastage:   14 bytes (per page)     Item size:   338 bytes.

Access: Can be read by anyone, edited by anyone.

Attributes: Record length is variable (threshold: 5 percent)
            Blanks are truncated
            Data is not compressed
            No pages were preallocated for the file
            File is not Key-Only
            Index-balancing flag is not set
            Duplicate-key pointers were not reserved
            VATs are not used

File currently contains 1705 records, on 421 pages.
```

reservation and use of VATs weren't available in the original version
and consequently appear in the display only when a file uses the new
format. A number of other differences between these two reports simply reflect differences between the two input files involved.

You may find the arrangement of functions within BTATR.C somewhat unconventional. I always place my main() routine at the end
of the file rather than at the beginning. Most C programmers make
the main() routine the first one in a source file. Consequently,
when writing ANSI C programs they must include prototypes (often
in a header file) to declare all other routines in the program.

Although I began putting main() last simply as a carryover from
a period in which I used Pascal almost exclusively, I've continued
the practice because it eliminates any need to declare prototypes for

internal procedures. When a program defines a routine before even invoking it, no prototype is necessary. I believe this makes programs easier to understand. To me, that's always an important consideration. It becomes especially significant when I must return to a program six months or a year after it was last modified to do maintenance.

The Include Files

Like all five sample programs, **BTATR.C** uses a standard block of **#include** statements at its beginning to declare all the standard C runtime library functions involved. (Some of the programs add one for **CTYPE.H** after the **STRING.H** inclusion.) The **BTRIEVE.H** header defines all of Btrieve's internal structures and several macro sequences to extract pointer information.

```
#include <stdio.h>
#include <conio.h>
#ifdef __TURBOC__
#include <alloc.h>        // Borland-specific
#else
#include <malloc.h>       // Microsoft version
#endif
#include <string.h>

#include "btrieve.h"
```

The only unusual thing in this block of statements is the test to determine whether a Borland or Microsoft compiler is in use. The functions declared by Borland in **ALLOC.H** and by Microsoft in **MALLOC.H** are essentially identical, but because the vendors chose different names for the header files it's necessary to determine which you're using.

Borland's products always define the macro **__TURBOC__** automatically each time the compiler runs, providing the indicator you need. For use with other than Borland or Microsoft compilers, this test may need changes. Refer to your compiler's detailed reference manual to find out how.

Program Constants and Variables

Besides the structures that `BTRIEVE.H` defines, this program needs to know each bit pattern that may appear in the file flags word. The following macro definitions at the start of the file provide descriptive names for each pattern:

```
#define AT_VARLEN   0x001   // file attribute bit patterns
#define AT_TRUNCBLK 0x002
#define AT_PREALLOC 0x004
#define AT_COMPRDAT 0x008
#define AT_KEYONLY  0x010
#define AT_BALANCE  0x020
#define AT_KEEP10   0x040
#define AT_KEEP20   0x080
#define AT_KEEP30   0x0C0
#define AT_DUPPTRS  0x100
#define AT_RESERVE  0x200
#define AT_SPECKEY  0x400
#define AT_USEVATS  0x800
```

Additionally, the program uses several global variables for convenience. Most authorities will tell you that it's poor practice to use globals. However, in special-purpose small programs such as these, it's frequently much easier to deal with globals than it is to carry everything around in huge parameter lists. Using globals also makes it easier to comprehend what each routine is doing, which is important here.

```
BYTE pgbf1[4096], pgbf2[4096];        // max page size
FILE *fp;
char outbuf[512];
int PageSize;
char *PgmName = "BTATR";
```

The two arrays `pgbf1[]` and `pgbf2[]` provide space for the largest possible FCR. BTATR never reads any other part of the file. File pointer `fp` provides the file identity. The `outbuf[]` array stores the file's name for display purposes. Other programs reserve only 80 bytes for the name; the limit imposed by MS-DOS itself is 67 bytes; Novell's NetWare allows filename specifications to reach 128 bytes. Finally, `PgmName` is a pseudo-constant that passes the program name to the `Usage()` and `Banner()` routines we'll meet a few pages later.

The dump() Procedure

The `dump()` procedure isn't actually used anywhere in the program; I left it in the file as a simple example of a useful diagnostic tool. When debugging earlier versions of the program, I used this routine to display any kind of variable or buffer content so that I could see exactly what was stored there (for example, it helped significantly in determining exactly what byte sequences a record pointer uses). If you modify any of the sample programs for special purposes, you may find it equally useful.

```
void dump( BYTE *x, int n )        // used only in debugging
{ int c = 0;
  while( n-- )
    { printf( " %02X ", *x++ );
      if( c++ && !(c & 15) )
        putchar( '\n' );
    }
  putchar ('\n' );
}
```

The only unusual thing about this little routine is the test for a multiple of 16 bytes having been output to force a newline character into the output stream. Declaring x as a pointer to type `BYTE` prevents sign extension of the bytes, which ANSI C automatically performs when promoting type `char` to `int`. `BTRIEVE.H` uses a typedef to make `BYTE` a synonym for `unsigned char`.

The swap() Procedure

The `swap()` procedure undoes Btrieve's word-swapping. I took advantage of special knowledge about the way in which the Borland and Microsoft compilers pass arguments into functions and

how the code returns values in the AX and DX registers to simplify
the swap operation. If it doesn't work with your compiler, replace
the two lines that begin **asm** with the single line that's commented
out.

```
long swap( long n )
{ asm les dx,n;                   // ASM trick for simplicity
  asm mov ax,es;
// return ((n>>16)&0xFFFF) | (n<<16);
}
```

Note that the absence of an explicit return keyword in this function
causes both Borland and Microsoft compilers to issue a warning
message that the function must return a value. It actually does do so
because these compilers return 32-bit values in the DX and AX registers. The high 16 bits are in DX, and the low 16 bits in AX. That's
what the two **asm** statements do: the first puts the high 16 bits of n
into register ES and the low 16 bits into DX, and the second moves
the high 16 bits into AX. This effectively does the word
swap, without using any shift operations.

The equivalent C code that I've commented out uses explicit shifts,
masking, and recombination to achieve the same results in a fully
portable manner.

The main() Procedure

The **main()** procedure appears, unchanged, in all five sample programs. I made this possible by putting all program-specific information in other functions that **main()** calls.

```
int main( int argc, char **argv )
{ int retval = 0;
  Banner();
  if( argc < 2 )
    { Usage();
      retval = 255;
    }
```

In addition to providing the language's required program entry point, this routine does three things. First, it displays the banner and copyright notice through a call to `Banner()`. Then it verifies that at least one parameter was passed on the command line. If not, the program aborts after calling `Usage()` to display a summary of what's needed to run the program.

```
else
  { int i;
    for( i=1; i < argc; i++ )
      { retval = Do_File( argv[i] );   // process each file
          if( retval )                  // if error, wait
            while( getch() != 13 )

              /* wait right here for CR */  ;
        }
    }
  return retval;
}
```

Finally, the routine passes each command-line parameter in turn to `Do_File()`. If `Do_File()` returns a nonzero value (indicating some kind of error), the processing loop waits for a keystroke before continuing. When it has completed processing of all parameters, `main()` returns to the operating system with the last return value from `Do_File()` as its exit code.

The Banner() Procedure

The `Banner()` procedure, called from `main()`, displays a standard banner heading each time the program runs. This procedure appears without change in all five sample programs. The only item that varies from one program to another is the program name itself, taken from the pseudo-constant `PgmName` declared at the top of each source file.

```
void Banner( void )
{ printf( "\n\t    %s - from \"Btrieve Complete\" by Jim Kyle\n",
          PgmName );
  printf( "\t    Copyright 1995 by Jim Kyle - All Rights "
          "Reserved\n" );
  printf( "\t    Use freely, but do not distribute "
          "commercially.\n\n" );
}
```

The Usage() Procedure

The `Usage()` procedure tells how to use the program. Like `Banner()`, this routine obtains the program's name from `PgmName` and plugs it into a standard explanation. The rather strange construction shown in the second `printf()` statement is simply to break the long string across two lines for clarity in the printed listing. This procedure appears unchanged in all five sample programs.

```
void Usage( void )
{ printf( "Usage: %s file1 [file2 [...]]\n", PgmName );
  printf( "\t where filenames can continue until command"
          " line is full\n" );
}
```

The Do_File() Procedure

The `Do_File()` procedure processes a single file, specified by the filename that `main()` passes into the routine. This is the first program-specific module. Although each sample program contains a function with this name and each of them returns an integer value (zero for success or nonzero for any error), the exact actions within each depend upon the specific program.

```
int Do_File( char * fnm )
{ int ret = 0;                          // assume success
```

The function begins by forcing the passed-in filename to upper case (for a professional appearance in the displays), then attempting to open the file.

```
strupr( fnm );
fp = fopen( fnm, "rb" );
```

If the open succeeds, `Do_File()` then copies the filename to the character array `outbuf` so that it can be used by other display functions and calls `GetFormat()` to determine whether the file is in fact a Btrieve file; if so, it identifies the format in use. The return value (0 if not a Btrieve file, 1 for original format, or 2 for the new format) goes into global variable `CurFmt` for subsequent use.

```
if( fp )
  { strcpy( outbuf, fnm );                      // save for reports
    CurFmt = GetFormat();
```

A switch statement controlled by `CurFmt` then executes code appropriate to each possible result.

```
switch( CurFmt )
        {
        case 0:
          printf( "%s is not a Btrieve file.\n", fnm );
          ret = 1;
          break;
        case 1:
          ret = Old_Format();
          break;
        case 2:
          ret = New_Format();
          break;
```

The default option should never occur, but it's nevertheless good defensive programming to include such "impossible" conditions just to be certain that you don't become misled if something goes seriously wrong with your program.

```
    default:
     puts( "Undefined format code, should never happen!" );
     ret = 99;
     break;
    }
  fclose( fp );
}
```

If an error occurs, the value of global variable `fp` after the `fopen()` call will be NULL. In this case, the routine uses the C library function `perror()` to report the nature of the error, then returns to `main()` with an error code of 2.

```
    else
      { perror( fnm );
        ret = 2;
      }
    return ret;
}
```

Regardless of which branch of the switch executes, `Do_File()` returns a defined value to its caller. In the case of the two Btrieve file format branches, this value will be zero for error-free operation. The other two branches return nonzero values to cause `main()` to wait while the user reads the error message displayed.

The GetFormat() Procedure

The `GetFormat()` procedure determines a file's type, then sets global variable `PageSize` and positions the file back to the top of the (first) FCR page.

```
int GetFormat( void )
( int fmt = 0;              // 0 not Btrieve
                            // 1 old, 2 new
   int testbuf[5];          // used to test 10 bytes
```

Local variable `testbuf[]` allows the function to read just the first 10 bytes of the file to determine page size and determine which format is in use. If the third and fourth bytes read (**test-buf[1]**) are any value other than zero, the file cannot be a valid Btrieve file. If they are zero, then the first and second bytes (**testbuf[0]**) indicate which format is present. If they are also zero, the original format is present. If they contain the signature values 'FC', then the new format is in use. If the value is anything else, it's not a Btrieve file.

```
fread( testbuf, 5, 2, fp );
if( testbuf[1] == 0 )                  // page sequence must be zero
  { if( testbuf[0] == 0 )
      fmt = 1;
    else if( testbuf[0] == 0x4346 ) // 'FC' signature
      fmt = 2;
  }
```

The result of the format test determines the value for global variable **PageSize**. If the file passes muster as a Btrieve file, the 16-bit value from bytes 9 and 10 is the page size in bytes. Otherwise, the global variable becomes zero to allow its use as a flag. Since global variable **CurFmt** serves the same flag function, this capability remains unused in BTATR but might be useful in applications derived from this code.

```
if( fmt )                             // set page length if Btrieve
  PageSize = testbuf[4];
else
  PageSize = 0;
```

Finally, GetFormat returns the file position to the front of the file to allow other routines to read from a known starting position, then returns the format code to its caller.

```
  fseek( fp, 0L, 0 );                  // rewind file in any event
  return fmt;
}
```

This version of GetFormat reflects my original design. Other sample programs use a later version that also initializes a global FCR buffer. BTATR doesn't use such a single buffer. Both approaches are valid. I left the early design in this program to show you alternate techniques for accomplishing the same results.

The Old_Format() Procedure

The `Old_Format()` procedure sets up parameters so that `ShowAttrib()` can process an original-format file. First, the routine sets local pointer `ValidFCR` to address `pgbf1[]` and reads the FCR page into array `pgbf1[]`.

```
int Old_Format( void )
{ int ret = 0;
  FCRTOP *ValidFCR = (FCRTOP *)pgbf1;
  fread( pgbf1, PageSize, 1, fp );
```

With the FCR data loaded into the array, `Old_Format()` then calls `ShowAttrib()`, passing in the values from the FCR.

```
  ShowAttrib( "Original",
            ValidFCR->r1.v5.Version,
            ValidFCR->RecLen ? ValidFCR->RecLen
                             : ValidFCR->ComprLen,
            ValidFCR->PhyLen,
            ValidFCR->PagSize,
            ValidFCR->Nkeys,
            ValidFCR->OwnerFlags,
            ValidFCR->UsrFlgs,
            ValidFCR->VRecsOkay,
            ValidFCR->Nrecs,
            ValidFCR->Npages,
            ValidFCR->PreAlloc );
  return ret;
}
```

Since no actual processing occurs in this routine, its return value is always zero (indicating success). In this program, there's no real need to return a value from either `Old_Format()` or `New_Format()`. However, doing so provides a consistency of architecture across the entire suite of utilities.

The New_Format() Procedure

The `New_Format()` procedure sets up parameters so that `ShowAttrib()` can process a new-format file. First, like `Old_Format()`, the routine reads the first FCR page into array `pgbf1[]`. However, it then reads the next page into array `pgbf2[]`.

```
int New_Format( void )
{ int ret = 0;
  FCRTOP *ValidFCR;
  fread( pgbf1, PageSize, 1, fp );
  fread( pgbf2, PageSize, 1, fp );
```

Next, `New_Format()` compares the `r1.v6.Usage` values from `pgbf1[]` and `pgbf2[]` to determine which should be addressed by `ValidFCR`, and sets `ValidFCR` to the appropriate address.

```
  if( ((FCRTOP *)pgbf1)->r1.v6.Usage >
      ((FCRTOP *)pgbf2)->r1.v6.Usage )
    ValidFCR = (FCRTOP *)pgbf1;
  else
    ValidFCR = (FCRTOP *)pgbf2;
```

With the FCR data loaded into the array and `ValidFCR` correctly set, `New_Format()` then calls `ShowAttrib()`, passing in the values from the FCR. Note the difference in the Version argument reference between the old and new formats.

```
  ShowAttrib( "New 6.+ version",
              ValidFCR->r7.v6.Version,
              ValidFCR->RecLen ? ValidFCR->RecLen
                               : ValidFCR->ComprLen,
              ValidFCR->PhyLen,
              ValidFCR->PagSize,
```

```
            ValidFCR->Nkeys,
            ValidFCR->OwnerFlags,
            ValidFCR->UsrFlgs,
            ValidFCR->VRecsOkay,
            ValidFCR->Nrecs,
            ValidFCR->Npages,
            ValidFCR->PreAlloc );
  return ret;
}
```

The IsSet() Procedure

The `IsSet()` procedure tells whether a bit pattern is set or not. It returns a true value (1) if every set bit of the pattern supplied as `Atr` is also set in the flag word `fflg`, and false (0) otherwise. This is a helper procedure, called only by `ShowAttrib()`.

```
int IsSet( int Atr, int fflg )      // true if bits match exactly
{ return (fflg & Atr) == Atr;
}
```

The ShowAttrib() Procedure

The `ShowAttrib()` procedure lists attributes of the file. Its argument list includes all the FCR variables required to generate the display. This routine is the heart of BTATR.C.

Local variables serve as arrays of character strings to translate codes into meaningful display language, and other variables provide internal flags that signal presence or absence of each possible attribute. The array `eng[]` includes three strings that never display; they're present simply to fill the space since the lowest valid version code is 3.

```
void ShowAttrib( char * fmt, int ev, int recsiz, int phylen, int
                 pagsiz, int nk, char oflags, int fflgs, char
                 vrec, long nrec, long npg, int pre )
{ char *eng[] = { "c=0", "c=1", "c=2", "4.0", "4.1", "5.0",
                  "6.0" };
  char *acc[] = { "by anyone", "only by owner" };
  char *yn[] = { " not ", " " };
  int pubr, pubw, encr, trun, cmpr, var, vthresh;
```

Immediately upon entry, `ShowAttrib()` sets local variables `cmpr`, `var`, and `trun` either TRUE or FALSE by using `IsSet()` to verify the corresponding bit patterns in the passed-in `fflags` value. These variables, when TRUE, indicate that data is compressed, that record length is variable, and that trailing-blank truncation is in use. It's necessary to make two tests to establish presence of variable-length records since some versions of Btrieve leave that portion of the file flag word clear after the file is created. Then, if `var` is TRUE, variable `vthresh` becomes the numeric percentage for the threshold value of free space (which applies only when record length is variable).

```
trun = IsSet( AT_TRUNCBLK, fflgs );
cmpr = IsSet( AT_COMPRDAT, fflgs );
var = vrec || IsSet( AT_VARLEN, fflgs );
if( var )
  { vthresh = (( fflgs >> 6 ) & 3 ) * 10;
    if( !vthresh )
      vthresh = 5;
  }
```

Next, `ShowAttrib()` establishes values for the three local variables dealing with access control, based on the existence of an owner name for the file as encoded into the Version word `ev`. This word is made negative if an owner name exists; it's left positive if the file has no owner. Any owned file may be written only by its owner, but the ability to read the file may be granted to anyone. Similarly, the content of an owned file may be encrypted if desired. The default values for these abilities are that the file may be read by all, and data is not encrypted. After access flags are set, the routine shifts `ev` to the low byte so that its value can be used to select an output string.

```
if( ev < 0 )
  { pubw = 1;
    pubr = !(oflags & 1);
    encr = (oflags & 2) == 2;
    ev = ( 0 - ev ) >> 8;
  }
```

```
else
  { pubr = pubw = encr = 0;
    ev >>= 8;
  }
```

Once the critical flag variables are established, `ShowAttrib()` begins displaying information on the screen. All output goes to `stdout` via `printf()` and `puts()` so that it may be redirected as you desire. First, the routine displays the filename, followed by the string that describes the output format. The third item displayed is the version number required by the file. This may differ from the version of Btrieve that created the file. If a file uses only those capabilities and format that existed at version 4.0, BTATR reports that version here, even if version 6.15 created the file.

```
printf( "Attributes for file %s:\n", outbuf );
printf( "Format: %-20.20s", fmt );
printf( "Requires Btrieve version %s (or later) engine.\n\n",
        eng[ev] );
```

After reporting the filename, format, and version information, the routine continues, displaying record size, page size, number of indexes, page wastage, and item size. The record size always displays the fixed-length value; variable-length records may be larger, but never smaller. For compressed files, this size is the uncompressed size of each record.

Item size includes all overhead associated with each data record on the data page. This normally will be equal to or greater than record size. When data compression exists, the item size is fixed at 5 bytes for the original format or 7 bytes for the new; record size normally is much larger.

A unique feature of BTATR is its display of the amount of space wasted, in bytes, on each data page. The program calculates this value by subtracting the fixed page header's 6 bytes from the page size, then dividing by the item size and reporting the remainder.

```
printf( "Sizes: Record: %4d bytes, ", recsiz );
printf( "Page: %4d bytes.    ", pagsiz );
if( nk )
  { printf( "Has %d index%s", nk, nk>1 ? "es" : "" );
    if( IsSet( AT_SPECKEY, fflgs ) )
      printf( ", prenumbered" );
  }
else
  printf( "Has no index" );
printf( ".\n            Wastage: %4d bytes (per page)\t"
        "Item size: %4d bytes.\n\n",
        (pagsiz - 6) % phylen, phylen );
```

With all size statistics complete, the next few statements display access rights to the data. The strings defined in array acc[], selected by the value in the corresponding flag variable, convert the rights into a verbal description as shown by Figures 10.1 and 10.2. Array yn[] provides either a single blank space or the word *not* for the encryption report. Since only an owned file can be encrypted, this part of the display occurs only when the file has an owner (flagged by pubw).

```
printf( "Access: Can be read %s, ", acc[ pubr ] );
printf( "edited %s.\t", acc[ pubw ] );
if( pubw )
  printf( "Data is%sencrypted.", yn[ encr ] );
printf( "\n\n" );
```

The remaining print statements report various attributes of the file as indicated (mostly) by the file flag word. The first indicates whether record length is fixed or variable and if it is variable also reports the threshold value. The remaining reports are largely self-explanatory, but it's worth noting the decision structure that substitutes the word *No* for the value 0 when some of the values aren't applicable to the file under examination.

```
if( var )
  printf( "Attributes: Record length is variable "
          "(threshold: %d percent)\n", vthresh );
else
  printf( "Attributes: Record length is fixed\n" );

if( var )
  printf( "            Blanks are%struncated\n", yn[ trun ] );
printf( "            Data is%scompressed\n", yn[ cmpr ] );

if( IsSet( AT_PREALLOC, fflgs ) )
  printf( "            %d pages were preallocated for " "the
          file\n", pre );
else
  puts( "            No pages were preallocated for"
        "the file" );

  printf( "            File is%sKey-Only\n",
          yn[ IsSet( AT_KEYONLY, fflgs ) ] );

  printf( "            Index-balancing flag is%sset\n",
          yn[ IsSet( AT_BALANCE, fflgs ) ] );
```

The final two attributes apply only to the new file format and are skipped entirely for versions earlier than 6.0.

```
if( ev > 5 )
  { printf( "            Duplicate-key pointers "
            "were%sreserved\n",
            yn[ IsSet( AT_DUPPTRS, fflgs ) ] );
    printf( "            VATs are%sused\n",
            yn[ IsSet( AT_USEVATS, fflgs ) ] );
  }
```

With all attributes reported, the final line BTATR displays is the current count of records and active pages. For the new format, the page count includes only those currently active, which may be significantly less than the total number contained in the file because of the shadow paging techniques. Both these values appear in the FCR as word-swapped 32-bit items, so swap() must reverse the word order before they can print accurately.

```
printf( "\nFile currently contains %ld records, "
        "on %ld pages.\n\n",
        swap(nrec),
        swap(npg) );
}
```

Unlike most of the other routines we've seen, `ShowAttrib()`
returns no value to its caller. It merely displays the desired information to `stdout`, then returns.

The Complete BTATR.C Listing

Now that we've examined in detail each of its component modules,
here's the complete listing for BTATR.C as it appears on the companion diskette:

```
/* * * * * * * * * * * * * * * * * * * * * * * * *\
 *                                               *
 *      BTATR.C - Jim Kyle - January 1995        *
 *                                               *
 *      Reports attributes from any version of   *
 *      Btrieve file without requiring Btrieve   *
 *      engine to be installed in system.        *
 *                                               *
\* * * * * * * * * * * * * * * * * * * * * * * * */

#include <stdio.h>
#include <conio.h>
#ifdef __TURBOC__
#include <alloc.h>        // Borland-specific
#else
#include <malloc.h>       // Microsoft version
#endif
#include <string.h>
#include "btrieve.h"
#define AT_VARLEN   0x001  // file attribute bit patterns
#define AT_TRUNCBLK 0x002
#define AT_PREALLOC 0x004
#define AT_COMPRDAT 0x008
#define AT_KEYONLY  0x010
```

```
#define AT_BALANCE    0x020
#define AT_KEEP10     0x040
#define AT_KEEP20     0x080
#define AT_KEEP30     0x0C0
#define AT_DUPPTRS    0x100
#define AT_RESERVE    0x200
#define AT_SPECKEY    0x400
#define AT_USEVATS    0x800
BYTE pgbf1[4096], pgbf2[4096];   // max page size
FILE *fp;
char outbuf[512];
int PageSize;
char *PgmName = "BTATR";

void dump( BYTE *x, int n )      // used only in debugging
{ int c = 0;
  while( n-- )
    { printf( " %02X ", *x++ );
      if( c++ && !(c & 15) )
        putchar( '\n' );
    }
  putchar ('\n' );
}


/* * * * * * * * * * * * * * * * * * * * * * * * *\
 *                                              *
 *      This procedure undoes Btrieve"s         *
 *      word-swapping.                          *
 *                                              *
\* * * * * * * * * * * * * * * * * * * * * * * * */
long swap( long n )
{ asm les dx,n;                          // ASM trick for simplicity
  asm mov ax,es;
// return ((n>>16)&0xFFFF) | (n<<16);
}
```

```
/* * * * * * * * * * * * * * * * * * * * * * * *\
 *                                             *
 *       This procedure tells if bit pattern   *
 *       is set or not.                        *
 *                                             *
\* * * * * * * * * * * * * * * * * * * * * * * */
int IsSet( int Atr, int fflg )     // true if bits match exactly
{ return (fflg & Atr) == Atr;
}


/* * * * * * * * * * * * * * * * * * * * * * * *\
 *                                             *
 *       This procedure lists attributes of    *
 *       the file.                             *
 *                                             *
\* * * * * * * * * * * * * * * * * * * * * * * */
void ShowAttrib( char * fmt, int ev, int recsiz,
                 int phylen, int pagsiz, int nk,
                 char oflags, int fflgs, char vrec,
                 long nrec, long npg, int pre )
{ char *eng[] = { "c=0", "c=1", "c=2", "4.0", "4.1", "5.0",
                  "6.0" };
  char *acc[] = { "by anyone", "only by owner" };
  char *yn[] = { " not ", " " };
  int pubr, pubw, encr, trun, cmpr, var, vthresh;
  trun = IsSet( AT_TRUNCBLK, fflgs );
  cmpr = IsSet( AT_COMPRDAT, fflgs );
  var = vrec || IsSet( AT_VARLEN, fflgs );
  if( var )
    { vthresh = (( fflgs >> 6 ) & 3 ) * 10;
      if( !vthresh )
        vthresh = 5;
    }

  if( ev < 0 )
    { pubw = 1;
      pubr = !(oflags & 1);
      encr = (oflags & 2) == 2;
      ev = ( 0 - ev ) >> 8;
    }
  else
```

```
    { pubr = pubw = encr = 0;
      ev >>= 8;
    }

printf( "Attributes for file %s:\n", outbuf );
printf( "Format: %-20.20s", fmt );
printf( "Requires Btrieve version %s (or later) engine.\n\n",
          eng[ev] );
printf( "Sizes: Record: %4d bytes, ", recsiz );
printf( "Page: %4d bytes.    ", pagsiz );
if( nk )
  { printf( "Has %d index%s", nk, nk>1 ? "es" : "" );
    if( IsSet( AT_SPECKEY, fflgs ) )
      printf( ", prenumbered" );
  }
else
  printf( "Has no index" );
printf( ".\n    Wastage: %4d bytes (per page)\t"
        "Item size: %4d bytes.\n\n",
        (pagsiz - 6) % phylen, phylen );

printf( "Access: Can be read %s, ", acc[ pubr ] );
printf( "edited %s.\t", acc[ pubw ] );
if( pubw )
  printf( "Data is%sencrypted.", yn[ encr ] );
printf( "\n\n" );
if( var )
  printf( "Attributes: Record length is variable "
          "(threshold: %d percent)\n", vthresh );
else
  printf( "Attributes: Record length is fixed\n" );
if( var )
  printf( "         Blanks are%struncated\n", yn[ trun ] );
printf( "         Data is%scompressed\n", yn[ cmpr ] );

if( IsSet( AT_PREALLOC, fflgs ) )
  printf( "         %d pages were preallocated for "
                "the file\n", pre );
else
  puts( "         No pages were preallocated for "
        "the file" );
```

```
   printf( "            File is%sKey-Only\n",
           yn[ IsSet( AT_KEYONLY, fflgs ) ] );
   printf( "       Index-balancing flag is%sset\n",
           yn[ IsSet( AT_BALANCE, fflgs ) ]);
   if( ev > 5 )
     { print( "      Duplicate-key pointers "
                "were%sreserved\n",
                yn[ IsSet( AT_DUPPTRS, fflgs ) ] );
       printf( "            VATs are%sused\n",
                yn[ IsSet( AT_USEVATS, fflgs ) ] );
     }

   printf( "\nFile currently contains %ld records, "
           "on %ld pages.\n\n",
           swap(nrec),
           swap(npg) );
}


/* * * * * * * * * * * * * * * * * * * * * * * *\
 *                                             *
 *    This procedure sets up original-format   *
 *    file.                                     *
 *                                             *
\* * * * * * * * * * * * * * * * * * * * * * * */
int Old_Format( void )
{ int ret = 0;
  FCRTOP *ValidFCR = (FCRTOP *)pgbf1;
  fread( pgbf1, PageSize, 1, fp );

  ShowAttrib( "Original",
             ValidFCR->r1.v5.Version,
             ValidFCR->RecLen ? ValidFCR->RecLen
                             : ValidFCR->ComprLen,
             ValidFCR->PhyLen,
             ValidFCR->PagSize,
             ValidFCR->Nkeys,
             ValidFCR->OwnerFlags,
             ValidFCR->UsrFlgs,
             ValidFCR->VRecsOkay,
             ValidFCR->Nrecs,
```

```
                    ValidFCR->Npages,
                    ValidFCR->PreAlloc );
      return ret;
    }


    /* * * * * * * * * * * * * * * * * * * * * *\
     *                                           *
     *      This procedure sets up a new-format  *
     *      file.                                 *
     *                                           *
    \* * * * * * * * * * * * * * * * * * * * * */
    int New_Format( void )
    { int ret = 0;
      FCRTOP *ValidFCR;
      fread( pgbf1, PageSize, 1, fp );
      fread( pgbf2, PageSize, 1, fp );
      if( ((FCRTOP *)pgbf1)->r1.v6.Usage >
          ((FCRTOP *)pgbf2)->r1.v6.Usage )
        ValidFCR = (FCRTOP *)pgbf1;
      else
        ValidFCR = (FCRTOP *)pgbf2;

      ShowAttrib( "New 6.+ version",
                    ValidFCR->r7.v6.Version,
                    ValidFCR->RecLen ? ValidFCR->RecLen
                                      : ValidFCR->ComprLen,
                  ValidFCR->PhyLen,
                  ValidFCR->PagSize,
                  ValidFCR->Nkeys,
                  ValidFCR->OwnerFlags,
                  ValidFCR->UsrFlgs,
                  ValidFCR->VRecsOkay,
                  ValidFCR->Nrecs,
                  ValidFCR->Npages,
                  ValidFCR->PreAlloc );
      return ret;
    }
```

```
/* * * * * * * * * * * * * * * * * * * * * * * *\
 *                                             *
 *    This procedure determines a file"s type, *
 *    then sets PageSize and positions to the  *
 *    start of the file.                       *
 *                                             *
\* * * * * * * * * * * * * * * * * * * * * * * */
int GetFormat( void )
{ int fmt = 0;                      // 0 not Btrieve
                                    // 1 old, 2 new
  int testbuf[5];                   // used to test 10 bytes

  fread( testbuf, 5, 2, fp );
  if( testbuf[1] == 0 )            // page sequence must be zero
    { if( testbuf[0] == 0 )
        fmt = 1;
      else if( testbuf[0] == 0x4346 )          // 'FC' signature
        fmt = 2;
    }

  if( fmt )                    // set page length if Btrieve
    PageSize = testbuf[4];
  else
    PageSize = 0;

  fseek( fp, 0L, 0 );          // rewind file in any event
  return fmt;
}


/* * * * * * * * * * * * * * * * * * * * * * * *\
 *                                             *
 *    This procedure processes a single file.  *
 *                                             *
\* * * * * * * * * * * * * * * * * * * * * * * */
int Do_File( char * fnm )
{ int ret = 0;                                  // assume success

  strupr( fnm );
  fp = fopen( fnm, "rb" );
  if( fp )
```

```
      { strcpy( outbuf, fnm );                    // save for reports
        CurFmt = GetFormat();
        switch( CurFmt )
          {
          case 0:
            printf( "%s is not a Btrieve file.\n", fnm );
            ret = 1;
            break;
          case 1:
            ret = Old_Format();
            break;
          case 2:
            ret = New_Format();
            break;
          default:
            puts( "Undefined format code, should never happen!" );
            ret = 99;
            break;
          }
        fclose( fp );
      }
    else
      { perror( fnm );
        ret = 2;
      }
    return ret;
}


/* * * * * * * * * * * * * * * * * * * * * * * * *\
 *                                               *
 *     This procedure tells how to use the       *
 *        program.                               *
 *                                               *
\* * * * * * * * * * * * * * * * * * * * * * * * */
void Usage( void )
{ printf( "Usage: %s file1 [file2 [...]]\n", PgmName );
  printf( "\t where filenames can continue until command" " line
          is full\n" );
}
```

```
/* * * * * * * * * * * * * * * * * * * * * * * *\
 *                                             *
 *  This procedure displays a standard banner  *
 *  heading each time the program runs.        *
 *                                             *
\* * * * * * * * * * * * * * * * * * * * * * * */
void Banner( void )
{ printf( "\n\t     %s - from \"Btrieve Complete\" by Jim Kyle\n",
                 PgmName );
  printf( "\t     Copyright 1995 by Jim Kyle - All Rights "
                 "Reserved\n" );
  printf( "\t     Use freely, but do not distribute "
                 "commercially.\n\n" );
}


/* * * * * * * * * * * * * * * * * * * * * * * *\
 *                                             *
 *     This procedure is program entry point.  *
 *                                             *
\* * * * * * * * * * * * * * * * * * * * * * * */
int main( int argc, char **argv )
{ int retval = 0;
  Banner();
  if( argc < 2 )
    { Usage();
      retval = 255;
    }
  else
    { int i;
      for( i=1; i < argc; i++ )
        { retval = Do_File( argv[i] );  // process each file
          if( retval )                  // if error, wait
            while( getch() != 13 )
              /* wait right here for CR */  ;
        }
    }
  return retval;
}
```

To compile BTATR.EXE, using Borland's compilers, use the command line

```
BCC -ml BTATR.C
```

The -ml switch specifies large memory model. No other special options are necessary.

Looking at Index Information

Another frequent need of both the developer and the system administrator is to determine a file's index structure. Our second sample program (BTKEY) extracts from the FCR record of any Btrieve file full details for all segments of all keys.

As is true for most of the information that BTATR shows, the data that BTKEY displays is also available by use of BTI's BUTIL -STAT utility option, but BTKEY doesn't require the presence of Btrieve to locate the information. The presentation differs somewhat from that of BUTIL, as shown in Figure 10.3. This capture displays index information for a renamed copy of the FILE.DDF data dictionary file.

Figure 10.3   *The BTKEY program displays full specifications for all segments of all keys.*

```
C:\SAMPLES>btkey file.btr

              BTKEY - from "Btrieve Complete" by Jim Kyle
              Copyright 1995 by Jim Kyle - All Rights Reserved
              Use freely, but do not distribute commercially.


Key specifications for File FILE.BTR:
Format: Original            Requires Btrieve version 4.0 (or later) engine.
This file has 2 indexes. The file contains 11 records, on 7 pages.
```

Key Nbr	Seg Nbr	Offset in rec	Segment Length	Data Type	Flags	Null Value	Unique Values	ACS Nbr
0	0	0	2	binary	(none)	0	11	0
1	0	2	20	ASCII	MC	0	11	0

```
Flags:  < = Descending Order          S = Supplemental Index
        D = Duplicates Allowed        A = Any Segment (Manual)
            rD = repeated             L = All Segments (Null)
            lD = linked               C = ACS used
        I = Case Insensitive              *C = Multiple ACS
        M = Modifiable
```

Since the key specification area of the FCR page is the only place within a Btrieve file where any indication of the type of data within a record occurs, a copy of the BTKEY report can be quite useful when you are trying to create data dictionary files without access to the original layout for a file that a third-party application has created. To create one, simply run BTKEY on the file in question, redirecting output to your printer by the command line

```
BTKEY MyFile.Dat >PRN
```

Reused Procedures

BTKEY reuses many of the procedures from BTATR without change. In addition, the included header files are the same, as are most of the declared constants and variables. The only significant changes in the variables are that PgmName is now BTKEY, and an array of data type names translates Btrieve's extended data type codes to the corresponding names (see Chapter 5):

```
static char * datatypes[] = {
  "String",
  "Integer",
  "Float",
  "Date",
  "Time",
  "Decimal",
  "Money",
  "Logical",
  "Numeric",
  "Bfloat",
  "Lstring",
  "Zstring",
  "Note",
  "Lvar",
  "Unsigned",
  "AutoInc",
  "Bit",
  "STS",
  "ASCII",                  // not extended types
  "binary"
};
```

The final two items in the `datatypes[]` array are not actual extended data names. Instead, these are the original two data types. When the segment's flag word indicates absence of any extended type, the appropriate bit of the flag word forces the program to modify its copy of the type code to one of these indexing values. This change occurs in the `ShowKeys()` routine, as it reads each segment into memory to create the display line and has no effect on the file itself.

Procedures that BTKEY reuses, unchanged, from BTATR are `main()`, `Banner()`, `Usage()`, `Do_File()`, `GetFormat()`, `IsSet()`, and `swap()`. (`Do_File()` and `GetFormat()` have one minor change, to show use of a local variable for `fp` instead of the global variable. This change also affects `Old_Format()`, `New_Format()`, and `ShowAttrib()`.) The `Old_Format()`, `New_Format()`, and `ShowAttrib()` routines undergo extensive simplification. Only `ShowKeys()` and `attrib()` are totally new for this program.

The Old_Format() Procedure

The `Old_Format()` procedure used in BTKEY differs from that of BTATR in only two details. First, it takes `fp` as a passed-in argument rather than using a global variable. The purpose of this change is simply to show alternate methods of accomplishing the same function. The other difference is that it passes far fewer values to `ShowAttrib()`.

```
int Old_Format( FILE *fp )
{ int ret = 0;
  FCRTOP *ValidFCR = (FCRTOP *)pgbf1;
  fread( pgbf1, PageSize, 1, fp );

  ShowAttrib( "Original",
              ValidFCR->r1.v5.Version,
              ValidFCR->Nkeys,
              ValidFCR->UsrFlgs,
              ValidFCR->Nrecs,
              ValidFCR->Npages,
              ValidFCR );
  return ret;
}
```

The New_Format() Procedure

Like `Old_Format()`, the `New_Format()` procedure used in BTKEY differs from that of BTATR in the same two details. All other actions are identical to those described for BTATR.

```
int New_Format( FILE *fp )
{ int ret = 0;
  FCRTOP *ValidFCR;
  fread( pgbf1, PageSize, 1, fp );
  fread( pgbf2, PageSize, 1, fp );
  if( ((FCRTOP *)pgbf1)->r1.v6.Usage >
      ((FCRTOP *)pgbf2)->r1.v6.Usage )
    ValidFCR = (FCRTOP *)pgbf1;
  else
    ValidFCR = (FCRTOP *)pgbf2;

  ShowAttrib( "New 6.+ version",
              ValidFCR->r7.v6.Version,
              ValidFCR->Nkeys,
              ValidFCR->UsrFlgs,
              ValidFCR->Nrecs,
              ValidFCR->Npages,
              ValidFCR );
  return ret;
}
```

The ShowAttrib() Procedure

The `ShowAttrib()` procedure lists several essential attributes of the file, then calls ShowKeys to report detailed data for each defined key. This routine is similar to the version used in BTATR, but has a much smaller list of arguments and uses only the version-level translation table. It prints only the file name, format, version level, and number of indexes, then reports file size and calls `ShowKeys()` to analyze the key segment specifications.

```
void ShowAttrib( char * fmt, int ev, int nk,
                 int fflgs, long nrec, long npg,
                 FCRTOP * ValidFCR )
```

```
{ char *eng[] = { "c=0", "c=1", "c=2", "4.0", "4.1", "5.0", "6.0"
                 };

  if( ev < 0 )
      ev = ( 0 - ev ) >> 8;
  else
      ev >>= 8;
  printf( "\nKey specifications for File %s:\n", outbuf );
  printf( "Format: %-20.20s", fmt );
  printf( "Requires Btrieve version %s (or later) engine.\n",
          eng[ev] );

  if( nk )
    { printf( "This file has %d index%s", nk, nk>1 ? "es" : "" );
      if( IsSet( AT_SPECKEY, fflgs ) )
        printf( ", prenumbered" );
      printf( ". " );
    }
  else
    printf( "Has no index. " );

  printf( "The file contains %ld records, on %ld pages.\n\n",
          swap(nrec),
          swap(npg) );
  ShowKeys( ev, nk, (SEGSPEC *)((char *)ValidFCR+0x110) );
}
```

The only point worthy of note in this routine is the rather convoluted typecasting necessary to establish a starting address for the segment specification information in the call to ShowKeys(). Although the new file format uses a Key Allocation Table that may (in some future version) allow segment specifications to appear elsewhere, all current versions of Btrieve place the segment information at offset 0x110 within the FCR page. BTKEY ignores the KAT complication.

The ShowKeys() Procedure

The ShowKeys() procedure reports detailed descriptions for each segment of each key defined in the FCR. This procedure is the heart of BTKEY. The routine takes three arguments. The first is the version code (ev), the second is the number of keys (nk), and the last is a pointer to the segment specification at which to start reporting (keyseg). A local variable (kn), initialized to zero at entry, holds the number of the key currently being processed.

```
void ShowKeys( int ev, int nk, SEGSPEC * keyseg )
{ int kn = 0;
```

The first two lines that ShowKeys() displays provide column headings for its tabular listing.

```
printf( "  Key  Seg  Offset  Segment Data Type  " );
printf( "Flags       Null      Unique    ACS\n" );
printf( "  Nbr  Nbr  in rec  Length             " );
printf( "            Value    Values    Nbr\n" );
```

After displaying the headings, ShowKeys() enters a key-processing loop that repeats so long as nk is greater than zero. Each time the loop returns to begin processing a new key, it resets to zero a local variable (sn) that identifies the current segment number. Next, the routine tests the Kflags word within the segment specification that keyseg addresses, for presence of extended data types (Bit 8, 256). If no extended data type code is present, the routine tests the ASCII/binary bit (Bit 2, 4) of Kflags and sets the data type code to 18 for ASCII, or 19 for binary. This allows the reporting routine to use the datatypes[] array for all text translation of data types, but will require change if BTI defines any additional data types in future versions of Btrieve.

```
while( nk-- )
  { int sn = 0;
    if( !(keyseg->Kflags & 256) )
      { if( keyseg->Kflags & 4 )
          keyseg->ExTyp = 19;
        else
          keyseg->ExTyp = 18;
      }
```

After adjusting if necessary, the routine displays the first line of the report for the current key, incrementing both `kn` and `sn` as it does so. It also calls `attrib()` within this `printf()` call, to translate the attributes of the segment into an appropriate code for display. The ACS-code display will be zero for all original-format files, but may vary for new-format files that contain multiple alternate collating sequences.

```
printf( "%6d %5d %8d %7d   %-13.13s %-9.9s %5X %8ld %6d\n",
        kn++,                                  // key
        sn++,                                  // seg
        keyseg->Beg,                           // position
        keyseg->Len,                           // length
        datatypes[ keyseg->ExTyp ],            // datatype
        attrib( ev, keyseg->Kflags ),
        keyseg->NulVal,                        // nulval
        swap( keyseg->Total ),                 // total
        *(int *)(keyseg->r1.v6.ACSPage) );     // ACS code
```

With the segment-0 information for the key displayed, the routine enters an inner loop that continues so long as Bit 4 of the `Kflags` word is set (indicating that another segment of the same key follows immediately). This loop performs the same adjustment of `ExTyp`, then displays a simpler report that omits the key number. If the key has no additional segments, the test fails immediately. No spurious report appears. The first statement within the loop increments the `keyseg` pointer to address the next complete segment, taking advantage of C's pointer arithmetic. When the loop completes, after displaying zero or more lines, the pointer increments again in order to move past the last segment displayed.

```
while( keyseg->Kflags & 16 )              // more segments
  { keyseg++;
    if( !(keyseg->Kflags & 256) )
      { if( keyseg->Kflags & 4 )
          keyseg->ExTyp = 19;
        else
          keyseg->ExTyp = 18;
      }
```

```
        printf( "%6s %5d %8d %7d  %-13.13s %-9.9s %5X\n",
                " ",                        // key is blank
                sn++,                       // seg
                keyseg->Beg,                // position
                keyseg->Len,                // length
                datatypes[ keyseg->ExTyp ],
                attrib( ev, keyseg->Kflags ),
                keyseg->NulVal );           // nulval
    }
  keyseg++;
}
```

After displaying all segments of all keys, in sequence, the routine
finally shows a legend that translates the single-character (mostly)
codes generated by **attrib()** into more complete descriptions of
the segment attributes:

```
  puts( "\nFlags:\t< = Descending Order                    "
        "S = Supplemental Index" );
  puts( "\tD = Duplicates Allowed                    A = Any "
        "Segment (Manual)" );
  puts( "\t    rD = repeated                    L = All "
        "Segments (Null)" );
  puts( "\t    lD = Linked                    C = ACS used" );
  puts( "\tI = Case Insensitive                 "
        "*C = Multiple ACS" );
  puts( "\tM = Modifiable" );
}
```

The attrib() Function

The **attrib()** function returns a string that describes the
attribute flags for each segment. This function simply tests each bit
pattern and, if set, adds an appropriate indicator character (or
sequence of characters, in the cases of a few new variations) to the
string it constructs.

```
char * attrib( int ver, int x )
{ static char ret[20];
  ret[0] = 0;
```

```
if( ((ver >> 8) == 5 ) && (x & 128) )
  strcat( ret, "S" );
if( x & 2 )
  strcat( ret, "M" );
if( x & 8 )
  strcat( ret, "L" );
if( x & 512 )                              // added at 6.0
  strcat( ret, "A" );
if( x & 32 )
  { if( x & 1024 )                         // added at 6.0
      strcat( ret, "*" );
    strcat( ret, "C" );
  }
else if( x & 1024 )
  strcat( ret, "I" );
if( x & 64 )
  strcat( ret, "<" );
if( x & 1 )                      // duplicate-key handling
  { if( (ver >> 8) >= 6 )
      { if( x & 128 )            // added at 6.0
                                 // made user-settable at 6.1
          strcat( ret, "r" );
        else
          strcat( ret, "l" );
      }
    strcat( ret, "D" );
  }
```

At the end of the analysis, if the string contains no indicators,
attrib() copies the word "(none)" to the string to indicate that
this segment has no special characteristics.

```
if( !strlen( ret ) )
  strcat( ret, "(none)" );
return ret;
}
```

The Complete BTKEY.C Listing

Now that we've examined each of its component modules, here's
the complete listing for BTKEY.C as it appears on the companion
diskette:

```
/* * * * * * * * * * * * * * * * * * * * * *\
 *                                          *
 *   BTKEY.C - Jim Kyle - January 1995      *
 *                                          *
 *   Reports key segment specifications from *
 *   any Btrieve file without requiring Btrieve *
 *   engine installed in system.            *
 *                                          *
\* * * * * * * * * * * * * * * * * * * * * */
#include <stdio.h>
#include <conio.h>
#ifdef __TURBOC__
#include <alloc.h>          // Borland-specific
#else
#include <malloc.h>         // Microsoft version
#endif
#include <string.h>

#include "btrieve.h"

#define AT_VARLEN   0x001   // file attribute bit patterns
#define AT_TRUNCBLK 0x002
#define AT_PREALLOC 0x004
#define AT_COMPRDAT 0x008
#define AT_KEYONLY  0x010
#define AT_BALANCE  0x020
#define AT_KEEP10   0x040
#define AT_KEEP20   0x080
#define AT_KEEP30   0x0C0
#define AT_DUPPTRS  0x100
#define AT_RESERVE  0x200
#define AT_SPECKEY  0x400
#define AT_USEVATS  0x800
BYTE *pgbf1, *pgbf2;
char outbuf[512];
```

```
int PageSize;
char *PgmName = "BTKEY";
static char * datatypes[] = {
  "String",
  "Integer",
  "Float",
  "Date",
  "Time",
  "Decimal",
  "Money",
  "Logical",
  "Numeric",
  "Bfloat",
  "Lstring",
  "Zstring",
  "Note",
  "Lvar",
  "Unsigned",
  "AutoInc",
  "Bit",
  "STS",
  "ASCII",                                    // not extended types
  "binary"
};


/* * * * * * * * * * * * * * * * * * * * * * * *\
 *                                             *
 *       This procedure undoes Btrieve"s       *
 *       word-swapping.                        *
 *                                             *
\* * * * * * * * * * * * * * * * * * * * * * * */
long swap( long n )
{ asm les dx,n;                          // ASM trick for simplicity
  asm mov ax,es;
  //return ((n>>16)&0xFFFF) | (n<<16);
}
```

```
/* * * * * * * * * * * * * * * * * * * * * * * *\
 *                                               *
 *     This function returns a string that       *
 *     describes the attribute flags for each    *
 *     segment.                                   *
 *                                               *
\* * * * * * * * * * * * * * * * * * * * * * * */
char * attrib( int ver, int x )
{ static char ret[20];
  ret[0] = 0;

  if( ((ver >> 8) == 5 ) && (x & 128) )
    strcat( ret, "S" );
  if( x & 2 )
    strcat( ret, "M" );
  if( x & 8 )
    strcat( ret, "L" );
  if( x & 512 )                  // added at 6.0
    strcat( ret, "A" );
  if( x & 32 )
    { if( x & 1024 )             // added at 6.0
        strcat( ret, "*" );
      strcat( ret, "C" );
    }
  else if( x & 1024 )
    strcat( ret, "I" );
  if( x & 64 )
    strcat( ret, "<" );
  if( x & 1 )                    // duplicate-key handling
    { if( (ver >> 8) >= 6 )
        { if( x & 128 )          // added at 6.0
                                 // made user-settable at 6.1
            strcat( ret, "r" );
          else
            strcat( ret, "l" );
        }
      strcat( ret, "D" );
    }
  if( !strlen( ret ) )
    strcat( ret, "(none)" );
  return ret;
}
```

```
/* * * * * * * * * * * * * * * * * * * * * * *\
 *                                            *
 *    This procedure reports details for all  *
 *    segments of each key defined in the FCR. *
 *                                            *
\* * * * * * * * * * * * * * * * * * * * * * */
void ShowKeys( int ev, int nk, SEGSPEC * keyseg )
{ int kn = 0;
  printf( " Key  Seg  Offset  Segment Data Type  " );
  printf( "Flags     Null    Unique   ACS\n" );
  printf( " Nbr  Nbr  in rec  Length            " );
  printf( "           Value  Values   Nbr\n" );

  while( nk-- )
    { int sn = 0;
      if( !(keyseg->Kflags & 256) )
        { if( keyseg->Kflags & 4 )
            keyseg->ExTyp = 19;
          else
            keyseg->ExTyp = 18;
        }

      printf( "%6d %5d %8d %7d  %-13.13s %-9.9s %5X %8ld %6d\n",
              kn++,                        // key
              sn++,                        // seg
              keyseg->Beg,                 // position
              keyseg->Len,                 // length
              datatypes[ keyseg->ExTyp ],  // datatype
              attrib( ev, keyseg->Kflags ),
              keyseg->NulVal,              // nulval
              swap( keyseg->Total ),       // total
              *(int *)(keyseg->r1.v6.ACSPage) ); // ACS code
      while( keyseg->Kflags & 16 )                      // more segments
        { keyseg++;
          if( !(keyseg->Kflags & 256) )
            { if( keyseg->Kflags & 4 )
                keyseg->ExTyp = 19;
              else
                keyseg->ExTyp = 18;
            }
          printf( "%6s %5d %8d %7d  %-13.13s %-9.9s %5X\n",
```

```
                    " ",                            // key is blank
                    sn++,                           // seg
                    keyseg->Beg,                    // position
                    keyseg->Len,                    // length
                    datatypes[ keyseg->ExTyp ],
                    attrib( ev, keyseg->Kflags ),
                    keyseg->NulVal );               // nulval
            }
        keyseg++;
      }
   puts( "\nFlags:\t< = Descending Order                          "
         "S = Supplemental Index" );
   puts( "\tD = Duplicates Allowed          A = Any "
         "Segment (Manual)" );
   puts( "\t    rD = repeated             L = All "
         "Segments (Null)" );
   puts( "\t     lD = linked             C = ACS used");
   puts( "\tI = Case Insensitive           "
         "*C = Multiple ACS" );
   puts( "\tM = Modifiable" );
}


/* * * * * * * * * * * * * * * * * * * * * * * * *\
 *                                              *
 *     This procedure tells if bit pattern      *
 *     is set or not.                           *
 *                                              *
\* * * * * * * * * * * * * * * * * * * * * * * * */
int IsSet( int Atr, int fflg ) // true if bits match exactly
{ return (fflg & Atr) == Atr;
}
```

```
/* * * * * * * * * * * * * * * * * * * * * * * *\
 *                                             *
 *    This procedure lists some attributes of  *
 *    the file, then calls ShowKeys to report  *
 *    detailed data for each defined key.      *
 *                                             *
\* * * * * * * * * * * * * * * * * * * * * * * */
void ShowAttrib( char * fmt, int ev, int nk,
                 int fflgs, long nrec, long npg,
                 FCRTOP * ValidFCR )
{ char *eng[] = { "c=0", "c=1", "c=2", "4.0", "4.1", "5.0", "6.0"
                };
  if( ev < 0 )
      ev = ( 0 - ev ) >> 8;
  else
      ev >>= 8;
  printf( "\nKey specifications for File %s:\n", outbuf );

  printf( "Format: %-20.20s", fmt );
  printf( "Requires Btrieve version %s (or later) engine.\n",
          eng[ev] );

  if( nk )
    { printf( "This file has %d index%s", nk, nk>1 ? "es" : "" );
      if( IsSet( AT_SPECKEY, fflgs ) )
        printf( ", prenumbered" );
      printf( ". " );
    }
  else
    printf( "Has no index. " );
  printf( "The file contains %ld records, on %ld pages.\n\n",
          swap(nrec),
          swap(npg) );
  ShowKeys( ev, nk, (SEGSPEC *)((char *)ValidFCR+0x110) );
}
```

```
/* * * * * * * * * * * * * * * * * * * * * * * *\
 *                                             *
 *     This procedure sets up original-format  *
 *     file.                                    *
 *                                             *
\* * * * * * * * * * * * * * * * * * * * * * * */
int Old_Format( FILE *fp )
{ int ret = 0;
  FCRTOP *ValidFCR = (FCRTOP *)pgbf1;
  fread( pgbf1, PageSize, 1, fp );

  ShowAttrib( "Original",
              ValidFCR->r1.v5.Version,
              ValidFCR->Nkeys,
              ValidFCR->UsrFlgs,
              ValidFCR->Nrecs,
              ValidFCR->Npages,
              ValidFCR );
  return ret;
}


/* * * * * * * * * * * * * * * * * * * * * * * *\
 *                                             *
 *  This procedure sets up a new-format file.  *
 *                                             *
\* * * * * * * * * * * * * * * * * * * * * * * */
int New_Format( FILE *fp )
{ int ret = 0;
  FCRTOP *ValidFCR;
  fread( pgbf1, PageSize, 1, fp );
  fread( pgbf2, PageSize, 1, fp );

  if( ((FCRTOP *)pgbf1)->r1.v6.Usage >
      ((FCRTOP *)pgbf2)->r1.v6.Usage )
    ValidFCR = (FCRTOP *)pgbf1;
  else
    ValidFCR = (FCRTOP *)pgbf2;
  ShowAttrib( "New 6.+ version",
              ValidFCR->r7.v6.Version,
              ValidFCR->Nkeys,
              ValidFCR->UsrFlgs,
```

```
            ValidFCR->Nrecs,
            ValidFCR->Npages,
            ValidFCR );
  return ret;
}


/* * * * * * * * * * * * * * * * * * * * * * * *\
 *                                             *
 *   This procedure determines a file's type,  *
 *   then sets PageSize and positions to the   *
 *   start of the file.                        *
 *                                             *
\* * * * * * * * * * * * * * * * * * * * * * * */
int GetFormat( FILE *fp )
{ int fmt = 0;                    // 0 not Btrieve
                                  // 1 old, 2 new
  int testbuf[5];                 // test first 10 bytes

  fread( testbuf, 5, 2, fp );
  if( testbuf[1] == 0 )        // page sequence must be zero
    { if( testbuf[0] == 0 )
        fmt = 1;
      else if( testbuf[0] == 0x4346 )
        fmt = 2;
    }
  if( fmt )                       // set page length if Btrieve
    PageSize = testbuf[4];
  else
    PageSize = 0;
  fseek( fp, 0L, 0 );           // rewind file in any event
  return fmt;
}
```

```
/* * * * * * * * * * * * * * * * * * * * * * * * *\
 *                                               *
 *     This procedure processes a single file.   *
 *                                               *
\* * * * * * * * * * * * * * * * * * * * * * * * */
int Do_File( char * fnm )     // opens file for processing,
                              //    and routes
{ int ret = 0;
  FILE *f;

  strupr( fnm );
  f = fopen( fnm, "rb" );
  if( f )
    { CurFmt = GetFormat( f );
      strcpy( outbuf, fnm );
// set up output-file buffer and open if Curfmt = 1 or 2
      switch( CurFmt )
        {
        case 0:
          printf( "%s is not a Btrieve file.\n", fnm );
          ret = 1;
          break;
        case 1:
          pgbf1 = (BYTE *)malloc( PageSize );
          ret = Old_Format( f );
          free( pgbf1 );
          break;
        case 2:
          pgbf1 = (BYTE *)malloc( PageSize );
          pgbf2 = (BYTE *)malloc( PageSize );
          ret = New_Format( f );
          free( pgbf2 );
          free( pgbf1 );
          break;
        default:
          puts( "Undefined format code, should never happen!" );
          ret = 99;
          break;
        }
// if fo open, close it...
      fclose( f );
```

```
      }
   else
     { perror( fnm );
       ret = 2;
     }
   return ret;
}


/* * * * * * * * * * * * * * * * * * * * * * * * * *\
 *                                                 *
 *      This procedure tells how to use the        *
 *      program.                                   *
 *                                                 *
\* * * * * * * * * * * * * * * * * * * * * * * * * */
void Usage( void )
{ printf( "Usage: %s file1 [file2 [...]]\n", PgmName );
  printf( "\t where filenames can continue until command line "
          "is full\n" );
}


/* * * * * * * * * * * * * * * * * * * * * * * * * *\
 *                                                 *
 *      This procedure displays a standard banner  *
 *      heading each time the program runs.        *
 *                                                 *
\* * * * * * * * * * * * * * * * * * * * * * * * * */
void Banner( void )
{ printf( "\n\t    %s - from \"Btrieve Complete\" by Jim Kyle\n",
                PgmName );
  printf( "\t    Copyright 1995 by Jim Kyle - All Rights" "
                Reserved\n" );
  printf( "\t    Use freely, but do not distribute "
                "commercially.\n\n" );
}
```

```
/* * * * * * * * * * * * * * * * * * * * * * * * * *\
 *                                                 *
 *      This procedure is program entry point.     *
 *                                                 *
\* * * * * * * * * * * * * * * * * * * * * * * * * */
int main( int argc, char **argv )
{ int retval = 0;
  Banner();
  if( argc < 2 )
    { Usage();
      retval = 255;
    }
  else
    { int i;
      for( i=1; i < argc; i++ )
        { retval = Do_File( argv[i] );  // process each file
          if( retval )                  // if error, wait
            while( getch() != 13 )
              /* wait right here for CR */  ;
        }
    }
  return retval;
}
```

To compile BTKEY.EXE using Borland's compilers, use the command line

```
                BCC -ml BTKEY.C
```

The -ml switch specifies large memory model. No other special options are necessary.

Listing Index Content

Sometimes it's not enough to just know the index structure of a file. You may want to examine the data stored in each item of each index tree. The LISTKEYS program fills this need. It lists actual values for every key item within the file, together with the associated record pointer (or pointers, if the file permits duplicate values for a key).

Figure 10.4 shows the first three items in key 0 for a FIELD.DDF file that has four keys. The header data (extracted from the FCR key specification) shows that the file contains seventeen unique values for this key and that each value occupies 2 bytes. With 4 more bytes for a lesser-than page pointer and 4 bytes for a pointer to the data record, the total key length is 10 bytes per item. Since each item has room for only one record pointer, we can deduce that this index requires key values to be unique.

For each item within the index, LISTKEYS displays either three or four columns. The leftmost column reports the lesser-than page pointer associated with the data field of that item. The next column displays the data field itself, in a four-line hex-ASCII format that lets you read both binary and text data readily.

The top line of the data field display, aligned with the page pointer, presents the first hex digit of the field value. The second line

Figure 10.4   *The FFFFFFFF at the left edge of the display is the Lesser-Page page pointer of the B-tree structure. When it's anything other than a string of eight Fs, it's the page pointer to the index page that contains the values listed since the last valid lesser-page pointer. If no item has a valid Lesser-Page page pointer, then all items for that index appear on its root page.*

```
C:\SAMPLES>listkeys field.ddf

          LISTKEYS - from "Btrieve Complete" by Jim Kyle
          Copyright 1995 by Jim Kyle - All Rights Reserved
          Use freely, but do not distribute commercially.

File FIELD.DDF has 4 keys.
At key 0, seg 0, Level = 1, count: 17, page at 00003000
datasize = 2, total key length = 10

FFFFFFFF    00
            10
            **
            --    00006:0006
FFFFFFFF    00
            20
            **
            --    00006:0038
FFFFFFFF    00
            30
            **
            --    00006:006A
```

presents the second digit. The third line displays the ASCII value if one exists, or a "*" character if the value is outside the ASCII range of printable characters. Finally, the fourth line is a row of dashes to separate adjacent displays from each other. If the data field exceeds 64 bytes in length, it wraps to a second four-line group immediately below the first.

The third column of the display contains the pointer to the first data record written for this index item. If the file prohibits duplicate key values, this will be the only record pointer and the display shows only three columns. If key values need not be unique, a fourth column displays the most recently written record for the item as shown in Figure 10.5.

Record pointers display in a logical page:page offset format. For the original file format, this is identical to the actual offset within the file to the first byte of the record, but for the new file format we must translate logical page numbers into physical page addresses to determine the file offset. Thus, LISTKEYS offers our first exposure

Figure 10.5 *LISTKEYS also shows quite clearly how Btrieve handles the duplicate-key situation within its indexes. This extract from a much larger listing indicates that the first key value, with a value of 0x0001, has at least two duplicate records in the file. The first one written is at offset 0x0006 of logical page 6, and the most recently written is at offset 0x009C also on logical page 6. The second item, with a value of 0x0002, was first written to logical page 6 at offset 0x00CE, and the most recently written record with this key is at offset 0x0038 of logical page 0x0C.*

```
At key 1, seg 0, Level = 1, count: 3, page at 00003200
datasize = 2, total key length = 14

FFFFFFFF    00
            10
            **
            --    00006:0006    00006:009C
FFFFFFFF    00
            20
            **
            --    00006:00CE    0000C:0038
```

to the actions necessary to retrieve information from a file that's
written in the new format.

Include, Constant, and Variable Differences

To help the new `dumpdata()` routine determine whether any specific byte value falls into the ASCII printable range, LISTKEYS adds
an additional header file to its block of files for inclusion:

```
#include <ctype.h>
```

LISTKEYS retrieves information from many pages within the file
rather than only accessing the FCR page. To simplify things, I chose
to use a global FCRTOP structure to contain all vital data concerning the file. This changed the global variable list:

```
FILE *fp;              // global for convenience
FCRTOP Fcr;
int PageSize, NbrKeys;
char *PgmName = "LISTKEYS";
char outbuf[80];       // holds filename for possible need
```

Finally, since LISTKEYS totally ignores all file and index attribute
bits, the constants used by BTATR and BTKEY aren't needed.

Reused Procedures

LISTKEYS reuses only the `main()`, `Banner()`, `Usage()`, and
`swap()` routines from BTATR and BTKEY. The `Do_File()` and
`GetFormat()` routines include significant changes, while all
other procedures appear for the first time in this program.

The Do_File() Procedure

As in BTATR, the `Do_File()` procedure processes a single file.
The routine uses the global FILE pointer `fp` to identify the file for
other procedures, sets global variable `CurFmt` to indicate the file
format in use, and deals with any file error condition encountered
while opening the file. Unlike BTATR or BTKEY, this version of

`Do_File()` processes both Btrieve file formats identically, by calling the `DoItToIt()` routine.

```c
int Do_File( char * fnm )
{ int ret = 0;                        // assume success

  strupr( fnm );
  fp = fopen( fnm, "rb" );
  if( fp )
    { strcpy( outbuf, fnm );          // save for reports
      CurFmt = GetFormat();
      switch( CurFmt )                // handle exceptions
        {
        case 0:
          printf( "%s is not a Btrieve file.\n", fnm );
          ret = 1;
          break;
        case 1:
        case 2:
          DoItToIt();                 // process the file
          break;
        default:
          puts( "Undefined format code, should never happen!" );
          ret = 99;
          break;
        }
      fclose( fp );
    }
  else
    { perror( fnm );
      ret = 2;
    }
  return ret;
}
```

The GetFormat() Procedure

The `GetFormat()` procedure determines a file's type, then loads the global FCRTOP structure `Fcr`, and positions the file to the start of the index specification area on the first FCR page. Unless a program has explicitly added indexes to a new-format file, the index specification area should be identical for both FCR pages.

```
int GetFormat( void )
{ int fmt = 0;                  // 0 not Btrieve
                               // 1 old, 2 new
  int testbuf[5];              // test first 10 bytes
  long ndxbeg = 0x110L;        // offset to seg specs in FCR
```

Unlike the versions of GetFormat() we've used before, this version does its own testing of usage counts to determine which FCR is the valid copy when it identifies a new-format file. If you're concerned about the possibility of an index having been added to a file after initial creation, you can modify this part of the routine to add PageSize to local variable ndxbeg when the second FCR is found to be the valid copy.

```
  fread( testbuf, 5, 2, fp );
  if( testbuf[1] == 0 )              // page sequence must be zero
    { if( testbuf[0] == 0 )
        { fmt = 1;                   // original format
          fseek( fp, 0L, 0 );
        }
      else if( testbuf[0] == 0x4346 )   // 'FC' signature
        { fmt = 2;
          fseek( fp, (long)testbuf[4]+4, 0 );   // check next FCR
          fread( &testbuf[0], 2, 1, fp );
          if( testbuf[0] > testbuf[2] ) // second is valid
            fseek( fp, (long)testbuf[4], 0 );
          else                         // use the first
            fseek( fp, 0L, 0 );
        }
    }
```

Once the file is identified as a valid Btrieve file (by fmt being non-zero), GetFormat() loads the global structure Fcr and sets variables PageSize and NbrKeys. The routine then positions the file to the start of its index specification area in preparation for the next stage of processing.

```
if( fmt )                              // load valid FCR
  { fread( &Fcr, 1, sizeof( FCRTOP ), fp );
    PageSize = Fcr.PagSize;
    NbrKeys = Fcr.Nkeys;
    fseek( fp, ndxbeg, 0 );        // position to index
  }
```

If the file turns out not to be a valid Btrieve file, `GetFormat()`clears `PageSize` to zero for possible use as a flag by other routines.

```
else
  PageSize = 0;
  return fmt;
}
```

The only values expected on return from `GetFormat()`are 0 for non-Btrieve files, 1 for a file in original format, or 2 for new format, just as with the other version of this function.

The DoItToIt() Procedure

The `DoItToIt()` procedure cycles through all keys of the file, calling the `ListKey()` routine for each in turn. Local variable `CurKey` holds the current key number, which increments each time that the routine calls `ListKey()`within the processing loop. This routine reports only the file name (from `outbuf`) and the number of keys (from `NbrKeys`).

```
void DoItToIt( void )
{ int CurKey=0;

  printf( "File %s has %d %s.\n",
          outbuf,
          NbrKeys,
          NbrKeys > 1 ? "keys" : "key" );
  while( CurKey < NbrKeys )
    ListKey( CurKey++, 1 );
}
```

The ListKey() Procedure

The `ListKey()` procedure initializes data for each key from all its segments, then starts `TraceKey()` for it to report each key item in the file. This routine maintains several local variables to control its actions and those of `TraceKey()`.

```
void ListKey( int keyno, int level )
{ int seg = 0;                    // seg nbr within key
  int datasize=0;                 // total data field size
  int keysize;                    // size of each key item
  long rootpage;                  // start of B-tree
  SEGSPEC spec;
```

To initialize the data for a key, `ListKey()` loops through all segments of the key reading each in turn and printing the segment number for each (the Level indicator is left over from early diagnostic efforts and should not change in this version). During this loop, the routine accumulates the total number of bytes in the data field by adding the length of each segment to local variable `datasize` (which is initialized to zero each time the routine runs). During the first pass (while processing segment 0 of the key, which always exists in any key) local variables `rootpage` and `keysize` also get values taken from the key specification. The routine also displays in this pass the total number of unique values for the key.

```
    do {
      fread( &spec, 1, sizeof( SEGSPEC ), fp );
      if( seg )
        printf( "            seg %d, Level = %d\n",
                seg++,
                level );
      else
        { rootpage = lp_pp( spec.Entry );
          printf( "At key %d, seg %d, Level = %d, "
                  "count: %ld, page at %08lX\n",
                  keyno,
                  seg++,
                  level,
```

```
                    swap( spec.Total ),
                    rootpage );
        keysize = spec.Klen;
      }
    datasize += spec.Len;
    } while ( spec.Kflags & 16 );          // process all segments
```

When the loop finishes processing all segments for the current key, ListKey() displays the values for data field size and total item size, then passes these together with the page pointer rootpage to TraceKey().

```
  printf( "datasize = %d, total key length = %d\n\n",
          datasize,
          keysize );
  TraceKey( rootpage, keysize, datasize, level );
  putchar( "\n" );
}
```

Once TraceKey() has traced out the complete tree for this index, ListKey() calls putchar() to add a new line to the display, then returns to its caller.

The TraceKey() Procedure

The TraceKey() procedure traces the B-tree for one key, reporting all information from each item. To be able to follow all branches of the B-tree, this routine calls itself recursively. The argument lv, passed in as the final parameter of each call, tracks the depth of recursion.

Although the routine doesn't use lv in any way, it's handy to have this information available in case you modify the code and then run into problems. Printing out all four parameters at the beginning of each instance helps show exactly what is happening inside the recursion.

Local variable savepos holds the file position each time you enter. This is necessary so that the routine can restore the same position at exit. The recursive calls can move the actual file position anywhere, but upon return from each, the routine expects to find the position exactly where it had been before the call.

```
void TraceKey( long ofs, int tl, int dl, int lv )
{ void *bfr;                        // holds malloc'ed buffer adr
  PGPTR *b1;                        // these address item fields
  char *b2;
  long *b3;
  long savepos;                     // save-restore position
  int dupes;
```

This structure defines the standard header used by each index page for either the original or the new format. It's left out of BTRIEVE.H since it's not necessary for many programs. Differences in the headers between the original and the new formats occur only inside the PGPTR structure. The pointer **above** points to the index page that contains the first data item that follows the last item on this page in the tree.

```
  struct {                         // index page header
    PGPTR pghdr;
    int usage;
    int count;
    PGPTR above;
  } pgtop;
```

The first action of **TraceKey()** is to save the current file position in **savepos**, followed by allocation of enough space to hold the total length of one key item. Since the structure of the item can vary between having three or four fields, and the length of the data field can vary from one index to another, all in the same file, no formal structure can be defined. Instead, pointer arithmetic and typecasting serve to keep things straight. That's why the program declares **bfr** as a pointer to **void**. Pointers **b1**, **b2**, and **b3** identify the types contained in each index item.

```
savepos = ftell( fp );                  // save file position
bfr = (char *)malloc( tl );             // get buffer space
```

If the space allocation succeeds, **bfr** will be nonzero and **Trace-Key()** then reads a key page header into the **pgtop** structure:

```
if( bfr )
  { fseek( fp, ofs, 0 );                // go to key page
    fread( &pgtop, 1, sizeof( pgtop ), fp );
```

Next, the routine enters a loop that continues while the count of items on the page exceeds zero. Each time around the loop, **TraceKey()** reads one more index item into the allocated **bfr** area.

```
while( pgtop.count-- )          // for each item on page
  { fread( bfr, 1, tl, fp );    // read the item
```

Before doing anything else, the routine assigns the address of **bfr** to pointer **b1** as a pointer to a PGPTR structure, then calls **lp_pp()** with this address to establish the physical offset in the file for the less-than page associated with this item. If the offset (saved in **ofs**) refers to an actual page, **TraceKey()** then calls itself recursively with the offset as the new page address and a level count one greater than the level of this call.

```
b1 = (PGPTR *)bfr;              // less-than pointer
ofs = lp_pp( *b1 );            // convert to phys offset
if( ofs != -1L )
   TraceKey( ofs, tl, dl, lv+1 ); // follow through
```

Upon return from the recursive call, or immediately if the value in **ofs** indicates no valid less-than page exists for this item, the routine prints the offset value. This second call to **lp_pp()** could be replaced by a reference to **ofs** with significant increase of performance, since the value of **ofs** cannot change as a result of the recursive call.

The routine then sets character pointer b2 to a value just 4 bytes past the start of bfr. This point is the first byte of the data field for the item. The somewhat arcane use of two statements to accomplish this was the only way I could get this operation past Borland C's error-detection capabilities. TraceKey() then calls dump-data() with pointer b2 and the passed-in total data field length dl, to generate the output display.

```
printf( "%08lX  ", lp_pp( *b1 ) );  // less-than page
b2 = bfr;                           // set up data pointer
b2 += sizeof( PGPTR );              // skip over PGPTR
dumpdata( b2, dl );                 // data part of key
```

When dumpdata() returns, TraceKey() sets b3 to the address of the first byte past the end of the data field, then calculates the number of bytes remaining in the item and converts this to the number of record pointers. The result goes to dupes, which controls a loop that reports all record pointer values. Within the loop, swap() first reverses the word order of the pointer, and the two calculations in the printf() statement split the pointer into its logical-page and record-offset components for display. After the loop finishes, the routine displays a newline character. This completes processing for a single index item and the outer loop closes to display the next item on the page.

```
b3 = (long *)&( b2[dl] );        // record pointers
dupes = (tl - (dl+4)) >> 2;      // number of pointers
while( dupes-- )
  { long rp = swap( *b3++ );
    printf( "  %05lX:%04lX",
            rp/PageSize,
            rp%PageSize );
  }
putchar( '\n' );
}
```

After displaying all items on a page (and, of course, processing all recursive calls caused by any item), the routine then converts the greater-than pointer **above** from the **pgtop** structure into a file off-set value in **ofs**; and if that refers to a valid page, the routine does another recursive call to process all parts of the tree that follow this page.

```
ofs = lp_pp( pgtop.above );      // greater-than pointer
if( ofs != -1L )
   TraceKey( ofs, tl, dl, lv+1 );
```

Once all recursive calls are complete, **TraceKey()** frees the allocated index-item buffer, which completes its processing. If the allocation attempt failed, **TraceKey()** simply displays an error message instead of attempting to process the page. In low-memory situations this may cause your report to have error messages embedded in it, rather than being complete, but you will at least see parts of the data.

```
      free( bfr );            // release buffer now
   }
  else                        // couldn't get buffer
    perror( "TraceKey" );
   fseek( fp, savepos, 0 );   // restore file position
}
```

The final action **TraceKey()** performs before returning to its caller is to restore the saved file position. Since it's quite easy to nest these calls several levels deep when processing a large data file, each instance of **TraceKey()** must restore the file position for itself.

The lp_pp() Function

The **lp_pp()** function converts a logical page number to a file offset, using the PAT for new format files. The method by which it does so is somewhat simpler than that used by the Btrieve engines, but is also much slower. You can see significant differences in speed between the processing of original-format files (which need no translation) and that for the new format.

Input to l p_pp ( ) is a logical page number, in the form of a PGPTR structure. The function returns the physical file offset in bytes to the start of that logical page, as a long integer.

```
static long lp_pp( PGPTR pgptr )
{ long ret, pat1, pat2, lp, svpos;
  unsigned short u1, u2, pppat;
```

If **CurFmt** indicates that the current file uses the new format, l p_pp ( ) extracts the logical page number from the input argument into local variable l p by use of the **PageNo6 ( )** macro, then saves the current file position in **svpos**. Next, the routine initializes the PAT pair's physical page number (in **ret**) to 2 since the first PAT pair is always at physical pages 2 and 3, calculates the number of pages each PAT page can hold based on the page size, and stores the result in **pppat**.

```
if( CurFmt != 1 )               // new format, lookup
  { lp = PageNo6( pgptr );       // get logical number
    svpos = ftell( fp );         // save file position
    ret = 2;                     // PAT pair at 2, 3
    pppat = (PageSize >> 2) - 2;  // pages per PAT
```

To ensure that the PAT pair containing the desired logical page is the one used for the lookup, l p_pp ( ) next processes a loop so long as the value of l p exceeds that of **pppat**. Each time around the loop, the value of l p goes down by the number of items each PAT can hold. At the same time, the base address for the PAT pair (in **ret**) goes up by the number of physical pages that separate adjacent PAT pairs.

```
while( lp > pppat )             // off current page
  { lp -= pppat;                 //    so tally down index
    ret += (PageSize >> 2);      //    and up the PAT page
    }
```

Upon exit from the scaling loop, l p contains a value that's the offset on the current page where the desired logical page's physical equivalent appears, and r e t contains the base physical page number for a PAT pair.

The next action is to determine which PAT within the pair is valid, by comparing their usage counts. First, the routine multiplies r e t by **PageSize** and stores the result in **pat1** as the file offset to the first PAT. Then it adds **PageSize** to this value to create the second PAT's offset and stores the result in **pat2**. The routine seeks to the usage-count offset (4 bytes) within the first PAT page of the pair, reads the value there into u1, then repeats for the second PAT to get its count into u2. Finally, the file offset of the PAT having the larger count goes into r e t for use.

```
pat1 = ret * (long)PageSize;    // first PAT of pair
pat2 = pat1 + (long)PageSize;   // second one right after
fseek( fp, pat1+4L, 0 );        // get both usage counts
fread( &u1, 2, 1, fp );
fseek( fp, pat2+4L, 0 );
fread( &u2, 2, 1, fp );
if( u1 > u2 )                   // choose most recent
   ret = pat1;
else
   ret = pat2;
```

With the correct PAT's base offset in r e t, the routine next converts l p into an offset value, adds that plus a fixed 4-byte bias to the base offset, and seeks to that point in the file. It next reads the page pointer at that offset into the original location of the **pgptr** argument, extracts the logical page portion into l p by using the **PageNo6()** macro again, and finally restores the saved file position. Upon exit from this part of the format-sensitive test, l p contains the physical page number that corresponds to the original logical page value.

```
ret += (long)(( lp << 2 ) + 4L ); // calculate position
fseek( fp, ret, 0 );
fread( &pgptr, sizeof( PGPTR ), 1, fp ); // read PGPTR
```

```
    lp = PageNo6( pgptr );
    fseek( fp, svpos, 0 );              // restore file position
}
```

Things are much simpler with the original format. The routine need only extract the page number into `lp` by using the `PageNo5()` macro:

```
    else                               // original format
        lp = PageNo5( pgptr );         // so just unswap
```

At this point, regardless of the format in use, `lp` contains a physical page number. All that remains is to test this number for the NULL pointer value. If it's indeed a NULL pointer, the routine will return a value of -1. If not, it will multiply the page number by the page size to return a file offset in bytes to the start of the specified logical page.

```
    if( lp == 0xFFFFFFFL || lp == -1L )  // NULL pointer values
        ret = -1L;
    else                                 // convert to offset
        ret = lp * PageSize;
    return ret;
}
```

The dumpdata() Procedure

The `dumpdata()` procedure dumps data to `stdout`, using the four-line combination hex-ASCII format described earlier in this section. This routine uses an internal character array to quickly translate numeric values in the range 0–15 to their hex-digit equivalents. This routine places a maximum of 64 bytes of data on each line of the display; if the field length passed in as argument `nbr` exceeds this size, the display automatically wraps every 64 bytes.

```
static void dumpdata( BYTE *data, int nbr )
( int i, j;
  char *h = "0123456789ABCDEF";
  for(i=0; i<nbr; i+=64)
```

For each group of 64 bytes or less, **dumpdata()** first takes each byte of the data field, shifts it right by 4 bits to extract the upper half, translates that value to a hex digit via the lookup table, and outputs the digit using **putchar()**. These actions occur only when index variable **j** is less than the value of **nbr**. At the end of the loop, **printf()** outputs a newline character, a horizontal tab, and two blank spaces, to align the next line with the first one.

```
{ for( j=0; j<64; j++ )
    if( (i+j) < nbr )
      putchar( h[ (data[i+j]>>4) & 15] );
  printf( "\n\t  " );
```

The second loop does almost the same thing, for the same group of 64 bytes or less. The difference is that this time, the byte's value does not shift, so the **putchar()** call displays the digit for the low half of the byte.

```
for( j=0; j<64; j++ )
  if( (i+j) < nbr )
    putchar( h[ data[i+j] & 15] );
printf( "\n\t  " );
```

The third loop follows the pattern that by now should be familiar. This time, the library function **isprint()** (declared in the include file **CTYPE.H** added for this program) determines whether the byte is within the ASCII printable range. If so, the byte itself goes to **putchar()**; if not, a "*" character goes instead.

```
for( j=0; j<64; j++ )
  if( (i+j) < nbr )
    putchar( isprint( data[i+j] ) ? data[i+j] : '*' );
printf( "\n\t  " );
```

The fourth and final loop simply displays a row of dashes, the same length as the previous three rows of data display. The primary purpose of this is to separate 64-byte groups from each other in case a data field exceeds 64 bytes in length.

```
      for( j=0; j<nbr; j++ )
        if( (i+j) < nbr )
          putchar( '-' );
    }
}
```

The `dumpdata()` procedure leaves the display cursor positioned at the character immediately following the last dash displayed by its fourth loop. This aligns the record pointer display vertically on the same line as shown in Figures 10.4 and 10.5.

The Complete LISTKEYS.C Listing

Now that we've examined each of its component modules, here's the complete listing for LISTKEYS.C as it appears on the companion diskette.

```
/* * * * * * * * * * * * * * * * * * * * * * * * * *\
 *                                                 *
 *       LISTKEYS.C - Jim Kyle - January 1995      *
 *                                                 *
 *       Lists all keys from any version of Btrieve *
 *       file without requiring Btrieve engine to  *
 *       be installed in system.                   *
 *                                                 *
\* * * * * * * * * * * * * * * * * * * * * * * * * */
#include <stdio.h>
#include <conio.h>
#ifdef __TURBOC__
#include <alloc.h>        // Borland-specific
#else
#include <malloc.h>       // Microsoft version
#endif
#include <string.h>
#include <ctype.h>

#include "btrieve.h"

FILE *fp;                 // global for convenience
FCRTOP Fcr;
```

```
int PageSize, NbrKeys;
char *PgmName = "LISTKEYS";
char outbuf[80];       // holds filename for possible need

/* * * * * * * * * * * * * * * * * * * * * * * * * * *\
 *                                                    *
 *      This procedure undoes Btrieve"s word-         *
 *      swapping.                                      *
 *                                                    *
\* * * * * * * * * * * * * * * * * * * * * * * * * * */
static long swap( long n )
{ asm les dx,n;              // ASM trick for simplicity
  asm mov ax,es;
// return ((n>>16)&0xFFFF) | (n<<16);
}


/* * * * * * * * * * * * * * * * * * * * * * * * * * *\
 *                                                    *
 *      This procedure dumps data, translating        *
 *      to ASCII if in printable range, else          *
 *      outputting as hex.                            *
 *                                                    *
\* * * * * * * * * * * * * * * * * * * * * * * * * * */
static void dumpdata( BYTE *data, int nbr )
{ int i, j;
  char *h = "0123456789ABCDEF";
  for(i=0; i<nbr; i+=64)
    { for( j=0; j<64; j++ )
        if( (i+j) < nbr )
          putchar( h[ (data[i+j]>>4) & 15] );
      printf( "\n\t   " );
      for( j=0; j<64; j++ )
        if( (i+j) < nbr )
          putchar( h[ data[i+j] & 15] );
      printf( "\n\t   " );
      for( j=0; j<64; j++ )
        if( (i+j) < nbr )
          putchar( isprint( data[i+j] ) ? data[i+j] : '*' );
      printf( "\n\t   " );
      for( j=0; j<nbr; j++ )
        if( (i+j) < nbr )
```

```
                    putchar( "-" );
        }
}

/* * * * * * * * * * * * * * * * * * * * * * * * *\
 *                                                *
 *      This procedure converts a Logical Page    *
 *      number to a file offset, using the PAT    *
 *      for new format files.                     *
 *                                                *
\* * * * * * * * * * * * * * * * * * * * * * * * */
static long lp_pp( PGPTR pgptr )
{ long ret, pat1, pat2, lp, svpos;
  unsigned short u1, u2, pppat;

  if( CurFmt != 1 )                   // new format, lookup
    { lp = PageNo6( pgptr );          // get logical number
      svpos = ftell( fp );            // save file position
      ret = 2;                        // PAT pair at 2, 3
      pppat = (PageSize >> 2) - 2;    // pages per PAT

      while( lp > pppat )             // off current page
        { lp -= pppat;                //    so tally down index
                                      //    and up the
          ret += (PageSize >> 2);     //   PAT page
        }
      pat1 = ret * (long)PageSize;    // first PAT of pair
      pat2 = pat1 + (long)PageSize;   // second one right after
      fseek( fp, pat1+4L, 0 );        // get both usage counts
      fread( &u1, 2, 1, fp );
      fseek( fp, pat2+4L, 0 );
      fread( &u2, 2, 1, fp );
      if( u1 > u2 )                   // choose most recent
        ret = pat1;
      else
        ret = pat2;
      ret += (long)(( lp << 2 ) + 4L); // calculate position
      fseek( fp, ret, 0 );
      fread( &pgptr, sizeof( PGPTR ), 1, fp ); // read PGPTR
      lp = PageNo6( pgptr );
      fseek( fp, svpos, 0 );          // restore file position
```

```
    }
  else                                // original format
    lp = PageNo5( pgptr );            // so just unswap

  if( lp == 0xFFFFFFFL || lp == -1L )  // NULL pointer values
    ret = -1L;
  else                                // convert to offset
    ret = lp * PageSize;

  return ret;
}


/* * * * * * * * * * * * * * * * * * * * * * * * * *\
 *                                                 *
 *      This procedure traces through the B-tree   *
 *      for one key, reporting all information     *
 *      from each item.                            *
 *                                                 *
\* * * * * * * * * * * * * * * * * * * * * * * * * */
void TraceKey( long ofs, int tl, int dl, int lv )
{ void *bfr;              // holds malloc'ed buffer adr
  PGPTR *b1;              // these address item fields
  char *b2;
  long *b3;
  long savepos;          // save-restore position
  int dupes;

  struct {               // index page header
    PGPTR pghdr;
    int usage;
    int count;
    PGPTR above;
  } pgtop;

  savepos = ftell( fp );             // save file position
  bfr = (char *)malloc( tl );        // get buffer space
  if( bfr )
    { fseek( fp, ofs, 0 );           // go to key page
      fread( &pgtop, 1, sizeof( pgtop ), fp );

      while( pgtop.count-- )         // for each item on page
        { fread( bfr, 1, tl, fp );   // read the item
```

```
            b1 = (PGPTR *)bfr;              // less-than pointer
            ofs = lp_pp( *b1 );             // convert to phys offset
            if( ofs != -1L )

              TraceKey( ofs, tl, dl, lv+1 );  // follow through

            printf( "%08lX  ", lp_pp( *b1 ) ); // less-than page
            b2 = bfr;                        // set up data pointer
            b2 += sizeof( PGPTR );           // skip over PGPTR
            dumpdata( b2, dl );              // data part of key

            b3 = (long *)&( b2[dl] );     // record pointers
            dupes = (tl - (dl+4)) >> 2; // number of pointers
            while( dupes-- )
              { long rp = swap( *b3++ );
                printf( "  %05lX:%04lX",
                        rp/PageSize,
                        rp%PageSize );
              }
            putchar( '\n' );
          }

        ofs = lp_pp( pgtop.above );          // greater-than pointer
        if( ofs != -1L )
          TraceKey( ofs, tl, dl, lv+1 );

        free( bfr );                          // release buffer now
      }
    else                                   // couldn't get buffer
      perror( "TraceKey" );
    fseek( fp, savepos, 0 );               // restore file position
}

/* * * * * * * * * * * * * * * * * * * * * * * * * * *\
 *                                                  *
 *      This procedure initializes data for each    *
 *      key, from all its segments, then starts     *
 *      TraceKey for it.                            *
 *                                                  *
\* * * * * * * * * * * * * * * * * * * * * * * * * * */
void ListKey( int keyno, int level )
{ int seg = 0;                     // seg nbr within key
  int datasize=0;                  // total data field size
```

```
  int keysize;                     // size of each key item
  long rootpage;                   // start of B-tree
  SEGSPEC spec;

  do {
    fread( &spec, 1, sizeof( SEGSPEC ), fp );
    if( seg )
      printf( "            seg %d, Level = %d\n",
              seg++,
              level );
    else
      { rootpage = lp_pp( spec.Entry );
        printf( "At key %d, seg %d, Level = %d, "
                "count: %ld, page at %08lX\n",
                keyno,
                seg++,
                level,
                swap( spec.Total ),
                rootpage );
        keysize = spec.Klen;
      }
    datasize += spec.Len;
    } while ( spec.Kflags & 16 ); // process all segments
  printf( "datasize = %d, total key length = %d\n\n",
          datasize,
          keysize );
  TraceKey( rootpage, keysize, datasize, level );
  putchar( '\n' );
}


/* * * * * * * * * * * * * * * * * * * * * * * * * * *\
 *                                                   *
 *      This procedure cycles through all keys,      *
 *      calling ListKey routine for each in turn.    *
 *                                                   *
\* * * * * * * * * * * * * * * * * * * * * * * * * * */
void DoItToIt( void )
{ int CurKey=0;
  printf( "File %s has %d %s.\n",
          outbuf,
          NbrKeys,
```

```
            NbrKeys > 1 ? "keys" : "key" );
  while( CurKey < NbrKeys )
    ListKey( CurKey++, 1 );
}


/* * * * * * * * * * * * * * * * * * * * * * *\
 *                                            *
 *     This procedure determines a file's type, *
 *     then sets CurFmt, loads Fcr, and       *
 *     positions to index specification area  *
 *     of FCR page.                           *
 *                                            *
\* * * * * * * * * * * * * * * * * * * * * * */
int GetFormat( void )
{ int fmt = 0;                   // 0 not Btrieve
                                 // 1 old, 2 new
  int testbuf[5];                // test first 10 bytes
  long ndxbeg = 0x110L;          // offset to seg specs in FCR
  fread( testbuf, 5, 2, fp );
  if( testbuf[1] == 0 )          // page sequence must be zero
    { if( testbuf[0] == 0 )
        { fmt = 1;               // original format
          fseek( fp, 0L, 0 );
        }
      else if( testbuf[0] == 0x4346 )   // 'FC' signature
        { fmt = 2;
          fseek( fp, (long)testbuf[4]+4, 0 ); // check next FCR
          fread( &testbuf[0], 2, 1, fp );
          if( testbuf[0] > testbuf[2] ) // second is valid
            fseek( fp, (long)testbuf[4], 0 );
          else                   // use the first
            fseek( fp, 0L, 0 );
        }
    }
  if( fmt )                      // load valid FCR
    { fread( &Fcr, 1, sizeof( FCRTOP ), fp );
      PageSize = Fcr.PagSize;
      NbrKeys = Fcr.Nkeys;
      fseek( fp, ndxbeg, 0 );    // position to index
```

```
      }
    else
      PageSize = 0;
    return fmt;
  }


/* * * * * * * * * * * * * * * * * * * * * * * * * *\
 *                                                 *
 *      This procedure processes a single file.    *
 *                                                 *
\* * * * * * * * * * * * * * * * * * * * * * * * * */
int Do_File( char * fnm )
{ int ret = 0;                     // assume success

  strupr( fnm );
  fp = fopen( fnm, "rb" );
  if( fp )
    { strcpy( outbuf, fnm );       // save for reports
      CurFmt = GetFormat();
      switch( CurFmt )             // handle exceptions
        {
        case 0:
          printf( "%s is not a Btrieve file.\n", fnm );
          ret = 1;
          break;
        case 1:
        case 2:
          DoItToIt();              // process the file
          break;
        default:
          puts( "Undefined format code, should never happen!" );
          ret = 99;
          break;
        }
      fclose( fp );
    }
  else
    { perror( fnm );
      ret = 2;
    }
  return ret;
}
```

```
/* * * * * * * * * * * * * * * * * * * * * * * * * * *\
 *                                                    *
 *       This procedure tells how to use the          *
 *       program.                                     *
 *                                                    *
\* * * * * * * * * * * * * * * * * * * * * * * * * * */
void Usage( void )
{ printf( "Usage: %s file1 [file2 [...]]\n", PgmName );
  printf( "\t where filenames can continue until command line "
          "is full\n" );
}



/* * * * * * * * * * * * * * * * * * * * * * * * * * *\
 *                                                    *
 *       This procedure displays a standard banner    *
 *       heading each time the program runs.          *
 *                                                    *
\* * * * * * * * * * * * * * * * * * * * * * * * * * */
void Banner( void )
{ printf( "\n\t    %s - from \"Btrieve Complete\" by Jim Kyle\n",
                  PgmName );
  printf( "\t     Copyright 1995 by Jim Kyle - All Rights" "
          "Reserved\n" );
  printf( "\t     Use freely, but do not distribute "
          "commercially.\n\n" );
}

/* * * * * * * * * * * * * * * * * * * * * * * * * * *\
 *                                                    *
 *       This procedure is program entry point.       *
 *                                                    *
\* * * * * * * * * * * * * * * * * * * * * * * * * * */
int main( int argc, char **argv )
{ int retval = 0;                       // assume success
  Banner();
  if( argc < 2 )                        // data missing
    { Usage();
      retval = 255;
    }
  else                                  // cycle thru data
```

```
{ int i;
  for( i=1; i < argc; i++ )
    { retval = Do_File( argv[i] ); // process each file
      if( retval )                 // if error, wait
        while( getch() != 13 )
          /* wait right here for CR */  ;
    }
  }
return retval;
}
```

To compile LISTKEYS.EXE, using Borland's compilers, use the command line

```
BCC -ml LISTKEYS.C
```

The -ml switch specifies large memory model. No other special options are necessary.

Tracing Available Space Information

Another utility that can help you discover problems in an existing Btrieve file is one to trace the chain of reusable records in that file. When you delete a record from any Btrieve file, the engine adds that record to the head of the reusable-record chain. Tracing the chain therefore shows you the record pointer for every record that has been deleted and not yet reused.

If you suspect that a file has become corrupted but there's a possibility that someone merely deleted several records, running DUMPFREE can help you determine what happened. If it's true file corruption, the chain is quite likely to be incomplete.

With the new file format, though, even a newly created file that has never contained a single record will have a reusable chain. When a version 6.0 or later Btrieve engine creates a new file, it builds one data page and one index page at the time of creation. The data page contains a chain of reusable records that have not, in fact, ever been used. The screen capture shown in Figure 10.6 to illustrate DUMPFREE's display is just such a case. Although this file does

Figure 10.6   *Here's the chain of data records available for reuse in one file, as reported by DUMPFREE. This utility is handy when you need to verify that records have actually been deleted from a file, rather than being lost through some system error. A record deletion will place its space on the reusable chain, but a system error will not.*

```
C:\SAMPLES>dumpfree index.ddf

        DUMPFREE - from "Btrieve Complete" by Jim Kyle
        Copyright 1995 by Jim Kyle - All Rights Reserved
        Use freely, but do not distribute commercially.

File INDEX.DDF is in new format; pagesize = 512, has 4 pages
The following data records are free for reuse:
        next at file offset 0x00000F02, byte 0x0102 of logical page  3
        next at file offset 0x00000F1E, byte 0x011E of logical page  3
        next at file offset 0x00000F3A, byte 0x013A of logical page  3
        next at file offset 0x00000F56, byte 0x0156 of logical page  3
        next at file offset 0x00000F72, byte 0x0172 of logical page  3
        next at file offset 0x00000F8E, byte 0x018E of logical page  3
        next at file offset 0x00000FAA, byte 0x01AA of logical page  3
        next at file offset 0x00000FC6, byte 0x01C6 of logical page  3
        next at file offset 0x00000FE2, byte 0x01E2 of logical page  3
End of record chain; free = 9.
```

have a number of records in it, the initial page hasn't yet been fully used and still has space for nine more records.

The way to detect this situation is to examine the byte offsets shown in the display. When they appear in sorted sequence on the same page, as they do in Figure 10.6, that's a reliable indication that you're looking at an initial-build chain. In practice, record deletion happens at random locations throughout the file, causing the chain's offsets and pages to be out of sort sequence.

When a file has become corrupted through some serious system error, the record pointer that DUMPFREE finds as the link to the next record in the chain may actually be either part of another record's data field or part of an index. As DUMPFREE attempts to follow such a spurious link, it's quite likely to encounter "impossible" page numbers such as –987315. Any time you see such numbers in a DUMPFREE display, you're safe in concluding that the file has been corrupted.

Another anomaly that can occur when a file becomes corrupt is for the chain to point back at a record already reported. That causes an infinite loop condition that will continue until you hit Control-C to interrupt the display.

Include, Constant, and Variable Differences

The block of include files that DUMPFREE uses is identical to that used by LISTKEYS. Like LISTKEYS, DUMPFREE defines no constants. The global variable list is somewhat shorter for DUMPFREE, however. Only three totally new variables occur: `compr` indicates whether the file contains compressed data or not, since compressed files in the new format flag record use differently than do files using other data storage techniques. `FreeRec` is a RECPTR, set to the first free record during program initialization. Finally, character pointer array `fmt` translates the file format into descriptive words for display.

Reused Procedures

Procedures reused from previous programs without change include `main()`, `Banner()`, `Usage()`, `Do_File()`, and `swap()`. Undergoing only minor change are `GetFormat()`, `DoIt-ToIt()`, and `lp_pp()`. Totally new for this program is `DumpFree()`.

The GetFormat() Procedure

The `GetFormat()` procedure determines a file's type, loads `Fcr` from the valid FCR page, and returns a format type code. The major difference between this version of `GetFormat()` and the version in LISTKEYS is that this version sets `compr` to indicate a file uses data compression.

```
int GetFormat( void )
{ int fmt = 0;                  // 0 not Btrieve
                                // 1 old, 2 new
  int testbuf[5];               // test first 10 bytes
  fread( testbuf, 5, 2, fp );
  if( testbuf[1] == 0 )         // page sequence must be zero
    { if( testbuf[0] == 0 )
      { fmt = 1;                // original format
```

```
                  fseek( fp, 0L, 0 );
            }
        else if( testbuf[0] == 0x4346 )    // 'FC' signature
            { fmt = 2;
              fseek( fp, (long)testbuf[4]+4, 0 ); // check next FCR
              fread( &testbuf[0], 2, 1, fp );
              if( testbuf[0] > testbuf[2] ) // second is valid
                fseek( fp, (long)testbuf[4], 0 );
              else                          // use the first
                fseek( fp, 0L, 0 );
            }
    }
```

If this is a Btrieve file, the routine determines whether data compression is active and sets `compr` accordingly. The reason for doing this is that data compression changes the way in which new-format files indicate that records are not in use.

```
  if( fmt )                          // load valid FCR
    { fread( &Fcr, 1, sizeof( FCRTOP ), fp );
      PageSize = Fcr.PagSize;
      if( Fcr.UsrFlgs & 8 )        // compressed data is
        compr = 1;                 // different format
      else                         // so set flag...
        compr = 0;
    }
  else
    PageSize = 0;
  return fmt;
}
```

The DoItToIt() Procedure

The `DoItToIt()` procedure first locates the free record chain and swaps the words of the pointer. Location of the free record pointer varies between the original and the new file formats.

```
void DoItToIt( void )
{ if(CurFmt == 1 )                    // save head of chain
    FreeRec = Fcr.NxtReuseRec;
```

```
else
  FreeRec = Fcr.r9.v6.Free[0].nxrec;
FreeRec.wl = swap( FreeRec.wl );
```

The routine then displays a header and calls `DumpFree()` to display the chain.

```
printf( "File %s is in %s format; pagesize = %d, "
        "has %ld pages\n",
        outbuf,
        fmt[CurFmt-1],
        PageSize,
        swap( Fcr.Npages ) );
printf( "The following data records are free for reuse:\n" );
DumpFree( FreeRec );                    // dump free-rec chain
}
```

The lp_pp() Procedure

The `lp_pp()` procedure converts a logical page number to a file offset, using the PAT for new format files. This version is similar to that used by LISTKEYS and shares its speed limitations.

The major difference is that this version defines its input argument as a variable of type `long` rather than as a `PGPTR`. Consequently, it does not use the `PageNo5()` and `PageNo6()` macros from BTRIEVE.H. Instead, it unpacks the page pointers with explicit code to show you another way to achieve the same end.

Note that `lp` has already been put into proper word sequence before being passed to this routine.

```
static long lp_pp( long lp )
{ long ret, pat1, pat2;
  unsigned short u1, u2, pppat;
  if( CurFmt != 1 )                  // only do lookup for new
    { ret = 2;                       // first PAT pair on 2, 3
      pppat = (PageSize >> 2) - 2;       // pages per PAT
```

This loop forces the appropriate PAT base page address into ret, and adjusts lp accordingly, just as in the previous version.

```
while( lp > pppat )              // off current page
  { lp -= pppat;                 //    so tally down index
    ret += (PageSize >> 2);      //    and up PAT pp nbr
  }
```

With the correct PAT base address in ret, determine which PAT of the pair is valid and copy its offset into ret.

```
pat1 = ret * (long)PageSize;  // first PAT of pair
pat2 = pat1 + (long)PageSize; // second right after it
fseek( fp, pat1+4L, 0 );      // get both usage counts
fread( &u1, 2, 1, fp );
fseek( fp, pat2+4L, 0 );
fread( &u2, 2, 1, fp );
if( u1 > u2 )                      // choose most recent one
  ret = pat1;
else
  ret = pat2;
```

Now add the offset and bias to the PAT offset and read the physical page pointer into lp.

```
ret += (long)(( lp << 2 ) + 4L);  // position in PAT
fseek( fp, ret, 0 );
fread( &lp, 4, 1, fp );           // read it into LP
```

Swap words of lp and mask off the page type code byte; this completes processing for new format files. Original-format files need no modification at all of lp.

```
lp = swap( lp );                     // and un-word-swap it
lp &= 0xFFFFFFL;
}
```

Test for an all-ones NULL pointer (original format has 32 bits but new format only 24); if true, return –1. Otherwise, return the file offset to the start of the page.

```
  if( lp == 0xFFFFFFL || lp == -1L ) // NULL pointer values
    ret = -1L;
  else                                  // convert to offset
    ret = lp * PageSize;
  return ret;
}
```

The DumpFree() Procedure

The `DumpFree()` procedure follows the free record chain and displays the pointer for each record it finds in the chain. This routine is the heart of DUMPFREE; everything else merely sets up the variables to let this procedure perform.

At entry to this routine, local variable `svps` gets the current file position, and at exit the routine restores the position. Since DUMPFREE does no other actions, these two operations aren't necessary in this program. However, if you modify the program to trace the free pages and free variable-length record areas, you'll need to retain file positions. That's why these useless actions appear.

Local variable `nxrec` holds the physical file offset to the next record in the chain. Local variable `n` counts the number of free records found. Local variable `u` serves as a buffer to test the record usage field for new-format records that aren't part of compressed files.

```
void DumpFree( RECPTR rp )                //trace free-record chain
{ long svps = ftell( fp ), nxrec;
  int n=0, u;
```

This loop continues until record pointer `rp` holds an end-of-chain flag (all ones in the low 24 bits). For new-format files, we must convert the logical page number extracted from `rp.wl` into a physical file offset by calling `lp_pp()`, then add the byte offset within the page. For files in the original format, record pointer `rp` already contains the physical file offset of the record. The routine then displays record details. These details apply to the record to which `rp` points.

```
while( ( rp.wl & 0xFFFFFF )            // go until END flag
        != 0xFFFFFF )
  { if( CurFmt == 2 )                  // translate new format
      nxrec = ( lp_pp( rp.wl / (long)PageSize )) +
                    ( rp.wl % (long)PageSize );
    else                               // original format OK
      nxrec = rp.wl;
    printf( "\tnext at file offset 0x%08lX, "
            "byte 0x%04lX of logical page %3ld\n",
            nxrec,                     // actual file offset
            rp.wl % (long)PageSize,  // logical record offset
            rp.wl / (long)PageSize );  // logical page number
```

With the detail line displayed, we position the file to that next record. If the file is both in new format and uses any storage type other than compressed data, we then verify that the new record has a usage count of zero (indicating that it's free). If not, the loop breaks without continuing. If the file is in old format or uses data compression, or if the record is truly free, we read its next-record link pointer into `rp`, swap the words of `rp.wl`, increment the count of free records, and close the loop.

```
        fseek( fp, nxrec, 0 );
        if( CurFmt == 2 && !compr ) // compr usage NOT first
          { fread( &u, 2, 1, fp );
            if( u )                    // break loop if bad
              break;
          }
        fread( &rp.wl, 4, 1, fp );  // get next pointer
        rp.wl = swap( rp.wl );       // un-wordswap it
        n++;                         // tally this record
      }
  printf( "End of record chain; free = %d.\n\n", n );
  fseek( fp, svps, 0 );
}
```

When the loop reaches an end-of-chain flag (or fails because of the usage-count test), the routine displays the count of free records. If the original record pointer held an end-of-chain flag, this will be the only line displayed, and the count will be zero.

The Complete DUMPFREE.C Listing

Now that we've examined each of its component modules, here's the complete listing for DUMPFREE.C as it appears on the companion diskette.

```c
/* * * * * * * * * * * * * * * * * * * * * * * * * *\
 *                                                 *
 *   DUMPFREE - Jim Kyle - January 1995            *
 *                                                 *
 *   Lists all free records from any version of    *
 *   Btrieve file without requiring Btrieve engine *
 *   to be installed in system.                    *
 *                                                 *
\* * * * * * * * * * * * * * * * * * * * * * * * * */
#include <stdio.h>
#include <conio.h>
#ifdef __TURBOC__
#include <alloc.h>       // Borland-specific
#else
#include <malloc.h>      // Microsoft version
#endif
#include <string.h>
#include <ctype.h>

#include "btrieve.h"

FILE *fp;                // global for convenience
FCRTOP Fcr;

int PageSize, compr = 0;
RECPTR FreeRec;
char *PgmName = "DUMPFREE";
char outbuf[80];

char *fmt[] = {
```

```
    "original",
    "new"
};

/* * * * * * * * * * * * * * * * * * * * * * * * *\
 *                                                *
 *      This procedure undoes Btrieve"s word-     *
 *      swapping.                                 *
 *                                                *
\* * * * * * * * * * * * * * * * * * * * * * * * */
static long swap( long n )
{ asm les dx,n;              // ASM trick for simplicity
  asm mov ax,es;
// return ((n>>16)&0xFFFF) | (n<<16);
}


/* * * * * * * * * * * * * * * * * * * * * * * * *\
 *                                                *
 *      This procedure converts a Logical Page    *
 *      number to a file offset, using the PAT    *
 *      for new format files.                     *
 *                                                *
\* * * * * * * * * * * * * * * * * * * * * * * * */
static long lp_pp( long lp )
{ long ret, pat1, pat2;
  unsigned short u1, u2, pppat;
  if( CurFmt != 1 )                   // only do lookup for new
      {ret = 2;                       //   first PAT pair on 2, 3
      pppat = (PageSize >> 2) - 2;    // pages per PAT
      while( lp > pppat )             // off current page
        { lp -= pppat;                //   so tally down index
          ret += (PageSize >> 2);     //   and up PAT pp nbr
        }
      pat1 = ret * (long)PageSize;    // first PAT of pair
      pat2 = pat1 + (long)PageSize;   // second right after it
      fseek( fp, pat1+4L, 0 );        // get both usage counts
      fread( &u1, 2, 1, fp );
      fseek( fp, pat2+4L, 0 );
      fread( &u2, 2, 1, fp );
      if( u1 > u2 )                   // choose most recent one
        ret = pat1;
```

```
      else
        ret = pat2;

      ret += (long)(( lp << 2 ) + 4L ); // position in PAT
      fseek( fp, ret, 0 );
      fread( &lp, 4, 1, fp );          // read it into LP
      lp = swap( lp );                 // and un-word-swap it
      lp &= 0xFFFFFFL;
    }
  if( lp == 0xFFFFFFL || lp == -1L ) // NULL pointer values
    ret = -1L;
  else                               // convert to offset
    ret = lp * PageSize;
  return ret;
}


/* * * * * * * * * * * * * * * * * * * * * * * * * * *\
 *                                                  *
 *      This procedure follows the free record      *
 *      chain and displays each record it finds      *
 *      in the chain.                               *
 *                                                  *
\* * * * * * * * * * * * * * * * * * * * * * * * * * */
void DumpFree( RECPTR rp )             // trace free-record chain
{ long svps = ftell( fp ), nxrec;
  int n=0, u;

  while( ( rp.wl & 0xFFFFFF )          // go until END flag
         != 0xFFFFFF )
    { if( CurFmt == 2 )                // translate new format
        nxrec = ( lp_pp( rp.wl / (long)PageSize )) +
                     ( rp.wl % (long)PageSize );
      else                             // original format OK
        nxrec = rp.wl;
      printf( "\tnext at file offset 0x%08lX, "
              "byte 0x%04lX of logical page %3ld\n",
              nxrec,                   // actual file offset
              rp.wl % (long)PageSize,  // logical record offset
              rp.wl / (long)PageSize ); // logical page number
```

```
        fseek( fp, nxrec, 0 );
        if( CurFmt == 2 && !compr ) // compr usage NOT first
          { fread( &u, 2, 1, fp );
            if( u )                     // break loop if bad
              break;
          }
        fread( &rp.wl, 4, 1, fp );        // get next pointer
        rp.wl = swap( rp.wl );            // un-wordswap it
        n++;                             // tally this record
      }
  printf( "End of record chain; free = %d.\n\n", n );
  fseek( fp, svps, 0 );
}


/* * * * * * * * * * * * * * * * * * * * * * * * *\
 *                                                *
 *      This procedure locates the free record    *
 *      chain and displays a header, then calls    *
 *      DumpFree to display.                       *
 *                                                *
\* * * * * * * * * * * * * * * * * * * * * * * * */
void DoItToIt( void )
{ if(CurFmt == 1 )                          // save head of chain
    FreeRec = Fcr.NxtReuseRec;
  else
    FreeRec = Fcr.r9.v6.Free[0].nxrec;
  FreeRec.wl = swap( FreeRec.wl );

  printf( "File %s is in %s format; pagesize = %d, "
          "has %ld pages\n",
          outbuf,
          fmt[CurFmt-1],
          PageSize,
          swap( Fcr.Npages ) );
  printf( "The following data records are free for reuse:\n" );
  DumpFree( FreeRec );                      // dump free-rec chain
}
```

```
/* * * * * * * * * * * * * * * * * * * * * * * * *\
 *                                                *
 *      This procedure determines a file's type,  *
 *      then sets CurFmt, loads Fcr, and positions *
 *      to index specification area of FCR page.   *
 *                                                *
\* * * * * * * * * * * * * * * * * * * * * * * * */
int GetFormat( void )
{ int fmt = 0;                    // 0 not Btrieve
                                  // 1 old, 2 new
  int testbuf[5];                 // test first 10 bytes

  fread( testbuf, 5, 2, fp );
  if( testbuf[1] == 0 )                // page sequence must be zero
    { if( testbuf[0] == 0 )
        { fmt = 1;                // original format
          fseek( fp, 0L, 0 );
        }
      else if( testbuf[0] == 0x4346 )   // 'FC' signature
        { fmt = 2;
          fseek( fp, (long)testbuf[4]+4, 0 ); // check next FCR
          fread( &testbuf[0], 2, 1, fp );
          if( testbuf[0] > testbuf[2] ) // second is valid
            fseek( fp, (long)testbuf[4], 0 );
          else                          // use the first
            fseek( fp, 0L, 0 );
        }
    }
  if( fmt )                       // load valid FCR
    { fread( &Fcr, 1, sizeof( FCRTOP ), fp );
      PageSize = Fcr.PagSize;
      if( Fcr.UsrFlgs & 8 )       // compressed data is
        compr = 1;                // different format
      else                        // so set flag...
        compr = 0;
    }
  else
    PageSize = 0;
  return fmt;
}
```

```
/* * * * * * * * * * * * * * * * * * * * * * * * *\
 *                                                *
 *        This procedure processes a single file.  *
 *                                                *
\* * * * * * * * * * * * * * * * * * * * * * * * */
int Do_File( char * fnm )
{ int ret = 0;                      // assume success

  strupr( fnm );
  fp = fopen( fnm, "rb" );
  if( fp )
    { strcpy( outbuf, fnm );        // save for reports
      CurFmt = GetFormat();
      switch( CurFmt )
        {
        case 0:
          printf( "%s is not a Btrieve file.\n", fnm );
          ret = 1;
          break;
        case 1:
        case 2:
          DoItToIt();
          break;
        default:
          puts( "Undefined format code, should never happen!" );
          ret = 99;
          break;
        }
      fclose( fp );
    }
  else
    { perror( fnm );
      ret = 2;
    }
  return ret;
}
```

```
/* * * * * * * * * * * * * * * * * * * * * * * *\
 *                                              *
 *      This procedure tells how to use the     *
 *      program.                                *
 *                                              *
\* * * * * * * * * * * * * * * * * * * * * * * */
void Usage( void )
{ printf( "Usage: %s file1 [file2 [...]]\n", PgmName );
  printf( "\t where filenames can continue until command line "
          "is full\n" );
}


/* * * * * * * * * * * * * * * * * * * * * * * *\
 *                                              *
 *      This procedure displays a standard banner *
 *      heading each time the program runs.     *
 *                                              *
\* * * * * * * * * * * * * * * * * * * * * * * */
void Banner( void )
{ printf( "\n\t    %s - from \"Btrieve Complete\" by Jim Kyle\n",
          PgmName );
  printf( "\t    Copyright 1995 by Jim Kyle - All Rights"
          " Reserved\n" );
  printf( "\t    Use freely, but do not distribute "
          "commercially.\n\n" );
}


/* * * * * * * * * * * * * * * * * * * * * * * *\
 *                                              *
 *      This procedure is program entry point.  *
 *                                              *
\* * * * * * * * * * * * * * * * * * * * * * * */
int main( int argc, char **argv )
{ int retval = 0;
  Banner();
  if( argc < 2 )
    { Usage();
      retval = 255;
    }
  else
    { int i;
```

```
    for( i=1; i < argc; i++ )
      { retval = Do_File( argv[i] ); // process each file
        if( retval )                      // if error, wait
          while( getch() != 13 )
            /* wait right here for CR */  ;
      }
  }
return retval;
}
```

To compile DUMPFREE.EXE, using Borland's compilers, use the command line

```
          BCC -ml DUMPFREE.C
```

The **-ml** switch specifies large memory model. No other special options are necessary.

A Data Dump Utility

The most useful of the five sample programs is DUMPDATA, which can either create a file in the BUTIL -SAVE format or can display each record of the file in a combination hex-and-ASCII format. This allows you to examine the records, regardless of data format.

The BUTIL -SAVE format creates a file that is identical with those that BUTIL itself generates. The difference is that DUMPDATA does not require the Btrieve engine to run. The display format presents up to 64 bytes of each record in a four-line group, repeating groups as necessary to show the entire record.

The first line of each group displays the hex value of the upper 4 bits of each byte, the second line shows the value of the low 4 bits, and the third line displays the ASCII value if the byte's value is within normal ASCII range. For out-of-range values, the third line simply displays a "*" character as shown in Figure 10.7. The fourth line serves only to separate groups when a record's length exceeds 64 bytes.

The display shows the file's page size, number of pages, record count, and the storage technique in use. The example in Figure 10.7

Figure 10.7   *DUMPDATA handles variable length and compressed records and reports the record type as part of its record count report. The file shown here used data compression.*

```
C:\SAMPLES>dumpdata cmp6.btr

           DUMPDATA - from "Btrieve Complete" by Jim Kyle
           Copyright 1995 by Jim Kyle - All Rights Reserved
           Use freely, but do not distribute commercially.

File CMP6.BTR is in new format; pagesize = 512, has 6 pages
Record count = 2 (Compressed).

Write SAVE file, or VIEW data on CRT (S or V )?V
100,       3333333333333333333333333333333333333333334444444444444444444
           1223334444555555666666677777778888888889999999999111111111112222222222
           122333444455555566666667777777888888888899999999999AAAAAAAAAABBBBBBBBBB
           ----------------------------------------------------------------
           44444444444444444444444444444442222222222
           2233333333333334444444444444444DDDDDDDDDD
           BBCCCCCCCCCCCCCDDDDDDDDDDDDDD----------
           ----------------------------------------------------------------

100,       66726727662766626672666266677677662766676727626627677662222222222
           EF70930485049D506F201CC03FD02533540253F24304F0250453454EEEEEEEEE
           now is the time for all compressed records to be tested.........
           ----------------------------------------------------------------
           22222222222222222222222222222222222222222
           EEEEEEEEEEEEEEEEEEEEEEEEEEEEEEEEEEEEEEEEEE
```

shows both records of a new-format file that uses 100-byte compressed records. The compression algorithm (see Chapter 8) converts runs of 5 or more identical bytes into a single copy of the byte, together with a repetition count. The two most serious challenges in getting DUMPDATA to work properly for all storage techniques were to reliably reverse the compression algorithm and to guarantee that variable-length records always went back together in proper sequence (with restoration of any truncated blanks at the end of each record).

The additional code necessary to meet these two challenges makes DUMPDATA by far the most complicated of our sample programs, but all the complications appear in a single procedure. Most of the other parts of the program show little if any change from the routines we've already examined.

Include, Constant, and Variable Differences

DUMPDATA.C includes the same set of header files used by
DUMPFREE. As in DUMPFREE, file pointer `fp` and FCRTOP structure `Fcr` are global variables, as are `PageSize`, `PgmName`, `out-
buf`, and string array `fmt[]`. New global variables include
`RecLen`, `PhyLen`, `fpout`, `rectype`, `Vrec`, `fragno`, `fragpg`,
`fragfo`, `fragpp`, `fragi`, `frago`, `fragl`, `Vbfr[]`, and `wrk-
buf[]`.

`RecLen` and `PhyLen` simply hold FCR information, similar to the
purpose of `PageSize`.

At startup, the program initializes file pointer `fpout` to the predefined standard output stream value, `stdout`. If you choose to create a SAVE-format output file, the program creates your file using
the `fpout` pointer. After processing that file, the program then uses
the fact that `fpout` is no longer equal to `stdout` to determine that
the output file needs closing. After closing the file, the routine sets
`fpout` back to `stdout`.

The `rectype` variable holds a code that indicates the storage technique in use. The code for fixed-length records is 0. Variable-length
records get a code of 1 (or 2, if they also use blank truncation). A code
of 3 indicates data compression, and files using the new VAT structures are flagged as record type 4. DUMPDATA doesn't support VAT
files; that's left as an exercise for any reader who feels it's needed.

The remaining new variables all deal with the complications of
reconstructing variable-length and compressed-data records. Variable record pointer `Vrec` stores the current variable-record pointer.
The fragment number from `Vrec` goes into `fragno`, and the logical page number portion of `Vrec` goes into `fragpg`. Variable
`fragfo` holds the true file offset to the corresponding physical
page. Integer pointer `fragpp` holds the calculated base address of
the offset pointer array (at the end of each variable-record page),
and `fragi` stores the current index into the `fragpp` array. The
value found there (after skipping any deleted fragment numbers)
goes into `frago` as the offset to the first byte of the fragment, and
`fragl` holds the calculated length of the fragment.

Two arrays, **Vbfr[]** and **wrkbuf[]**, each **MAXBTRPG** bytes long, hold the current variable record page and any other needed page, respectively. BTRIEVE.H defines **MAXBTRPG** equal to 4096, the largest possible Btrieve file page at present.

Reused Procedures

Procedures from DUMPFREE or LISTKEYS that remain unchanged are **swap()**, **lp_pp()**, **Do_File()**, **Usage()**, **Banner()**, and **main()**. Slightly modified procedures are **dumpdata()** and **GetFormat()**. **DoItToIt()** is heavily modified. Finally, **DumpRecs()**, **oflomsg()**, and **DmpRec()** are entirely new. The complications of record restoration are all in **DmpRec()**.

The dumpdata() Procedure

The **dumpdata()** procedure dumps data in the combination hex-ASCII format we met in LISTKEYS. The only change for this program is to modify the amount of space left at the start of each output line.

```
static void dumpdata( BYTE *data, int nbr )
{ int i, j;
  char *h = "0123456789ABCDEF";
  for(i=0; i<nbr; i+=64)
    { for( j=0; j<64; j++ )
        if( (i+j) < nbr )
          putchar( h[ (data[i+j]>>4) & 15] );
      printf( "\n\t  " );
      for( j=0; j<64; j++ )
        if( (i+j) < nbr )
          putchar( h[ data[i+j] & 15] );
      printf( "\n\t  " );
      for( j=0; j<64; j++ )
        if( (i+j) < nbr )
          putchar( isprint( data[i+j] ) ? data[i+j] :
                 '*' );
      printf( "\n\t  " );
      for( j=0; j<64; j++ )
```

```
        if( (i+j) < nbr )
          putchar( '-' );
      if( j == 64 )
        printf( "\n\t   " );
    }
}
```

The GetFormat() Procedure

The `GetFormat()` procedure determines a file's type, then loads `Fcr` and establishes the record type that the file employs. The change to this routine was addition of the record-type testing and setting of `rectype`.

```
int GetFormat( void )
{ int fmt = 0;                        // 0 not Btrieve
                                      // 1 old, 2 new
  int testbuf[5];                     // test first 10 bytes
  fread( testbuf, 5, 2, fp );
  if( testbuf[1] == 0 )               // page sequence must be zero
    { if( testbuf[0] == 0 )
        { fmt = 1;                     // original format
          fseek( fp, 0L, 0 );
        }
      else if( testbuf[0] == 0x4346 )   // 'FC' signature
        { fmt = 2;
          fseek( fp, (long)testbuf[4]+4, 0 ); // check next FCR
          fread( &testbuf[0], 2, 1, fp );
          if( testbuf[0] > testbuf[2] ) // second is valid
            fseek( fp, (long)testbuf[4], 0 );
          else                          // use the first
            fseek( fp, 0L, 0 );
        }
    }
```

If it's a Btrieve file, we now test `Fcr.UsrFlgs` and `Fcr.VRecsOkay` to determine the type of data storage it uses, and set `rectype` accordingly.

```
  if( fmt )                            // load valid FCR
    { fread( &Fcr, 1, sizeof( FCRTOP ), fp );
      PageSize = Fcr.PagSize;
      if( Fcr.UsrFlgs & 8 &&
          ( Fcr.VRecsOkay || Fcr.UsrFlgs & 1 ))
        rectype = 5;                   // compressed variable data
      else if( fmt == 2 && Fcr.UsrFlgs & 0x0800 )
        rectype = 4;                   // uses VATs
      else if( Fcr.UsrFlgs & 8 )
        rectype = 3;                   // compressed data
      else if( Fcr.VRecsOkay || Fcr.UsrFlgs & 1 )
        { if( (BYTE)Fcr.VRecsOkay == 0x00FD || Fcr.UsrFlgs & 2 )
            rectype = 2;               // var trunc
          else
            rectype = 1;               // variable length
        }
      else
        rectype = 0;                   // fixed length
    }
  else
    PageSize = 0;
  return fmt;
}
```

The DoItToIt() Procedure

The `DoItToIt()` procedure displays a file header that tells the file name, page size, and number of pages. It then asks which output format you want and waits for either S (BUTIL SAVE format) or V (viewing format). Pressing either the Escape key or Control-C at this time halts processing of the file, but the routine ignores all other keystrokes. Once you have specified the output format, `DoIt-ToIt()` cycles through all pages of the file, calling the `DumpRecs()` routine for each data page in turn.

```
void DoItToIt( void )
{ long x, fps = 0L, pgct;
  unsigned u, u1, u2;
  int lpg=1;
  char *rt[] = { "Fixed Length", "Variable Length",
```

```
                    "Variable, truncated", "Compressed",
                    "Uses VAT, not supported",
                    "Compressed variable-length" };
```

Immediately upon entry, the routine copies the information it needs from the FCR.

```
RecLen = Fcr.RecLen;                // save global values
PhyLen = Fcr.PhyLen;
pgct = swap( Fcr.Npages );     // get number of pages
Fcr.Nrecs = swap( Fcr.Nrecs );
```

The next action is to display the file information to the user. If the file has no records, or uses VATs, DoItToIt() quits at this point without doing anything else.

```
printf( "File %s is in %s format; pagesize = %d, "
        "has %ld pages\n",
        outbuf,
        fmt[CurFmt-1],
        PageSize,
        pgct );
printf( "Record count = %ld (%s).\n\n",
        Fcr.Nrecs, rt[rectype] );
if( Fcr.Nrecs < 1L || rectype == 4 )   // VATs not
                                       //    supported
    return;
```

If, however, records exist and it's not a VAT file, DoItToIt() prompts for the format choice. The routine then goes into a loop controlled by variable u, which remains set until you make a valid format choice. If your choice is S for SAVE output, another prompt asks for a name to use when creating the output file. The program then searches for the end of the name string and sets an end-of-string marker into place.

If you hit S by mistake and really want to view the file, you can press the Enter key without entering a name. The program detects this condition and falls through to the view choice. If you do enter a name, the routine opens a new file with the name you supply and stores the file pointer in `fpout`, replacing the original value `stdout`. Control then falls through to the view choice, which simply clears variable `u` and sends a newline to the CRT. With `u` set to zero, the `for` loop breaks.

```
printf( "Write SAVE file, or VIEW data on CRT (S or
        V )? " );
for( u=1; u; )
  switch( getch() )
    {
    case 's':
    case 'S':
      printf( "\nSave to filename: " );
      gets( wrkbuf );                      // get filename
      for( u=0; wrkbuf[u] > 0x1F; u++ )  // find end of name
        ;
      wrkbuf[u] = 0;
      if( strlen(wrkbuf) )              // no name means view
        fpout = fopen( wrkbuf, "wb" );
    case 'v':                          // fall through
    case 'V':
      u = 0;
      putchar( '\n' );
      break;
```

If you press the Escape key, an ASCII code of 27 comes back from `getch()`; pressing Control-C generates a value of 3. In either case, `DoItToIt()` returns immediately with no additional action.

```
    case 27:
    case 3:
      return;
    }
```

To process the file, `DoItToIt()` must cycle through each logical page of the file. In the original format, every page (including the FCR) has a logical page number, so the count must start at zero. In the new format, neither FCRs nor PATs bear logical page numbers, and logical page zero isn't used. Therefore, the count starts at one if `CurFmt` indicates the file uses the new format.

```
if( CurFmt > 1 )
  lpg = 1;                        // new starts at one
else
  lpg = 0;                        // old starts at zero
```

The following loop steps through the file logical page by logical page. First, it converts the page number to a physical file offset by calling `lp_pp()`. If a NULL pointer value comes back, the file must be corrupted; therefore, `DoItToIt()` breaks the loop prematurely. Otherwise, the loop positions to the start of the page, reads its 4-byte header and 2-byte usage count, then checks the usage count to determine whether its high bit is set.

Btrieve sets this bit of the usage count for every data page, whether original format or new format, so that the Get Direct functions can identify data pages without using any index. We use it for essentially the same reason. If the bit is set, `DoItToIt()` calls `DumpRecs()` to process all records on the page.

```
for( ; lpg < (unsigned)pgct; lpg++ ) // do rest of pages
  { fps = lp_pp( lpg );           // convert to file offset
    if( fps < 0L )
      break;                      // NULL-pointer, get out
    fseek( fp, fps, 0 );          // seek to start of  page
    fread( &x, 4, 1, fp );        // read header & usage
    fread( &u, 2, 1, fp );
    if( u & 0x8000 )              // dump data records
      DumpRecs();
}
```

After processing all active pages in the file, `DoItToIt()` compares `fpout` to `stdout` to determine whether a data file needs closing. If they are unequal, `DoItToIt()` writes an EOF byte (0x1A, required by BUTIL) to end the file, closes `fpout,` and restores the value of `fpout` to be `stdout`.

```
  if( fpout != stdout )              // close data file
    ( fprintf( fpout, "%c", 0x1A ); // after adding EOF mark
      fclose( fpout );
      fpout = stdout;
    }
}
```

The DumpRecs() Procedure

The `DumpRecs()` procedure goes through all possible records on a page and calls DmpRec for each. To determine how many records the page can hold, the routine first subtracts the 6-byte header size from the total page size, then divides by the physical length of a single record. A `for` loop then calls `DmpRec()` repeatedly.

```
void DumpRecs( void )
( int recpg = (PageSize - 6) / PhyLen;  // page capacity
  int currec;                            // current record
  for( currec=0; currec < recpg; currec++ )
    DmpRec();
}
```

The oflomsg() Procedure

The `oflomsg()` procedure writes a message to the CRT, then waits for the user to press the Enter key. Only the `DmpRec()` procedure ever calls `oflomsg();` the call passes in the name of the action where the overflow happened, the count, and the saved file position. The routine displays the error message to `stdout`, waits, calls `dumpdata()` to display the bad buffer, then restores the file position.

```
static void oflomsg( char * p, int r, long cpos )
{ printf( "\07%s buffer overflow!\07\n"
```

```
            "Press ENTER to continue\n%d\t   ", p, r );
  while( getch() != 13 )
    /* wait for user */ ;
  dumpdata( wrkbuf, r );
  fseek( fp, cpos + (long)PhyLen, 0 );
}
```

The DmpRec() Procedure

The `DmpRec()` procedure checks one record for validity and then outputs its data, expanding as necessary. Because it includes full code for dealing with variable-length records, blank truncation, and data compression, this is by far the most complicated single procedure in this book. However, each portion of the routine is no more difficult to comprehend than the simpler procedures of the previous four programs. That is, the listing looks far more complicated than it actually is.

```
void DmpRec( void )           // dumps single record
{ long cpos = ftell( fp );    // save position at entry
  int i, b, r = RecLen, count, state;
```

At entry, the current file position points to the first byte of a record. For the first record on each page, this positioning is inherent in the layout of a data page. We save the position in local variable `cpos`. We'll restore the file to the position of the next record, before leaving the routine. We also initialize local variable r to be equal to the size of the fixed-length portion of each record.

Next, if the file uses the new format and doesn't use data compression, we read its record-usage field (the record's first 2 bytes) into test variable `i`. If the count is zero, the record is currently unused. We set the file to the start of the next record and return immediately. Otherwise, the record is valid, and we read its remaining bytes into `wrkbuf`. Using `wrkbuf` rather than some smaller buffer provides plenty of room for reconstructing long records (although new-format files can have records much larger than 4,096 bytes; DUMP-DATA cannot handle such large records as written but could easily be modified to do so).

```
if( rectype != 3 && CurFmt == 2 )  // new format usage test
  { fread( &i, 2, 1, fp );
    if( !i )                              // ignore unused records
      { fseek( fp, cpos + (long)PhyLen, 0 );
        return;
      }
    fread( wrkbuf, PhyLen-2, 1, fp ); // load workbuf with data
  }
```

If the file is in original format or uses data compression, we test for unused records by another method. Btrieve clears all data out of a deleted record, leaving it filled with zeroes except for the record pointer at the front. Therefore, we read the record into **wrkbuf** and check every byte beyond the first four. If we find any byte nonzero, the record is valid. If not, we position the file to the next record and return.

```
  else                               // test for empty record
    { int empty = 1;
      fread( wrkbuf, PhyLen, 1, fp );  // load wrkbuf with data
      for( i=4; i<PhyLen; i++ )        // skip over pointer
        if( wrkbuf[i] )                // something there
          { empty = 0;                 // so not empty
            break;
          }
      if( empty )                      // restore file, ignore
        { fseek( fp, cpos + (long)PhyLen, 0 );
          return;
        }
    }
```

Once we have a valid record in **wrkbuf**, we check the value of **rectype**. If it's zero, the file uses fixed-length records and we can skip over all the expansion code.

```
  if( rectype )                      // var, trunc, compr
    { long fps = ftell( fp );        // save file position
      int lofs;
      BYTE cmpalg, savect;
```

If `rectype` isn't zero, we choose between variable-length rebuilding (cases 1 and 2) or compressed-data expansion (cases 3 and 5) by means of a switch statement. For rebuilding variable-length records, the first step is to copy the variable-record pointer that immediately follows the fixed-length portion of the record into `Vrec`. The value that follows the pointer goes into `count`. If blank truncation is in effect, this is the number of blanks to put back; if not, `count` is ignored. Next, we set integer pointer `fragpp` equal to the address of the first byte of `Vbfr` so that we can index directly into the fragment offset pointer table at the end of each variable record page.

```
switch( rectype )
  {
  case 1:                    // VARIABLE LENGTH DATA
  case 2:                    // BLANK TRUNCATION
    memcpy( &Vrec, wrkbuf + r, 4 );
    memcpy( &count, wrkbuf + r + 4, 2 );
    fragpp = (int *)Vbfr; // set pointer
```

Although most authorities consider it dangerous to use a goto statement in modern programming, sometime it's the clearest way to do a job. That's why this routine has four of them. It's possible to write this procedure in totally structured form without using a goto, but the result is much more difficult to comprehend.

The label `nxvr` identifies a loop point; each time we find a new fragment pointer, we'll return to this location. Here, we split the record pointer in `Vrec` into its fragment and page components, using macros defined in BTRIEVE.H. The results go into `fragno` and `fragpg`. We then translate the page number into a file offset and store that in `fragfo`. If `fragfo` holds a NULL pointer or `fragno` is greater than 254 (the highest valid fragment number), we've reached the end of the expansion loop and control passes to label `vrdun`. Otherwise, we load buffer `Vbfr` with the page that `fragfo` addresses. Reading a full 4,096 bytes does no harm here.

```
nxvr:     fragno = VRFrag( Vrec );  // for multiple frags
          fragpg = VRPage( Vrec );
```

```
fragfo = lp_pp( fragpg );
if( fragfo == -1L || fragno > 254 )
  goto vrdun;                 // no more to do
fseek( fp, fragfo, 0 );     // read page into buffer
fread( &Vbfr, MAXBTRPG, 1, fp );
```

Next we calculate the index to the desired fragment number by first halving the page size (minus 1 to convert to zero-based counting) and then subtracting fragno. Remember that the fragment offset pointer table starts at the end of the page and works back toward the front. This calculation determines the actual index value to use, which goes into fragi.

With this index and pointer fragpp, we obtain the true offset within the page to the first byte of the data fragment. Since original-format files indicate the presence of additional fragments by setting the high byte of the offset value to 1 for every fragment except the final one, we must mask that bit out before storing the offset at frago.

To determine the fragment's length, we subtract its offset from the next valid offset in the fragment offset pointer table. However, any entry in that table may be -1, indicating a deleted fragment number, so we must first discard any such fragments that lie in between. That's the job of the empty for loop. The first entry we find that's not equal to -1 is the one to use; masking off its high bit also, then subtracting frago, gives us the value for fragl.

```
fragi = ((PageSize - 1) >> 1 ) - fragno;
frago = fragpp[ fragi ] & 0x7FFF;
for(lofs=1; fragpp[fragi - lofs] == -1; lofs++)
  /* all done in test! */ ;
fragl = (fragpp[ fragi - lofs ] & 0x7FFF ) - frago;
```

If additional fragments exist for this record (and even if they don't, in the new file format) the first 4 bytes of the fragment will be the variable record pointer to the next fragment. For the last fragment of a new-format file, this pointer is 0x00FFFFFF. We copy the pointer into `Vrec`, then adjust both `frago` and `fragl` to account for it, before proceeding.

```
if( CurFmt == 2 || fragpp[fragi] & 0x8000 )
 { Vrec = *(VRECPTR *)(&Vbfr[ frago ]);
   frago += sizeof( VRECPTR );
   fragl -= sizeof( VRECPTR );
 }
```

If the file is in original format and no more fragments exist for this record, no next-fragment pointer exists. We fake an end-of-chain marker by filling all 4 bytes of `Vrec` with 0xFF.

```
else
 { Vrec.lo = Vrec.mid = Vrec.hi = Vrec.frag = 0x00FF;
 }
```

Once we're done with the arithmetic, the record reconstruction becomes anticlimactic. We simply use the library routine `mem-cpy()` to move `fragl` bytes, from `Vbfr` starting at `frago`, to offset `r` in `wrkbuf`. We then add `fragl` to `r` in preparation for any additional fragment and loop back to label `nxvr`.

```
memcpy( wrkbuf + r, Vbfr + frago, fragl );
r += fragl;
goto nxvr;                 // check for next frag
```

When the loop finds the end-of-chain marker, control comes to label `vrdun`. If blanks were truncated, we put them back. Otherwise, we merely break out of the switch statement. The record is fully reconstructed in `wrkbuf`.

```
vrdun:    if( rectype == 2 )           // restore blanks
           { while( count--  && r < 4095 ) // stay in buffer!
             wrkbuf[ r++ ] = ' ';
           }
          break;
```

If the file contains compressed data, the code to expand it is almost identical to that used for variable-length records right up to the point at which we move data into the working buffer. The differences, however, are critical. One of them occurs right at the beginning of cases 3 and 5 (the only difference between the two is the message displayed about data format; the expansion technique is the same whether record length is fixed or variable).

We copy the variable record pointer to the compressed data into Vrec and initialize fragpp just as before, but we set local variable cmpalg equal to the fifth byte of the data record in wrkbuf. This byte holds the compression algorithm code, and a zero value here indicates a deleted record. The new format includes a record usage field in its sixth and seventh bytes, but we need not examine it. This greatly simplifies testing for deleted records. We also clear count and the local variable savect to guarantee they are both zero at the start of a record and set state to 1 since the compression algorithm always starts with a copy string (even if the first byte is a repeat). After copying out the data, we set r to zero because none of the actual record data is yet in wrkbuf. It's all in the record to which Vrec points (and any fragments that follow that record).

```
case 3:                         // COMPRESSED DATA
case 5:                         // COMPRESSED, VARIABLE
  memcpy( &Vrec, wrkbuf + r, 4 );
  fragpp = (int *)Vbfr;  // set pointer
  cmpalg = wrkbuf[4];
  if( !cmpalg )                 // deleted record, ignore
      { fseek( fp, cpos + (long)PhyLen, 0 );
        return;
      }
  count = 0;                    // clear count vars
  savect = 0;
  r = 0;                        // expansion index
  state = 1;                    // copy strings first
```

Processing the variables that control fragment addressing and the loops that deal with multiple fragments is exactly the same as those for variable-length records, except that we read only `PageSize` bytes into `Vbfr`, rather than the maximum possible.

```
nxcr:      fragno = VRFrag( Vrec );   // for multiple frags
           fragpg = VRPage( Vrec );
           fragfo = lp_pp( fragpg );  // actual file offset
           if( fragfo == -1L || fragno > 254 )
             goto crdun;
           fseek( fp, fragfo, 0 );     // read page into buffer
           fread( &Vbfr, MAXBTRPG, 1, fp );
           fragi = ((PageSize - 1) >> 1 ) - fragno;
           frago = fragpp[ fragi ] & 0x7FFF;
           fragl = (fragpp[ fragi - 1 ] & 0x7FFF ) - frago;
           if( CurFmt == 2 || fragpp[fragi] & 0x8000 )
             { Vrec = *(VRECPTR *)(&Vbfr[ frago ]);
               frago += sizeof( VRECPTR );
               fragl -= sizeof( VRECPTR );
             }
           else
             { Vrec.lo = Vrec.mid = Vrec.hi = Vrec.frag
                                             = 0x00FF;
             }
```

However, once we've loaded a fragment that holds compressed data, we must use a decompression loop to either copy or expand that fragment, one portion at a time. If things become murky here, refer to Chapter 8 for details of the compression algorithm. The first fragment of a record begins with a 2-byte value, which we will copy into local variable count. We will then adjust the loop count to allow for the 2 bytes.

However, when a record spans multiple fragments, the breaks between them can come anywhere. One particularly troublesome break can be between the 2 bytes of the count value. That's why we use `savect`. Initially its value is zero, but if a fragment ends between the first and second bytes of a count, we save the first in `savect`. The following code then becomes active immediately after the next fragment loads (this technique fails for a count value of 0x0000 that spans a fragment boundary; a separate flag really should be used. I never encountered the failure in my testing and caught the design flaw only during final editing of this description, too late to correct the text. It is corrected in the code on the diskette, however).

```
if( savect )                // count spans frags
  { frago--;                // adj offset, length
    fragl++;
    Vbfr[frago] = savect;   // set first byte in
    count = 0;              // clear out count
    savect = 0;             // clear save/flag byte
  }
```

This puts the saved byte immediately ahead of the just-loaded second byte, in Vbfr, and adjusts the offset and length values. It then zeroes out both savect and count. Zeroing savect assures that the adjustment won't be made again unnecessarily. Zeroing count forces reading of the new count value.

It's also possible for the break between fragments to happen immediately after the count word or in the middle of a copy string. In either case, the count variable will be greater than zero, so we leave its value unchanged. In normal operation, count decrements to zero during the copy or repeat loops, and so we read a new value at the start of the next string. The test against fragl is to detect the situation in which the break follows the second byte.

```
for( i=0; i<fragl; )    // decompression loop
  { if( count < 1 )     // get new count
      { count = *(int *)(Vbfr + frago + i );
        i += 2;         // advance pointer
      }
    if( i >= fragl )    // at fragment end
      break;            // so get another
```

The compression algorithm forces copy and repeat strings to alternate; the program keeps track of this by using variable state. When state equals one, a copy string follows the count. When

state is zero, it's a repeat byte. The **if()** selects the appropriate action:

```
if( state )           // process data pair
```

The copy loop is relatively straightforward; the only complication is that it's possible for the fragment to end before the count runs out, so the library **memcpy()** routine isn't usable here. We must test after each byte to verify that we're still within the fragment. We also test to be certain that possible corruption can't cause the output buffer to overflow; you should never see this message in practice however. When the copy completes and count is down to zero (or below; it should never get there but I found that it would do so under at least one combination of values), the loop then switches **state** so that the next pair will repeat rather than copy.

```
{ while( count-- )        // copy is state 1
   { wrkbuf[ r++ ] = Vbfr[ frago + (i++) ];
      if( r > 4090 )    // error trap...
        { oflomsg( "Copy", r, cpos );
           return;        // skip this record
        }
      if( i == fragl && // string spans frags
          count )        //    and isn't done yet
         break;          // get next fragment
    }                    // copy loop
  if( count < 1 )
     state = 0;          // repeat next pair
}
```

When **state** is zero, we must repeat the following byte **count** times. In this case, we don't have to test for running off the end of the fragment because the fragment pointer never advances. We do, however, have to test for possible output buffer overflow. When the count runs out, we advance the fragment pointer past the repeated byte, change **state** back to copy the next pair, and we're done with the loop.

```
        else
          { while( count-- )                    // repeat is state 0
             { wrkbuf[ r++ ] = Vbfr[ frago + i ];
                if( r > 4090 )                   // error trap...
                  { oflomsg( "Repeat", r, cpos );
                    return;                      // skip this record
                  }
             }                                   // repeat loop
          i++;                                   // over repeat byte
          state = 1;                             // copy next pair
        }
```

However, it's still possible that we might have only 1 byte of the next count word left in the current fragment. If so, we must save that byte in `savect` for use at the start of the next fragment as we've already seen.

```
        if( i == fragl-1 )                       // count spans frags
          { savect = Vbfr[ frago + i++ ];
            break;                               // get next
          }
      }                                          // decompression loop
```

When the fragment index pointer i reaches the value in `fragl`, the `for()` loop runs out, so we loop back to `nxcr` to get the next fragment.

```
        goto nxcr;                   // to get next fragment
```

When no fragments remain to be processed, record expansion is complete. Upon breaking out of the switch statement, `DmpRec()` restores the saved file position from `fps`.

```
crdun:   break;
      }
    fseek( fp, fps, 0 );
  }
```

No matter what the value of rectype, control eventually reaches this point. For fixed-length records it happens immediately. Other types must pass through the switch statement and its nested loops. Here, we tally down the total number of records to process and switch between two different routines depending on the output format we selected earlier. For viewing, we simply display the record length, call dumpdata(), and then output a newline.

```
Fcr.Nrecs--;                        // tally down count
if( fpout == stdout )
  { printf( "%d,\t  ", r );         // human-readable format
    dumpdata( wrkbuf, r );
    putchar( '\n' );
  }
```

For the save-file option (the only alternative to viewing), we write the record length, all valid bytes from wrkbuf, and a CR/LF pair to file fpout. Masking the output against 255 prevents any possible sign extension from corrupting the output file.

```
else
  { fprintf( fpout, "%d,", r );              // BUTIL -SAVE format
    for( i=0; i<r; i++ )
      { b = 255 & wrkbuf[i];
        fprintf( fpout, "%c", b );
      }
    fprintf( fpout, "\r\n" );
  }
```

With processing of a single record now complete, we adjust the file position to be the start of the next record, and return to the caller.

```
    fseek( fp, cpos + (long)PhyLen, 0 );  // restore file position
}
```

The Complete DUMPDATA.C Listing

Now that we've examined each of its component modules, here's the complete listing for DUMPDATA.C as described in this chapter:

```
/* * * * * * * * * * * * * * * * * * * * * * * * *\
 *                                               *
 *    DUMPDATA - Jim Kyle - January 1995         *
 *                                               *
 *    Lists all data records from any version of *
 *    Btrieve file without requiring Btrieve engine *
 *    to be installed in system.                 *
 *                                               *
\* * * * * * * * * * * * * * * * * * * * * * * * */
#include <stdio.h>
#include <conio.h>
#ifdef __TURBOC__
#include <alloc.h>        // Borland-specific
#else
#include <malloc.h>       // Microsoft version
#endif
#include <string.h>
#include <ctype.h>
#include "btrieve.h"

FILE *fp;                 // global for convenience
FCRTOP Fcr;

int PageSize, RecLen, PhyLen;
char *PgmName = "DUMPDATA";
char outbuf[80];


FILE *fpout = stdout;
int rectype = 0;   // 0 fixed, 1 variable, 2 var trunc,
                   //   3 compressed, 4 uses VAT
VRECPTR Vrec;      // current vrec pointer
int  fragno;       // fragment number from Vrec
long fragpg;       // vrec logical page number from Vrec
long fragfo;       // file offset to physical page
int *fragpp;       // fragment index array base
int  fragi,        // index into fragpp array
     frago,        // offset to start of fragment
     fragl;        // length of fragment
BYTE Vbfr[MAXBTRPG];
char wrkbuf[MAXBTRPG];  // for reading anything into
```

```
char *fmt[] = {
  "original",
  "new"
};

/* * * * * * * * * * * * * * * * * * * * * * * * * *\
 *                                                 *
 *      This procedure undoes Btrieve"s word-      *
 *      swapping.                                  *
 *                                                 *
\* * * * * * * * * * * * * * * * * * * * * * * * * */
static long swap( long n )
{ asm les dx,n;                  // ASM trick for simplicity
  asm mov ax,es;
// return ((n>>16)&0xFFFF) | (n<<16);
}


/* * * * * * * * * * * * * * * * * * * * * * * * * *\
 *                                                 *
 *      This procedure dumps data, translating     *
 *      to ASCII if in printable range, else       *
 *      outputting as hex.                          *
 *                                                 *
\* * * * * * * * * * * * * * * * * * * * * * * * * */
static void dumpdata( BYTE *data, int nbr )
{ int i, j;
  char *h = "0123456789ABCDEF";
  for(i=0; i<nbr; i+=64)
    { for( j=0; j<64; j++ )
        if( (i+j) < nbr )
          putchar( h[ (data[i+j]>>4) & 15] );
      printf( "\n\t  " );
      for( j=0; j<64; j++ )
        if( (i+j) < nbr )
          putchar( h[ data[i+j] & 15] );
      printf( "\n\t  " );
      for( j=0; j<64; j++ )
        if( (i+j) < nbr )
          putchar( isprint( data[i+j] ) ? data[i+j] : '*' );
      printf( "\n\t  " );
```

```
      for( j=0; j<64; j++ )
        if( (i+j) < nbr )
          putchar( '-' );
      if( j == 64 )
        printf( "\n\t   " );
    }
}


/* * * * * * * * * * * * * * * * * * * * * * * * *\
 *                                               *
 *      This procedure converts a Logical Page   *
 *      number to a file offset, using the PAT   *
 *      for new format files.                    *
 *                                               *
\* * * * * * * * * * * * * * * * * * * * * * * * */
static long lp_pp( long lp )
{ long ret, pat1, pat2;
  unsigned short u1, u2, pppat;
  if( CurFmt != 1 )                   // only do lookup for new
    { ret = 2;                        // first PAT pair on 2, 3
      pppat = (PageSize >> 2) - 2;  // pages per PAT

      while( lp > pppat )           // off current page
        { lp -= pppat;              // so tally down index
          ret += (PageSize >> 2);   // up the PAT pp nbr
        }

      pat1 = ret * (long)PageSize;  // first PAT of pair
      pat2 = pat1 + (long)PageSize; // second right after it
      fseek( fp, pat1+4L, 0 );           // get both usage counts
      fread( &u1, 2, 1, fp );
      fseek( fp, pat2+4L, 0 );
      fread( &u2, 2, 1, fp );
      if( u1 > u2 )                      // choose most recent one
        ret = pat1;
      else
        ret = pat2;
      ret += (long)(( lp << 2 ) + 4L ); // position in PAT
      fseek( fp, ret, 0 );
      fread( &lp, 4, 1, fp );                   // read it into LP
      lp = swap( lp );                          // and un-word-swap it
```

```
      lp &= 0xFFFFFFL;
    }
  if( lp == 0xFFFFFFL || lp == -1L )      // NULL pointer values
    ret = -1L;
  else                                    // convert to offset
    ret = lp * PageSize;
  return ret;
}

/* * * * * * * * * * * * * * * * * * * * * * * * *\
 *                                               *
 *      This procedure writes a message to CRT   *
 *      and then waits for user to press ENTER   *
 *      key.                                      *
 *                                               *
\* * * * * * * * * * * * * * * * * * * * * * * * */
static void oflomsg( char * p, int r, long cpos )
{ printf( "\07%s buffer overflow!\07\n"
          "Press ENTER to continue\n%d\t   ", p, r );
  while( getch() != 13 )
    /* wait for user */ ;
  dumpdata( wrkbuf, r );
  fseek( fp, cpos + (long)PhyLen, 0 );
}


/* * * * * * * * * * * * * * * * * * * * * * * * *\
 *                                               *
 *      This procedure checks one record for     *
 *      validity and then outputs its data,      *
 *      expanding as necessary.                  *
 *                                               *
\* * * * * * * * * * * * * * * * * * * * * * * * */
void DmpRec( void )                      // dumps single record
{ long cpos = ftell( fp );               // save position at entry
  int i, b, r = RecLen, count, state;

  if( rectype != 3 && CurFmt == 2 )  // new format usage test
    { fread( &i, 2, 1, fp );
      if( !i )                           // ignore unused records
        { fseek( fp, cpos + (long)PhyLen, 0 );
          return;
```

```
            }
        fread( wrkbuf, PhyLen-2, 1, fp ); // load workbuf with data
    }

  else                                    // test for empty record
    { int empty = 1;
      fread( wrkbuf, PhyLen, 1, fp );    // load wrkbuf with data
      for( i=4; i<PhyLen; i++ )          // skip over pointer
        if( wrkbuf[i] )                  // something there
          { empty = 0;                   // so not empty
            break;
          }
      if( empty )                        // restore file, ignore
        { fseek( fp, cpos + (long)PhyLen, 0 );
          return;
        }
    }

  if( rectype )                          // var, trunc, compr
    { long fps = ftell( fp );            // save file position
      int lofs;
      BYTE cmpalg, savect;

      switch( rectype )
        {
        case 1:                          // VARIABLE LENGTH DATA
        case 2:                          // BLANK TRUNCATION
          memcpy( &Vrec, wrkbuf + r, 4 );
          memcpy( &count, wrkbuf + r + 4, 2 );
          fragpp = (int *)Vbfr;    // set pointer

nxvr:     fragno = VRFrag( Vrec );  // for multiple frags
          fragpg = VRPage( Vrec );
          fragfo = lp_pp( fragpg );
          if( fragfo == -1L || fragno > 254 )
            goto vrdun;                  // no more to do
          fseek( fp, fragfo, 0 );  // read page into buffer
          fread( &Vbfr, MAXBTRPG, 1, fp );

          fragi = ((PageSize - 1) >> 1 ) - fragno;
          frago = fragpp[ fragi ] & 0x7FFF;
```

```
              for(lofs=1; fragpp[fragi - lofs] == -1; lofs++)
                /* all done in test! */ ;
              fragl = (fragpp[ fragi - lofs ] & 0x7FFF ) - frago;

              if( CurFmt == 2 || fragpp[fragi] & 0x8000 )
                { Vrec = *(VRECPTR *)(&Vbfr[ frago ]);
                  frago += sizeof( VRECPTR );
                  fragl -= sizeof( VRECPTR );
                }
              else
                { Vrec.lo = Vrec.mid = Vrec.hi = Vrec.frag
                    = 0x00FF;
                }
              memcpy( wrkbuf + r, Vbfr + frago, fragl );
              r += fragl;
              goto nxvr;                   // check for next frag
vrdun:        if( rectype == 2 )          // restore blanks
                { while( count--  && r < 4095 ) // stay in buffer!
                    wrkbuf[ r++ ] = ' ';
                }
              break;

          case 3:                     // COMPRESSED DATA
          case 5:                     // COMPRESSED, VARIABLE
            memcpy( &Vrec, wrkbuf + r, 4 );
            fragpp = (int *)Vbfr;     // set pointer
            cmpalg = wrkbuf[4];
            if( !cmpalg )                   // deleted record, ignore
              { fseek( fp, cpos + (long)PhyLen, 0 );
                return;
              }
            count = 0;                  // clear count vars
            savect = 0;
            r = 0;                      // expansion index
            state = 1;                  // copy strings first

nxcr:       fragno = VRFrag( Vrec );  // for multiple frags
            fragpg = VRPage( Vrec );
            fragfo = lp_pp( fragpg ); // actual file offset
            if( fragfo == -1L || fragno > 254 )
              goto crdun;               // end of chain
```

```
fseek( fp, fragfo, 0 );    // read page into buffer
fread( &Vbfr, PageSize, 1, fp );
fragi = ((PageSize - 1) >> 1 ) - fragno;
frago = fragpp[ fragi ] & 0x7FFF;
fragl = (fragpp[ fragi - 1 ] & 0x7FFF ) - frago;

if( CurFmt == 2 || fragpp[fragi] & 0x8000 )
  { Vrec = *(VRECPTR *)(&Vbfr[ frago ]);
    frago += sizeof( VRECPTR );
    fragl -= sizeof( VRECPTR );
  }
else
  { Vrec.lo = Vrec.mid = Vrec.hi = Vrec.frag
      = 0x00FF;
  }
if( savect )              // count spans frags
  { frago--;              // adj offset, length
    fragl++;
    Vbfr[frago] = savect; // set first byte in
    count = 0;            // clear out count
    savect = 0;           // clear save/flag byte
  }
for( i=0; i<fragl; )      // decompression loop
  { if( count < 1 )       // get new count
   {count = *(int *)(Vbfr + frago + i );
    i += 2;               // advance pointer
  }
 if( i >= fragl )         // at fragment end
   break;                 // so get another

 if( state )              // process data pair
   { while( count-- )     // copy is state 1
     { wrkbuf[ r++ ] = Vbfr[ frago + (i++) ];
        if( r > 4090 )   // error trap...
          { oflomsg( "Copy", r, cpos );
            return;       // skip this record
             }
        if( i == fragl && // string spans frags
            count )       //   and isn't done yet
          break;          // get next fragment
     }                    // copy loop
```

```
                    if( count < 1 )
                      state = 0;              // repeat next pair
                 }
               else
                 { while( count-- )          // repeat is state 0
                     { wrkbuf[ r++ ] = Vbfr[ frago + i ];
                       if( r > 4090 )   // error trap...
                         { oflomsg( "Repeat", r, cpos );
                           return;        // skip this record
                         }
                     }                       // repeat loop
                   i++;                      // over repeat byte
                   state = 1;                // copy next pair
                 }

                 if( i == fragl-1 )          // count spans frags
                   { savect = Vbfr[ frago + i++ ];
                     break;                  // get next
                   }
               }                             // decompression loop
           goto nxcr;                        // to get next fragment
  crdun:    break;                           // record complete now
         }
       fseek( fp, fps, 0 );
     }

   Fcr.Nrecs--;                              // tally down count
   if( fpout == stdout )
     { printf( "%d,\t   ", r );              // human-readable format
       dumpdata( wrkbuf, r );
       putchar( '\n' );
     }
   else
     { fprintf( fpout, "%d,", r );           // BUTIL -SAVE format
       for( i=0; i<r; i++ )
         { b = 255 & wrkbuf[i];
           fprintf( fpout, "%c", b );
         }
       fprintf( fpout, "\r\n" );
     }

 fseek( fp, cpos + (long)PhyLen, 0 );  // restore file position
 }
```

```
/* * * * * * * * * * * * * * * * * * * * * * * * * *\
 *                                                 *
 *      This procedure goes through all possible   *
 *      records on a page and calls DmpRec for     *
 *      each.                                       *
 *                                                 *
\* * * * * * * * * * * * * * * * * * * * * * * * * */
void DumpRecs( void )
{ int recpg = (PageSize - 6) / PhyLen;  // page capacity
  int currec;                              // current record

  for( currec=0; currec < recpg; currec++ )
    DmpRec();
}


/* * * * * * * * * * * * * * * * * * * * * * * * * *\
 *                                                 *
 *      This procedure cycles through all pages,   *
 *      calling DumpRecs routine for each data     *
 *      page in turn.                              *
 *                                                 *
\* * * * * * * * * * * * * * * * * * * * * * * * * */
void DoItToIt( void )
{ long x, fps = 0L, pgct;
  unsigned u, u1, u2;
  int lpg=1;
  char *rt[] = { "Fixed Length", "Variable Length",
              "Variable, truncated", "Compressed",
              "Uses VAT, not supported" };,
              "Compressed variable-length" };
  RecLen = Fcr.RecLen;           // save global values
  PhyLen = Fcr.PhyLen;
  pgct = swap( Fcr.Npages );     // get number of pages
  Fcr.Nrecs = swap( Fcr.Nrecs );

  printf( "File %s is in %s format; pagesize = %d, "
          "has %ld pages\n",
          outbuf,
          fmt[CurFmt-1],
          PageSize,
          pgct );
```

```
    printf( "Record count = %ld (%s).\n\n",
            Fcr.Nrecs, rt[rectype] );
    if( Fcr.Nrecs < 1L || rectype == 4 )  // VAT's not
        supported
      return;

    printf( "Write SAVE file, or VIEW data on CRT (S or V )? " );
    for( u=1; u; )
      switch( getch() )
        {
        case 's':
        case 'S':
          printf( "\nSave to filename: " );
          gets( wrkbuf );                    // get filename
          for( u=0; wrkbuf[u] > 0x1F; u++ )  // find end of name
            ;
          wrkbuf[u] = 0;
          if( strlen(wrkbuf) )               // no name means view
            fpout = fopen( wrkbuf, "wb" );
        case 'v':                            // fall through
        case 'V':
          u = 0;
          putchar( '\n' );
          break;
        case 27:
        case 3:
          return;
        }

    if( CurFmt > 1 )
      lpg = 1;                               // new starts at one
    else
      lpg = 0;                               // old starts at zero

    for( ; lpg < (unsigned)pgct; lpg++ ) // do rest of pages
      { fps = lp_pp( lpg );                  // convert to file offset
        if( fps < 0L )
          break;                             // NULL-pointer, get out
        fseek( fp, fps, 0 );                 // seek to start of page
        fread( &x, 4, 1, fp );               // read header & usage
        fread( &u, 2, 1, fp );
        if( u & 0x8000 )                     // dump data records
```

```
        DumpRecs();
    }
  if( fpout != stdout )                    // close data file
    { fprintf( fpout, "%c", 0x1A );        // after adding EOF mark
      fclose( fpout );
      fpout = stdout;
    }
}


/* * * * * * * * * * * * * * * * * * * * * * * * * *\
 *                                                 *
 *     This procedure determines a file's type,    *
 *     then loads Fcr, and establishes record      *
 *     type.                                        *
 *                                                 *
\* * * * * * * * * * * * * * * * * * * * * * * * * */
int GetFormat( void )
{ int fmt = 0;                      // 0 not Btrieve
                                    // 1 old, 2 new
  int testbuf[5];                   // test first 10 bytes

  fread( testbuf, 5, 2, fp );
  if( testbuf[1] == 0 )             // page sequence must be zero
    { if( testbuf[0] == 0 )
        { fmt = 1;                  // original format
          fseek( fp, 0L, 0 );
        }
      else if( testbuf[0] == 0x4346 )   // 'FC' signature
        { fmt = 2;
          fseek( fp, (long)testbuf[4]+4, 0 ); // check next FCR
          fread( &testbuf[0], 2, 1, fp );
          if( testbuf[0] > testbuf[2] ) // second is valid
            fseek( fp, (long)testbuf[4], 0 );
          else                      // use the first
            fseek( fp, 0L, 0 );
        }
    }
  if( fmt )                         // load valid FCR
    { fread( &Fcr, 1, sizeof( FCRTOP ), fp );
      PageSize = Fcr.PagSize;
      if( Fcr.UsrFlgs & 8 &&
```

```
             ( Fcr.VRecsOkay || Fcr.UsrFlgs & 1 ))
        rectype = 5;              // compressed variable data
     else if( fmt == 2 && Fcr.UsrFlgs & 0x0800 )
        rectype = 4;              // uses VATs
     else if( Fcr.UsrFlgs & 8 )
        rectype = 3;              // compressed fixed data
     else if( Fcr.VRecsOkay || Fcr.UsrFlgs & 1 )
        { if( (BYTE)Fcr.VRecsOkay == 0x00FD || Fcr.UsrFlgs & 2 )
           rectype = 2;           // var trunc
          else
           rectype = 1;           // variable length
        }
     else
        rectype = 0;              // fixed length
    }
  else
    PageSize = 0;
  return fmt;
}


/* * * * * * * * * * * * * * * * * * * * * * * * *\
 *                                              *
 *      This procedure processes a single file. *
 *                                              *
\* * * * * * * * * * * * * * * * * * * * * * * */
int Do_File( char * fnm )
{ int ret = 0;                    // assume success

  strupr( fnm );
  fp = fopen( fnm, "rb" );
  if( fp )
    { strcpy( outbuf, fnm );      // save for reports
      CurFmt = GetFormat();
      switch( CurFmt )
        {
        case 0:
          printf( "%s is not a Btrieve file.\n", fnm );
          ret = 1;
          break;
        case 1:
        case 2:
```

```
            DoItToIt();
            break;
        default:
            puts( "Undefined format code, should never happen!" );
            ret = 99;
            break;
        }
      fclose( fp );
    }
  else
    { perror( fnm );
      ret = 2;
    }
  return ret;
}


/* * * * * * * * * * * * * * * * * * * * * * * * *\
 *                                               *
 *      This procedure tells how to use the      *
 *      program.                                 *
 *                                               *
\* * * * * * * * * * * * * * * * * * * * * * * * */
void Usage( void )
{ printf( "Usage: %s file1 [file2 [...]]\n", PgmName );
  printf( "\t where filenames can continue until command line "
          "is full\n" );
}



/* * * * * * * * * * * * * * * * * * * * * * * * *\
 *                                               *
 *      This procedure displays a standard banner *
 *      heading each time the program runs.      *
 *                                               *
\* * * * * * * * * * * * * * * * * * * * * * * * */
void Banner( void )
{ printf( "\n\t    %s - from \"Btrieve Complete\" by Jim Kyle\n",
          PgmName );
  printf( "\t    Copyright 1995 by Jim Kyle - All Rights" "
          Reserved\n" );
```

```
     printf( "\t    Use freely, but do not distribute "
           "commercially.\n\n" );
}

/* * * * * * * * * * * * * * * * * * * * * * * * * *\
 *                                                 *
 *        This procedure is program entry point.   *
 *                                                 *
\* * * * * * * * * * * * * * * * * * * * * * * * * */
int main( int argc, char **argv )
{ int retval = 0;
  Banner();
  if( argc < 2 )
    { Usage();
      retval = 255;
    }
  else
    { int i;
      for( i=1; i < argc; i++ )
        { retval = Do_File( argv[i] );  // process each file
          if( retval )                  // if error, wait
            while( getch() != 13 )
              /* wait right here for CR */  ;
        }
    }
  return retval;
}
```

To compile DUMPDATA.EXE using Borland's compilers, use the
command line

`BCC -ml DUMPDATA.C`

The `-ml` switch specifies large memory model. No other special
options are necessary.

Conclusion

In this chapter, we've used the information about Btrieve file internal organization to create five sample programs and have gone through each of the five in detail. My intent is to provide you ample data from which you can create your own utilities to meet any special need you may run into.

In Chapter 11, we explore a completely different facet of dealing with Btrieve. We'll look at ways to achieve optimum performance from your Btrieve applications by applying the knowledge of internal structure. We'll also examine some little-publicized aspects of performance tuning.

11

Getting the Best Out of Btrieve

This chapter describes methods and techniques for obtaining optimum performance from Btrieve. The information in this chapter comes from a number of sources. Some is based on the official manuals, some comes from experienced Btrieve users, and some items evolved from my experiences in learning how to get the best out of the Btrieve system. A number of points presented here originated with discussions on CompuServe, in the BTRIEVE forum.

Because of the diversity of the material, you'll find this chapter is more like a collection than an organized presentation. Major topics appear in order of apparent interest to most Btrieve users, not as part of a tree-like outline structure, but as independent entities. Let's start by looking at the two faces of **optimum performance,** since this term always implies a tradeoff between features that conserve space and those that improve speed.

Optimum = Tradeoff

Before you can begin to tune a design for optimum performance, you must decide whether optimum means fastest or smallest. This decision should occur long before any detailed design begins because it impacts nearly every facet of the Btrieve file structure for the application.

Not every fast operation requires additional space, just as not all space-conservation techniques make an application slower. In fact, if it's possible to meet your needs by keeping page size relatively small, the application is likely to run faster than it will with larger page sizes. However, this isn't true for all applications. It depends to a great degree on the exact pattern of user actions, how often they create new records, and how frequently they access records. In general, though, the methods that provide most effective space conservation will take a little longer both to create new records and to retrieve existing data. In many applications this makes no difference, of course.

Getting the most rapid response is more dependent upon the choice of hardware involved than on any other factor, but several techniques can be implemented at the program-design level to help in this respect. The ideal, of course, is to come up with a design that's fast enough to meet all your users' needs and uses no more system resources than necessary to do so. System resources include both the RAM necessary at run time and the mass storage (usually disk) that holds the data itself. Most designs wind up somewhere between the two extremes of fastest and smallest to reach this goal. Note, too, that the environment in which the system runs can also have great impact on what's needed to get optimum performance. Especially with regard to speed, networked multiuser applications show major differences from systems that run on isolated computers and serve only a single user. We examine network needs as a separate topic later in this chapter, but must also deal with them to some degree here.

Even though most applications will fall between the extremes of smallest and fastest, we separate the two goals into individual topics in this discussion. First, let's see how we can minimize the space used by an application.

Using Minimum Space

Many of the principles mentioned in this section apply even when you don't care about storage space, since if all else is equal, bigger pages take longer to read or write than do smaller ones. Therefore, you should take enough time at the outset to establish the correct page size for your application, based on the record length required, the number of keys, and the length of each key's data field.

Page Size Determination   Selecting the proper page size for an application requires you to determine the best fit between a number of factors. These factors include the size of each record, the size of each index, the number of indexes, and the number of keys that allow duplicate values.

I'm continually amazed at the number of software developers who simply pick both their record size and the page size from thin air, with no attempt to estimate real requirements. Applications "designed" in such a haphazard manner cannot possibly approach optimum performance, unless it happens by accident. For example, the first Btrieve application I encountered used a page size of 2,048 bytes and a record size of 1,024 "just to be on the safe side," although less than 500 bytes of each record held actual data. The designer obviously thought it a good idea to make everything possible a power of two. Equally obvious is the fact that he had never bothered to look at the section in the Btrieve manual that describes how many records a page can hold. Had he done so, he would have realized that nearly half the space in his data file was wasted, since each page could hold only one record.

Even worse, that same file defined five different indexes, and most of them used huge fields. Two of the indexes duplicated the same 60 bytes of record data, but one of them added 2 more bytes to pick up an identifying number. Although the wastage per index page wasn't anywhere near as drastic as that on the data pages, the near-duplicate index specifications doubled the number of items kept in indexes. The designer apparently didn't realize that he could have used the 62-byte field anywhere in place of the 60-byte field just by using the Get Equal or Greater search function instead of Get Equal and filling the extra 2 bytes with zeroes.

Since four of the five indexes permitted duplicate key values, each data item's physical length was 1,024 plus 32, or 1,056 bytes. The header on each data page added 6 more bytes, so the file used a total of 1,062 bytes on each 2,048-byte page. The remaining 986 bytes went to waste.

Had he reduced the record length from 1,056 bytes to 1,021, each page would have been able to contain exactly two records. That could have been achieved by reducing the record length to 989. Another way to get there would have been to eliminate the near-duplicate keys, which would reduce the space taken by duplicate-key chains from 32 bytes to 24. The 8 bytes gained could be added to the record size, bringing it to 997.

Since the real size requirement, though, was less than 512 bytes, things could have been greatly improved by using shorter records. With a record length of 512 bytes, and three duplicate-key chains, the physical length of each record would be 536. Dividing the 2,042 bytes available for data on each page by 536 gives us three full records, with 440 left over. Again, our wastage is high, but we're getting three records in the same space that could hold only one in the original file.

To find out what record size would allow four records per page, we can plug numbers into one of the following equations. All of them represent the same relation we've been using, but I've factored it into separate rules to make it easier to do "what-if" designing.

```
PageSize = 6 + MaxCount * (MaxRecLen + (8 * NumDup) + R)
MaxRecLen = ((PageSize - 6)/ MaxCount) - (8 * NumDup)- R
MaxCount = ((PageSize - 6)/ (MaxRecLen + (8 * NumDup) + R)
```

The first of these three equations simply defines the data page layout. The constant **6** is the number of bytes the header occupies. The **8 * NumDup** expression accounts for the duplicate key pointers if any. The **R** term accounts for the new-format record usage count field; it's zero for files in the original format, or 2 for new format files. We use this first equation to determine how much of the page is actually used; any left over is wastage.

The second equation lets us calculate the maximum record length when we know the page size, the number of records we want to fit onto the page, and the number of duplicate keys. When we plug in figures to find out what record length would allow four records on a 2,048-byte page, we get $(2042/4) - 24$. This reduces to 486.5. Since we cannot use a half-byte, we must discard the fraction and set the record length to 486. This wastes 2 bytes on each page (the half-bytes we had to discard, times the four records per page).

The third equation tells us the maximum number of records we can fit onto a page if we must use a specific record length. Any fraction, again, represents wastage since Btrieve won't split a data record across a page boundary. (Although the fragments of variable-length and compressed records do go on multiple pages, they never span a page boundary.)

When the record size is cast in concrete by requirements of the application and cannot be modified to optimize the design, the only adjustment possible is to modify page size. The third equation is the one to use in this situation. You can try it for every possible value of page size between the minimum possible for the file and 4,096 and use the page size that gives the smallest amount of waste space.

Determining that "minimum possible" page size depends on the size of your largest index field and whether it allows duplicate key values. Btrieve requires that each index page in a file be able to contain at least eight index items. If your largest index field is 62 bytes long, each item's length will be 74 bytes if the index prohibits duplicate values; it will be 78 bytes if they're allowed. The additional bytes include 4 for the Less-Than page pointer, 4 more for the Record pointer, and another 4 for the additional Record pointer when using duplicate keys.

To find the minimum possible page size, we first multiply the item size by 8 (getting 592 or 624), then add 12 more bytes for the index page header (for a total of 604 or 636), and finally pick the first multiple of 512 that's larger than our result. In this case, the minimum page size would be 1,024 bytes.

While this may seem like too much trouble to go through just to pick a file's page size, it can easily make the difference between an application that simply runs and one that runs well. If a program isn't designed with careful attention to details, it will always be difficult to maintain and may well be a breeding ground for mysterious bugs. This is one of the most basic design details for any Btrieve application.

Btrieve's Space Requirements   If you're new to Btrieve, you may be startled to find that the Btrieve files appear to be significantly larger than those used by some other data management systems. This is most likely to happen when you are converting existing files from some other database to one built on Btrieve. One such puzzled newcomer posted on BTI's CompuServe forum the question of why this happens. After noticing the file size difference, he reported he had performed repeated trials of inserting a record, then checking file size while holding constant everything possible. He found that file size failed to increase the same way each time he did this. "In fact," he wrote, "file size can be considerably different for the same file description, record size, indexes, and number of records." He concluded his question by noting that his CEO had become "a little concerned when he saw that Btrieve v6.15 file sizes were, on average, about 34 percent larger than those in our proprietary system."

The reason (as you know from Part II of this book) is the shadow-imaging technique, which always leaves several unused pages in the file. These pages will, of course, be used when the next transaction takes place, so they don't represent waste space. Instead, think of them as replacing the older separate pre-image files. But Davin

Church, a user of Btrieve since SoftCraft days, answered the forum inquiry with a response that was tailored for passing along to the concerned executive:

"Well, Btrieve *does* use considerably more space than many other file managers," wrote Davin. "It keeps up with lots more internal information and makes it rapidly accessible, and that takes more room than just the data alone. The more indexes you define (plus other advanced features you use), the more apparent overhead you'll see."

Davin is in many respects typical of the majority of Btrieve users. He owns and operates a consulting business, Creative Software Design, and works with Btrieve and SSQL every day. "I do custom programming, mostly for small businesses who need specialized apps to fit their business rather than the other way around."

Although he had no official connection with BTI at the time I contacted him, Davin expects to be a volunteer staff member on the BTRIEVE forum by the time you see these pages. He performed those duties for Novell for a number of years, and when I contacted him for permission to quote his advice here, he told me he had just agreed to do the same for BTI. His CompuServe UserID will be 74777,1360.

Data Compression: Yes, or No?   Btrieve provides one data storage method that compresses repeated strings of identical characters into a 5-byte code for storage. In one test, I found that simply using compression reduced one 890K data file to slightly over 400K, which meant a saving of nearly 40 percent in the storage need for that file. However, everything has its price and data compression is no exception.

Adding a new record to the file took noticeably longer (when reloading the file from a BUTIL -SAVE backup, the compressed file seemed to take approximately twice as long as did the uncompressed original file), and retrieving the record also is slightly slower, although the difference at this point was not noticeable in practice.

It's only reasonable that data compression would be slower, since extra processing is necessary to compress the data initially, and also to expand it back to the original form. This means that if speed is already a problem, using compressed data might be the straw that would break the camel's back for your application.

Additionally, the anticipated data format significantly impacts the degree of space savings you can expect from compressing the data. My test file was similar to a blank form, with many records almost totally blank. These runs of blanks (more than 900 on each record in extreme cases) compress down to just 5 bytes, so my results were better than I expected. If your data doesn't have long repeating runs of identical byte values, you won't get much if any benefit from the Btrieve compression algorithm.

Using compression will increase your need for system RAM, because Btrieve requires a decompression buffer at least twice as long as the longest record to be decompressed. This buffer must be allocated when starting the Btrieve engine. For files that use VATs, the buffer must be even larger: 16 times the largest page size to be used!

Because of all these factors, you can decide whether to use data compression only on a case-by-case basis. When it's applicable, though, no other single technique can give such a great saving in storage space at so little cost in response speed.

Sometimes speed is more important that file size, so let's look now at techniques you can use to achieve faster response from Btrieve and its relatives Xtrieve and SSQL.

Achieving Fastest Response

A number of techniques for improving response speed exist. Most of them apply more to network installations than to single-user systems, since the greatest single cause for observed slow operation comes from heavy multiuser loading. Some, however, apply to all Btrieve applications.

For instance, keeping page size and record size as small as possible consistent with the application's needs will always produce at least some speed improvements. Similarly, providing as much memory as possible for Btrieve's internal cache and buffers will usually produce faster operation.

Any time that speed is essential, of course, you'll need to avoid any techniques that are known to slow down the action of Btrieve (for example, data compression).

Keep Files Open for Speed   One technique for improving the speed of any Btrieve application that uses multiple files is to open all the files upon entering the program and leave them open until the program ends.

This is the exact opposite of conventional practice, which recommends leaving any file open for only the minimum time necessary. However, Btrieve protects file integrity by its pre-imaging and shadow-imaging techniques. This makes it unnecessary to take additional steps within your programs.

Opening a file is one of the slowest operations in Btrieve's repertoire, so by eliminating repeated open operations on the same file you will gain noticeable improvement in speed. This affects not only the application itself, but any other Btrieve applications running on the same server. When the server's attention is devoted to an open operation, all other operations must wait.

Leaving files open throughout an entire session of the application also allows Btrieve to do a better job of enforcing integrity in case of system failure since the data recovery functions built into Btrieve are much more reliable than those of most networks (and infinitely more so than the nonexistent recovery functions of DOS, for single-user systems).

Use Extended Operations   When you need to retrieve an entire group of records in response to a single user request, and especially if you need only portions of each record to satisfy the requirement, you can use the extended Get functions such as Get Next Extended. You must first position to either the first or the last record of the group by conventional operations, then build a specification of exactly what you want back, in the data buffer, and issue the extended function. The Btrieve engine then processes the extended request, gathering the data as you specified it, and returns the entire batch of data to your data buffer as a single packet. On a network, this greatly reduces the amount of traffic between server and workstation. Even on a single user system, it offers a distinct improvement in speed because of the smaller number of function calls needed to satisfy the user request.

While processing an extended function, Btrieve can perform a number of logical filtering operations for you to select only those records that meet specified criteria. However, the parsing built into the Btrieve engine is far from being sophisticated. It does the filtering by strict left-to-right evaluation of the conditions you specify. There's no capability at all to group the logic operations, which means that such tests as the "exclusive OR" simply can't be done. Here are the rules used: For each candidate record, Btrieve evaluates the first logic expression in your specification. If the evaluation returns TRUE and the next logic operator in your specification is OR, Btrieve accepts the record without any more evaluation taking place. If the evaluation returns FALSE and the next operator is OR, Btrieve evaluates the next expression. The loop continues until reaching either an evaluation of TRUE or a next operator of AND.

If the evaluation returns TRUE and the next logic operator is AND, Btrieve evaluates the next expression in your specification. So long as the evaluation returns TRUE and the next operator remains AND, this evaluation loop continues. If no expressions remain for evaluation, Btrieve accepts the record. If the next operator after a TRUE evaluation is OR, Btrieve accepts the record without additional evaluation. If an evaluation returns FALSE before reaching a next operator of OR, Btrieve rejects the record.

Thus, if you specify four logic expressions, which I'll represent as A, B, C, and D, and connect them as "A or B and C or D" with the intention of retrieving all records in which either A or B is true and also either C or D is true, you'll be disappointed. The rules will select every record in which A is true without ever testing C or D. If A is false, the rules then require both B and C to be true to select a record. If B is true but C is false, Btrieve rejects the record without ever evaluating D. The only way for D to be evaluated is for C to be true, which is the exact opposite of the intended test condition.

When you're aware of this simplified parsing method, you can program around it, but it has been the downfall of many developers in their first attempts to use the extended methods. The current Btrieve manuals describe the situation quite well, but the manuals furnished before version 6.0 left things more than a bit murky.

Another pitfall you must be aware of when using extended operations is that they can produce serious *loss* of speed when they run into either the end or the beginning of the file. If you use an extended operation within a loop (to provide additional filtering, for example) be sure to test for the EOF/BOF condition and break the loop the first time it happens.

Partition Server Memory Properly   We noted earlier in this section that Btrieve will run faster when given more memory. On a network installation, this leads directly to the question of how to partition the server's RAM between Btrieve and the network disk operations themselves. As one user put it when raising the question, "Is it best to allocate the server's memory to cache Btrieve, or leave that low and let the memory be used for disk cache? My servers have at least 64 megabytes of RAM." BTI support replied, "Whatever you give to Btrieve it will use. The level of performance must be monitored so that your overall configuration will benefit from the settings you use. Concerning Btrieve, too much cache is wasteful. However, too little cache can result in slower performance. That is also true of NetWare. Since cache buffers are configurable, you may gauge performance by assuming reasonable settings as an initial starting point and seeing what happens; then adjust as necessary."

Tom Ruby, another Btrieve user, also responded with suggestions drawn from years of experience: "It seems to depend on what else the server is doing. If the server is only (or mostly) servicing Btrieve requests, then you may want to make the Btrieve cache use most of the server's memory. If you have much other activity, you'll want to be sure to leave enough cache buffers for it also."

Tom's observations continued with a not widely publicized point: "If you're doing many Btrieve inserts or updates, Btrieve seems to dump all the dirty pages out of its cache at one time. This drives the number of dirty-cache buffers, current disk requests, and utilization very high. The server's response goes down the tubes, until the number of dirty-cache buffers gets back down to a reasonable figure. These slowdowns occur less often, but last longer, if the Btrieve cache is big. To keep our users from thinking the system has locked up, we currently have our Btrieve cache set fairly small."

Preallocated Pages Help   When an application creates many new records, you can speed this part of the process by preallocating pages at file creation time. Doing so makes it unnecessary for Btrieve to ask DOS or the network server for additional file space. Preallocation also keeps all pages of the file in one contiguous block, which speeds all disk actions even after creating the new records.

The maximum number of preallocated pages that Btrieve permits is 65,635. However, even with the smallest possible page size of 512 bytes, this allows a file to grow to more than 33.5 MB before running out of preallocated space. With larger page sizes, the maximum preallocated file size increases accordingly. For 4,096-byte pages, up to 268 MB can be preallocated.

Preallocation can occur only when the file is created. The disk must be able to provide the requested file size as one contiguous block. If this requirement isn't met, file creation fails.

Another point worth remembering is that Btrieve provides no method for releasing pages back to the system once they're allocated to a file. This applies to preallocated pages as well as to pages added during ordinary file growth. If you plan to preallocate space, try to make the best possible estimate of the amount you'll need. Allocating too much simply wastes resources and won't save any time.

Working with Windows

One major difference between using Btrieve in the Windows environment and the more familiar DOS-based applications that most developers associate with Btrieve is the lack of any need to install the Btrieve TSR package before starting an application. Under Windows (and the other advanced operating systems such as Windows NT and OS/2), Btrieve uses a DLL that loads automatically when an application initializes itself. The only precaution users must take is to be certain they have the correct DLL available in the Windows system directory. In the original version 5 releases of Btrieve for Windows, the local client- and server-based engines occupied separate DLLs that had the same name. The only way to distinguish one from the other was by file size: the server DLL was only about 13K, but the local engine DLL's size was 51K. For applications requiring both local and remote support, you had to rename the local version of WBTRCALL.DLL.

With release of version 6 engines, BTI combined the two DLLs into a single library and changed the method of determining which type of support to provide. Now, entries in the BTI.INI file indicate support requirements. Details appear in the Btrieve for Windows manual for version 6.15 and later.

The only major problem remaining concerning DLL installation is that many applications use installation or setup programs that will blindly overwrite your existing DLLs with older and possibly incorrect versions. Never install a new application under Windows until you have a current backup copy of your existing system-directory files so that you can put things right if this happens to you. And be absolutely certain that you don't have multiple copies in different directories. This is especially troublesome when the copies involve different versions!

You can run into other kinds of problems, though, when using Btrieve under Windows. Here are some of them. Every newly written application seems to create its own set of problems, though, so the list can never be truly complete.

The ODBC Situation

One of the problems most often voiced by individuals and firms attempting to use Btrieve in the Windows environment deals with Microsoft's ODBC specification. Virtually all Microsoft products and many third-party applications use ODBC to be able to support a wide variety of database products. While ODBC support exists for Btrieve, most users and developers find it less than satisfactory.

What Is ODBC?   ODBC (the acronym for Open DataBase Connectivity) is a Microsoft standard. ODBC defines function calls that allow an application to connect to a data source, execute SQL statements, and retrieve results. The SQL syntax used is based on the X/Open and SQL Access Group (SAG) SQL CAE specification (1992).

As Microsoft describes it in their Open Database Connectivity SDK Version 2.0, the ODBC architecture comprises four components. These are (1) the application, (2) the driver manager, (3) the driver, and (4) the data source. The application is any program that calls ODBC functions to submit SQL statements and retrieve results. To send a SQL statement, the program includes the statement as an argument in an ODBC function call. The statement need not be customized for any specific data source.

The driver manager, a DLL furnished by Microsoft, loads drivers on behalf of an application. The driver processes ODBC function calls, submits SQL requests to a specific data source, and returns results to the application. A driver may modify an application's request, if necessary, so that the request conforms to syntax supported by the associated data source. The driver manager and driver appear to an application as a single unit that processes ODBC function calls. When we speak of an ODBC driver, we're referring to this combination.

Microsoft defines the data source as "the data the user wants to access and its associated operating system, DBMS, and network platform (if any) used to access the DBMS." For Btrieve users, this means the data files themselves together with the associated Btrieve engine.

An ODBC driver must perform, as a minimum, the following tasks in response to ODBC function calls from an application.

1. Establish a connection to a data source.

2. Submit requests to the data source.

3. Translate data formats, if requested by the application.

4. Return results to the application.

5. Format errors into standard error codes and return them to the application.

6. Declare and manipulate cursors if necessary. (This operation is invisible to the application unless there is a request for access to a cursor name.)

7. Initiate transactions if the data source requires explicit transaction initiation. (This operation is invisible to the application.)

Note that nothing in this list of requirements specifies any need for a driver to perform its tasks efficiently. Neither does the specification suggest the use of features available in the data source to best advantage, where possible. All emphasis in the ODBC specification is on portability; performance is not addressed, even indirectly.

Available Drivers   At the time this book was written, only two firms (Microsoft and Intersolv's Q&E division) supplied ODBC drivers for Btrieve. One disgruntled user described both drivers as "the worst ODBC driver each of the vendors offers." That user went on to justify his statement, posted on CompuServe: "Their drivers for many other systems allow an application to have multiple connections with the database (to support more than one active transaction) and to have multiple statements active for each connection. The Btrieve ODBC drivers don't support this. I don't even think that the Btrieve drivers use indexes to speed data retrieval. The available drivers for Btrieve have minimal functionality. They don't support the building of industrial strength apps."

Most, if not all, developers who have attempted to access Btrieve data through the ODBC interface share that opinion. While it's an excellent idea, in theory, the current practice falls far short of acceptable performance. This sad state of affairs has not gone unnoticed at BTI headquarters.

BTI on ODBC   BTI originally came to a conclusion that ODBC drivers should be the domain of third-party utility vendors, but after hearing repeated complaints from their most devoted customers, reversed that position. In late 1994, following a high-level user meeting at which he made the commitment orally, CEO Ron Harris posted the following message on CompuServe: "Btrieve Technologies is going to resolve the ODBC performance issues related to accessing Btrieve data. We spent our first sixty days as an independent company making good on our promise to release the next generation Btrieve6 engines for Windows and DOS. Those products are shipping, and the initial feedback is great! Our accounting customers are reporting core functions running ten times faster.

During the next thirty days we will announce plans for moving Btrieve Technologies beyond NetWare boundaries. ODBC is a critical part of the plan. We will formally announce our ODBC strategy in the coming weeks and will deliver solutions shortly thereafter."

At the time this was written (January 1995), the promised ODBC strategy was scheduled for beta testing in the summer of 1995. No more details were available.

Potential Problems   Lack of adequate ODBC drivers poses both potential and actual problems for developers and for end users. Here's a typical situation that befell one developer who tried to extend his system: "We currently use," said this developer, "a medium-sized accounting, payroll, and benefit package built on the Btrieve record manager. This application supports approximately 1,000 employees and is processed over a pair of NetWare servers (the NLM Btrieve) and a dozen DOS/Windows client workstations. Btrieve has never been anything but a stable, rock-solid performer. However, I'm interested in performing queries against the Btrieve data files with Borland's PDOXWIN and ObjectPAL. According to the PDOXWIN documentation this is possible, given the proper ODBC driver. But will the penalties preclude me from deriving any real benefit from this?"

Until better ODBC drivers that take advantage of the strengths of Btrieve become available, the answer to his question is "yes."

If, like another user who inquired, you only want to get access to a Btrieve database running on a Novell Server through ODBC, you can do so. However, the response time to even the simplest queries can be agonizingly slow. One developer reported that an operation that required only about thirty seconds using Xtrieve remained incomplete after five minutes using ODBC and Microsoft Access. "It was as if Access could use the Btrieve keys to display the records in order," he reported, "but it could not use them in a join. Access had to read all the records and join them in a work file, but it could not read just the five records that satisfied the key."

It seems only fair to balance out this litany of complaints about poor performance of the available ODBC drivers with at least a few reports of good results. Unfortunately, in searching four months of user discussions on the Btrieve forum of CompuServe, I couldn't find even a single one!

Visual Basic

Visual Basic provides a fast and simple way to create a "front end" for any kind of database application, and Btrieve applications are no exception. However, you can run into problems unless you take special care when tying Btrieve and Visual Basic together.

To make the connection, you can use any of several techniques. The simplest (but also the least satisfactory) is to establish an ODBC connection between your VB program and the Btrieve files. As we've already noted, though, at this time ODBC cannot provide professional levels of performance because of inadequacies in the available drivers. While this technique allows you to use the data control in VB, response time is likely to be so slow as to render your program unusable.

Next simplest would be to buy one of the many VBX packages available from third-party vendors (see Chapter 9 for several) and use that. Most of these VBX controls access Btrieve functions directly rather than going through ODBC, so response time is much faster. This technique precludes use of VB's data control, but the performance gain definitely pays back the extra programming effort required.

If your budget won't support additional special controls and you have the professional version of VB that supports full database operations, you can draw on the VISDATA example that Microsoft furnishes and create your own interface. This technique uses ODBC for some of its actions but bypasses it for others. Consequently, it can provide acceptable performance so long as you restrict your needs to simple queries. When you require data joins and other exotic SQL actions, though, it falls into the ODBC tar-pit along with the first technique.

Possibly the best solution is to either write your own "wrapper" library for Visual Basic, or buy one of those listed in Chapter 9 and use that to connect Btrieve directly to your program, bypassing both the ODBC interface and all of VB's own data facilities. That's the solution my company has been using for the past five years. We've found it to retain the excellent performance for which Btrieve is noted and to be easy to maintain. If you choose to write your own wrapper library, you can do so using Visual Basic itself to create a module that you then include in each project. If you're comfortable with the Basic language, this is probably the simplest way to go. The Btrieve developer kits include appropriate Btrieve interface modules for Basic, and these are usable virtually without change in a VB module also.

You can also create such a module as a DLL, writing it either in C or in Pascal, then declare the library to your VB programs. This will reduce the overhead in each VB program, but requires that you be comfortable creating a DLL for Windows.

Either approach yields comparable results; the choice is yours, depending on your comfort level with each of the languages involved.

The 32-Bit Future

You don't have to be a close observer of the microcomputer industry to see that it's rushing toward a future based entirely on 32-bit hardware and software. Already, the 80386 is obsolescent, and most entry-level systems include 80486 processors. Windows 95 gets most of the publicity in the software area, but its big brother Windows NT competes head-to-head with Novell now in the server marketplace, and IBM's presence remains significant with the Warp revision of OS/2.

WinNT   The joint announcement from Microsoft and BTI that Btrieve would become available to Windows NT Server users has sparked intense interest in the Btrieve community about migrating applications into the WinNT universe. The most frequently asked question in this area is simple: "Is there any way for an NT workstation to access Btrieve files on the NT Server from a Windows program since you can't run BREQUEST before a Windows program?" The normal answer to this is that you should execute the DOS BREQUEST.EXE from the AUTOEXEC.NT file that WinNT runs automatically each time the workstation logs in its user. This, however, often brings up a secondary problem: BREQUEST seems unable to load. Two users finally tracked down the applications that caused this problem and posted the following three-step procedure for making BREQUEST run under NT.

1. From the NT control panel, remove the NWLINKIPX service (unfortunately, this will mess up your NetWare client as well, they noted).

2. Power the system down, then bring it back up, to get the existing copy of NWLINKIPX out of the way. Then reinstall NWLINKIPX. This rewrites portions of the AUTOEXEC.NT file.

3. In AUTOEXEC.NT, place the line that loads BREQUEST line *after* the lines relating to the virtual network drivers. Do *not* try to load BREQUEST high, even though the help file for NT says that this can be done.

This technique forces Btrieve to use the 16-bit Windows DLL. A 32-bit DLL that will operate directly from NT, with no need for a separate DOS requester, was undergoing beta testing as this was written and should be available by the time you read these pages.

OS/2   OS/2 support for Btrieve was also just completing its beta test phases as this book went to press. At a late 1994 meeting in Austin I saw demonstration copies of both 32-bit systems in operation. The speeds were impressive in both cases, but especially so for the OS/2 version.

Network Needs

Running any Btrieve application on a network implies that several users may attempt to work with it at the same time, so any networked application must concern itself with the problems of multi-user access. This usually turns into a discussion of the file and record locking techniques that protect data from simultaneous update attempts.

Other factors come into play also, however. A frequent cause of problems is that a user will need to access files located on his local disk drives and also need data from files on a network server. With older versions of Btrieve, this could become serious. The newer versions offer much improved solutions, but you can still get into trouble if a user attempts to run an old-version local server and you have version 6 or later on the network server.

Finally, several vendor-specific situations need to be addressed when searching for the best possible performance.

File and Record Locking

Users familiar with other data management systems often ask Btrieve support reps, "Where is the information about Btrieve locks kept? Is it in the Btrieve files, or somewhere else?" One reason this question is asked so often is that many other systems do provide their own internal locking mechanisms to prevent two or more users from attempting to write to the same record or page of a file at the same time.

For Btrieve, however, locking is essentially left up to the operating system itself. Under DOS-based networks such as Lantastic, SHARE.EXE provides the protection. On any Novell network, the network's file-sharing capabilities do the job. For optimization, Btrieve implemented LCK files at version 6.0 and later. These files come into play for multiengine file accesses, along with being used for normal record lock control.

A point that seems not to be well understood is that Btrieve actually performs page locking rather than record locking. When you execute a Get operation with the WAIT lock option (function code 105), Btrieve locks the entire page on which that record appears. This causes all attempts to retrieve other records on that page to return with status code 84, indicating that the record is locked.

The code of 84 should not be considered an error, but rather a notification of the situation. The recommended technique for dealing with this situation is to establish an acceptable number of times for retrying the access and have the program repeat the Get WAIT that many times while code 84 returns.

If the retry count runs out before the Get succeeds, the program can then ask the user whether it should try again or abandon the attempt. Since the lock duration is normally measured in milliseconds, most operations will succeed within five attempts and the user will never know that a conflict arose. A file lock, on the other hand, remains in effect so long as the file is kept open after being locked. This prevents any other users from modifying the file, although they may still be able to read records from it. For most applications, the file lock should be reserved for such operations as repair of a damaged database. For normal transactions, record locks usually suffice.

Tom Ruby, of Legal Files Software, posted in the BTRIEVE forum one of the best short guides to use of record locks and transactions that I've come across. Responding to a question from a new Btrieve user who was having problems with an order-entry application, Tom advised: "The trick is to *NEVER* lock anything while waiting for a user to do something. Most people, when creating a multiuser program, lock each record when the user calls the record up to edit. Here's what to do instead: Call up the record and let the user see it *unlocked*. Other users can still see this record, because they're not locking it either. Once the user doing the edit makes a change to the record and is ready to write it back, reread the record into a different data buffer, *locking* it this time. Now, you can examine the record to see if the change is still valid, or whether someone else made a change to it while the first user was viewing it, which would invalidate the first user's change.

"If it's still appropriate to make the change," Tom concluded, "copy the change to the reread record, write it back out, and release the lock."

Tom's recommendations continued, covering additional situations: "If the order had been entered before, and the user is calling it up to add or change line items, you want to make sure nobody else tries to change them at the same time. Let the user call up the record and view it without locking it. If they need to change line items, let them *then* lock the record, and edit the line items. This violates the general principle, but in this case you're *intentionally* reducing concurrency. You might store the user's ID in the locked record, so that if you're trying to lock a record and can't do so, you can show who has abandoned the computer leaving a record locked.

"Do you have a batch order processor, which you would not want to pick up an order that is being changed? Have it read each order record, locking it. If the lock fails, the program knows somebody's working on it. The batch processor can now read the record *unlocked* (Btrieve will allow this) and create a log entry noting that order such-and-such wasn't processed because so-and-so was editing it. The batch processor can then go on to the next order."

"Perhaps the process could set a flag in each order so it can tell whether the order was already processed, and then on another later run find this order again because the flag wasn't set. Of course, the process would only keep the order locked while processing it, maybe printing the shipper or something, then unlock it. A user would have to be calling this specific record up at this specific moment to notice any delay, and then it's only a couple of seconds, which they might not even notice."

Record locking can create network-wide problems if an application that has network pages locked through the BTRIEVE.NLM server engine happens to crash beyond recovery. Because of the application crash, the workstation disconnected without clearing the locks. The server then maintains the locks on the Btrieve files that were open. This can prevent others from modifying those pages, but even more seriously can prevent the file from being backed up by system backup programs. One way to clear such abandoned locks is to unload BTRIEVE.NLM, then reload it, but this disrupts all other users. Tom Ruby has a better solution: "We have a small program that issues a RESET command that closes files and releases locks. We run this program immediately after loading the requester, during the workstation's login sequence. Now, any locks and open files remain in place only until the station is rebooted."

Tom's solution is ideal in a development environment, where frequent crashes of applications under construction are normal events. For more stable areas, he suggests that "there's an easier way to clear locks. Use the BTRMON NLM to look at the active users, and press DELETE on the user that crashed. Sometimes, the user name will vanish from the display, but there'll be a telltale blank line in the list, which you can delete."

Both Local and Remote Btrieve Files

When a workstation must access some Btrieve files from local drives and others from the network file server, the situation can become confusing. If you become sufficiently confused, you can even induce serious problems.

If all operations will be done from the command line, you can provide both local and remote support by loading BTRIEVE.EXE first to support the local files, then loading BREQUEST.EXE to pass remote requests on to the server. The sequence of loading is essential.

All Btrieve executable files must be at the same major version levels. Version 5.x requesters aren't compatible with version 6.1 server engines, and neither are version 5.x local engines. Only a few days ago I temporarily lost some 200 MB of data because of an unexpected interaction between a version 6.15 local engine and an accidental attempt to load a version 5.1 engine on top of it. Version 6 uses a DOS extender, but version 5 does not; DOS became so confused that it dumped a copy of the version 6 engine right on top of the root directory of my hard drive. Fortunately, I was able to recover everything, but the incident brought home quite sharply the dangers that lie in accidental version mixing.

If running under Windows, the BTI.INI file (for Btrieve for Windows version 6.15) or the WIN.INI and NOVDB.INI files (for versions 5.x) must have both *local=Yes* and *requestor=Yes* lines established. These settings tell the Windows DLLs how to route requests.

To use version 6.15 products in this way, you need version 6.16 of BREQUEST.EXE. This version contains some modifications so that BREQUEST would work correctly with the new architecture of the 6.15 products when run at the same time as the local engine. In terms of the way BREQUEST communicates to the server, nothing changed. Thus, you can use BREQUEST v6.16 with the 6.10c NLM, or any prior version, as well as with the 5.15 VAP. Functionally, from a DOS workstation point of view, BREQUEST v6.10e and v6.16 do not differ.

Server File Shareability

A question that comes up repeatedly involves Novell's "shareable" file attribute. It seems only logical that any Btrieve file should be flagged as shareable, since many users share access to the file, but this isn't the way things work. It's essential, in fact, that files managed by a server engine be flagged as "nonshareable" so that only the server engine itself can access them. The server then makes sure that no two workstations interfere with each other.

The client based BTRIEVE.EXE handles multiuser file access by using exclusive DOS calls to briefly lock the entire file, or the page that contains a specific record. If different copies of BTRIEVE.EXE are loaded on different workstations, each has no direct knowledge of what the other is doing. The file and "record" (actually page) locks ensure there is no conflict between the isolated applications. The single engine at the server, however, functions as a central manager of file access requests. Running in a multithreaded environment, it is aware of all file activity. This allows it to queue up and process requests in the most efficient manner that avoids conflicts.

If files on the server are flagged as SHARE and are accessed through multiple client-based Btrieve engines, then more than one person can be updating the file at the same instant. The results are unpredictable but can be disastrous. That's why server-based files should always be flagged nonshareable.

Novell NetWare Specifics

Since Novell owned Btrieve for many years, by far the majority of Btrieve users also use Novell's network products. Many optimization points are specific to the interactions between NetWare and Btrieve; we cover a few in this section.

Version 6.1 Upgrade Kit   For several years now, a no-cost upgrade kit for bringing the Novell-supplied Btrieve server engine BTRIEVE.NLM from version 5.x to version 6.10 has been available for downloading from CompuServe. This package is normally quite straightforward to install, but some users have had problems when doing so. Almost invariably, these problems seem to be based on missing key items in the detailed instruction sheet that's part of the upgrade kit. One reason that such things are easy to overlook is that the kit is built to support both version 3.11 and version 3.12 of NetWare, and the two versions require different program sets. In addition, the upgrade requires that you replace additional NLMs to support the 6.10 version of Btrieve, and these other modules are easy to overlook. If you attempt the upgrade and then find that BSPXCOM generates several errors that say "loader cannot find public symbol," then you do not have the proper versions of the supporting NLMs. These include CLIB, AFTER311, and others. If symbols are not found, the load for that NLM will fail. Make certain you are loading everything you need.

Once the updated version loads properly, run BSETUP.NLM to configure both Btrieve and Bspxcom. This is both easier and more reliable than attempting to edit the BSTART.NCF and BSTOP.NCF files by hand.

Btrieve 87 error   NetWare users may run out of available file handles, made evident by the Btrieve status code 87. One user, running a Btrieve product with five files, on a 16MB server using Btrieve 6.1 under Netware version 3.12 and supporting ten workstations, sees this at a specific time each day when all machines are accessing files. His query to Btrieve support reps indicated a clear understanding of the problem; he wanted to know whether he should increase the number of handles available by increasing the setting of the -h option in his BSTART.NCF file.

The advice from Btrieve support was to remember that for each session, accessing the same file requires an additional handle. Thus, for ten sessions, opening just one file in each session requires a total of ten handles. For five files, fifty handles would be needed if all five are open at the same time in each session.

The true number of files each workstation is trying to use will determine the number of handles you need to reserve. In reality you must set it for the highest value ever needed, based on the number of workstations and the number of files that are active at any one time.

Other Networks

Even while Novell owned Btrieve, some customers ran the record manager on other networks. While client-server operation is supported only under NetWare, OS/2, and soon under Windows

NTAS, peer-to-peer operation is possible for any network that complies with the record and file locking conventions of MS-DOS version 3.31 and later. Btrieve is not tied to any particular network.

Users also report that it's possible to work on a peer-to-peer network like Windows for Workgroups, using the Btrieve engine for Windows version 6.15. To be successful, it's necessary to allow access to the whole disk on the "server"-station (the one containing the engine and data files), not just to a special directory.

With Artisoft's Lantastic network, it's essential to run SHARE.EXE on the server machine, but *not* on the workstations.

Designing for Defense

One of the most important items to consider when optimizing a data management system is to make the system as robust and reliable as possible. Although Btrieve includes many features to assist you in reaching this goal, it's never possible to totally eliminate Murphy's law. In every system, if *anything* can go wrong, it will. The wise designer, knowing this, includes many layers of defense in the design of every system.

Most such defensive design techniques, being applicable to all kinds of data management systems, are well documented elsewhere. Several, however, are unique to Btrieve systems, and those are the ones we'll concentrate on here.

Prevent Corruption by Using Reset Instead of Close

Before the arrival of version 6, with its shadow-imaging technique, Btrieve systems that used large numbers of separate files and underwent frequent revision sometimes seemed to just corrupt themselves for no apparent reason. The problem never reached alarming levels since it happened only rarely and could be corrected by keeping good backup copies. Nevertheless, the tendency indicated need for an adequate defensive measure.

After long study, a number of users concluded that the corruption appeared to occur during the process of closing the multiple files. By closing each file individually, it was possible to create short timing "windows" in which the multiple files of the application could lose their synchronization. It was even possible, in some cases, to confuse the underlying operating system and cause a file to no longer be recognizable by the Btrieve engine. If all files could be closed in a single Btrieve operation, the timing windows would no longer exist. That action is part of what the RESET function does. Sure enough, using a single RESET just before leaving the Btrieve system, without closing any files first, seemed to solve the file-corruption problems completely.

Although the technique never made it into the official manuals, it became a staple recommendation of the technical support crew, and today many experienced Btrieve developers continue to use RESET rather than close files individually. While the shadow-imaging technique may have significantly reduced the possibility of this problem's survival, they prefer to stay with a technique that has been reliable in past years.

Using RESET has additional advantages as well. It not only closes all open files and releases all locks that the workstation may have established, but tells Btrieve to release any other system resources it may have been using for the application. It's still the most highly recommended defensive-design technique for Btrieve applications.

Planning to Simplify Recovery

Sometimes you can organize your data structures in a way that can simplify recovery of the information should file corruption strike your system. For instance, unless there's a pressing need to store data in binary or floating-point format, you might consider storing everything in ASCII string format. Files that have only ASCII characters in them are much simpler to reconstruct. While this isn't unique to Btrieve systems, you'll also find it easier to rebuild files if you organize everything in what the relational folks call Third Normal Form. A database in this form (usually written as 3NF to save keystrokes) never (or hardly ever) repeats information. Instead, such repeating information items as street names, directions, area codes, ZIP codes, and geographical names all go into separate tables. Individual records then include only the "foreign keys" to those tables; the applications then rebuild full data records by replacing the keys with the data to which they refer.

This approach reduces rebuilding effort primarily by reducing the exposure of your data to any chances of corruption. A system organized in 3NF normally is much smaller than the same system would be with the more often encountered repetitive full data records.

Avoid Encryption If Possible

Our final defensive design tip is simple: If possible, avoid using the encryption capability of Btrieve. When an encrypted file becomes so corrupted that it's beyond the abilities of the BUTIL -RECOVER option, it's essentially impossible to recover its data. If data is so sensitive that it absolutely must be encrypted, consider placing it on a totally secure computer system and limiting access to the system. If your user community has access to a system that contains encrypted data, the security of that data is always at risk because no really secure technique that's rapid enough to support production database activities yet exists.

Importing and Exporting Data

While it doesn't deal directly with achieving optimum design for your systems, one question that arises quite frequently is that of how to import or export data from Btrieve files. Since Btrieve is a record manager rather than a full DBMS, it doesn't include within itself any import or export capability. It does provide all the functions necessary to let you build these features into any application, but many potential users tend to be concerned about this issue before they allow you to create applications built on Btrieve. Other users question the possibility of retaining existing non-Btrieve data should they migrate to the Btrieve environment.

Using Microsoft Access As a Translator

A typical question might be, "I have an old inventory database in dBase format. I also have a new inventory system that uses Btrieve. How can I convert from one format to the other? I have Microsoft Access, Quattro Pro, and Excel, if any of these would help."

The answer to that one is quite direct. You can use Access to import from dBase and export out to Btrieve. Attach the first (.DBF) table in dBase format. Then attach the second (Btrieve) table, in Btrieve format. You may need an intermediate table if the field layouts are different.

If you use Access to create that table in Btrieve format, by choosing "Export to Btrieve," the Btrieve table will have an extra integer field (the first field) full of 0s, named "M_I_C_R_O_S_O_F_T." This field appears to have no use, but you can't stop Access from creating it. Now just use Access, according to its instructions, to get your data into the new file. Access will treat the dBase and Btrieve files just as though they were Access files. You'll need to consider relational/referential integrity and other issues, of course. This may be a serious point if the applications are not from the same vendor. However, the actual data transfer can be done with no special programming tools or additional utilities.

Doing It the Hard Way

In the more general situation when neither your Btrieve application nor the other system with which you need to exchange data offers explicit import or export facilities (or possibly one does while the other does not), you may need to become a bit more creative.

Most of the third-party utility packages discussed in Chapter 9 include some sort of import and export capability. Using one of them can handle the Btrieve end of the communications channel. The DUMPDATA program described in Chapter 10 provides export capability, and BUTIL can import files that are in the format DUMPDATA provides.

If you want to move data into Btrieve and the other system has no export facilities, you might consider using DUMPDATA as a model from which to create a similar program to gather the content of the other system's files and write it in the BUTIL format. If the task is to go the other way, you may find that the near-universal "comma delimited format" used by xBase systems (and many others also) can do the job. At least a couple of the packages mentioned in Chapter 9 include the capability to create files in this format.

Just getting the data, of course, isn't adequate. You also must take into account the record layouts of both the old application and the new application, and quite probably you'll have to perform extensive editing of the intermediate files to get everything into the right locations. The task is definitely not trivial. It is, however, both possible and practical, and is usually a better choice than just printing out data from one system and typing it into the other. Manual data entry virtually guarantees multiple typographical errors, which can slip by and create havoc days or even months after the data transfer is done!

Assorted Tips and Tricks

To conclude this discussion of methods and techniques for obtaining optimum performance from Btrieve, here are a couple of useful tidbits of information that seem to fit nowhere else in this book.

Purging Old Pre-Image Files

Before version 6.0, Btrieve used pre-image files to safeguard data while modifying records. Although the design called for deletion of all pre-image files when they had served their purpose, that did not always happen (for a multitude of reasons). Consequently, many users found their servers or their non-networked systems becoming clogged with files bearing the extension PRE.

Just blindly deleting such files can lead to serious problems. Many corporate developers and system administrators learned this lesson the hard way. Others were content to be more cautious and ask questions like this one: "As I understand it, a pre-image file is left on the disk if power goes down, or if someone reboots a workstation without first closing all Btrieve files. Am I right? Is there a graceful way to use some utility to find out which pre-image files could be deleted without ill effects? If there is a way, do I have to kick everybody out of Btrieve to do this magic trick?"

"Yes, you are correct," BTI technical support replied to the user who asked that question. The reply went on to list a sequence of steps that can safely get rid of any old pre-image files that are hanging around, with no danger to the data.

1. Make certain all users are out of Btrieve. This will close all data files. On a network, use BTRMON to verify that no files remain open.

2. If any pre-image files remain after closing all data files, check the data file dates and times against those of the matching pre-image files. If the data files are newer, you can probably delete the pre-image file without a problem. However, make a backup (both data and pre-image files) before you do so that all can be restored should a problem arise.

3. Next, run BUTIL -STAT on each of the data files. If this fails (most probably with a status code of 14), the data file may have inconsistent internal flags that mistakenly indicate something must be backed out. To cure this, create an empty pre-image file by typing COPY CON <data file name>.PRE at the command-line prompt, pressing the Enter key, and then immediately pressing Ctrl-Z. This puts an EOF marker in the new dummy file. Then use DIR *.PRE to make certain the new file's size is "0 Bytes." Now repeat the BUTIL -STAT action, and the file will open correctly, clearing those internal flags as it does so.

Error 22 with Brequest in Version 6+

Sometimes, correcting an oversight creates more problems than it cures. That happened to Btrieve with the release of version 6.10. Due to an oversight when creating the 5.x versions of BREQUEST.EXE and BTRIEVE.EXE, the engines failed to check the data buffer length parameter when performing the Version operation.

At version 6.10 of BREQUEST.EXE the correction took place; the length is now verified. As a direct result, some customers began getting status 22 failures (data buffer too short) on Version operations after upgrading to BREQUEST.EXE v6.10. The same programs had worked perfectly, without error, when using the 5.x versions of BREQUEST.EXE or BTRIEVE.EXE.

To prevent that status 22, specify the data buffer length on version operations, just as on all other operations. It should always be the size, in bytes, of the data buffer passed on the call.

Conclusion

In this chapter, we've explored methods and techniques you can use to achieve optimum performance with Btrieve. In the next and final chapter, we examine ways to recover data from files that have become corrupt for any reason.

12

Data Corruption:
Causes, Prevention, Repair

This final chapter discusses some known causes of data corruption, techniques for anticipating and preventing the problem, and finally a few methods for recovering if it happens to your files. The best protection, however, is to keep frequent and complete backups of all critical data.

Causes of Data Corruption

Data corruption can stem from many causes. This fact, in itself, greatly complicates the problem of preventing it from happening at all, since when the problem does strike it's often next to impossible to determine the culprit. The cases described in this section come from a sampling of support questions appearing in BTI's support forum on CompuServe. The first, in particular, provides a litany of frequent causes that you can check your situation against should you find files going wrong for no known reason.

Hardware Can Cause Problems

When a system experiences data corruption, it usually falls into one of two extremes. Either it's the result of a single, known catastrophe, such as a fire, an earthquake, or a power failure at a critical time during system operation, or it's an insidious thing that seems to just creep in and get worse as time goes by.

The first situation is relatively easy to diagnose and deal with, although the data recovery problem that results may be immense. There's no question of prevention when events like earthquakes are involved, though it's possible to improve fire protection, and a good uninterruptable power supply is almost total protection against power failures.

The second situation, however, causes system administrators to age before their time. Here's a typical incident of this kind of data corruption, together with the responses both from BTI technical support folks, and from an experienced system administrator (Legal Files Software's Tom Ruby, also quoted extensively in Chapter 11).

"I have a continual problem," wrote the system administrator, "with one of my Btrieve files being corrupted. It is a rather large file of 150,000 records and is heavily used by a number of users. The corruption shows up as errors with status code 2. Can anyone tell me the causes of Btrieve file corruption and how this can be avoided? I am using version 6.10 networked and version 6.10e requester."

"Many things can lead to a status 2," replied BTI developer support. "If the Btrieve data files are flagged SHAREABLE, for example, this could potentially cause a status 2. If a network interface card, especially the LAN card, is bad, or is using an old driver, this can cause a Btrieve data file to go bad. You would have to give us more specifics as to the environment you are in and the frequency with which you encounter the error and at how many sites."

Tom Ruby's response was somewhat more specific and underscores the importance of close attention to detail. He wrote: "First off, make sure you have the newest of everything. The current Btrieve is 6.10c. Is the file server abending? You didn't say which version of

Netware you're using, but patches already exist for NetWare 3.12. We had a server that gave us fits with 6.10c. Often, a file being rebuilt (to recover from corruption) would have an error 2 before the rebuild could complete! Since this was a huge file, our users were not happy. The server had worked for a long time, with no such problems, using the version 5.15 NLM. This was an ISA-bus computer with 16MB RAM and a recently installed 1-GB IDE drive. I had been strongly opposed to installing an IDE drive, but was overruled by a recently hired guru. We changed over to a SCSI drive, and the problem vanished. Users are happy now, and the server is much faster than ever before. But the (recently fired) guru swore I was wasting money on that SCSI drive."

One moral that can be drawn from this is to always check out the effects of any changes to either hardware or software, and see if any correlation exists between such changes and the onset of data corruption. Often, as was Ruby's experience, this is all that's required to cure the problem.

Incompatible Interface Module Corrupts Data

It's not always hardware that's to blame for corruption. Sometimes it's a software problem. If it happens to be in some of the tools supplied by BTI, they're quick to put things right. Consider this lament received from a developer who works exclusively with the Basic language:

"I'm using Btrieve for DOS, version 5.10a. Since I changed my Basic compilers from QB45 to VBDOS 1.0, I've been getting random corruption of variable page data. I get low characters and extended characters. I'm searching the string for them, right before the Btrieve call, and not catching them. The problem is rare, but frequent enough that it's a real problem. I've downloaded the patches for BTRIEVE.EXE. Are there any patches for the interface .OBJ?"

The response from BTI Developer Support came back within a few hours: "Make sure you're linking in the BC7RBTRV.OBJ file dated 11-26-90 that is 810 bytes. The file with the same name that was released with Btrieve for DOS v5.10a (dated 4-13-90, 869 bytes) has a bug in it that could be causing your problem."

It was indeed the cause of the problem, and when the developer could not locate a copy of the correct version (because version 5 is no longer the current version), Developer Support sent the file to him by E-mail. Most other firms' support operations could take lessons from this event.

Beware NLM Version 6.10a; Use 6.10c Instead

Several sites have reported random status code returns of 2 and 4 when multiple users attempt to simultaneously retrieve data from files that were written under version 5.1 or earlier, but are now being retrieved by the version 6.10 server engine supplied by Novell. The problem was finally traced to errors in the version 6.10a engine. Version 6.10c is the current version and should always be the one in use.

The 6.10a NLM frequently causes this problem, according to one user's report, when doing a record Insert inside a Transaction.

The problem can be serious if your site upgrades to Netware 3.12 since the bad version 6.10a comes with NW3.12. You can download the correct version from the BTRIEVE forum of CompuServe at no cost other than connect time. It seems to be free of such problems.

Prevention's the Best Cure

One of the best ways to deal with data corruption is to prevent it whenever possible. If that fails, the next best thing is to detect it as rapidly as possible after the corruption does occur so that it can be corrected before its effects propagate throughout the information system.

Pack Files Once a Year

A long-time user of Btrieve offers this technique for preventing problems, which he reports has served him well: "Once a year, as maintenance, I run BUTIL -SAVE on my main Btrieve files. Then I initialize them and run BUTIL -LOAD to put the data back. This reorganizes the records by the first primary key and eliminates any unused space from deleted records. I consider this year-end maintenance."

Other utilities described in Chapter 9 can replace the two BUTIL options; BTFILER, in particular, includes the ability to do the entire job in a single pass, which could provide significant time savings for large files.

Detect Corruption ASAP

Another user was thinking ahead, when he asked about availability of utilities that could help detect corruption immediately after it happened.

"I am curious," wrote this system administrator, "whether anyone knows of any utilities available that can scan Btrieve databases and notify me if any corruption has occurred. I have a large number of Btrieve databases spread across three servers. When a server goes down, I need to know right away if any corruption took place, before I let any users get back into the system. I am running Client/Server Btrieve version 6.10, and all the utilities I have seen are for version 5.x. Thanks in advance."

Doug Reilly, of Access Microsystems Incorporated, responded: "My BTFILER will do just that. Results can be logged to a file. Index testing is quite complete. BTFILER is shareware, and if you like it, it may be registered through the SWREG forum on CompuServe."

Repairing Corrupted Data

No matter how it happens, nor how diligently you strive to prevent it, the chance that you will have to try to recover a corrupted database at least once in your career as a system administrator is very close to certainty. Depending on the nature of the damage to the files and the techniques by which you attempt the repair, you may be able to preserve all the data, or you may not be able to save any of it. The average result is somewhere between these extremes, but many times the lost data can be held to a small percentage.

If the damage involves actual damage to the underlying DOS or NetWare file system, such as the scrambling of the DOS File Allocation Table, your chance of recovering any data at all is slim. If, however, the file structure remains intact and the damage affects only the Btrieve file, it's likely that the loss will be small and quite possible that you may achieve full recovery given the proper tools.

Since well over half the space in most Btrieve files goes to the B-tree index pages, there's more than an even chance that random corruption to only a few sectors of a file may have damaged only index information. Such index damage can render the file unreadable by Btrieve itself (at least by way of the damaged index). However, a number of utilities can read the data and reconstruct the records in a form you can use to build a new file. You might also be able to recover all data records by using another key, or you could write a special program using only Get First, Get Next, Get Last, and Get Previous calls, to copy the data into a new file.

Using BUTIL to Recover

One of the utilities that's able to recover data from a damaged Btrieve file comes free with any of the Btrieve products. That's BUTIL (or the corresponding executable for platforms other than DOS), which includes a -RECOVER option switch, When you run BUTIL -RECOVER, the program attempts first to access the first physical data record in the file, using Get First to avoid any index reliance. It then writes the content of that record to an output file in the format used by the SAVE and RESTORE option switches, and calls Get Next to retrieve the next record. So long as it's successful, this loop continues until reaching the end of the file, writing each record in turn to the output file and then fetching the next.

If the retrieval runs into an error before reaching the end of the file, the program notes the physical address of the record that gave the error. It then uses Get Last to move to the last record in the file, writes that to the output, and backs up one record by means of the

Get Previous function. If successful, it writes that record also and backs up again. This loop continues until either reaching the record that caused the error during the forward-stepping loop, or until running into another error.

When the second loop ends, BUTIL quits looking for more data. If only one page of the file happens to be damaged, this strategy is effective and recovers most of the records from the file. However, if damage is widespread, BUTIL may salvage only a few records from the situation. In at least one case, only 6 out of the 8,000 records originally in the file could be saved.

How to Go Around the Indexing

It's possible to bypass indexing in a different way that doesn't use a Btrieve engine at all. The sample program DATADUMP described in Chapter 10 does exactly this, and might be able to do data recovery quite effectively. Providing just such a capability was the primary reason for adding to DATADUMP the ability to write a BUTIL -SAVE format output file in addition to merely displaying data on the CRT.

Both the Btrieve Get functions and the DATADUMP program use the fact that every data page has the high bit of its usage count word set to 1 to distinguish between data pages and other kinds of pages in the file. Most of the time this works perfectly, but it's possible that a file could suffer a kind of damage that would make an index or PAT page appear (to this test) to be a data page.

If this happened, the recovery program would generate many spurious "data" records. The only times that this would create serious problems, though, would be when the file originally stored data in either compressed or variable-length formats. All of these formats embed pointers to data within the records (described in Chapter 8), and attempting to follow invalid "pointers" in such spurious data pages could cause the recovery programs to crash.

The chances are extremely great that any file damaged in that manner won't be recoverable by any method. If the data is important enough, though, and irreplaceable, it could be worthwhile to use a binary file editor (such as those supplied in the Norton Utilities or PC Tools) to locate the specific pages that generate such spurious data records and manually modify the usage count word to remove its "this is data" indicator bit. Be sure to have backup copies of the file, even in its damaged state, if you attempt this route. You may find it necessary to restore the file several times while attempting to modify the data indicator bits, especially if apparently good data pages then point to damaged pages that prevent the recovery program from continuing.

Btrieve and Backups

By far the best way to recover from a case of file corruption, of course, is to just restore the system from a current (and accurate) set of backup files. Unfortunately, maintaining accurate backup data sets isn't always possible in the real world of 24-hour system operation and multiuser networks.

Most backup programs refuse to make a backup copy of any file that's in use. This, in itself, may prevent you from keeping completely current backup copies. While other backup programs and network features exist to help you overcome the "file in use" problem, these solutions bring with them a whole new set of problems. These new problems include the possibility of inducing file corruption should the server crash during the backup operation.

Files Always in Use

Besides the "file in use" problem, extremely large data files add an extra dimension of difficulty simply because of the time required to make a complete backup. For example, a 24-hour operation using files with sizes in the multiple-gigabyte region, updating tens of thousands of records each day, takes appreciable time to back up even with the fastest tape drives currently available.

Possible solutions include using the incremental-backup approach, saving only those records that have changed. This, however, could involve almost as much activity as a total backup because of the way that Btrieve uses its file pages. Another solution could be to take a snapshot of all changed records, possibly at the end of each transaction. Yet another technique might be to enable the logging feature of Btrieve and then back up the log file so that it would be possible to reconstruct any file changes if need be.

When this question arose recently, involving just such a large file and 24-hour operation, several experienced system administrators offered opinions and recommendations.

"My first thought would be continuous mode," said Tom Ruby, referring to a feature available in Btrieve version 6.0 and later server-based engines. "Your updates will be slower during the backup, but then everything will be slower during the backup. One thing requires caution. Currently (version 6.10c), if the server crashes while you're in continuous mode, the data file will be corrupted as soon as NetWare backs out transactions. The next version of the Btrieve NLM will fix this."

"Another thought," Ruby continued, "would be to enable logging and back up the log file. You'd have to stop the operation every now and then, back up the real data file, and erase the log file. There's a problem with using continuous mode and logging together. Otherwise you could switch to continuous mode to do this backup, say once a week, and just back up the log file daily."

Doug Reilly, of Access Microsystems Inc., described how he solved a similar problem for a hospital client that required 24-hour operation:

"I use my BTUTIL utility," wrote Doug, "to do an -XSAVE of the files while they are in use. The problem with this is that you do not have a snapshot of a specific moment in time. This is not a problem for me, since the records are structured in such a way that there is no need for multirecord update transactions (that is, records where one will make no sense without the other). The one instance where that is the case (all records "report" to a patient master record) can easily be recovered from other sources. Also, space is not an issue. The -XSAVE saves the data to another server in a different building, not to tape. I have not needed to do a -XLOAD except in testing, but

I am sure I could recover all 100+ megabytes of information in a very short period of time. Multigigabyte files would be another story, but then tape backup would be lengthy as well."

Reilly is the author of BTUTIL, described in Chapter 9 and included on the companion diskette.

Still another developer suggested that he might solve such a problem by modifying the application to write duplicates of all changes out to a separate server that could be closed, backed up, and purged periodically. "Then," he wrote, "you would just need to write a restore routine that would apply those changes back to your master database."

Using Continuous Mode Backup

The continuous mode operation that Ruby referred to offers one solution to the backup problem, if you run on a Novell NetWare system. However, using it with Btrieve version 6.10x server engines involves a number of known problems.

In version 6.10, the one currently provided by Novell, the continuous operation feature uses NetWare's sparse files, which can create problems if the server itself crashes. Novell is not believed to be planning to fix this problem any time soon. Consequently, BTI is introducing a new method with the release of Btrieve 6.15 (which should have happened by the time you read this). The new method avoids use of sparse files and is also platform independent. It works for the NT product, and others not yet announced.

Automatic continuous mode operation cannot be started from a workstation-based backup. It has to initiate at the server. It does, however, work with files created in the original format just as well as with those in the new format.

The End of the Trail

Here we are, at the end of Chapter 12 and of the book itself. The accompanying companion diskette includes all the program examples from the text, together with evaluation copies of several well-known shareware utilities mentioned in Chapter 9. Full instructions for installing the files and for using the example programs appear in the Appendix.

I fear that the title *Btrieve Complete* is one that's not very possible to live up to totally, though. The product called Btrieve continues to evolve. Even if I had been able to completely cover all facets of the package as of today, the new enhancements already in the pipeline together with those in the labs would render this book somewhat less than complete by the time it reaches you.

The title does, however, convey the essence of what I hope I've done here: to give you a well-rounded view of Btrieve, and by laying bare most of its internal detail, to help you make more informed and effective use of this tool to improve your own applications.

Appendix

The Companion Diskette

This appendix describes the files contained on the companion diskette and provides suggestions for installing any or all of the files on your fixed drive.

Installing Any or All Files

Unlike many book-diskette packages that are intended for use by nontechnical readers, this diskette contains no customized installation programs. Most of the files are either ZIP files created by means of PKWare's popular PKZIP program, or are self-extracting archives. The ZIP files use the new compression method introduced with PKZIP version 2.04 and are not compatible with version 1.10 PKWare products or their equivalent.

To install any ZIP file on your fixed drive, you can use PKUN-ZIP version 2.04 or later. If you don't already have a copy of

PKUNZIP.EXE on your system, you can use the UNZIP.EXE program from the root directory of the diskette instead.

UNZIP.EXE is part of a "portable ZIP package" created by the Info-ZIP group. This volunteer group, reachable through the Internet at zip-bugs@wkuvx1.wku.edu, encourages use of the package for software distribution. More details about the Info-ZIP effort, including how and where to obtain the source code, appear in files COPYING and WHERE (also in the root directory of the diskette). The following notice is adapted from a suggested version contained in the COPYING file:

> Info-ZIP's software (Zip, UnZip and related utilities) is free and can be obtained as source code or executables from various bulletin board services and anonymous-ftp sites, including CompuServe's IBMPRO forum and ftp.uu.net:/pub/archiving/zip/*.

Installation of the self-extracting files is described later in this appendix, in the section that describes the files themselves.

Using PKUNZIP.EXE

To extract all files from one of the ZIP files using PKUNZIP, go to (or create) the subdirectory into which you want the files extracted, then use this command (if the diskette is in your A: drive; if not, change the drive letter appropriately):

```
PKUNZIP A:\dir\zipfile
```

No special option switches are necessary for any of the files contained on the diskette. Replace the dir and zipfile portions of the command with the appropriate directory name and filename. It's not necessary to add the ".ZIP" suffix to the filename.

To extract a specific file from one of the ZIP files using PKUNZIP, go to (or create) the subdirectory into which you want the files extracted, then use this command (assuming that the diskette is in your A: drive; if not, change the drive letter appropriately):

```
PKUNZIP A:\dir\zipfile progfile.exe
```

Replace the dir, zipfile, and progfile.exe portions of the command with the appropriate directory name, filename, and name of the desired program. Wildcard characters are acceptable in the name of the desired program.

Using UNZIP.EXE

To extract all files from one of the ZIP files using UNZIP, go to (or create) the subdirectory into which you want the files extracted, then use this command (if the diskette is in your A: drive; if not, change all drive letters appropriately):

```
A:\UNZIP A:\dir\zipfile.zip
```

To extract a specific file from one of the ZIP files using UNZIP, go to (or create) the subdirectory into which you want the files extracted, then use this command (assuming that the diskette is in your A: drive; if not, change the drive letter appropriately):

```
A:\UNZIP A:\dir\zipfile progfile.exe
```

Replace the dir, zipfile, and progfile.exe portions of the command with the appropriate directory name, filename, and name of the desired program. Wildcard characters are acceptable in the name of the desired program. Alternatively, you can copy UNZIP.EXE from the diskette to your BIN or utility directory, and use it exactly as you would PKUNZIP. The ".ZIP" suffix isn't required by UNZIP, but adding it to the command shaves a few microseconds from the time it takes to start. When running direct from the diskette, the time saved is more than microseconds; it's noticeable!

The Diskette's Layout

The diskette is organized into four subdirectories, each named for the author of the programs contained therein. These directories are ENG, KYLE, LARMET, and REILLY. The respective authors are Bob Eng, Jim Kyle, Andre Larmet, and Doug Reilly.

The ENG Directory

This directory contains a free trial version of the commercial product Bbug from Access Technology Corporation.

The KYLE Directory

This directory contains all example programs from Chapter 10, plus a bonus package not described in the text.

The LARMET Directory

This directory contains limited capacity evaluation copies of shareware from C-Soft Inc.

The REILLY Directory

This directory contains two freeware packages and three shareware applications from Access Microsystems Inc.

What's in the ENG Directory

This directory contains a free trial demonstration of bBUG from Access Technology Corporation, together with two text files describing its use. None of the files is compressed.

The bBUG program is a task-specific memory resident monitor/debugger targeted to the needs of software developers using the popular Btrieve file manager.

BBUGDEMO.EXE

During the development cycle bBUG allows the programmer to monitor file manager operations and his program's interface to the manager. Complete transparency and language independence is maintained. No special procedures or coding are required on the part of the programmer. The finished program is identical to the program under development.

This free trial version of BBUG (BBUGDEMO.EXE) has the following limitations:

- no selective trace control is possible
- no table reset can be done
- a maximum of 200 Btrieve operations may be observed

BBUGDEMO.EXE is otherwise a complete version of the product, compiled from the same source code. BBUG release 2.0 will be updated to match the latest versions of Btrieve and to include support for a new VGA split screen 60-line mode.

The Text Files

The two text files, BBUG.ASC and BBUGDEMO.ASC, provide installation and operating instructions for the program. BBUG.ASC contains the full instructions; it's the manual for the complete version. BBUGDEMO.ASC is an abbreviated version describing only the most immediately useful features.

What's in the KYLE Directory

The KYLE directory contains the following seven files, totaling 99,917 bytes before expansion:

BTATR.ZIP	BTKEY.ZIP	BTRIEVE.H
DUMPDATA.ZIP	DUMPFREE.ZIP	LISTKEYS.ZIP
MAKCRE.ZIP		

I recommend extracting all the source files (*.C in each ZIP file) into a single subdirectory and placing the executable versions into the directory from which you run Btrieve (or into a general utility directory, if you use one). This will preserve the original versions as you experiment with the source code. If you only want to use the utilities, and have no need for the *.C files, you don't need to extract them. All of these utilities operate without any dependence on any other files (except, of course, the Btrieve data file that you are examining).

BTRIEVE.H

The BTRIEVE.H, an uncompressed text file 7,875 bytes in size, is the header file used by all the example programs. This file also documents the internal structure of both Btrieve file formats. Copy it into your normal INCLUDE directory, along with your C compiler's standard header files, or into the same directory as your example source files.

BTATR.ZIP

The BTATR.ZIP file contains BTATR.C (11,447 bytes when expanded) and BTATR.EXE (18,616 bytes when expanded). See Chapter 10 for details of this program.

BTKEY.ZIP

The BTKEY.ZIP file contains BTKEY.C (13,550 bytes when expanded) and BTKEY. EXE (18,810 bytes when expanded). See Chapter 10 for details of this program.

DUMPDATA.ZIP

The DUMPDATA.ZIP file contains DUMPDATA.C (21,615 bytes when expanded) and DUMPDATA.EXE (20,390 bytes when expanded). See Chapter 10 for details of this program.

DUMPFREE.ZIP

The DUMPFREE.ZIP file contains DUMPFREE.C (10,376 bytes when expanded) and DUMPFREE.EXE (17,682 bytes when expanded). See Chapter 10 for details of this program.

LISTKEYS.ZIP

The LISTKEYS.ZIP file contains LISTKEYS.C (13,401 bytes when expanded) and LISTKEYS.EXE (18,636 bytes when expanded). See Chapter 10 for details of this program.

MAKCRE.ZIP

The MAKCRE.ZIP file contains the bonus utility, MAKCRE.C (6,076 bytes when expanded) and MAKCRE.EXE (17,306 bytes when expanded). This program extracts information from the FCR page of any Btrieve file and writes a description file to st dout in format acceptable to the BUTIL -CREATE option. Normally st dout addresses the CRT, but it may be redirected to create a file.

Operation of this program is similar to that of BTATR and BTKEY described in Chapter 10; the difference is in the output format.

What's in the LARMET Directory

The LARMET directory contains two self-extracting archive files, BTEDXT.EXE and BTCRXT.EXE, each of which holds a separate shareware application from C-Soft Inc. Unlike the other files on the diskette, you install these by first creating or choosing the directory where you want them, then typing the filename at the command prompt (that is, A:BTEDXT or A:BTCRXT) and pressing the Enter key. It's not necessary to copy the file to your hard disk before doing the extraction. Both packages in this directory are limited-capacity shareware; they include all features of the complete versions, but are restricted to relatively small files. When you register, the final version has no such limitations.

BTEDXT.EXE

Self-extracting archive file BTEDXT.EXE contains these 3 files, totaling 145,070 bytes:

BTEDIT.EXE   BTEDITFT.TXT   ORDERFRM.TXT

Here's an excerpt from the BTEDITFT.TXT file that explains what the package does:

BTedit is designed for software developers who use Btrieve as the database manager. In addition BTedit is extremely helpful to QA and support staffs. Its primary use is to be able to look at Btrieve records and to be able to search for a particular record for analysis.

If editing is required, it is very easy to look at a record in detail format (HEX and ASCII) and to apply a change in either format. BTedit was designed to get you there simply and fast. Its user interface is probably not the fanciest, but it is to the point.

There is very little need for documentation since every function available is shown at the bottom of the screen when appropriate. The only exception to that rule is the list menu, which consists of three rotating menus. Note that when on the list screen, ALL rotating menu functions are AVAILABLE although only one menu is displayed.

Help is available when necessary. New users should scan all the help at least once to become familiar with some time-saving features.

BTCRXT.EXE

Self-extracting archive file BTCRXT.EXE contains these ten files, totaling 375,845 bytes:

BTAPPIDS.TXT   BTCREATE.EXE   BTCREATE.TXT

BTSOURCE.510   BTSOURCE.615   BTSOURCE.EXE

BTSOURCN.510   BTSOURCN.615   ORDERFRM.TXT

SETUP.BAT

The files with extensions 510 and 615 are used by SETUP.BAT to configure the package for either original-format (510) or new-format (615) Btrieve files.

Here's an excerpt from the BTCREATE.TXT file that explains what the package does:

BTsource and BTcreate are designed to create and maintain DDF (dictionary) and Btrieve files. BTsource creates and maintains the source information necessary to describe the Btrieve file you want to create while BTcreate uses that information to create the files.

BTsource contains all the information necessary to use both programs as on-line help. Be sure to read all the screens shown by the About function from the main menu of BTsource as well as the F1 and F2 help screens.

What's in the REILLY Directory

The REILLY directory contains two files with freeware applications, together with three files containing evaluation copies of shareware products. The freeware files are BLDBTB.ZIP and BU2.ZIP. The shareware applications are in BTFL14.ZIP, BTUTIL.ZIP, and BTVIEW.ZIP.

BLDBTB.ZIP

The BLDBTB.ZIP file contains these two files, totaling 34,794 bytes when expanded:

BLDBTB.DOC   BLDBTB.EXE

Here's an excerpt from the BTBLD.DOC file that explains what the package does:

First things first. If you don't use BTFILER (currently BTFL14.ZIP) this program is about as useful as tap shoes would be to a fish. Don't despair: you can download BTFL14.ZIP and then you can use this program. Of course, all this assumes that you have Btrieve and some Btrieve files.

BTFILER allows you to create files using description files (.BTrieve Build or .BTB files). Description files are in some ways more useful than interactive file creation tools, in that the results can be repeated by reusing the description file, or the results can be altered by modifying the description file.

Using BTBLD is pretty straightforward: Simply type BLDBTB followed by the name of the Btrieve file that you want the .BTB file created for and the filename for the .BTB file. You may also specify an owner name by using a third parameter in the form of -Oowner-name. As I have said, the most useful thing about building .BTB files is that you can use the .BTB file as a template for creating a similar but not identical file with minimal retyping.

If you forget the usage pattern, simply type BLDBTB and press the Enter key. The syntax will be displayed.

This is copyrighted material, but you may distribute it as you see fit.

BTFL14.ZIP

The BTFL14.ZIP file contains these twenty-five files, totaling 421,367 bytes when expanded:

AMIMAP.EXE	BTCLONE.BAT	BTCOPY.BAT
BTCREATE.BAT	BTFILER.BER	BTFILER.BOP
BTFILER.CF1	BTFILER.DOC	BTFILER.EXE
BTFILER.HLP	BTFILER.MNU	BTFILER.MSK
BTPACK.BAT	BTREBLD.BAT	BTRESET.BAT
BTTEST.BAT	CINSTALL.DAT	POL.ASC
POL.DAT	POL.DOC	POL.INX
README.BTF	REGISTER.DOC	SAMPLE.BTB
SAMPLE.BTS		

Here's an excerpt from the BTFILER.DOC file that explains what the package does:

BTFILER allows you to TEST and RECOVER data from Btrieve files. In addition to standard sorts of Btrieve testing (Test for consistent prev/next links, etc.) BTFILER also has a DOS File test that reads the entire file and reports if a DOS Critical error (ABORT, RETRY, or FAIL) error occurs. You may also rebuild a damaged Btrieve file header, and if really desperate, use our Recover EVERY POSSIBLE Record recovery method, which painfully tries to get every possible record in the file by guessing where the data might be.

BTFILER allows you to view, edit, search, and delete records in a Btrieve file.

BTFILER allows you to Clone a Btrieve file (that is, create an empty Btrieve file with the same key structure and record size as the original).

BTFILER allows you to Pack a Btrieve file (that is, create a copy of a Btrieve file less the space left by deleted records) as well as Copy a file (that is, copy records from one Btrieve file to another, with the destination file possibly having a different record length and key structure).

BTFILER allows you to Import and Export records in an Unformatted ASCII format, a format like BUTIL, Novell's Btrieve Developer's Utility, or NEW with version 1.40, comma-delimited ASCII!

BTFILER allows you to create a Btrieve file with a BTrieve Build file (.BTB) file and create a supplemental index using a BTrieve Supplemental (.BTS) file. You may also DROP a supplemental index.

BTFILER allows you to begin and end transactions within a single session and will prompt you to end the transaction if you try to do something that can't be done in a transaction.

BTFILER allows you to repeat repetitive tasks by creating keystroke files that are passed back to the keyboard buffer as the program is run. This also allows more technical users to provide easy to use batch files for those less comfortable operating BTFILER directly.

BTFILER allows you to Set and Clear owners of Btrieve files, displays Btrieve version information, and shows file statistics and key structure.

BTFILER lists Btrieve Error codes (arranged numerically) and Operation codes (arranged alphabetically). You may also get details on Btrieve error codes.

BTUTIL.ZIP

The BTUTIL.ZIP file contains these five files, totaling 120,183 bytes when expanded:

BTUTIL.DOC   BTUTIL.EXE   REGISTER.DOC

SAMPLE.BTB   SAMPLE.BTS

Here's an excerpt from the BTUTIL.DOC file that explains what the package does:

BTUTIL comes about as a result of a request for a command-line Btrieve file recovery utility. A customer had over 400 sites in need of such a utility, and our full scale Btrieve File Maintenance and Recovery Utility program BTFILER was too much (from a cost and user-interface standpoint) for their requirements. We already had a partial replacement program for Novell's BUTIL called BU. BU does some of the simpler BUTIL operations, such as -CLONE, -LOAD, -STOP, -STAT, and -VER. BU is freeware. BU was upgraded, new features were included, and BTUTIL was born.

BTUTIL allows you to SAVE data to ASCII files compatible with Novell's BUTIL. BTUTIL also allows you to LOAD BUTIL format ASCII files into a Btrieve file.

BTUTIL allows you to RECOVER data from damaged Btrieve files. Unlike Novell's BUTIL, BTUTIL recovers records from the damaged file directly to another Btrieve file that is a clone of the damaged file.

BTUTIL allows you to Clone a Btrieve file (that is, create an empty Btrieve file with the same key structure and record size as the original).

BTUTIL allows you to Copy a file (that is, copy records from one Btrieve file to another, with the destination file possibly having a different record length and key structure).

BTUTIL allows you to create a Btrieve file with a BTrieve Build file (.BTB) file.

BTUTIL allows you to RESET, STOP and display the currently loaded Btrieve VERSION.

BTUTIL allows you to do an XSAVE or XLOAD using extended gets or inserts. In environments using BTRIEVE.NLM and BREQUEST, these operations are up to 33 percent faster than their nonextended counterparts.

BTVIEW.ZIP

The BTVIEW.ZIP file contains these eighteen files, totaling 492,758 bytes when expanded:

AMIMAP.EXE	BTCLONE.BAT	BTCOPY.BAT
BTCREATE.BAT	BTVIEWER.BER	BTVIEWER.BOP
BTVIEWER.CF1	BTVIEWER.DOC	BTVIEWER.EXE
BTVIEWER.HLP	BTVIEWER.MNU	BTVIEWER.MSK
CINSTALL.DAT	README.BTV	REGISTER.DOC
SAMPLE.BTB	SAMPLE.BTS	SAMPLES.ZIP

Here's an excerpt from the BTVIEWER.DOC file that explains what the package does:

BTVIEWER allows you to create, save and restore "views" of your data. "Views" include a file, a set of fields, a sorting order, and a set of restrictions. Data is viewed and edited in a convenient format (dates like 06/17/1992, binary numbers presented like 123.45, and so on). You also may edit fields in a HEX format as an option.

BTVIEWER allows you to JOIN two files based upon a field in a primary file and an index in a secondary file, including all records, all records with a match in the secondary file, or all records without a match in the secondary file.

BTVIEWER allows you to restrict your "view" of a file using a "query by form" screen. You may also modify all records in the view with a "modify by example" screen, or delete all records in a view.

BTVIEWER allows you to generate summary information (MIN, MAX, SUM, AVG) and allows a calculated field, that is, a field in a view that is calculated from constants and other fields.

BTVIEWER allows you to RECOVER data from damaged Btrieve files. BTFILER, our Btrieve File Maintenance and Recovery Utility, offers more complete file rebuilding, so consider it if you have severe data corruption problems.

BTVIEWER allows you to Clone a Btrieve file (that is, create an empty Btrieve file with the same key structure and record size as the original).

BTVIEWER allows you to Pack a Btrieve file (that is, create a copy of a Btrieve file less the space left by deleted records) as well as Copy a file (that is, copy records from one Btrieve file to another, with the destination file possibly having a different record length and key structure).

BTVIEWER allows you to Import and Export records in comma-delimited ASCII! You may Export into dBASE III compatible files.

BTVIEWER allows you to create a Btrieve file with a BTrieve Build file (.BTB) file and create a supplemental index using a BTrieve Supplemental (.BTS) file. You may also DROP a supplemental index.

BTVIEWER allows you to begin and end transactions within a single session, and will prompt you to end the transaction if you try to do something that can't be done in a transaction.

BTVIEWER allows you to repeat repetitive tasks by creating keystroke files that are passed back to the keyboard buffer as the program is run. This also allows more technical users to provide easy to use batch files for those less comfortable operating BTVIEWER directly.

BTVIEWER allows you to Set and Clear owners of Btrieve files, displays Btrieve version information, and shows file statistics and key structure.

BU2.ZIP

The BU2.ZIP file contains these 2 files, totaling 37,006 bytes when expanded:

BU.EXE   README.BU

Here's an excerpt from the README.BU file that explains what the package does:

BU is a partial replacement for BUTIL. It implements the -STOP, -RESET, -CLONE, -LOAD, and -VER commands of BUTIL. To see the format of the commands, simply type BU<Press ENTER> at the command line with Btrieve loaded.

Index

Symbols
2-3 tree, 78
32-bit hardware and software, 461
@Trieve, 289

A

Abort Transaction (Code 21) function
    operation, 146–147
Aborting all transactions, 108–109
Access, 43, 49, 52
ACS (Alternate Collating Sequence)
    pages, 166, 179, 184, 225–226
    multiple, 225
Addition group operations, 116–118
Algorithm 1, 271
All-or-none operations, 144–147

API (application programming inter-
    face), 43, 94–152
    backward compatibility, 94
    data buffer, 95
    File Control block, 95
    HLL languages, 99–101
    parameter block, 94–95, 98–99
    position block, 95–98
    primitive operations, 101–152
    16-bit variable, 95
Applications
    defensive design, 469–471
    minimum space, 445–448
    page size, 445–448
    terminating, 109
    transactions, 144
Arctco, Inc., 23–25